Louis Charles Casartelli

Louis Charles Casartelli

A Bishop in Peace and War

⁂

Martin John Broadley

Koinonia
Manchester

Published by Koinonia
70 Sandown Road, Bury, Lancashire BL9 8HW, UK

British Library Cataloguing-in-Publication Data
A catalogue record for this book is available from the British Library

EAN 978 0 86088 035 6

First published 2006

Typeset in Dante with Golden Cockerel display by
Koinonia, Manchester
Printed in Great Britain by
Bell & Bain Limited, Glasgow

Contents

⟨⟩⟨⟩⟨⟩

Part Two   The Episcopal Years 1903 to 1925

Abbreviations

AAB	Archdiocesan Archives Birmingham
AAL	Archdiocesan Archives Liverpool
AAS	Archdiocesan Archives Southwark
AAW	Archdiocesan Archives Westminster
ACA	Arundel Castle Archives
ASEQ	Acta Salfordiensia Episcopi Quarti
ASV	Archivo Segreto Vaticano
BOL	Brompton Oratory Library
CF	Catholic Federationist
CO	Catholic Opinion
COT	Catholic Opinion and Times
DAA	Downside Abbey Archives
EOS	Egyptian and Oriental Society
GP	Gasquet Papers
JRL	John Rylands Library
MA MOU	Moulton Papers
MG	Manchester Guardian
NLW	National Library of Wales
PFA	Propaganda Fide Archives, Rome
SDA	Salford Diocesan Archives
SDCM	Salford Diocesan Chapter Minutes
UCA	Ushaw College Archives, Durham
VG	Vicar General

Acknowledgements

I would like to renew my gratitude to Dr Peter Nockles, who oversaw the original thesis with unfailing care, help, and enthusiasm. I would also like to thank Dr Geoffrey Price, Dr Dorothy Clayton and Christine Hill who very kindly read drafts of this book and made invaluable suggestions. I am grateful to Anthony Barrett who made possible the photographs of Bishop Casartelli contained herein.

I would like to express my appreciation to the Catenian Association, especially Philip Barnes, and Peter Purdue of Koinonia Press, and also of the generous assistance from Association members: The Manchester Circle, the Provincial Council of Province 1, Peter and Denise Baldwin, Tom Ball, Phil and Pat Barnes, Anne Barnes (in memory of Robbie), Brian Cann, Michael and Isabel Cusack, Bob and Stephanie Dunbar, Frank and Bebe Hinds, Jim and Barbara Kelly, Jim and Lisa King, Mike and Anne-Marie O'Malley, Pat O'Neill (in memory of her husband Ron and her father Joe Murphy), Peter and Frances Purdue, Frank and Mary Rafferty, Gerald and Pauline Soane, Jack and May Tootle, John and Maria Woodhouse and Stephen Wright.

The photographs reproduced in this book are by kind permission of the following: front cover: the Rector, St Bede's College, Manchester; frontispiece: Salford Diocesan Archives; page 2, The John Rylands Library, University of Manchester; page 10, the Rector, St Bede's College, Manchester; page 14, Manchester Central Reference Library, Local Studies; page 90, The John Rylands Library, University of Manchester.

Dedication

In Memory of Geoffrey Price

And I tell you, if you have the desire for knowledge and the power to give it physical expression, go out and explore. If you are a brave man you will do nothing: if you are fearful you may do much, for none but cowards have need to prove their bravery. Some will tell you that you are mad, and nearly all will say, 'what is the use?' For we are a nation of shopkeepers, and no shopkeeper will look at research which does not promise him a financial return within a year. And so you will sledge nearly alone, but those with whom you sledge will not be shopkeepers: that is worth a good deal. If you march your Winter Journeys you will have your reward, so long as all you want is a penguin's egg.

Apsley Cherry-Garrard, *The Worst Journey in the World.*

Introduction

> One delightful trait in his character was his conversance with any subject discussed, however trivial; it was founded on that wonderful humanity which felt interest in the smallest details of every day life; the most ignorant could talk to the Bishop and receive the same courteous attention given to the most erudite. Truly in his relation with his flock as well as with the large number of scientific, literary, and other organisations, his Lordship proved in the words of Terence: *Homo sum et humani a me nil alienum puto (sic).*[1]

A photograph taken on the occasion of the 25th anniversary of the founding of the Manchester Geographical Society[2] aptly portrays Frances Zanetti's[3] vignette of Louis Charles Casartelli, the Fourth Bishop of Salford. The Society brought together different sections of the population of Manchester: financial, commercial, educational, and missionary. Here we see the wide compass of Casartelli's interests. His ability to take a place among the intelligentsia and leading men of Manchester is represented by the presence of the Vice-Chancellor of the University of Manchester and members of the Geographical Society. Casartelli was a founder member of the Society, along with Herbert Vaughan,[4] then Bishop of Salford, and played an inspired and significant rôle in its development. A fundamental reason why the Society was founded was in response to Vaughan's observation that British overseas trade was beginning to wane due to foreign competition.[5] The interest of Vaughan in this matter, together with that of Casartelli, his prodigy, is symptomatic of their shared wish to see Catholics play an active rôle within society and to strike a blow at a commonplace attitude of Victorian England – that Catholics were uninterested in the commercial prosperity of the country.[6]

This book explores the life and times of Louis Charles Casartelli from the perspectives of citizen, educationalist, scholar, and churchman. On the occasion of Casartelli's death the *Manchester Guardian* commented: 'Manchester, no less than learning and piety, has lost a distinguished son by the

Sir E. H. Shackleton, CVO, and the Officers of the Manchester Geographical Society

Back: D. A. Little, F. Zimmern, J. Howard Reed, The Vice-Chancellor of the University, Harry Sowerbutts

Front: Bishop Welldon, Dean of Manchester, Sir Ernest Shackelton, Harry Nuttall, MP and Bishop Casartelli, Bishop of Salford

death of Dr Casartelli. He was a great scholar and in the first rank of Orientalists.'[7] The task of research in this instance has benefited from the good fortune of access to ample primary sources, the vast majority of which were, until now, unused or not previously available. This has enabled a detailed and original study to be made of this Russian-speaking, Persian-teaching, Chinese-learning prelate, who found inspiration in John Henry Newman, Henry Edward Manning, and Herbert Vaughan. Although it is a study of a leader of a local Church, it is not restricted to the field of local, nor indeed, denominational, history.

First as a priest, and later as a bishop, Casartelli was advised by Vaughan to enter into the intellectual and civic life of the city and community at large. In those 'pre-ecumenical' days he was willing to assume a rôle on public platforms along with other Christian leaders. He joined with them in the pursuit of knowledge through the University of Manchester and in the defence of denominational schools. Casartelli built up relations with other Christians in various other ways. For example, he was a member of the 'Police-Aided Clothing Association' for destitute children. In 1903 the Rev. James Mounihan, of The Vicarage, Werneth, invited Casartelli to attend a dinner at the Midland Hotel, Manchester, to be hosted by Trinity College, Dublin. He also enjoyed the friendship of the eminent Free Church scholar James Hope Moulton.[8] This is an example of how Casartelli, especially in his academic interests and pursuits, was not confined by denominational limits and was able to find common ground with other Christians.[9] His ability in this regard was obviously impressive; although, as the biographer of J. H. Moulton wrote: 'sacerdotalism left him either cold or irritated,'[10] yet he made special mention of his friendship with Casartelli.[11] Casartelli was a vice-president of the Manchester and Salford Citizens Association.[12] He was invited to become a vice-president of the Canterbury and York Society, and was the only Catholic cleric on the committee.[13] The presence of the Vice-Chancellor in the photograph of the Geographical Society is symbolic of Casartelli's link with the University, where he taught Persian languages in the Theology Faculty. Through the Geographical Society he played a part in the development of a Geography Department within the University. In these, and in other ways, Casartelli led by example as he encouraged his fellow Catholics to assume their duties as citizens. He advocated a 'pacific penetration', whereby through 'their example and intellectual influence,' Catholics could be a benign presence in the society in which they live.[14]

Casartelli was also an original-thinking Zoroastrian scholar; his status as such was to receive European recognition. Prior to his appointment at Manchester University, he had held a similar part-time post at the University of Louvain. Even today his scholarship and expertise has been deemed worthy of a substantial entry in the latest edition of the *Encyclopaedia Iranica*.[15] However, his brilliance was never allowed to reach fruition in a full academic career. From his latter days as a student for the priesthood, he was destined by Vaughan to become a member of staff at St Bede's Commercial College, Manchester. On his own admission he found this a difficult and wearying task, and one that would not have taxed him intellectually. Nevertheless, as we shall see, as a teacher and by his pioneering work with the Geographical Society, Casartelli was an active educationalist promoting advanced ideas on commercial education. He saw the advancement of the teaching of geography as a means to further the prosperity of Britain's, and in particular Manchester's, overseas trade.

Much against his will and despite his vehement protestations of inability and lack of aptitude, Casartelli was named the fourth bishop of Salford in 1903. He made his unsuitability for the task clear at every level: to Vaughan, who strongly supported his nomination; to the Prefect of Propaganda Fide in Rome, before whom he appeared in person in the hope of avoiding being nominated; and in the first pastoral letter addressed to the people of his diocese after his reluctant appointment. On his own admission, he would much rather have remained at St Bede's, or, even better, have dedicated himself more fully to scholarship. Vaughan later concurred that Casartelli lacked personal ambition, and noted how he had always shunned becoming a Canon of the Diocese. Casartelli's rôle in the Church was a source of continual personal conflict. Nevertheless, he remained obedient to his ecclesiastical superiors, and saw Rome's wish that he become a bishop as a sign of the will of God. His acceptance of the bishopric of Salford is evidence of the strength and simplicity of his unostentatious piety. He chose as his episcopal motto: *fiat voluntas tua*.

The Catholic Church in England at the beginning of the twentieth-century was becoming more confident and beginning to take its place on the national stage. By appointing a scholarly bishop like Casartelli, it was hoped to give the Church in Manchester and Salford, and throughout the diocese, a sense of self-worth and a certain amount of kudos. The fact that he was among the handful of Catholic scholars at the time, and one who enjoyed good relations and standing with the non-Catholics of Manchester, was particularly mentioned in Vaughan's letters of recommendation. However, because of his lack of aptitude and experience, Casartelli initially feared failure as a bishop. This early lack of confidence, coupled with utter intellectual honesty, had earlier prevented him accepting the offer of the post of chaplain to the University of Oxford. However, as this thesis will show, he went on to be an influential if cautious leader of his Diocese. Although he tended throughout to look to Vaughan his predecessor as a rôle model, there is much evidence of his capacity to make his own reforms. Thus he strove to not only implement the liturgical reforms of Pius X but also to set his diocese in the vanguard of progress in this respect.

Despite Casartelli's initial reluctance to assume leadership, his intellectual abilities were well suited to the task. As an educated thinker with a European background, he was able to address his natural audience – as evident from 'The Signs of the Times', his first pastoral letter on the Church and civic institutions – the new Catholic middle-class which was beginning to form in the predominantly working-class diocese of Salford. Indeed, as a thinker, Casartelli was of an open, one might even say, progressive mind: in Oriental Studies he sought to chart new territory and to venture forth into a discipline that was uncommon and therefore, to some degree, 'dangerous ground'. However, his heart reflected his background; by temperament he was conservative and keen to be seen to conform. Although in principle he favoured openness towards the rôles that could be played by the laity, in practice he remained timid, fearful that groups such as Catholic teachers might go beyond the controlling reins of the hierarchy. Casartelli wanted to see an organised laity ('organise' was the motto of his episcopate), he therefore thought it necessary that authority was seen to be exercised in order to guarantee unity. His conservative disposition was uppermost when – in the midst of national campaigns to preserve Catholic school education – he considered that Francis Bourne[16] as Archbishop of Westminster had failed to restrain lay Catholics from unwise public statements. Casartelli preferred strong leadership by the hierarchy – and at times this difference of opinion caused the two men to be at odds. During the War, Casartelli's conservatism was also apparent in his eagerness to conform and to portray the Catholic community as patriotic; only with extreme caution did he allow his underlying pan-European sentiments as a scholar and intellectual to be heard.

Charles Bolton in his history of the Salford Diocese wrote: 'no doubt the fact that he was one of the favourite disciples of Cardinal Vaughan must have influenced the appointment,' and, 'much of the administrative work must have been uncongenial to the learned man of many books.'[17] Despite being slightly acerbic, both comments are accurate. Casartelli was a disciple of Vaughan, but he never had any desire to follow him into the episcopate. On the rare occasions when Casartelli mentioned his work as a bishop, it is clear that he saw it as an uncongenial burden. On one occasion he acknowledged to a fellow bishop that if he had the financial means to support himself he would resign his see. The boxes of unsorted 'Vicar General Correspondence' in the Salford Diocesan Archive show that Casartelli devolved much of the administration to his Vicar/s General.[18] Evidence of this type suggests that to his clergy he remained a distant figure. Almost certainly, he was at his happiest in Bexhill-on-Sea, where he spent approximately six weeks per year on holiday, or at meetings of the various learned societies[19] of which he was a member. Ill health[20] repeatedly kept him from his episcopal duties. During these periods when he was ill, he would often convalesce at the home of his sisters close by his residence at St Bede's College. It must not be imagined that because of his temperament and ill health that Casartelli was a loner. He had many friends and acquaintances as can be seen from the following entry in his diary for Christmas 1909: 'busy all day receiving Xmas cards and *presents*, – never received so many of latter before, some very beautiful and even valuable ones. How kind and generous friends are! Answering all took a very long time.'[21]

Nothing to date has been written specifically on Casartelli. He is mainly remembered for being the instigator of the Catholic Federation[22] and the Catenians[23] and for having an outlook that was European and non-parochial.[24] A more recent work has seen Casartelli as taking a strongly anti-Socialist stance – a position that caused him to be somewhat isolated from the rest of the bishops.[25] This article – which will be evaluated in the course of this thesis – is valuable for the light it sheds on the undoubted force and vigour which he brought to the episcopate, and the tensions with his underlying training as a scholar. However, a thorough study of the life of Louis Charles Casartelli can reveal – as the following chapters seek to demonstrate – much more of the conflicts and the trials of his times. He was eager to show that the Catholic Church was a loyal and integral part of English society. Hence his life is something of a prism, refracting the upheavals and struggles of the contemporary Catholic community. These include its allegiance to the State, its struggle to provide religious education from elementary to university level, its response to the Great War, the need for proper scientific study of ancient texts and exegesis, politics and party allegiance – especially the Irish Question – and the rise of the Labour Party. Modernism, of the intellectual kind, was not a problem within the Salford diocese.[26] But Casartelli did react strongly to the Modernistic idea that it was impossible to subordinate the temporal to the spiritual.

His life is also of great intrinsic interest as evidence of what could be achieved by a determined religious leader in the newly-modernising twin cities of Salford and Manchester. Moreover, he did much to promote a Catholic presence in the learned circles of Manchester; this was no small achievement when one considers that the University of Manchester was and is founded on a secular charter. As a pioneering intellectual, he left a distinguished legacy in the field of Oriental Studies. As a public preacher and speaker, his efforts, particularly during the First World War, did much to dispel misconceptions about the Catholic Church. As a Church administrator –

despite his distant manner and preference for delegation – his diocese prospered: twenty-four new parishes were created during the time he was bishop; ninety priests were ordained and eighteen Catholic organisations founded. Moreover, his success as a well-respected citizen who did much to dispel misunderstanding and hostility is reflected in the fact that Manchester had two Catholic Lord Mayors whilst Casartelli was bishop.

We now turn to the task of testing and exemplifying these preliminary judgements of Casartelli's life and influence. J. D. Holmes, in an article written shortly after a small collection of Casartelli's papers had been deposited at Ushaw College, commented that if Casartelli had been a bishop in the nineteenth century then it is likely that a biography would have already been written.[27] This comment presupposes the general trend to ignore the history of twentieth-century Catholicism. One reason for this could be because the administration of the Church during this period has been perceived as bland. Furthermore, the bishops of the past century have been acknowledged as administrators, rather than men of intellect and vision. Such perceptions do little to inspire researchers to venture forth and explore the period.

The ample primary sources held in the Salford Diocesan Archives, consisting of diaries, correspondence, and episcopal *acta* are an invaluable source in helping to understand the development of English Catholicism in the twentieth century. For the early part of Casartelli's life, his diaries and letters to his father have provided an invaluable insight into his character. His academic pursuits are well documented in three bound volumes of his various learned papers and newspaper articles, which he had made for his personal library. The details of his nomination as bishop and the discussion surrounding this event are to be found in the 'Hedley Papers' in the National Library of Wales, Aberystwyth, and in the Archives of Propaganda Fide, Rome. These sources help us to construct and re-construct a history that is a challenge to the so-often-accepted view that the Catholic Church of this period was insular and inward-looking. Despite the fact that one of Casartelli's continual struggles was with parochialism, there is ample evidence that the Church under his leadership was also trying to be outward-looking. Even those institutions that have been traditionally seen as the bastion of the English Catholic parochial structure – the parish schools – were based on a philosophy of education which saw denominational schools as serving the common good of education and the nation as a whole. The present study of Casartelli's life and work will, it is hoped, help make good the *lacuna* in historical scholarship of modern English Catholicism.

PART ONE

The Years 1852 to 1903

Bishop Turner, Bishop of Salford, 1850–1872
Left to right: Provost Croskell, Canon Benoit, Bishop Turner, Bishop Casartelli as a boy, Canon Roskell, later Bishop of Northampton

Chapter One

The Formative Years
1852–1877

⤛⟑⤜

Manchester streets may be irregular, and its trading inscriptions pretentious, its smoke may be dense, and its mud ultra-muddy, but not any or all of these things can prevent the image of a great city rising before us as the very symbol of civilisation, foremost in the march of improvement, a grand incarnation of progress.[1]

Ronald L. Greenall when speaking of Manchester and Salford in relation to the Industrial Revolution speaks of a 'double-barrelled' city. Of Salford he writes: 'taken together with Manchester it was part of the biggest urban concentration in Great Britain outside London, Glasgow and Birmingham ... Victorian Salford lay at the hub of one of the first industrial concentrations.'[2] The Casartelli family played a prominent rôle in the life of Manchester, one of Europe's first commercial capitals. As a bishop, Louis Charles Casartelli would extend this influence to include the no less important city of Salford.

Louis Charles Casartelli was born on 14 November 1852, at 2, Clarence Street, Cheetham Hill, an affluent area of Manchester.[3] His baptism took place at the church of St Augustine, Granby Row, on 16 November. He was the eldest of six children born to Joseph Louis Casartelli and Jane Henrietta Casartelli (née Ronchetti). Joseph, his father, was born near Lake Como in northern Italy on 9 September 1822. He was a man of many interests – scientific, artistic, and commercial. He was skilled and well-informed in mechanics, chemistry, meteorology, and astronomy, and also became one of the earliest photographers in England. But these abilities flowered far from home. For around the age of fourteen he moved to England as, according to an obituary in *The Harvest*, 'an involuntary exile.'[4] His migration followed a request from an uncle to assist him in his optical and scientific instrument-making business in Liverpool. The proven success of this enterprise inclined Joseph's parents to agree.[5] Eventually, his ingenuity and resourcefulness led to him being made a partner in the firm. Further success enabled him to purchase a similar business in Manchester. The business, founded *circa* 1790 in the respectable shopping area of Market Street, (see below p. 14), had at one time supplied precision instruments for the eminent chemist, John Dalton. J. T. Slugg described the business thus: 'Joshua Ronchetti was a noted maker of barometers, thermometers, and specially of hydrometers, the latter of which he had a large sale, in which at that time handsome profits were made.'[6] Ronchetti sent rainfall readings to the *Manchester Guardian*, a tradition later maintained by his son-in-law and later by his grandson, Louis Charles.[7] In the same year, 1851, that Joseph Casartelli moved to Manchester, he married Joshua Ronchetti's daughter, Jane Henrietta.

The Casartelli and Ronchetti families formed part of a small but significant circle of Italian artisans who had lived in Manchester since the early nineteenth century. This community offered particular skilful expertise in barometer making, optical equipment manufacture, picture framing, and gilding.[8] Paul de Felice writes of them, 'The earliest arrivals in Manchester made a significant contribution to the industrial development of the city. However, their settlement can be seen independently from the Ancoats[9] Italians. The Italian artisans did not settle in Ancoats, but were dispersed around the city.'[10]

The construction and expansion of the network of railways and canals, along with wider interests in dyeing, bleaching, and chemical processes, placed Casartelli's name at the heart of Manchester's industry where he became one of its most important precision instrument manufacturers of the nineteenth century.[11] A trade directory described Joseph Casartelli as an 'optician, and philosophical instrument and hydrometer maker.'[12] The following description appeared in 1888:

> It is the oldest and most important firm of its kind in the city, and, indeed, has no equal outside of London ... The Trade connection is principally in the mining and manufacturing districts of Lancashire, Yorkshire, Cumberland, Durham, and South Wales; and a large export trade to all parts of the world is maintained through the shipping firms of this city and the metropolis...The business in Market Street consists of stock – show – and salesrooms, warehouses, offices, and experimental workshops...The larger works are situated at Clarence Street, Cheetham Hill.[13]

Between 1855 and 1897 Joseph Casartelli applied for twelve patents, ranging from an apparatus for testing the lubricating quality of oils, to miners' dials and eye-glasses. His range of products was, at the time, at the forefront of technology. 'Philosophical instruments,' such as microscopes and barometers, were an integral part of the important and popular pursuit of natural philosophy. In 1868 he published a pamphlet on another topical subject of the day – the human eye.[14] A trade catalogue detailing Casartelli's goods includes several magic lanterns.[15] At an exhibition in 1876, these instruments were described as, 'an almost indispensable part of the apparatus of instruc-tion in nearly every department of human knowledge.'[16] Louis Charles would often illustrate his public lectures by using one of these magic lanterns.

Joseph Casartelli became a member of the Manchester Literary and Philosophical Society in January 1858, and to its proceedings, '...in spite of his shrinking from publicity, he was prevailed upon to contribute a paper.'[17] He was a friend of the physicist James Joule, for whom he supplied scientific instru-ments. Joule was Vice-President of the Literary and Philosophical Society, and Chairman of the meeting at which Casartelli was elected as a member.

Thus the middle-class family into which Louis Charles Casartelli was born, was one with extensive interests and involvement in technology, foreign trade, and natural philosophy. It might be said that it was here, within the family and under the influence of his father, that he was first introduced to a 'wider vision' of both the world and of learning. Throughout his adult life he strove, by word and example, to promote an effective and influential Catholic middle class. For instance, he become a member of institutions closely related to the *milieu* of the 'Manchester Man', such as the Manchester Statistical Society and the Manchester Geographical Society.[18] Therefore when he was nominated bishop of Salford, his already established position within Manchester society, partly inherited from his family and also due to his own intellectual prowess and ability, was significant.

When, in later years Casartelli presented his ground-breaking papers on commercial education he did so as one who came from a commercial back-ground and was well aware of the need to expand Manchester's overseas trade in the face of foreign competition. He gained this experience in the period when the 'Manchester Men' dominated the city: a new order of businessman – merchants, manufacturers, and bankers – who were the creators of the industrial era in this one of its key cities. Out of these years had grown the 'Manchester School,' with its ideology of free trade and the national campaign against the Corn Laws. Alan Kidd remarks that, 'it was the town's rôle in the campaign to achieve a government policy in the middle class interest which secured its national importance. Central to this was the agitation against the Corn Laws and the activities of the anti-Corn Law League.'[19] The Corn Laws, introduced in 1815 to maintain farm prices *via* the imposition of duty on imported corn, were part and parcel of the landowners' political dominance. The manufacturers objected to the Corn Laws because they caused demands for wages increases and so reduced profits. In Kidd's words – 'Manchester was thus the symbol of a new order of society and a new economic philosophy.'[20]

FAMILY BACKGROUND

Louis Charles Casartelli's family was devoutly Catholic. An obituary described his father as 'a beautiful exemplar of Catholic life in the world,' and bore testimony to his sense of philanthropy and public service.[21] This example is an important influence in the formation of his son's life-long aim to extend the spirit of Catholicism beyond the confines of parochial boundaries.

> When he [Joseph Casartelli] came to Manchester, although the wave of Anti-Catholicism, consequent upon the re-establishment of the Hierarchy in England, was at its height, Catholicism itself was well established there ... But the spirit of Catholicism had extended beyond its parochial missions. The most pitiable and helpless of all conditions, the double affliction of poverty and orphanage, had moved the Catholics of Manchester and Salford to open a House in which young orphan girls could find shelter from their loneliness and miseries.[22]

This house became known as St Bridget's Orphanage. Joseph Casartelli was a long-serving member of its management committee. When Bishop Herbert Vaughan[23] wrote to Bishop Hedley[24] recommending Louis Charles for the episcopate, he described Mr. Casartelli as having been 'highly respected'; of Mrs. Casartelli, he wrote that she 'was a real old Catholic matron and poured good sense and virtue into her children all day long.'[25] An impression of the home background, and the mutual affection between father and son, can be gained from a letter written by Louis Charles shortly after his arrival at Ushaw College. It was '... so happy a home, where I have enjoyed a life, thank God! unchequered by misfortune and sustained by the society and affection of the most loving of parents...I know it is a severe trial and painful separation for you and for myself.'[26]

His close relationship with his father, whom he called his 'confidant', remained throughout his life. Two accounts taken from his diaries are particularly moving and reflect the depth of this relationship. In the first, relating the sudden and serious illness Casartelli senior suffered in 1874, both the son's concern and the father's faith are palpable:

> one of the most trying and dreadful ordeals I have ever passed through ... all at once the idea rose in his mind that he was probably on his death bed! ... He called me to his bedside, and solemnly gave me what he thought might be his last injunctions. He committed his soul to God; he left his wife and children, I must always do my best for them, specific messages with regard to each, to brothers and relations; so full, so calm, orderly, so thoughtful, kind, above all Christian and Catholic! Never let any of his blood forsake the Holy Roman Church![27]

The second account tells of his father's last days prior to his death. At the time Louis Charles was teaching in Louvain and had to return hastily to England. On his return to Belgium he wrote:

> Alas! This long gap covers the saddest epoch of my life. On Thursday March 15th, at breakfast I received the telegram that told me of the critical state of my dear father...The end came on Tuesday morning 5.15 a.m. A beautiful, edifying Christian death![28]

Another highly significant person in his life was his mother's sister, Mary Elizabeth Ronchetti. On the 25th anniversary of her death in 1905, Casartelli wrote of her as 'my second mother.'[29] Of his natural mother he remained largely silent; she figured very little in either his diaries or letters. There is no evidence to explain why this was so.[30] Throughout his life he remained close to his siblings. When he became a bishop, he would spend several weeks a year staying at his sisters' house close by St Bede's College. There he found the warmth and affection that was so necessary to sustain him in his work as bishop of the diocese. As will be made clear, practical responsibility and administration left him isolated and lonely.

Among the outstanding features of Louis Charles Casartelli's life, evident from its earliest days, were the remarkable brilliance of his mind, the retentiveness of his memory, and his gift as a polyglot. It is to these that we now turn.

THE SALFORD CATHOLIC GRAMMAR SCHOOL

Bishop William Turner,[31] the first bishop of Salford, founded the Salford Catholic Grammar School in the stables behind his house situated on The Crescent, Salford, in 1862; it was later merged with St Bede's College, Manchester. The Bishop's intention was to provide a classical education for boys destined for the priesthood. It was not, however, a junior seminary. The pupils were to be taught French, natural philosophy, drawing, and bookkeeping. On the day the school opened its doors for the first time, Casartelli was the second of six pupils to enrol, after a boy who proved to be a faster runner deprived him of the distinction of being the first. During the time he spent at the Grammar School he lodged with his 'Aunt Elesa' (Elizabeth Ronchetti) who also lived on The Crescent, at number 24; and while living with his aunt he received the first rudiments of his education.[32]

A fellow-student described the young Casartelli as, 'a neatly dressed boy with a handsome Italian face, a brilliant mind, a clear voice and remarkably refined manners'.[33] Another student recalled his having a wonderfully retentive memory, great power of concentration, and the ability to synthesise. Whilst at the Grammar School he taught himself Flemish in order to speak to his teachers, *émigré* priests from Belgium, in their mother tongue.

Bishop Turner exercised a profound influence upon the young and impressionable Casartelli. Years later, in a retrospect written for *Baeda*, he referred to him as 'the saintly old bishop.'[34] In a letter written to his father shortly after receiving news of the bishop's death, he called him a 'near relation' and actually described him as 'his godfather.'[35] The depth of feeling he had for Turner can be seen in his strong desire to attend the funeral:

> But I must be at the funeral, and see him again before he is closed up. I am sure you will make no objection to this, for the position in which I stand to Dr Turner and all the kindnesses I owe him have made me as it were in the position of a near relation to him, and I feel I ought to be at the funeral.[36]

The cordiality between Turner and Casartelli is reflected in a picture painted in 1862 by an artist called Mercier (see above p. 10).[37] Turner is portrayed presiding at the episcopal throne in Salford Cathedral, assisted by Canon Peter Benoit;[38] Casartelli is depicted as the bishop's train-bearer. During the years at the Grammar School, under the good influence of his Aunt Elesa and Canon Peter Benoit, Casartelli began to feel an attraction for the priest-hood.[39] With this end in view he continued his education at Ushaw College.

USHAW COLLEGE

Casartelli arrived at Ushaw College,[40] near Durham, on 21 September 1867. This seminary for the northern dioceses of England and Wales traces its history back to the college founded in Douai, France, by William Allen for the education of Catholics forced to flee England due to religious persecution. Shortly after arriving Casartelli wrote to his sister saying, 'this is a splendid college.'[41] Despite this impression, and the fact that he was perfectly happy there, he later admitted in his diary that he was nervous about breaking the college rules.[42] This is indicative of his sensitivity and eagerness to conform, apparent in his later life when he accepted the episcopate out of a sense of obedience.

What other traits can be known of his character? In his early days at Ushaw he was shy, retiring, and something of a recluse: 'but when the cloud-let lifted, his companions recognised what a loyal, loving school-fellow they had, how intimately he knew the character of each of us, how charitable he was in seeing only the good in us all, and what keen appreciation he showed for all the fun that was constantly enlivening life.'[43] His diaries give the impression of a youth who was able to make friends, who enjoyed studying, playing football, and taking part in other college 'pastimes.' One diary entry reads:

Went with Stokes and Dunne to Biggins. After dinner seven of us returned forming in two lines arm-in-arm; we got very jovial and extremely boisterous, singing quite wildly, despite our Roman collars etc. We rather startled the natives. When we got into the fields we took to things spiritual, the litany, several hymns, etc., and so we got to Alma Mater![44]

Another fellow pupil remembered that, despite a high intellectual capacity and an ability to 'study at any time and in any place, even in the Playroom,' Casartelli was no bookworm; on the contrary, he was eminently human.[45] He never took himself too seriously: once he admitted good-naturedly to his father that he had been teased because of his Lancashire accent.[46]

Casartelli's academic achievements at Ushaw

Further signs of Casartelli's academic excellence, first displayed at the Salford Grammar School, soon became apparent. He was put into the 'Grammar' stream, but was soon raised to 'Syntax,' and allowed to study privately without the assistance of a pedagogue.[47] His college reports show that he was consistently among the top five of his class. He excelled at Greek, Latin, and French. As 'a private amusement' he secretly began to learn Hebrew.[48] By reading Dante he became proficient in Italian.[49] This interest in the four-teenth century Italian poet and philosopher was to last the whole of his lifetime; in 1906 he became a co-founder of the Manchester Dante Society.[50]

The Prefect of Studies advised him of the dangers of over-work and suggested, as a means of relaxation, that he take part in a college retreat. During this he read what was to be for him a seminal book – Roger Vaughan's *Life of St Thomas Aquinas*. This book introduced him 'to the new world of the Middle Ages...peopled with plenty of great objects, so that my head is now full of new acquaintances – St Thomas and St Albert. St Thomas was a great man, such massive genius.'[51] Some time later he bought a copy of Aquinas' *Summa Theologica*, which he described as, 'a fabulous thing ... It reminds me of a great journey through the universe. One can see Dante's progress in it.'[52]

Casartelli was a clear candidate for the London University examinations for the degrees of BA and MA. He was one of the brightest jewels in Ushaw's academic crown, and through his outstanding success in the examinations was a significant figure in its relationship with the University of London. Ushaw College gained its affiliation to London University in 1840, thus enabling its students to take the degree of B.A.[53] After a while this custom fell into disuse. Dr Robert Tate,[54] by making the preparation for the degree a central feature of the college's curriculum, restored the link in 1863. However, the link between the two institutions was not without its critics. For example, W. G. Ward[55] considered the London Matriculation and BA to be superficial and lacking scholarship.[56] Further objections were raised because the philosophy the students had to study was not Christian philosophy, and the examiners were 'Sophists and Sceptics.'[57] This fear was allayed in 1872 when Francis Wilkinson[58] pointed out to the hierarchy, in regard to the objections about the philosophy examination, that 'Neither was the idea right in theory nor was it right in practice; for London University had no set syllabus which candidates were forced to follow, and in fact candidates had passed the examinations without the study of either Mill or Bain, even when Bain himself was an examiner!'[59]

When a member of staff at Ushaw pointed this out to Casartelli he found it a little difficult to credit,[60] although ironically, by his outstanding success in the examinations he proved it to be true.

In July 1870 Casartelli took the first part of the BA degree. He was awarded Honours and an Exhibition in Latin. The results of his year's work, noted in the College Diary, were: *Ludovicus Casartelli: Acol. 1 B.A. Honores et Exhib. In Litteris Latinis adeptus est Jul '70; rediit Mart. 8 '71.*[61] He did not take the second part until 1872. This absence is explained by Casartelli being given a vacation after the examinations. The subjects he studied were extremely wide:

> My five months' absence has caused me to lose a great deal of ground ... Astronomy has been completely finished, and they have a capital course of it...the texts they followed were Herschel and J. Norman Lockyer. As for Physics, I have totally lost my chance for one essay which is to be given in three weeks last Friday. Subject: 'The Undulatory Theory of Light'. I am at present studying Spectrum Analysis and Polarisation. Physiology I haven't lost so much...[62]

The science course met with his approval, and was 'most liberal ... the authors put into our hands are the very best and the latest.'[63] He studied Logic, Moral Philosophy, and Classics, too. The philosophy studied, he told his father, '...is not Christian philosophy but 'London' philosophy; the authors are Mill and Bain.'[64] He took the pass degree paper at Ushaw in October 1872. In his diary he described the examination and how he had answered the questions,

> The pass examination is over at last. Subjects today were logic and moral philosophy. I was highly satisfied with both papers, and I think I wrote good ones; sixty-four pages in all morning and afternoon...What an interesting study philosophy is, there is always a great charm about it for me. I freely gave my opinion, I mean the Scholastic; and fully criticised Mr. Bain, their great authority.[65]

He took the honours papers in London. Prior to his departure Casartelli was bed-ridden with measles. In order that he might travel more comfortably, his father hired a First Class railway carriage and had a temporary bed made up for his still-ailing son. In the examinations he gained a First in Classical Honours, (with the award of a Scholarship) and a First (with the award of a prize) in Scripture (Hebrew).

Casartelli's record of achievement is remarkable by any standards. It is even more so when one takes into account his five months absence from Ushaw. He was one of only eight Ushaw students, out of sixty, to gain honours in the examinations, and one out of only seven from Ushaw to take the MA. By 1896 he was still one out of only two to have ever been awarded the Gold Medal since the foundation of London University. Nevertheless, within a relatively short space of time, despite his outstanding success, he came to criticise the London University system. He described the external degree system, and the general principle of coaching students for examinations, as a 'tyrannous fetish' and destructive of true culture.[66] We shall return to this issue in chapter three.

Casartelli left Ushaw in November 1872. His diary for 21 September shows that his time there had been truly happy: 'It is 5 yrs. to the day since I came to the college. How well I remember that wonderful day in my life!'[67] His departure was accompanied with more than academic trophies. He had been formed in its tradition of mixed-education, first begun in Douai, i.e. the education of lay and Church students in the same establishment. This experience deeply impressed him; he saw it as a means of unifying the Catholic body. As will be seen, the idea of unity and its accompanying strength was fundamental to his way of thinking and proved to be the key to his policy as a bishop. Casartelli saw the tradition as serving a dual purpose:

> [It] has had a great deal to do with the remarkable development of the Catholic Church in England this century … It assured lay people of a fundamentally religious education and trained them to have a deeply Catholic mind. It linked the clergy to Catholic lay leaders by that link so powerful of a common education, and giving it a very great influence on the latter.[68]

This tradition found favour with John Henry Newman and Herbert Vaughan.[69] Newman had wanted to involve the laity in the governing of the Catholic University of Ireland. He wrote

> You will be doing the greatest possible benefit to the Catholic cause all over the world, if you succeed in making the University a middle station at which clergy and laity can meet, so as to learn to understand and to yield to each other – and from which, as from a common ground, they may act in union upon an age, which is running headlong into infidelity.'[70]

Casartelli lauded this tradition, and would see it as one of the most valuable aspects of St Bede's College, where he was to spend the years 1876 – 1903 as a member of staff.[71] In this way he was able to maintain in his educational projects in Manchester something of Newman's ideas.[72]

Two rôle models shaped Casartelli's life and intellectual development: John Henry Newman, whose works he had begun to collect at Ushaw, and Herbert Vaughan, the second Bishop of Salford. Casartelli's theological outlook found Newman more sympathetic, but in practical affairs, Vaughan came to be the dominant influence on him – with some resulting tension, as we shall see. Before continuing to trace Casartelli's academic career, attention will be paid to these two influential figures.

THE INFLUENCE OF JOHN HENRY NEWMAN

To be a reader of Newman, while studying at Ushaw College in the 1870s, was to be out of step with a strong current of opinion in the Ultramontanist wing of the Church, which distrusted any reliance on the opinion of the laity in matters of doctrine.

J. D. Holmes, in his study of English Ultramontanism in this period, argued that the training and development of the clergy dramatically reflected the spread and development of this movement.[73] Holmes's interpretation represents 'Ultramontanism' as a somewhat monolithic phenomenon, involving the imposition of Italianate devotions and practices upon the Church in England by Roman authorities.[74] Jeffrey Von Arx has called this view into question.[75] He maintains that Ultramontanism is a phenomenon that can only be studied and defined within a particular context, in a specific place and for a specific function.[76] Despite these necessary qualifications, Holmes's study remains valuable in assessing the early circumstances of Casartelli's career. Arguing that during this period, the theological teaching and opinions of English priests began to shift away from Gallicanism and move toward the Ultramontane direction, Holmes points to John Gillow, professor of dogmatic theology at Ushaw, who '… thought nothing of attacking … John Henry Newman's essay 'On Consulting the Faithful.''[77] This attack was only partial – Newman's essay dealt with the place of the laity within the Church and suggested that the bishops ought to 'really desire to know the opinion of the laity on subjects with which the laity are especially concerned.'[78] By 'consulting' Newman meant not, 'asking the opinion of,' but rather, 'ascertaining facts,' as a 'physician consults the pulse of his patient; but not in the same sense in which his patient consults him.'[79] It was against this element of Newman's teaching that John Gillow reacted,[80] while in other matters retaining high regard for Newman's work.[81] Among the staff at

Ushaw, Newman was regarded with 'grave suspicion ... To be a Newmanite was almost to be suspect.'[82] Despite being made a cardinal by Leo XIII, a certain element of suspicion still surrounded Newman, until 1906 open conflict was a distinct possibility, as Casartelli noted in his diary.[83] Whilst at Ushaw Casartelli not only read Newman, which he had been advised to do in order to improve his English style, he also began to collect his works, which became a lasting influence. 'Received Dr. Newman's 'Historical Sketches' (just out) – the first steps towards a collection of J.N.'s work I hope to make. The greater part of the vol. is his 'Universities' (office and work). It is very charming. Only what a contrast to London!'[84]

A few days later, when out walking with one of his fellows, he discussed what he had read:

> It is a great pity and I think that in his letters with Capes he said he firmly believed in the infallibility, but it gave him pain it had been defined. This gives scandal and people say 'He believes the infallibility yet calls it in question at once, *viz.* on the opportunists'. However, I reject this. No, infallibility refers to dogma, i. e. to truth in *se;* the question of opportunities is one depending on human positions, dispositions and states of mind.[85]

The debt Casartelli owed to Newman was not only intellectual. In a letter written in 1875, shortly after the two had met, Casartelli acknowledged the part Newman had played in his personal formation,

> For many years (to me), from the very dawn of my thinking life, I have grown to cherish a reverence and an affection for you, which springs from a thorough and intense sympathy with you, (if you will forgive my saying so), in all your beliefs, feelings, and positions, so far as they have been known to me; and I have long looked forward to a personal acquaintance with yourself as the height of my hopes.[86]

The depth of Newman's influence is evident in a lecture given in 1919 when Casartelli stated that, 'by the time I left Ushaw for Louvain there had grown up a regular cult for this marvellous master of pure and pellucid style and thought, and consequently for his views.'[87]

THE INFLUENCE OF HERBERT VAUGHAN

Herbert Vaughan became the second Bishop of Salford in September 1872.[88] Copies of his letters to Casartelli, preserved in the Salford Diocesan Archives, permit an insight into the formative influence which he exercised over his prodigy and how he encouraged him to use his gifts and talents to further his own plans and ambitions in matters of commercial education. Not least important about these documents is the evidence which they contain of

Vaughan's universal understanding of the rôle of the episcopate, and his hopes for a commercial college in Manchester. These are crucially important issues in understanding the life and work of Casartelli in the sphere of the organised public work of the Church: in his episcopate, he adopted Vaughan's stance, and as an educator, he was intimately connected with plans for a commercial college.

Before continuing his studies at Louvain, Casartelli spent eighteen months with his family, who by 1861 had removed to Egerton Terrace, Higher Ardwick, Manchester.[89] Here he prepared for his MA, which he gained with the rarely granted Gold Medal. His diary conveys to the reader the obviously comfortable lifestyle enjoyed by his family. His time was spent in a leisurely and genteel way – reading, taking tea with family friends, studying, visiting 'town', etc. He mentioned with certain regularity Quarant' Ore, or 'Forty Hours'; Benediction; and other devotions.[90] He also recorded having read or written in some twenty-four languages; for example he bought a copy of the Book of Jonah written in Chaldee, Syriac, Ethiopic and Arabic as well as a copy of the Psalms in Armenian. It was during this period that he first came under the influence of Vaughan, who entrusted him with numerous literary tasks, including writing book reviews for The Tablet and articles for the Catholic Opinion. The reviews exhibit the breadth of Casartelli's interests, ranging from George Mivart's Man and Apes, to Ancient and Modern Atomic Theories, and The Zend-Avesta.

The warmth with which Vaughan speaks of Casartelli's relatives suggests that he was on familiar terms with the family.[91] Vaughan became also a rôle model for Casartelli in many ways, but especially as a bishop. Nevertheless, in other ways Casartelli demonstrated an ability to think independently, and in ways at variance with Vaughan. This was particularly marked in the way that Casartelli valued the ideas of Newman. His admiration for Newman was unbounded: whereas his episcopal mentor summed up Newman's Apologia thus: 'I have read it with a mixture of pain and pleasure. The egotism may be disgusting if it is venial. There are views put forward which I abhor, and which fill me with pain and suspicion.'[92] Despite Casartelli's youth, inexperience, and independent mind, Vaughan held his judgement in high esteem. For example, he asked him to send notice of any books that he might come across during his studies, because these could be new to the Tablet and thus useful to others. He also asked him to recruit priests from the continent who would be willing to come and spend time working in Salford diocese.[93]

The most important part played by Vaughan in Casartelli's early life was to appoint him to the staff of St Bede's College, Manchester. Vaughan wanted a commercial college in his diocese to educate the children of the Catholic commercial classes. This endeavour very soon brought him into dispute with the Society of Jesus who also wanted to establish a college in Manchester.[94] Robert O'Neil describes the argument between Vaughan and the Jesuits as 'a struggle for influence over the growing middle-class community in the nineteenth century. The school the Jesuits opened in Manchester was repeatedly stated to be one for the middle classes.'[95] Father Peter Gallwey, the Jesuit Provincial, wrote to Vaughan saying that the Cardinal Prefect of Propaganda Fide had asked the Father General of the Jesuits 'to do all he could in England for middle-class education, and named Manchester among other places.'[96] Gallwey maintained that it was the special privilege of his Order, granted by the Holy See, to establish schools and colleges without the permission, and despite the objection, of the local bishop. Vaughan contested this right. For him the point at issue was who was to be the judge of the needs of a diocese; in his mind this should be the local bishop. He spent eighteen months in Rome clarifying the matter and pleading his cause against the Jesuits.[97] The result of this dispute was the pronouncement by Pope Leo XIII, *Romanos Pontifices*, defining the relationship between the bishop and the regular clergy working within his diocese.[98]

Casartelli's intended rôle on the staff of St Bede's was obvious from the outset. Vaughan took him into his confidence and drew him into his plans. He wrote personally to inform him of the purchase of the Manchester Aquarium in order to convert it into a college, and to say that a museum was to be an integral part. He encouraged him to undertake a fact-finding tour around Belgium and Germany to collect information useful for the Manchester venture. He wrote,

> The more I have thought of your future the more convinced I am that you had better devote your time almost exclusively to direct preparation of it. Besides the prestige this will give you it will furnish you with many suggestions and a standard of attainment.
>
> The technological system is only recently introduced into England, and the superiority of the continental in this respect has been fully admitted.
>
> I would advise you and do as I did 24 yrs. ago when I visited some thirty seminaries. I had a book in which I recorded everything that seemed worth knowing – and had a list of questions which I asked in each...in order to test the ideas that prevailed in each.[99]

Vaughan explained to Casartelli what his hopes and designs were for St Bede's. In so doing he provided the contemporary reader with a most significant insight into the breadth of his vision and thinking. He had a wide understanding of the universal mission of the Church, as well as an appreciation of society's educational needs and wants which extended beyond the immediate concern of the local Church to educate her children. In a letter of 1877, Vaughan wrote:

I take it that we must aim rather at a commercial and practical course than a purely technical one in Manchester; for the reason that Manchester is essentially commercial and practical and that we shall hardly be likely to attract except in the direction of Manchester in its character as a commercial centre ... considering that there exists nowhere a Catholic Commercial College – that Catholics from all parts of America, Australia and Europe are sent to England to learn commerce, and that they either fail to obtain what they require by being sent to our colleges which are exclusively classical, or lose their faith and morals by being sent to Protestant schools or families, and then considering the beneficial mission of the Church to the whole world it has always seemed to me that we ought to make a provision in Manchester to meet the general want. I wish to provide for the children of my own flock in the first place, but at the same time I cannot fail to bear in mind that a bishop ought, as St Alphonso somewhere says, to be interested in and to work for objects which extend far beyond his own dioceses. He who is of the Apostolic line ought to have the universal spirit of an Apostle.[100]

In this statement by his mentor, two things are particularly significant for Casartelli's later career. Firstly, Vaughan's purpose was to provide 'a practical course' rather than 'a purely technical one.' In order to realise this aim, Casartelli dedicated much time and effort in teaching commercial subjects and generally promoting commercial education as a means of providing a true education in the face of the diminution in the teaching of *litterae humaniores*. We shall return to this theme in chapter three. Secondly, Vaughan's mention of the 'universal spirit of the Apostle' shows a freedom from the debilitating constraints of a narrow view of the Church's mission. Casartelli as a bishop was imbued with this same spirit: he imitated Vaughan by constantly striving to inspire among the clergy and people of his diocese a wider vision and understanding of the work and mission of the Church.

However, differences did emerge. Casartelli, the thinker and scholar with great capacities as a linguist, preferred to draw his pupils on by enthusing them at the intellectual level. One of them later remembered how Casartelli, when teaching Latin, 'did not believe in using exercise books; all that he insisted on was any clean piece of paper, legible writing, and 'sign your paper.''[101] Vaughan's preferred method reflected the way that he constantly drove himself to achieve his goals and fulfil his ambitions: teaching should be organised and systematic. Thus, after the college had been opened for a number of years, Vaughan placed before Casartelli 'two or three considerations ... which I hope may tend to fix your attention upon certain points and thus secure a general improvement.'[102] He advised that Casartelli, as Prefect of Studies, ought to apply more constant pressure upon the students.

He felt there was need of 'a little more of the driving power' and that the boys must be encouraged to 'reach the almost unattainable goal.' Encouragement alone was not enough to make them reach the highest standard; Vaughan could not 'resist the conviction that very much more might be got out of your boys than we get out of them at present.' Casartelli, therefore, was encouraged to visit other schools, Catholic or Protestant, where he might observe 'modes of forcing boys to work.' The problem lay in the fact that Casartelli was of 'such quick, ready and versatile genius' that he was apt to 'undervalue the need of the driving grinding power, already referred to.' Although bluntly stated, these observations were not meant to undermine Casartelli's rôle as Prefect of Studies. They were meant to augment his lack of experience and serve the general good of the college. In summing up his feelings, Vaughan spoke appreciatively of Casartelli's efforts,

> I should however be very neglectful of facts and of my estimate of them if I did not say how much I value the devotedness and zeal with which you have always given yourself to your work and how much indebted I feel to you for what you have done during the past six or seven years. It is because your work becomes more important year by year that I have put down these observations, with a view to helping you on.

Notwithstanding this evidence of a good working relationship with Vaughan, who recognised Casartelli's 'quick, ready and versatile genius,' nothing could hide the fact that the post of Prefect of Studies was uncongenial to him, and far below his capabilities. Casartelli was in fact eminently suited for a university post: Bishop John Keane, the first rector of the Catholic University of Washington, had tried to recruit Casartelli to his staff. Vaughan, the practical organiser, did not fully grasp the potential of the young scholar whom he had recruited to his programme: and he could only respond to the American request with an eye to his own local interests. His swift and curt reply contrasts with the more generous spirit noted above.

> It is quite useless for Bishop Keane to seek my consent to your going to America. I should like to know on what principle the United States should draw continually on Europe when it does nothing whatsoever for the Foreign Missions of the Church. The States are big enough, boastful enough, rich enough and strong enough to provide for themselves. Why should they 'covet their neighbour's ass'? Let them try, *date debitor vobis.*[103]

Nevertheless, Casartelli approached his routine work at St Bede's, according to Vaughan, with 'devotedness and zeal,' and would show the same qualities when later appointed to another task even further removed from his taste – that of being a bishop.

After having spent a year and a half at his parent's house, Casartelli continued his studies at Louvain – the place where he was to be most happy and for which he maintained, throughout his life, feelings of deep affection.

LOUVAIN

Vaughan provided Casartelli with a 'very full and flattering'[104] reference recommending him to the authorities of the *College St. Esprit*, at Louvain. He entered into residence there on 21 April 1874. The President and Rector Magnificus, whom Casartelli thought 'very kind', advised him 'to speak as much French, German, etc. as I could.'[105] The first thought he committed to his diary was – 'would be good if I could get into Degree Course!'[106] The Faculty of Theology allowed him the liberty of following whatever courses he wished to choose. He opted for the ordinary course for his first year with a view to taking the superior course the year following. Casartelli developed his talents with languages; his diary mentions his having made attempts at speaking or learning German, Icelandic, Assyrian, Dutch, and Syrian. Whilst in Louvain he came into contact with another formative influence in the person of Charles de Harlez,[107] Professor of Oriental languages. Casartelli described their first meeting in his diary,

> At 5.00 p.m. went to call on Prof. de Harlez, 25, Rue des Recollects. He is the new professor of Sanskrit. A tall man, old, with spectacles. A great invalid (delicate throat) and solaces himself when ill with music: as he is a good pianist. He is a priest. Very affable and charming. Is to teach Sanskrit and also Iranian languages: Zend, Pahlevi, Old Persian, etc. I engaged to follow his course and thus make the eleventh student.[108]

There was a certain similarity between the characters of the two men. Both were extremely gifted linguists and both suffered ill health throughout their lives. Due to his delicate constitution, de Harlez's bishop had allowed him to devote his life to Sanskrit, Zend, and 'cognate languages'. If Casartelli had been allowed to occupy a similar position his scholarly talents and inclinations would have been far more fulfilled. At any event, it was through de Harlez's influence that he became interested in Zoroastrianism. He was very impressed with the Professor's translation of the Zend-Avesta[109] and took special note of the Zoroastrian doctrine of the One, Spiritual, Invisible God, of its morality and doctrine of original sin, expiation, and resurrection of the body. De Harlez became Casartelli's supervisor when, in 1884, he wrote his doctoral thesis, *The Philosophy of the Mazdayasnian Religion under the Sassanids*.[110] On de Harlez's death Casartelli succeeded him as Professor of Iranian languages.[111]

De Harlez nurtured Casartelli's love of Oriental languages.[112] So deep was this passion that during his second year he sought a dispensation so that he might take his bachelorship in theology a year early and so be free to devote himself totally to the subject. Failure to secure the dispensation did not cause him any undue disappointment. On hearing of the decision he wrote:

> Myself at last free! That is to say I went to see Prof. Moulart this morning about a dispensation for a year's theology and so as to take the bachelorship this year. He assured me it would be useless to try as the faculty would not and could not grant it: *ergo* no degree this year, *ergo* practically none at all. I also talked it over with Lamy,[113] and suggested the giving up and returning next year to devote myself to Oriental Studies. He very much encouraged me. I feel quite happy now'.[114]

His father, however, 'was much disappointed' by this decision.[115]

Casartelli now suffered another breakdown in health and had to return to England. No details of his complaint are available, beyond the fact that it consisted of a swelling on the neck. During this stay in England he went to see Vaughan and 'talked over [his] scheme of abandoning degrees and taking to Oriental Studies. His Lordship quite approves of it, I am glad to say.'[116] Despite his initial approval, within a matter of two months Vaughan had changed his mind; the organisation of Manchester education took precedence. He wrote to Casartelli telling him to prepare himself instead, 'almost exclusively to direct preparation,' for his work at St Bede's.[117]

Casartelli was ordained a priest in Salford Cathedral on 10 September 1876; he recorded the day with great joy,

> The thrice-happy day of my ordination. I surely never felt so happy as today! The ceremony took place at 11 o'clock in the Cathedral, a grand function. I had the immense privilege of having my whole family, together with cousins from Liverpool, most of my friends.[118]

On returning to finish his studies he entertained the hope of extending his stay, and thus remaining within his chosen scholarly field.

> I am very glad I have returned to Louvain, at least for one more year: would I could stay longer! The lectures are simply invaluable. Also my Oriental Studies will greatly profit.[119]

However, his hopes of staying longer in Louvain did not come to fruition. Vaughan, concerned as always with practical organisation, decided otherwise. Casartelli noted wrote in his diary:

> Today it was decided by the Bp. that I should at once prepare to leave Louvain and to visit technical schools and similar institutions in Germany for benefit of St Bede's.[120]

Thus ended the happiest years of Louis Charles Casartelli's life.

CASARTELLI AS A MEMBER OF STAFF AT ST. BEDE'S COLLEGE

Casartelli took up the post of Prefect of Studies in September 1877. The subsequent years were to be amongst the most trying and difficult of his life, as can be appreciated from one of the most self-revealing entries he ever made in his diaries:

> What a gulf between the time at which my diary breaks and today! And looking back fills me with sadness and regret – I was then a student; I am now a professor. My thrice-happy student life is over, 'rolled up like a shepherd's tent', never to return. This is what makes me so sad. Experience has taught me only too truly that many thorns are in the life of the superior; what loss of companionship, sympathy, light-heartedness, freedom from responsibility! ... to me the life as a professor has been to some degree bitter and is continually full of anxieties, troubles, disappointments. What would I not give for the exchange, and could I but throw up my functions and become a student at St. Esprit again.[121]

Nothing could have expressed more clearly his distaste for administration and responsibility, and at the same time, by inference, indicate where his heart and tastes really lay – in the study of Oriental languages and the intellectual companionship of college life. At this point in his life he was obviously lonely. His isolation was increased by the hard, uphill task of trying to improve standards in the college, a task which would inevitably have brought him into conflict with some of his colleagues. He suffered a further emotional blow and loss of companionship when his aunt, Elizabeth Ronchetti, who had become the matron of the college, decided to leave after only one year because she had been badly treated by certain members of staff.[122] The frankness and heavy-heartedness with which Casartelli expressed himself in this difficult situation gives some idea of how he must have felt when he was later nominated bishop of Salford.

In September 1887, Casartelli, for reasons that are not clear, resigned his post as Prefect of Studies.[123] The position was offered to Fr Henry Newton, formerly Prefect of Studies at Ushaw; however, he declined the offer.[124] On hearing of this, Casartelli withdrew his resignation and wrote in his diary: 'Suppose I shall continue as before, and as all the professors strongly desire.'[125] Some indication of the amount of tension and unrest there must have been in the college can be surmised by the fact that a member of staff, Fr William Hill, in the presence of several witnesses, admitted to having burned the College diary for 1887 – 1891. With the amalgamation in 1891 of St Bede's College with the Salford Catholic Grammar School, and the subsequent appointment of Casartelli as rector, a new diary was begun with the following prefix:

The present entry prefixed to this bound volume of the New Series is made both to record and to solemnly protest against this unjustifiable destruction of one of the most valuable possessions of the College.[126]

Was Casartelli a success in this uncomfortable period at St Bede's? If the opinion of Canon George Richardson, one of the diocesan religious inspectors of schools and colleges, was accurate, then it would seem that only a qualified answer can be given. When Richardson wrote to Bishop Hedley at the time of Casartelli's name being put forward as one of the candidates for the new post of Catholic chaplain to the University of Oxford, he stated, 'He has not been a great success as head of St Bede's as a guide to the staff nor advisor either to boys or parents and to my mind St Bede's would not lose much by Dr. Casartelli's resignation.'[127]

Richardson assured Hedley that his opinion was unbiased and one which he 'was not alone in holding amongst Dr. Casartelli's friends, of which I am one of the oldest.'[128] However, a series of recollections[129] written by *alumni* of St Bede's gives a different picture. One recounts Casartelli's wonderful way of imparting knowledge and how he formed a small club for pupils who wished to learn Spanish. The same person recalled that, 'One Protestant friend admitted to me that he would rather spend an evening with Fr. Casartelli than with anyone in the world! With all his knowledge and responsibilities he was just one of us in play time. He was very keen on handball, and I enjoyed hundreds of games with him.'[130]

Another former pupil remembered Casartelli as 'the outstanding personality of the College', under whom 'it was a delight and a pleasure to study.'[131] Others remember a humble, kind, and gentle person. Casartelli's method of teaching, despite Vaughan's insistence that he be more demanding, was clearly of benefit to one student who stated: 'I have always felt that so much better studies would be done if only masters knew how to work up the enthusiasm of boys as Casartelli did in so many ways.'[132] Yet another pupil remembered a slightly different Casartelli, one who was reserved and never seen on the football field: 'Yet, somehow, we each of us felt that we knew him well and that he knew us better. For he was mightily interested in every boy, and watched our successes and failures with fatherly solicitude. He had a strange gift of being at once remote and familiar. In consequence we all stood in great awe of him, and yet, in familiar moments, could talk easily to him.'[133] These contrasting estimates typify the paradox of Casartelli, the intense, dedicated scholar thrust into the uncongenial work of educational administration.

During this long and difficult period, and six months after the severe reprimand which he had received from Vaughan concerning his teaching methods,[134] Casartelli was allowed, in 1884, to return to Louvain for as he put it, a 'six month's supplementary stay and work, *gratia episcopi*.'[135] During this time he wrote his doctoral thesis and was awarded the unusual degree of Doctor of Oriental Languages. Characteristically, he gained it, according to the university's records, *'avec grande distinction.'*[136]

CONCLUSION

What conclusions can be drawn from these formative years of Louis Charles Casartelli's life? From the earliest days, his qualities as a sensitive, observant, somewhat introspective, but gifted individual were apparent. The brilliance of his mind for which he was to be particularly known was evident during his time at the Salford Catholic Grammar School. His contemporaries also commented upon his reserve, kindness, and gentleness, the same qualities for which he was to be remembered by his pupils at St Bede's. To these must be added his social graces. At Ushaw he gave the impression of being distant and perhaps aloof. Because of his academic background this was how he also appeared to many of the clergy of the diocese. In reality he was very perceptive in social matters. One of his former pupils recalled, he was 'mightily interested' in individuals.[137] At the same time, it should be recognised that his highly organised, determined outlook left him to a large degree in awe of authority: it was whilst at Ushaw that he recorded his fear of breaking the college rules.[138]

The most influential people in his earliest days were his father, Elizabeth Ronchetti his aunt, and Canon Peter Benoit. In this company, he thrived: they nurtured his sensitive personality and nature, as well as his vocation to the priesthood. Casartelli was the product of a highly-skilled Italian *émigré* family, who felt equally at home in a wider European setting as in his native city of Manchester, for which he held a great devotion. His family remained the mainstay of his emotional life.

The importance of a supportive, intelligent circle for Casartelli is apparent also from the record of his years at Ushaw, which were among the happiest of his life. He was at his most comfortable in academia, having the ability to study in any environment or situation. He left Ushaw convinced by his own experience of the benefits of the education of Church and lay students in the same establishment: mutual understanding, lasting friendships, and above all the creation of a united Catholic body with a truly Catholic mind.

The limitations of Casartelli's early formation should also be recognised. Although he was delighted to be able to pursue advanced studies at Louvain, the experience also gave him first-hand experience of continental anticlericalism. He once recorded that he '... was publicly insulted. I had passed a school of biggish boys out walking, when one of them threw a pebble and struck me full on the left ear.'[139] He also recounted to his father the attack upon a procession in the city of Liège by anti-clerical university students.[140] These experiences probably contributed to his fear of socialism, which was later manifest in his mistrust of the nascent Labour Party – an issue on which he was later to clash with Archbishop Bourne of Westminster. On this issue, Peter Doyle comments valuably on the negative aspects of Casartelli's dual experience of England and continental Europe:

> There is, perhaps, evidence here of the debit side of what may be called Casartelli's continentalism. His links with the Continent and his interest in its concerns put him in touch with the latest developments in Catholic social thought, and gave him a wider vision than most of his fellow bishops. But they also brought him into contact with the routine refrain of anti-clericalism in continental Socialism.[141]

The tension which was to affect Casartelli's life most profoundly, was also evident in his early years. The perceptive scholar and linguist, to whom the equally sensitive but isolated figure of Newman was a lifelong inspiration,[142] came under the influence of a determined, expansionist organiser: Bishop Herbert Vaughan. If Casartelli had been able to remain under the tutelage of Charles de Harlez, he would have progressed still further as an accomplished Oriental scholar. This was to be his 'other life.' It was, we might say, his natural habitat: but he was not allowed to inhabit it. Instead, Vaughan's influence and plans became dominant in his life. Vaughan was a very forceful character, full of ambition and constantly making plans. In the intellectually gifted Casartelli he acquired a great asset. Moreover, just as Vaughan was forceful, so Casartelli was compliant. In the normal course of events, it was to be expected that, with the authority of a bishop, Vaughan would shape and direct a young priest's life. However, in Casartelli's case, the effects of Vaughan's guidance and direction were particularly far-reaching. The two positions that Casartelli held for longest – prefect of studies, and bishop – were both due to Vaughan. It spoke well of Casartelli's sense of duty that in both, even though he accepted them with a sense of resignation, he gave of his best. Despite these tensions between Casartelli the scholar and thinker, and Vaughan the ecclesiastical organiser, some evidence of resolution and the formation of a common project, can be discerned in these early years. For very early in his adult life, Casartelli was introduced to the 'apostolate of the press' when Vaughan asked him to write a series of articles for the *Catholic Opinion*.[143] On this task, he thrived: he was able to present the Catholic interest on issues of the day in a stream of articles for the general public. In the next chapter, we examine how Casartelli put his many talents to an – initially unexpected – use: as an apologist and writer.

Chapter Two

Apologist and Writer

E videncefor the years, 1873 to 1900, in which Casartelli became an active
public writer for the Catholic cause is somewhat restricted, because at
an early stage he ceased to keep what had already become a rather sporadic
diary.[1] He felt that he had allowed his journal to 'degenerate down to mere
dry bones, to a useless list.'[2] This is partly explained by his sense of caution:
'By reading up on a diary of time gone-by one learns its value, and the truth
of A.K. and B's advice about 'never keeping a skeleton in the cupboard.'[3]

In spite of this infrequency, and the apparent added difficulty that very
few letters relating to this time have survived, the available sources still
make it possible to construct a clear and definite picture of his thoughts and
ideas on prominent issues of the day. His papers and pamphlets on Oriental
studies and commercial education show him to have been a scholar with a
gift for originality and an awareness of contemporary needs in these fields.
His numerous and wide-ranging newspaper articles[4] are characteristic of his
ability to synthesise and evidence of the scope of his interests and intellectual
rigour. In these sources, aspects of his character come clearly to the fore. We
find Casartelli to have been a man of feelings, sensitive in his dealings with
others, yet capable of being firm and rigorous in argument. His intellectual
honesty was apparent in his decision to decline the offer to become chaplain
to the Catholic students at Oxford.

The present chapter concerns itself with that aspect of his intellectual life
which found expression in his rôle as writer and apologist. Two aspects of his
apologetics will be looked at: firstly, the validity of the double allegiance of
Catholics to the authorities of Church and State. Casartelli argued that there
was no inconsistency between obeying the Pope in matters of faith and
morals, and being a loyal citizen of the Crown. The second aspect stems
largely from the first: his engagement with the anti-Catholic feeling that
followed in the wake of the Decrees of the First Vatican Council.

THE RESURGENCE OF ANTI-CATHOLICISM IN THE 1870S

Casartelli's apologetical articles for the *Catholic Opinion*[5] were written at the request of Herbert Vaughan, who was utterly convinced of the value of the press as an instrument for defending and furthering the work of the Church. Casartelli was writing not only at Vaughan's behest and under his direct authority; he also had to submit drafts for his approval before they were printed.[6] This suggests that he was more of a mouthpiece than a writer who was given a free rein. Nonetheless, this should not disguise the formative effect the writing of these articles had on Casartelli.

The 1867 Reform Act, with the subsequent expansion of the electorate, coupled with the Education Act of 1870, resulted in the press becoming the most important medium for the communication of ideas. To some degree Vaughan feared this expansion and the effect it might have on the masses. To counter such adverse influence he purchased the *Catholic Opinion* and *The Tablet.*[7] Vaughan deliberately introduced Casartelli to the 'apostolate of the written word.' This early work as Catholic advocate-writer was one that Casartelli would constantly call upon and seek to encourage in others.[8]

Vaughan's request for help came at a time not only of general public criticism of the Catholic Church, but also of attacks levelled at him personally and at his brother, Kenelm.[9] Herbert Vaughan was under attack from supporters of the Liberal Party who objected to his ideas about how Catholics ought to vote.[10] The majority of Casartelli's articles were written to address political issues. Simultaneously, Kenelm Vaughan was in dispute with an Anglican parson about the use of Scripture in the Catholic Church.[11] Central to later expressions of the long tradition of anti-Catholic feeling in Victorian England was the reaction of W. E. Gladstone to the Syllabus of Errors and the First Vatican Council. He was bitterly opposed to both, and used them as a basis for questioning the allegiance of Catholics to State authority. Casartelli addressed the above issues in a series of responses that covered three disputed areas: how the Catholic and Protestant understandings of the Bible differed, the way Catholics ought to vote in the face of certain issues, and the allegiance of Catholics to civil authority in the light of the First Vatican Council's definition of Papal Infallibility.

The new form of anti-Catholicism, which Casartelli confronted, was of a more intellectual type, and found expression in the newspapers, rather than in physical violence which had been the case in earlier manifestations, for example the 'Ashton Riots' and the 'Murphy Riots' of the 1860s.[12] Nonetheless, fear of violent attack was still a factor among the Catholics of Manchester, as Casartelli's letters and diaries show.[13] An example of the new style of attack was the attempt in 1870 by C. N. Newdegate, MP for North

Warwickshire, who called for a Select Committee to enquire into 'Catholic Conventual and Monastic Institutions.'[14] His efforts to organise a Parliamentary Bill to this effect were opposed by members of the Manchester Catholic Club,[15] led by Canon Toole, who lobbied the four MPs for Manchester and Salford to oppose the Bill. Two Members supported the Club's motion; two were non-committal.[16] Although Newdegate's Bill failed, it highlighted how Catholicism could still be subjected to calls for strict statutory control. Accompanying this political antipathy was a deliberate re-opening of more common tensions and fears aroused by recalling the Massacre of St Bartholomew,[17] and spreading the opinion that Catholics were bad at trade because their religion was indifferent to the advancement of national wealth. The veneration of relics was also vilified. D. G. Paz comments on the vitality of this phase of anti-Catholicism: 'The mass media of the day produced a torrent of tracts, books, magazines, and newspaper stories that reviled their beliefs, challenged their political loyalty, and depicted them as the deluded dupes of men who lusted for sex, money, and power.'[18]

Those who had converted to Catholicism were not spared criticism. Casartelli cited as an example the case of the Marquis of Ripon,[19]

> The Times, did not think it beneath it to repeat that threadbare calumny, lately added to the stock, that nobody could become a Catholic without selling away his freedom of conscience and intellect in exchange for the mess of pottage of the Pope's infallibility.[20]

THE FIRST VATICAN COUNCIL AND W. E. GLADSTONE: CASARTELLI'S RESPONSE

Casartelli's first series of apologetical articles were largely an exposition and a defence of the Syllabus of Errors (1864)[21] and the First Vatican Council (1869 – 1870). In the words of Pius IX the object of the Council was, 'by means of joint discussion and united efforts, to discover with God's help the necessary remedies against the many evils which oppose the Church.'[22] As well as condemning naturalism[23] and rationalism,[24] the Syllabus and the Council had reiterated the teaching of the Council of Trent on Tradition, Scripture, and the authority of the Church to be the guardian and teacher of what Scripture contained.[25] Many critics saw the Syllabus and the Council as the Church's rejection of 'modern learning, science, individual freedom, and the liberal state.'[26] The Church's reaction can however be understood, in large part, as a response to questioning of the traditional authority of the Bible as a result of contemporary discoveries in palaeontology and Near Eastern Studies. Further unsettling challenges came with the publication of Charles Darwin's theory of 'Natural Selection' in his Origin of Species of 1858. In comparison with the resources developed by Protestant biblical scholarship, particularly the Tübingen School,[27] the Catholic Church lacked expertise to counter these challenges to the fundamentals of Christianity. Over forty years ago the wide-ranging historian and commentator H. Daniel-Rops pointed out that,

> It is surprising to discover that at a time when Strauss,[28] Baur and Renan[29] were overthrowing the traditional bases of exegesis, [Catholic] scriptural studies were negligible both in quality and in quantity. Indeed exegesis had little or no place in the curricula of seminaries...Nor were the strictly religious sciences in better condition.[30]

The accuracy of this judgement is supported by evidence from Casartelli himself in his recorded discussions with students at Ushaw College about the extent of the deluge over the earth, and how long it took to build the pyramids, given that mankind had all but been destroyed.[31] For someone of Casartelli's ability, who was self-taught in Flemish and Turkish[32] and had learned Hebrew 'as a pastime,'[33] it is hardly surprising that he chose to abandon theology in order to concentrate on Oriental languages.[34] Given that confrontation was not in his character, his excursion into Persian languages may have been a way of skirting this intellectual paucity in the Church. A similar move was made years later by Cuthbert Butler[35] who wanted to avoid the constraints of the anti-Modernist measures.[36]

It was Gladstone's attack[37] on the First Vatican Council's decree on Papal Infallibility[38] which really crystallised and focussed attention on the civil allegiance of Catholics. He claimed that the decrees had radically changed this allegiance and was 'convinced that there actually was a 'vast conspiracy' organised by the Roman Catholic hierarchy to direct a European war to the end of forcible restoration of the Pope's temporal power.'[39] On the impact of Gladstone's attack on the Catholic Church, Norman has commented:

> it illustrates how, even to a man of such well-known liberalism as Gladstone, with his past record of righteous opposition to anti-Catholic bigotry and intolerance, it was possible for Catholicism to appear in a guise apparently so monstrous as to allow all the old arguments against Rome to assume once more the proportions of great, almost self-evident truths.[40]

What effect did this criticism have on the Church? R. L. Greenall says that it imprisoned Catholics 'inside a psychological ghetto, giving it [the Church] a mentality quite different to [sic] that of any other religious denominations [...] 'No popery' did most to keep Catholics and Catholicism on the defensive, and out of the mainstream of civic life for the rest of the century.'[41]

Further contemporary evidence is found in Bishop Bilsborrow's[42] statement of 1892: 'At the present day, we the Catholics of England are but a 'remnant saved according to the election of grace' (Rom., XI.5) weak, isolated, and scattered in the midst of others enjoying almost the monopoly of wealth and power and worldly privilege'.[43]

The defensive stance of Catholics at this period was reflected in the way the Church presented its theology. Apologetics had increased in significance in the latter part of the nineteenth century owing to the Church's need to defend its doctrine in the face of naturalism and rationalism. As a result, this was not an era noted for its theological and philosophical developments.

In this difficult situation, there were exceptions, Casartelli and his colleague, Charles de Harlez, at Louvain being prominent among them.[44] The former was able to serve as an apologist in a double sense, being involved in its popular form, as seen in his work for the Catholic press, and in its more academic sense, as in his important contribution to the field of Oriental studies. Casartelli grasped the need to counter the arguments of the Tübingen School[45] by use of the same weapons – facts, texts, and documents – to defend the uniqueness of Christianity. Casartelli also had the great advantage of being fully aware of the situation in which the lay Catholics of Manchester and Salford found themselves. He constantly strove therefore to encourage the laity to take their place within civic life and to avoid isolation. His apologetic writings took the first step in this direction.

By correcting misconceptions and refuting error Casartelli supplied the basis for a useful body of knowledge, enabling his fellow Catholics to have greater confidence in their allegiance and citizenship and so be better able to assume civic responsibility. As a result, his apologetics were neither aggressive nor triumphant in tone; they display a far more irenical approach than that of Vaughan.[46] The last article of the first series, 'Consolations for Catholics,'[47] was an appeal to co-believers not to assume, in the face of opposition, an enclosed and defensive position and so avoid becoming, as he called it, 'a mere party.' He was strongly against the Church becoming an *imperium in imperio*.[48] Nevertheless, he certainly approached the apologetic task with vigour. Pius IX believed that, 'Catholic newspapers do in modern times what the mendicant orders did in time gone by.'[49] Vaughan and Casartelli certainly shared this enthusiasm and exemplified it to defend the Church and to render an account of its beliefs.

CASARTELLI: 'APOSTLE OF THE PRESS'

Why did Casartelli write as he did? Who were his readership? What was his message? His series of articles, printed between December 1873 and February 1875, took its name from the pseudonym under which they were written: 'John Pearl's Lay Sermons.' These dealt with the authority of the Church and the civil allegiance of Catholics. A second series was simply entitled 'Difficulties of the Day' and sought to counter the usual anti-Catholic rhetoric of the popular press. This series appeared between November 1875 and March 1876.[50]

Casartelli believed that the press was inherently neutral, and could therefore be a force for great good or evil. However, its potential for good had been nullified by its attack upon Catholic loyalty. By its uncritical repetition of opinions, common among those whose minds had become corrupted by doctrines condemned by the Syllabus – Materialism, Republicanism, and Communism – it had become an enemy of the Church. Casartelli argued that it was these philosophies, and not the theological beliefs of Catholics, which had diluted the sentiment of true allegiance. Therefore, anyone corrupted by these false philosophies 'will not ... think much about such deep and noble things as truth, and chivalry, and loyalty.'[51] The charge of disloyalty had been falsely assigned to Catholics because,

> We call ourselves Catholic first and then English, and because we drank the health of the Pope before that of the Queen,[52] [it was asserted that] we were disloyal, cared nothing for our country, and would very likely some fine day or other, if only we could, to get up another Gunpowder Plot or Spanish Armada'[53]

Casartelli countered such assertions vigorously. He adduced the example of the republicanism of Charles Wentworth Dilke,[54] which, he claimed, was so widespread that people had become accustomed to hear seditious talk, to the extent 'that when any one coolly discusses the chances of getting rid of the throne for the sake of a Republic, or spouts with indecent violence against a grant to one of Her Majesty's children, you don't find that people are so suddenly shocked as they used to be.'[55]
Casartelli was in fact exaggerating the extent of republican feeling for it did not extend nearly so far as he claimed. Dilke's biographer has noted that the country was not 'seething with republicanism'[56] and there was a very strong reaction against Dilke from many quarters.[57] For example, in Bolton in 1871, where he was to speak, the feeling of anger against him boiled over into a riot.[58] His attempt in 1872 to set up a Select Committee to enquire into the Civil List was defeated by 276 to 2.

Casartelli, by comparing the fact that one never heard Catholics calling for the abolition of the House of Lords or for the rejection of the Constitution, with the supposed widespread acquiescence in republican ideas, was trying to show where the true charge of disloyalty should be laid. Whilst there might have been no clamour for republicanism among Catholics, the evidence suggests that neither was there such a call outside the Catholic body. Furthermore, Casartelli was writing in 1874, two years after Dilke's defeat in the Commons and subsequent silence about republicanism.

'John Pearl's Lay Sermons' provide the clue as to why Casartelli wrote as he did. In these sermons, his primary aim was to establish that Catholicism and the modern liberal state were not mutually exclusive. He wanted to show that there was no contradiction between loyalty to the Pope and to one's country. To do this he delineated the proper boundaries of the Church, and thus explained how Catholics could properly hold a double allegiance to both ecclesiastical and civil authorities. Arguing that the Church only claimed authority in matters spiritual and eternal, as he later maintained in his Sermons on Biblical questions (see below p. 42), he showed that there was no reason to suspect any desire by this same authority to try to interfere in the political sphere. However, his Protestant opponents were permanently suspicious of Ultramontanism, fearing that its supporters would try and undermine the Constitution. Such perceptions are evident in Gladstone's harsh warning to Bishop Ullathorne: 'those who extend religious authority or the claims of it, into the civic sphere must be prepared for the *lex talionis*.'[59] Rebutting this view, Casartelli maintained that the term 'Ultramontanism' referred only to the Church's authority in her sphere of competence, and her freedom from the coercion of temporal power as understood by the Syllabus and the First Vatican Council.[60]

The argument contained in 'John Pearl's Lay Sermons' is drawn largely from two sources: Manning's paper 'Caesarism and Ultramontanism'[61] and Newman's letter to the Duke of Norfolk, dated 27 December 1874.[62] Casartelli readily acknowledged his debt to Manning's paper; he said that it 'expounded in the most fitting and powerful way ideas which had long been hovering in his own mind, but which he had never been able to put forward in such a clear and solid manner.'[63] Manning had sought to define the true meaning of 'Ultramontanism' in order to clarify any misconception there might be about its purpose and ramifications, and to defuse its use as 'a nickname to kindle persecution against the Church by false accusations and misleading the public opinion of this country.'[64] According to Manning, the enemies of the Church had a tendency to use the civil power as a means of persecution. When the civil power had supremacy over the spiritual, the Sovereign Prince or State had the unrestrained power to create and control everything, whether it be the political constitution, the ruling of domestic life, or the education of children. This despotic power, which necessarily excluded God, Manning referred to as 'the deification of man' or 'Caesarism.'[65] The Incarnation, and the institution of the Church by Christ, was the antidote to 'Caesarism.'

Casartelli utilised Manning's ideas to show how he personally understood 'Ultramontanism.' He presented his case through the fictional character of 'John Pearl,' representing one who drew his faith from the Church, but who also recognised the rightful place of civil authority and his dutiful allegiance towards it. John Pearl is described as an ordinary member of society and 'a respectable and intelligent tradesman' whose custom it was to attend various lectures on scientific and literary instruction – habits which had won him the respect of his non-Catholic companions.[66] The clear implication was that Catholics, contrary to popular misconception, were interested in learning and scientific pursuits. It is possible that this character was loosely based on Joseph Casartelli, Louis Charles' father, who was a member of the Manchester Literary and Philosophical Society. Casartelli (jnr.) set the scene for Pearl's conversations in a shop: he may well have had in mind the very conversations he had had with members of the Manchester Catholic Club in Market Street, near to his father's business premises.

John Pearl was both a 'practical Catholic' and an 'Ultramontane' who desired to learn the arguments and reasonings that supported the truths he held.[67] In other words he was a 'thinking man' who could justify his faith and beliefs and prove that they were not irrational obedience to an erroneous authority. He was a model Catholic layman, docile to the Church's authority. This recognition of legitimate authority saved him from being 'guilty of intellectual conceit…and consequently of trying to subject all things, even matters of faith, to the feeble light of (his) narrow lantern.'[68] Finally, he was a teacher and instructor of his peers who looked to him as a sort of oracle in matters they discussed with their non-Catholic neighbours or read in the newspaper.

For whom was Casartelli writing? The articles' technical nature suggests that they were meant for a more specific audience rather than the general reader. There is an obvious disjunction therefore between the general reader and those who held the more articulate and ideological expressions of anti-Catholicism which were the target of his writing. Norman reminds us that even Gladstone's pamphlet against the Decrees of the Vatican Council failed to stir the great mass of the British working public; what agitation there was, happened among 'men of influence,' such as politicians, priests, and journalists.[69] Indeed, the *Annual Register* of 1874 commented at the time on the restriction of anti-Catholic feeling to certain groups:

> Turning to the working-class of society in England this year, we find them occupied with very different disputes from those which exercised the minds of theorists on civil and religious allegiance. The practical question with labourers in all branches of industry, was how to secure what they considered sufficient high remuneration for their labour.'[70]

Such comments are still more pertinent, when read in the setting of the Catholic community of Manchester and Salford. There, the vast majority of

Catholics belonged to the working class and a significant proportion of those were Irish immigrants whose occupations were precarious. Far more pressing primary considerations weighed on them. This observation invites the question: how relevant were Casartelli's articles and how many people read them? They may well have been aimed partly at the clergy, with the intention of giving them material for sermons and instructions. But Vaughan was very much aware of the need for an educated Catholic middle class; there is no doubt that Casartelli would have had this group in mind as he wrote his articles. His presumption was that those who read his 'Lay Sermons' were conversant with the attacks upon Catholicism which had appeared in the pages of *The Times* and similar newspapers. This strongly suggests that the intended readership was indeed the members of the nascent Catholic middle class, who were being encouraged to take an active part in civic affairs. Moreover, the format of the sermons was that of 'Question and Answers' between the imaginary non-Catholic friends of John Pearl who were seeking clarification and he in turn endeavouring to respond. In this way Casartelli armed his educated readers with ready-made replies should they be asked similar questions. He was also trying to reach those Catholics who were supporters of the Liberal Party, and appealing to them to vote on political issues such as education according to conscience and not according to party loyalty. An example was the correspondent who, at the time Vaughan issued instructions on the way Catholics ought to vote, wrote to the *Manchester Guardian*: 'I sincerely hope that no Irishman will be found taking such advice.'[71]

Lastly we may ask: what was Casartelli trying to say? Effectively he was acting as rhetorician, in the task set him by Vaughan. Devising the character 'John Pearl', he used his skill with words to enter into the heart of the arguments which Catholics needed to refute. The device he used was to turn his opponent's own argument, and its innate error, back upon itself. For example, he deliberately used the Authorised King James Version of the Bible to show that Christ spoke of and founded a Church with a recognisable authority, and to demonstrate that Scripture itself did not allow individual interpretation. He dealt with Gladstone's pamphlet by carefully analysing the text and trying to tease out the inconsistencies. By this approach Casartelli hoped to present a form of Catholicism that was seen to be loyal and respectful of civil authority and which was not, as its Protestant denigrators implied, an attempt at an *imperium in imperio*.

Casartelli was involved with the defence of the true authority of the Church, while at the same time asserting that Catholics were loyal to State authority. His argument was based on the fact that Christianity had liberated mankind from being dominated. This had been achieved by Christianity withdrawing the control of religion from civil rulers with the effect of tempering their power. This liberation is what Manning meant by Ultramontanism, i.e. 'the liberty of the soul divinely guaranteed by an infallible Church.'[72] It was liberty because the Church cannot err or mislead; the same cannot be said of the temporal power. Ultramontanism was not the subversion of the State's temporal power, but rather 'the proper check and restraint of Caesarism, as Caesarism is the proper antagonist of the sovereignty of God.'[73] Ultramontanism was the guarantor of the Church's inalienable right to define faith and morals, to set the limits of its authority, and the universality of its jurisdiction.

Defence of true authority: the biblical arena

The first key issue for Casartelli as apologist and rhetorician, was to demonstrate the Church's divinely appointed authority as interpreter of Sacred Scripture, a point of Catholic doctrine rejected by Protestants.[74] In the first of four sermons on this issue, he challenged the Protestant belief that Scripture had no need of interpretation by any other authority other than the individual reader. Stepping onto his opponents' ground, he summarised their view in graphic terms.

> God has uttered once and for all in a certain set form of words...all that He ever intended to reveal or in any way make known directly to mankind, and this His voice is just photographed, so to speak, in the words, phrases, and narratives which go to make up the Bible.[75]

The metaphor of God's voice being photographed, conveyed well the naïve idea that in order to understand the meaning of Scripture it was sufficient to simply read the text without reference to any other authority. Casartelli attacked the underlying assumptions of this view. Contrary to Protestant belief, Catholics held that 'God has never ceased to speak to His people, and that there is no proof that He made known all He had to make known by means of those certain writings we call the Bible. They affirm that He goes on speaking with a living voice.'[76] This living voice was the Tradition of the Church and acted as the infallible interpreter of the written word. Can this be shown to be true, even using the magisterial Protestant translation, the Authorised Version? Yes, argued Casartelli, who highlighted the references that refer to Christ founding a Church with a recognisable authoritative hierarchy, and which speak against individuals interpreting the Scriptures for themselves.[77] He concluded, echoing the teaching of the First Vatican Council, 'we are not to build our belief on what we read in the Bible, but upon what the Church teaches us that the Bible means to say.'[78]

A second common ground of contention was the hostile assertion that Catholics were discouraged from reading the Bible.[79] Casartelli countered this charge in Sermon II, where he explained how the Church's authoritative interpretation of the Bible ranked before that of an individual: 'The real meaning of the Bible's words cannot differ from the Church's teaching.'[80] The Church did not put itself above Scripture, only above an individual's solitary interpretation. Extending this argument, Casartelli then attacked the Protestant view of *sola scriptura* as a sufficient rule of faith. This he did by carrying forward the line of argument he had begun in previous sermons – evidence from Scripture that Christ founded a recognisable Church with a visible authoritative structure. The practical ramifications of this were as follows.

Casartelli noted how Catholics 'have just been doing battle in the School Board Elections' with the Unsectarians.[81] Sermon V, 'A Church and a Bible,' was directly linked to the discussion between those who favoured denominational schools, with definite religious instruction, and those who preferred secular schools with religious 'instruction' restricted to 'simple Bible teaching,' such as the Birmingham League and the Unsectarians. John Pearl was brought in again to ask the rhetorical question, 'if the Bible is the only rule of faith why did Christ go to the trouble of founding a Church?'[82] Attacking directly the views of the Trinitarian Bible Society, he argued that the Church was not founded merely to spread the habit of bible-reading.[83] If that were the case then there would be no difference between trained ministers of the Church and book vendors. Rather, it was founded to be 'an infallible visible authority teaching the true and only faith, and deciding on all questions of the interpretation of the Written Word.'[84] Completing his defence, he declared that to take the Bible as the sole rule of faith was to render the Church superfluous. The Church used the Word of God as 'the text and groundwork of her teaching, dealing it out and expounding it, according to her mother-like prudence, to her children.'[85] The Catholic faith was thus founded on two principles: Scripture and Tradition.

A third area where it was vital to define a Catholic outlook was that addressed by the Protestant literature of self-help and moral education. In Sermon VI, Casartelli's John Pearl effectively tackled John Cassell,[86] the Manchester-born publisher of the *Bible Dictionary*, and *The Bible Educator*, and editor of *A Book of Martyrs*. He sought to counter what he regarded as the mistaken ideas contained in books from Cassell's house, which were 'expressly for working men.'[87] This kind of literature represented exactly that which Vaughan feared would spread among the labouring classes as a result of their increased desire for education and learning. The reader of this erroneous literature is typified in the Sermons in the character of 'a Bible Christian.'

The nub of Casartelli's rebuttal asked the question, 'what is the Bible,' and addressed the related question of the divergence between the Catholic and Protestant versions of the Canon of Scripture. He juxtaposed the First Vatican Council's declaration of the Vulgate as the standard version,[88] with the claim of the Bible Christian that 'priests and Popes [cram] the *Apocrypha* among the real books of the Bible.'[89] To this Pearl countered that the error in actual fact was on the part of the 'reformers [for] cutting off great pieces from God's Word.'[90] He ended by asserting that even Bible Christians admitted a visible earthly authority in the case of deciding which books were to be included in the Canon of Scripture. Authority had been exercised in the formation of the 'King James Bible.' His opponents were therefore inconsistent, for any appeal to authority, including that made in relation to the King James Version, showed the emptiness of the Bible Christian's argument based on the assertion 'the Bible, the Bible only, and nothing but the Bible.'[91]

Defence of true authority: the political arena

Extrapolating from his defence of the Church's infallible teaching authority, Casartelli next defined the authority appropriate to the temporal and spiritual spheres, and the loyalty of Catholics to both. Here again he took the attack directly to his opponents' ground. His two sermons on politics and education, 'Unpolitical Politics' and 'Politics and Education,'[92] were written in the weeks prior to the General Election of 1874, when the overall loyalty of Catholic subjects was under attack. The question of vital interest to Catholics was the provision of denominational schools. The issue divided the political parties: the Radical members of Gladstone's Liberal Party were very unsympathetic to the demand for church schools with religious teaching based on sectarian doctrine, whereas the Tories were more amenable. Herbert Vaughan had laid down a sharp challenge in a pastoral letter: 'no Catholic can vote for any candidate who proposes to saddle the country with a secular and godless system of education.'[93] In a letter to Lady Herbert of Lea, Vaughan showed where his anxieties arose:

> It has been a hot time for me down here. Gladstone is thrown out by the Radicals. I hope you will try and persuade him of that. The Radical creed was precisely three condemned propositions in the Syllabus and on popular Education. How could Catholics vote for that? *Non possumus.* Better suffer a little tyranny from the Tories than vote for the Radical programme in Education. The Catholics would have supported Gladstone but they could not support his Radicals.[94]

Vaughan's pastoral letter provoked an angry response from Gladstone's supporters, which included Irish Catholics, who accused him of using church pulpits for political purposes. Certain letters in the *Manchester Guardian* are evidence of how some Catholics were not receptive to Vaughan's advice and understood it for what it was – 'a direct command for all Catholics to vote either in the Conservative interest or abstain from voting altogether.'[95] One contributor synthesised the political issue with the anti-Catholicism discussed in the earlier part of this chapter:

> The political pastoral read throughout this diocese on Sunday last must have roused in your minds intensive indignation, astonishment and pain … His Lordship asks you to send to Parliament tomorrow, in Salford and Manchester, and elsewhere men who are the persistent enemies of your religion and country. Are the Murphy riots at Ashton-under-Lyne erased from your memories…Dr. Vaughan is an Englishman who has nothing in common with us on [the] questions [of freedom of Ireland and the Irish Land Act.][96]

Although Casartelli's 'John Pearl's Lay Sermons' were not direct replies to these correspondents, they were representative of the people, the issues, and the mode of thought over which he was trying to exert an influence *via* his articles for the *Catholic Opinion*.

Casartelli realised that his opponents would seek to redefine the Catholic vote as a litmus test of civil allegiance and sense of citizenship, thus furthering their aim of representing Catholics as disloyal to the Protestant Constitution. In his rôle as a controversialist, Casartelli again stepped into the public arena to challenge Protestant suspicion. On the practical matter of voting behaviour, he stressed that Catholics as a body did not have any politics. Thus they had no intention nor wish to become an *imperium in imperio*. He stressed, however, that Catholics were not apolitical; rather, they practised 'unpolitical politics.' This stance we may call 'practical Ultramontanism;' it fits in with the thrust of Manning's argument in *Caesarism and Ultramontanism* that religious power must prevail over the political power. Casartelli laboured as Vaughan's *aide-de-camp* and tried to convince his readers of the validity of the latter's opinion as expressed in his pastoral letter. On what was 'unpolitical politics' based?

The creed of self-help propagated by Samuel Smiles and John Cassell, among others, sought to focus attention on man's temporal well-being. Against their tenets, Casartelli appealed to the teaching of the Catechism of the Council of Trent and repeated by the First Vatican Council: the end of Man was 'everlasting happiness in the next life, and in this life his temporal well-being as a means towards his happiness in the next.'[97] The purpose of religion was to promote directly this eternal happiness. It was clearly distinguishable from the business of the State, commonly known as 'politics,' which was to promote directly mankind's material well-being. In the hierarchy of values man's eternal end must come before his temporal end and religion must come before politics.[98] However, this point in no way detracted from the importance of temporal affairs.

The ground upon which the Radical Liberals were to be opposed was thus laid. Casartelli argued that 'everything that assists material well-being in such a way as to conduce to eternal happiness, is good and commendable, and by all means to be sought after.'[99] On the other hand, anything that assisted material well-being but was contrary to eternal happiness must be avoided, for example secular education. Matters like this had not to be treated purely as a political question, but rather as a religious one because 'of all things in this world nothing affects his [man's] future eternal welfare more deeply than a child's education. Therefore education *directly* affects his future life. Therefore it is a *religious* affair.'[100]

Catholics should approach education and its political implications 'as members of the Church' and allow political preferences to give way to religious conviction.[101] In the past Catholics had been unjustly and wrongly accused of 'treason' and 'treachery to party,' for having acted in this way.[102] It would precisely be attachment to one political party that would lay Catholics open to the accusation of treason, he considered:

> if we as a body, as a portion of the Catholic Church, were to attach ourselves definitely to one of the two great political parties, and thus become a political body, having an influence in things political, we should then be really guilty of treason, because we should be really establishing an *'imperium in imperio.'*[103]

But this was not the right he claimed. 'If [the] Ashantee War, Court of Judicature, Mr. Disraeli's Bath Letter, or Mr. Gladstone's Budget, are political affairs, what business has the Church to meddle with them?'[104] The Church had the right to act in a unified manner on a religious issue, for example education, since it involved not merely 'political action,' but also 'religious action,' affecting not only 'policies' but also 'rules of conduct.'

In retrospect, it is possible to see that Casartelli's way of thinking put Catholics in a dilemma. In matters of pure politics they were left free to support the party of their choice; but, if this party proposed a policy that was against Catholic principles, then support should be withdrawn. This obviously created difficulties when it came to the question of denominational schools. What were Catholics to do when faced with the dilemma of Gladstone's Liberal Party, sympathetic to Irish Home Rule but less inclined to support church schools, and Disraeli's Tory Party, a supporter of denominational schools but not of Home Rule? Casartelli wrestled with this dilemma throughout his episcopate and it was a major factor in his later decision to found the Catholic Federation in order to try and unite Catholic forces when there was a clash between the temporal and the religious spheres.

The tensions in Casartelli's definition of 'unpolitical politics' are clear. It is difficult to avoid the conclusion that Catholics were in fact being told which way to vote. Issues that straddle the political and religious spheres are not patient of neat and easy distinction. Take for example another of Casartelli's conclusions,

> But supposing that we are followers of Mr. Gladstone as politicians, and Mr. Gladstone's Government supports a measure which affects our children's education in a manner adverse to their eternal welfare; or supposing we are followers of Mr. Disraeli, and his party are guilty of a like attempt; then it is evident that our political and our religious interests are at issue...We have shown above that our political interests must yield. It follows that we must oppose in the matter the Government which in purely political matters we support.[105]

The Liberal Government at the time was advocating secular education. No doubt Casartelli was alluding to this very fact as he wrote the above.

Defence of true authority: the loyalty of Catholics

After his defeat in the General Election, Gladstone wrote a pamphlet outlining his understanding of the significance of the Syllabus of Errors and the Decrees of the First Vatican Council. This was published in November 1874, and, as was to be expected from such an active debater, Casartelli's reply followed shortly. In four published sermons,[106] he took issue with Gladstone on the open charge of disloyalty, summed up in the phrase, 'A Catholic first, an Englishman afterwards,' and the Church's supposed 'pretensions.'

In order for Catholics to confirm their loyalty, Gladstone had called upon them to reject certain teachings of the Holy See,

> It seems not too much to ask of them (Roman Catholics) to confirm the opinion which we as fellow-countrymen entertain of them, by sweeping away ... the presumptive imputations which their ecclesiastical rulers at Rome, acting autocratically, appear to have brought upon their capacity to pay a solid and undivided allegiance.'[107]

This attack, Casartelli replied, begged the question at issue. He acknowledged the phrase 'presumptive imputations' to mean 'you may take it for granted beforehand that [Catholics] are very likely to be disloyal because they obey Vatican decrees.'[108] This is precisely what Gladstone meant. He believed that certain principles laid down by an ecclesiastical party within the Church were adverse to the purity and integrity of civil allegiance. He was convinced that the definition of the Vatican Council on Papal Infallibility meant that 'no one can now become [Rome's] convert without placing his own civil loyalty and duty at the mercy of another.'[109] Casartelli challenged Gladstone as to the foundations of these assertions. He had confirmed in his pamphlet that the slur he alleged on the allegiance of Catholics did not stem from anything the English Hierarchy had said nor from anything the laity in England had done. Yet Gladstone had alleged that Rome had acted 'autocratically', but gave no evidence for such a statement. What was the source of such imputations, then? Casartelli concluded that they could only have come from the clash between Bismarck and his liberal Catholic opponent, Döllinger. Given that these persons were of little consequence to the Catholics of Great Britain, Casartelli further concluded that Gladstone's charge carried little real weight.

In dealing with Gladstone's argument, Casartelli used logical distinctions and rules of interpretation in order to highlight the fallacies in the arguments which the Church's opponents put forward, and he also advocated that his readers 'keep as close as we can in all cases to the real meaning of words.'[110] For example, the way Catholics interpreted the word 'loyalty' differed entirely from the way it was used and understood by Gladstone. For the former it signified 'a thing so delicate that, like truthfulness, or uprightness, or charity, it is stained by the least breath, altogether ruined by the smallest flaw.'[111] For Gladstone to accuse Catholics of 'half-loyalty' was unacceptable: to them, half-loyalty was self-contradictory and therefore could not exist. In Gladstone's definition of loyalty Casartelli detected a tone of menace, for the way he used the term carried with it the implication of 'entire devotion of soul and body to State,' and a 'slavish submission to the supreme dictates of this governing power.'[112] This, Casartelli countered, resulted in the State having limitless authority and was unacceptable to Catholics, as indeed to any Christian. By putting their religion before the State, Catholics were acknowledging the supremacy of God. In this they were no different from other believers and their loyalty should therefore not be in question. This was Manning's preferred way of replying to Gladstone's criticism of Catholic loyalty. His reply, printed in The Times, on 7 November 1874, was to the effect that Catholic loyalty was not compromised by the teaching of the Church – this included the Vatican Decrees – because all who acknowledged the existence of God had a divided allegiance since they recognised the existence of a divine law. Using Manning's Caesarism and Ultramontanism, Casartelli further buttressed his own arguments with an extensive discussion of the spheres of competence of secular and Church authority.[113]

What of Gladstone's second attempt to deal a mortal blow to the Catholic self-understanding: his call to Catholics to reject certain teachings of the

Holy See, as inconsistent with their loyalty? In Sermon XI, 'Mr. Gladstone's Mistake and Somebody Else's', Casartelli claimed 'that of all the papers and letters which took up the task of quizzing or refuting this pamphlet, none to my knowledge, appeared to have noticed what struck me so forcibly at first sight.'[114] In this approach Casartelli was more original; he could not at this point have read *Newman's Letter to the Duke of Norfolk*, as it was not finished until 27 December 1874 and not printed publicly until early 1875. Nor could he have read Manning's response, *The Vatican Decrees in their Bearing on Civil Allegiance* since this was not published until February 1875.[115] Once again, Casartelli had detected a lack of logic in Gladstone's position. Gladstone's usage of the term 'Holy See' evidently signified 'merely a scheming Italian Bishop, or the President of a big sect, something of that kind.'[116] But this was an utter misconception. The Church was in actuality, 'the Chair of Peter, the Chair of Our Lord's Vice-regent, of the Visible Head of the Church on earth; who just on account of his office, is nothing else than the mouthpiece of the Church and of Christ her Founder.'[117] Gladstone, despite his vehement attacks upon Catholics, was not able to prove that the teachings of the Holy See were false. Therefore, his accusation that Catholics were susceptible to disloyalty begged the question; the Church's claim to be what it was had not been disproved, nor had the disloyalty of Catholics been proved.

Defence of true authority: papal infallibility

Casartelli concluded his sequence of sermons by addressing Gladstone's claim that thanks to the Vatican Council there were now two infallibilities: that of the Church and that of the Pope. In defending Papal Infallibility and refuting Gladstone's charge, Casartelli paraphrased Newman's ideas on the development of Christian doctrine, and his *Letter to the Duke of Norfolk* (1875.)

Casartelli recalled how it had been the constant teaching of the Church that when the liege lord of the spiritual power taught as God's representative, i.e. within the limits of his office and in his capacity, he must be obeyed since he cannot err. This had always been the case and had never affected the way Catholics were loyal to civil authority. As Newman put it in his *Letter to the Duke of Norfolk*: 'there is no real increase [in the Pope's authority]; he has for centuries upon centuries had and used that authority, which the Definitions now declare to have belonged to him.'[118] Reaffirming his earlier argument in the education controversy, Casartelli declared that only when the Church and State collide on matters of belief or religious practices were Catholics obliged to defer to the former.[119] He imagined the question of what would happen if someone claimed they could not, in conscience, accept the doctrine of Infallibility. Echoing Newman, he wrote:

'conscience is the rule and guide of our conduct ... with our doing or not avoiding what is good or what is bad. It can have nothing to do with telling us that a fact is true or false.'[120] The question of the Pope's Infallibility is one of truth or untruth; as such it is not a part of one's conscience. Therefore we cannot speak of it being against conscience. Newman put it thus: 'Conscience is not a judgement upon any speculative doctrine, but bears immediately on conduct, as something to be done or not done.'[121]

According to Casartelli, Gladstone was mistaken: the definition of infallibility did not constitute any change in the deposit of Catholic belief; the Council had not defined a 'second Infallibility;' nor was infallibility divided into two parts. Rather, the decree on Infallibility was best seen from the point of view of a development, an unfolding or making explicit of what was previously implicitly believed. It did not represent a declaration of new dogmas or facts. Casartelli traced the development of doctrine in three stages. Firstly, there was the passive stage when the dogma was accepted uncritically. This was followed by a period of conflict, which was also a time of purification and clarification. Finally, there was the definition of the doctrine and the making explicit of what was previously implicitly believed.[122]

In his Sermon on conscience, Casartelli followed Newman's example of trying to minimise any clash between conscience and State.[123] Newman believed that 'the amount of the Pope's authoritative enunciations has not been such as to press heavily on the back of the private Catholic.'[124] The practical implication was that the Pope figured very little in the regulation of ordinary life; so much so 'that the weight of his hand upon us, as private men is absolutely unappreciable.'[125] Casartelli echoed the same sentiments: 'this dreadful doctrine of infallibility, which seems such a bugbear to so many of our friends, does not really make so great a difference, practically speaking, as is thought.'[126]

In his opinion that the Church as a whole was infallible in its belief, Casartelli reflected the ideas of Newman to whom he had looked from early days.[127] The *ecclesia docens* ('teaching Church'), as distinct but not separate from the *ecclesia discens* ('learning Church'), was infallible in teaching and the definition of doctrine.[128] In this terminology the term *ecclesia docens* refers to the Pope and the bishops; the term *ecclesia discens* refers to all other members of the Catholic Church. However, in the position which he took on the Church's authority in matters of faith and morals, and the separation of the teaching office of the Church from the sphere of the State, whereby it had authority to set its own limits, Casartelli followed Manning.[129]

Casartelli ended his series of sermons on a sober yet confident note. He compared the present state of Catholics, accused of disloyalty and open to public criticism, with that of the Christians in the Epistles of St Peter. The lesson that Casartelli drew was that through practical loyalty Catholics, like their forebears, must be able to silence their critics. 'Honour all men. Love the brotherhood. Fear God. Honour the King.'[130] The risk of political or social persecution was not to be allowed to drive the Church into a defensive and enclosed position,

> We, as members of the one Church must be on our guard against the danger of making ourselves merely into a party. We are *not* a mere party. We must have charity for all men; because we must hope and try to bring all men to the truth. If we are suspected and hated, as we are by many outsiders, as a dangerous band of men, to be tabooed and fought shy of, why, hard as it may be, we must still try to be respectful, kind, and long-suffering to all.[131]

Catholics in England both enjoyed and were proud of their liberty. This theme Casartelli would introduce in his very first pastoral letter, 'The Signs of the Times.'

POPULAR APOLOGETICS: 'DIFFICULTIES OF THE DAY'

Casartelli was just as capable of addressing a general audience as he was of a detailed rebuttal of Gladstone. His 'Difficulties of the Day' engaged directly with key public matters of religion, and responded to the great interest, both negative and positive, then being shown in the Catholic Church and its doctrine. He intended these articles for two groups: Catholics who wished to learn more about their faith and how to refute criticism, and general seekers of truth.[132] His replies to the difficulties of belief constituted a powerful apologetic for the uniqueness of the Catholic Church in the face of industrial society and the growing independence of individuals, for example, the education of women.

The integrity of the Church

A common criticism aimed at the Church stemmed from the pain caused to the families of converts and her claim to be the Church founded by Christ. What sort of religion was Catholicism if it was the cause of such pain and suffering? In regard to the first point Casartelli struck a conciliatory note, regretting the harsh reply of a Catholic priest against a father whose son had converted to Catholicism. The priest's tone, 'brusque and overbearing ... was much lamented by Catholics as by Protestants.'[133] He suggested that the pain which the families of converts felt was a specific form of suffering and ought to be understood as a trial and therefore a means of merit since suffering was a constituent element of Christianity. However, on opposition to the claim of the Catholic Church to be the Church founded by Christ, Casartelli was unyielding. Criticisms came from all sides:

> Here we are persecuted because we teach disobedience; there because we fetter human liberty with trammels of obedience. The Protestant proves that we have innovated upon the truth, because we refuse to limit our faith to the letter of the Scriptures; the Freethinker that we have stuck in the mud far behind the progress of the age, because we pin our faith to a Sacred Book.[134]

Casartelli claimed these alleged criticism were in fact distinctive marks of the Catholic Church's claim to be what it was.[135] Indeed, Christ had warned that the Church would be subject to persecution and hatred; the fact that this was happening proved her divine foundation:

> For what does Jesus Christ foretell about his Church? He foretold that it should be in constant conflict. First with evil. When he said, 'The gates of Hell shall not prevail against her,' he clearly alluded to her continual struggle with the powers of darkness…He also told that she should be in conflict with the *Synagogue* and with *false prophets*; with *kings* and *governors*; that she should be *hated of all men*; and this universal hatred was to be a proof that her members were His members.[136]

Other churches did not suffer in the same way either because they enjoyed the favours of government and rulers or because they were acceptable to the world. All shared one thing in common – opposition to the Catholic Church. Such universal opposition could not emanate from the fact that the Church was evil since it opposed all evil, for example it had played a part in the eradication of the slave trade, duelling, and paganism. Consequently, the only reason for, and explanation of, such opposition was the simple truth that the Catholic Church was the one true Church of Christ.

The attack on Catholic teaching had considerable contemporary weight, because – as a result of condemning the evangelical campaign of Moody and Sankey – the Church had to face the counter accusation of not having at heart the propagation of the truths of Christianity.[137] Dwight Moody and Ira Sankey were American evangelists who made their first tour of England in 1873 and enjoyed particular fame for their use of hymns to excite emotion and convert people to the Gospel. They made a second revival tour in 1874/5. At times they were able to command at their rallies crowds of up to 20,000. In the face of such a strong popular movement, Casartelli presented a vigorous counter-argument. He began by stating that the Church condemned the mission because it taught 'half truths,' preferring 'a natural morality, joined with a certain vague belief in a Creator, a Redeemer, and a Rewarder.'[138] The evangelists saw as an encumbrance 'a definite Church, with a living sacrifice and living priesthood, with ever-flowing sacramental fountains of grace, with an exact and sure teaching of dogmatic truth.'[139] These enthusiastic claims were to be viewed calmly and rationally. The mission of the Church was as 'far removed from excitement and furore as possible,'[140] whereas the work of Moody and Sankey had merely excited popular interests and transitory excitement. The true success of the Church's mission should be measured in terms of one that was 'continual, [and] an ordinary one,' consisting of the directing of the whole of a person's life through the sacraments, the education of children, the relieving of the poor, tending the sick and dying, and housing the destitute.[141] The evidence of the ever-growing number of schools, churches, and converts was proof enough of such success. It was not to be forgotten, moreover, that the Church had had her own times of revival. During the General Mission in Manchester and Salford organised by Herbert Vaughan, 116,000 people were present at all the services on one particular Sunday; 53,000 approached the sacraments of Confession and Communion, 5,000 were Confirmed and 330 converts were received into the Church.[142]

The Church and women's suffrage

Casartelli observed that, 'There seems to ... be a very general impression that the Catholic Church is opposed to the modern movement for the higher education of women; and this is looked upon as a reproach to her, as being an evidence of her general opposition to progress and civilisation.'[143]

Initially, he doubted whether the Church held any teaching on the question of women becoming learned in certain subjects, as it apparently fell outside the ambit of faith and morals. However, he conceded that the Church was 'inclined to look with disfavour upon the movement towards educating *all* women like men.'[144] Casartelli judged that the education of women ultimately did enter into the sphere of the Church's competence because the ever-increasing desire for women's education affected the '*domestic* character of women at large and thus impinges on the family...By affecting the family [it] affects eventually the moral condition of mankind, which is particularly in the Church's keeping.'[145] Casartelli saw no objection to there being '*exceptional* cases,' whereby women received 'profound education and becoming really erudite persons.'[146] He believed, however, that 'outside of these phenomenon, the general result of universal higher education in women was epigrammatically summed up in a sentence of the late Mrs. Gaskell: 'A woman who speaks Greek can never cook a pudding well.'[147]

Casartelli feared the indiscriminate higher education of women, his reason being the possibility that they would become too interested in 'Virgil and mathematics' and so be unable, in later life, for the task of 'looking after the kitchen or managing the house.'[148] This typical Victorian attitude to women, and the tendency to view womanhood from the point of view of domesticity, was not the sum total of Casartelli's thinking on the subject. As in other matters he cannot be easily categorised. He believed that a woman's greatest work was the training and forming of her children; it followed, therefore, that exceptionally learned women should not be held as rôle models. Moreover, he did not apply this to the question of their general education, which he recognised as 'one of the gravest questions we have to deal with.'[149] A certain intellectual education was 'quite necessary for woman to fill her part in society, but the difficulty is in determining it.'[150] He saw women as a vital element in the teaching process because 'teaching is that great lever that is to raise the world; and its fulcrum is *Woman*.'[151] She was an educator in the sense that 'in the mould of her soul (Man's) mind is cast.'[152] Therefore a woman held a decisive influence over the destiny of Man – 'it is the mother who fertilises and trains in the soul of her children the first germs of intellectual, moral, and religious life.'[153] In this way Casartelli did not entirely reduce women to passivity, but recognised their vital rôle in the well-being of society. Quoting Eduardo Calcano, whom he described as an eminent lawyer, he spoke of 'the education of woman [as] the standard of the culture and morality of nations, the thermometer of their civilisation. Why should the pride of human philosophy and the haughtiness of our sex obstinately refuse to recognise…the decisive influences of woman over the destiny of man?'[154]

Overall, the tone of Casartelli's 'Difficulties of the Day' conveyed a confident rebuttal of the popular arguments used by the Church's enemies. He moved easily into the rôle of ecclesiastical journalism, using the press to echo the thoughts and ideas of his mentor Herbert Vaughan. His attitude toward the education of women reflected his background; none of his sisters was occupied in paid employment. He refused a request in 1874 to sign a petition in favour of university education for women.[155] In later life, his public outlook moderated; in 1924, he actively supported the setting up of a women's hostel for students at the University of Manchester[156] which later became St Gabriel's Hall. Was this because the attendance of women at universities had become inevitable and he had therefore to make provision for the pastoral care of Catholic women students, or was it because of a fundamental change of heart?[157] The evidence is unclear.

CONCLUSION

Casartelli was born a Victorian and remained so in many ways throughout his life. There was something quaint about his manner and style; at times it seems as though he yearned for earlier days as is especially apparent in the pastoral letters he wrote during the First World War. Yet he was equally capable of being open-minded: for example, his general understanding of university education and in particular his interest in Oriental Studies. 'John Pearl's Lay Sermons' were, in large part, an amalgam of certain ideas of Manning and Newman; but, in the context of the life of Casartelli, their importance goes far beyond this. The way he combined the two strands of thinking is indicative of how he is intellectually elusive and cannot easily be categorised. Manning in *Caesarism and Ultramontanism* wanted to assert the authority of the Pope and the supremacy of the spiritual sphere over the political. For Vaughan this had particularly important practical consequences in the light of the educational issue of Church schools and the Irish Catholics who, in support of Gladstone, might vote in such a way as to jeopardise parliamentary support of all such denominational schools. On these issues, Casartelli adopted Manning's stance, and was a very useful ally for Vaughan in the intellectual struggle to convince Catholic voters of the need to vote according to a non-political agenda. But at the same time, and within the very same series of sermons, Casartelli used Newman's *Letter to the Duke of Norfolk* to buttress his arguments. In that document Newman, in comparison with Manning, minimised any clash between fidelity to the Pope and civil authorities because, as he says,

> the circumference of State jurisdiction and of Papal are for the most part quite apart from each other; there are just some few degrees out of the 360 in which they intersect, and Mr. Gladstone, instead of letting these cases of intersection alone, till they actually occur, asks me what I should do, if I found myself placed in the space intersected.[158]

The question of the loyalty of Catholics and the prevailing of the religious power over the political were issues which persisted, and which Casartelli would have to tackle later as a bishop. His opportunity to parade his loyalty came with the Great War. His attempts at a practical implementation of non-political politics, or practical Ultramontanism, came – as we shall see – in his founding of the Catholic Federation. It can be concluded that much of what Casartelli later acted on in crucial matters, he learnt whilst writing his synthesis known as 'John Pearl's Lay Sermons.' His action on these issues forms the content of the following chapters.

Chapter Three

Casartelli and Education:
Advocate, Promoter and Pioneer

⋙ ⚜ ⋘

A chorus of voices, almost distressing in their harmony, [was] raised in favour of the doctrine that education is the great panacea for human troubles, and that, if the country is not shortly to go to the dogs, everybody must be educated.[1]

This observation by T. H. Huxley, made during the course of an address in 1868, shows how, in the second half of the nineteenth century, the issue of education and its provision was just as important and no less vexed a question than it is today. Politicians, men of business and commerce, and not least the Church all saw education as the remedy for society's many ills.[2] Given that it was such a vital issue for the Church, it understandably occupied a primary place in Casartelli's thinking and writing. Moreover, his intellectual ability and academic aptitude made it a central feature of his life. Prior to becoming a bishop, the whole of his adult years had been dedicated to teaching. Both as priest and bishop he was utterly convinced of the rôle of education in the mission of the Church.

In the march for development in national education Casartelli did not want to see the Church left behind or out of step. He was, therefore, not only a great advocate of Catholic schools *per se*; he also envisaged the Church being actively involved in the process of growth and expansion of education in general, and playing a leading rôle whenever possible. Secondly, he did not advocate a separatist policy: for example, he was a supporter of the removal of the ban on Catholics attending the universities of Oxford and Cambridge.[3] Later, when a bishop, he endeavoured to secure an adequate provision of secondary schools within his diocese, in order better to place lay Catholics on the 'ladder of education'. Thirdly, by his membership of the Manchester Geographical Society and by means of the papers which he gave to various learned societies, Casartelli pioneered the cause of commercial education, arguing for its recognition at university level and demonstrating how it could be the means of providing a valid intellectual culture.

Casartelli drew his ideas on education from three discernible sources, which he then synthesised. At various times, and in varying situations, one or the other tended to be the more influential. The sources are the same as those outlined in chapter two: Vaughan, Newman, and Manning. Vaughan was the most prominent practical influence. Casartelli was instrumental in putting into effect Vaughan's hopes for a commercial college in Manchester. He dedicated much time and effort in demonstrating that commercial education could form a credible syllabus for those destined for a career in commerce. Newman was the second influence – but here we are faced with another reason against neatly assigning Casartelli to a single category. For the influence of Newman, which he plainly acknowledged as of primary importance in the genesis of his intellectual development, does not sit easily with Casartelli's public advocacy of commercial education. McClelland has succinctly pointed out that 'Newman never became fully alive to the scientific and industrial needs of the age.'[4] This criticism could certainly not be levelled at either Manning or Vaughan, both of whom Casartelli followed on this issue. It is on the question of university education, and what constituted a university where we shall find the influence of Newman. Manning, his third source helped to form Casartelli's thoughts on the purpose of Catholic education. His ideas about Ultramontanism, and the freedom which this ensured for the Church in its teaching rôle, were used by Casartelli in his articles for the *Catholic Opinion* that dealt specifically with the question of education. As we shall see in this chapter, however, on the specific issue of the education of the clergy and seminary formation, Casartelli took the side of Vaughan, and criticised Manning's policy of preferring each diocese to have its own seminary, which in Casartelli's judgement contributed to the poor intellectual quality of the diocesan clergy.[5]

BACKGROUND TO THE EDUCATION QUESTION AND THE 1870 EDUCATION ACT

Casartelli's articles for the *Catholic Opinion* were composed in the three or four years after the passing of the 1870 Education Act. As we have seen already, he sought to educate the Catholic members of the electorate on the implications of the Act, and to influence their voting habits in relation to the provision of Catholic schools. It was vital that they should exercise their right to educate their children in consonance with their faith and not allow this to become the primary task of the State. In this regard, Casartelli was dealing with the same challenges which faced English Protestant Non-conformity: what form of religious instruction were children to be given in schools? Were they to receive credal or non-sectarian Bible instruction? What version of the Bible should be used?[6] How could Catholics resist Protestant doctrines of *sola scriptura* in rivalry with the *Magisterium*? These were not least among the difficulties Casartelli addressed in his 'Lay Sermons'.[7]

Friction on these issues was greatly increased by contemporary rapid industrialisation, and by the great influx of the massive number of refugees fleeing the famine in Ireland during 1845/6. By 1849 the number of Irish residents in Manchester had risen to about 80, 000.[8] This influx revived old suspicions of Catholicism, and irrational 'No-Popery' added more fuel to the educational controversy. As a measure to alleviate the crisis, regulations governing State aid had been widened in 1847 to include Catholic schools; hitherto these schools had been built and maintained entirely by voluntary offerings.[9]

By 1870, the problem of how to educate the impoverished masses now living in the industrial towns was comprised of two elements, one social and economic, the other religious. The situation was evidently beyond the capabilities of the religious bodies, even when assisted by the State. Following the widespread franchise granted by the 1867 Reform Act, advocates of State intervention in education seized their opportunity. The case they made was pragmatic and secular. Thus William Edward Forster, the initiator of the 1870 Act, declared that,

> Upon the speedy provision of elementary education depends our industrial prosperity. It is no use trying to give technical teaching to our citizens without elementary education; uneducated labourers – and many of our labourers are utterly uneducated – are, for the most part, unskilled labourers, and if we leave our work-force any longer unskilled, notwithstanding their strong sinews and determined energy, they will become overmatched in the competition of the world.[10]

These secular arguments posed a major challenge to the Church, which was no less aware of the need that society faced, but nevertheless understood education as being intimately and irrevocably related to eternal salvation.[11] The First Provincial Synod of Westminster, held in 1852, had recognised that it was 'the good school that secures the virtuous and edifying congregation.'[12] Similarly, Cardinal Manning insisted that the secular liberal State had no remit to teach religion and so ought to allow parents a free choice of schools for their children.[13] Education was a vital component in the Church's mission to effect regeneration; it acted like leaven in the midst of society; its influence for good would be achieved through, among other things, seminaries for the education of the clergy, schools for the poor and middle classes, and an adequate provision of higher education.

Given these deep disagreements, it was inevitable that the greatest conflict in the drafting of elementary education provision should centre on the question of what type of religious instruction was to be given. The situation demanded a solution that would reconcile religious and secular education.[14] The Education Bill published in February 1870, which later became the Forster Education Act, tried to steer a middle course between conflicting issues. In the end neither of the two great contending parties, the Nonconformists who wanted unsectarian education and simple Bible teaching, and the denominationalists who wanted credal teaching according to the doctrines of the Church, was satisfied. The tension caused by, on the one hand, the general public's desire for religious education, and, on the other, the Nonconformist's threat to organise a hostile campaign against rate-aid for denominational schools, was resolved by the 'Cowper-Temple' amendment.[15] This prohibited rate-aided schools using any 'catechism or religious formularies distinctive of any particular denomination.'

The 1870 Education Act established local School Boards, elected by the ratepayers, whose function it was to assess educational deficiency in their particular area. This created an opportunity for Catholics to become involved in the Boards, which enjoyed a great deal of discretion in regard to setting fees and the extent of religious instruction. Stemming from the Act, two types of school differing in the types of religious instruction, and in the ways of control and management, were established. Prior to 1870 the State had insisted upon the union between education and religion inasmuch as no school could be the beneficiary of a grant unless it was connected to a religious body. In the post 1870 era the situation was different: 'State responsibility was confined to the secular sphere; school managers might, if they wished, arrange for religious instruction, but such instruction would no longer be examined or rewarded by the State.'[16] Catholics saw this innovation in State education as a denial of the primary duties of parents.[17] Against such a background Casartelli laid out his strategy for Catholic education.

CASARTELLI: ADVOCATE OF CATHOLIC EDUCATION

As we have outlined, the main source for Casartelli's philosophy of education was Manning's 'Caesarism and Ultramontanism',[18] which he also used to help formulate his ideas on the limits of the State's competence. In this paper, Manning had spoken of mixed-questions, i.e. where the subject matter concerned both Church and State. In such cases the question was both religious, and civil or political, in nature. By referring to Manning's exposition of the limits of authority, Casartelli demonstrated that education was indeed the example *par excellence* of a mixed-question. Therefore, the Church's authority *vis-à-vis* education was supreme over that of the State because 'the *chief* interests which depend upon it [education] are religious interests, that is to say, the interests of the soul.'[19]

Casartelli resisted any view of education as a merely useful attribute, or of knowledge being reduced to its mechanical aspects. Characteristically, he differentiated between erudition and knowledge and education proper. To educate did 'not mean merely to stuff into the mind a great mass of 'facts' [...] Call this *information*, if you like; one of the means of education, but don't call it *education*.'[20] His philosophy of education was based upon the question of the very purpose of education. This was intrinsically linked to another question: what was the end of man, for what was he created? Education properly understood was the development of the whole person in order for him or her to attain the end for which they had been made. It was something dynamic and necessarily involved a relationship between teacher and pupil. In essence education was a, '*bringing into play*, or a development. A development of what? Thus, notice, the whole question turns upon the answer to this. *We* hold that education is a development of the *whole man*, of the faculties of every part of his body ... the soul (heart), the mind, and the body. Education must develop each and all of these parts and their faculties.'[21]

Interestingly, this is how Casartelli had viewed his own rôle as a teacher. His former pupils remembered how he would enthuse them into learning something, thus drawing them on and encouraging their development.[22] The mere teaching of the Catechism or Scripture could not in itself be sufficient to impart moral and religious education.[23] This type of training was for Casartelli, 'essentially practical and therefore needs constant exercise and training, so as to steep the whole soul with an habitual sense of religious truths and duties.'[24] The fruits of this moral training were not restricted to the individual's personal moral life. An educational system that was inclusive of this way of thinking would be, he maintained, beneficial for the general welfare of the State. It was vital that qualities such as justice, truthfulness, honesty, diligence, and reverence be an integral part in the education system. Here was the distinctive Catholic understanding of education, to be defended against 'a great many theorists of the day who confined education to mind and body.'[25] The teaching of morality was a religious task which fell outside the competence of the State. The State or civil power was dependent upon the religious power to fulfil this rôle, and in exchange, the Church could influence secular society by an influx of moral teaching. The Church thus had a vital place in the educational developments of the day. Casartelli's conviction was that in order to influence more effectively the moral and intellectual life of the nation and to strengthen its own position, the Church ought to speak with a unified voice. As a practical implementation of this policy, he supported the idea of a meeting of Catholic headmasters, first mooted in the pages of the *Downside Review*[26] by the editor. Casartelli, who had outlined his own policies earlier,[27] now went on to point out that a meeting of Catholic colleges would facilitate a uniformity in the syllabus, a corresponding 'parallel systemisation of the classical and modern' sides of education, and a uniformity in textbooks.[28] It would also assist the task of gaining adequate representation to bodies such as the University of London. Although he was not

> a worshipper of the London University [it was at present] almost our sole resource for 'academic' distinction. It is, therefore, of some considerable importance that Catholic colleges should have some chance of exercising a legitimate influence on the system of examinations, such as the authorities of the University are always ready enough to admit. Numerous questions crop up from time to time, strongly affecting Catholic education in its relations to 'London'. It is evident that the best machinery for the influence desiderated would be some kind of a Union, representative of our secondary and higher educational establishments. Here, as elsewhere, *l'union fait la force.*'[29]

This last phrase was to become the 'watchword' of his episcopal years. His career can be read as a practical translation of this motto because of his constant seeking of 'strength in unity,' by making the Catholic Federation the central work of his episcopate.

Ten years elapsed before any practical steps were taken to implement the proposal for a Headmasters' Association. Thanks to 'the statesmanlike initiative of Cardinal Vaughan,'[30] the first meeting took place at Westminster on 3 January 1896;[31] twenty-three colleges were represented. Casartelli, who was nominated secretary, observed that those present were largely unknown to one another – the situation first perceived by the editor of the *Downside Review* in 1886 – and he urged a better organisation of their forces.[32] The motive prompting the convening of the meeting was the increased demand for education and the recently issued Report of the Royal Commission on Secondary Education which gave increased hope to the advocates of State education.[33] It was recognised that 'it would never do for Catholics to be outside the national movement.'[34] Vaughan urged that the meeting should discuss first the possibility of a scheme to enable poorer children to gain the advantages – as in the Middle Ages – of secondary education. Casartelli had addressed this theme in the *Dublin Review* a year earlier,[35] so it is quite possible that Vaughan, given his high opinion of Casartelli, was drawing upon this as a source for his ideas. Likewise, Casartelli saw Vaughan as a model to follow. When Vaughan stated that the Church's 'success in carrying out the great mission of her Divine Founder must depend, humanly speaking, upon the due organisation of her forces and upon her ability to educate her children', Casartelli would probably have connected this with the motto he had quoted earlier: *vis unita fortior.*[36]

The second topic for discussion was the improvement of Catholic secondary education. The Royal Commission had set a major challenge to Catholics: arguing that private endeavour had failed to produce an adequate supply of secondary schools, it had recommended that the only means of achieving such provision was by State intervention. However, an opening for reforming Catholics could still be perceived, for the Commission had conceded that the provision of a more literary education might be prejudiced by its programme.

> There is little danger at the present day that we shall fail to recognise the necessity of improving and extending scientific and technical instruction. It is less certain that we may not run some risk of a lopsided development in education, in which the teaching of science, theoretical or applied, may so predominate as to entail comparative neglect of studies which are of less obvious and immediate utility.[37]

Catholic educators could claim – and in the conference called by Vaughan did so – a rôle in meeting this difficulty. Hence they suggested as a necessary step in this improvement that Catholic teachers should make up any deficiency in their professional training and ability by taking advantage of a university education. This proposal received unanimous agreement.[38]

CASARTELLI: PROMOTER OF CATHOLIC EDUCATION

Oxford and Cambridge: opportunity or peril?

When Casartelli – influenced by Newman – advocated the participation of English Catholics at the Universities of Oxford and Cambridge, the position that he took was a bold one. Undoubtedly, English Catholics had for some time asked if, 'taking advantage of the gradual abolition of religious tests at Oxford and Cambridge – [they should] throw in their lot with the national universities and face all the rocks and shoals of English university life as it then was, or should they attempt to create a university of their own in which a specifically Catholic learning and culture might arise.'[39]

The idea of a specifically Catholic university college had arisen, again, in 1873, in the wake of the hierarchy's reiteration in the previous year of Rome's directive of 1865, prohibiting Catholics attending the ancient Universities.[40] The Roman authorities had earlier requested that the English bishops deal with the question of the higher education of Catholic youth. In reply, and in order to elevate the standard of higher studies, it was suggested that a Board of Examiners be formed.[41] In consequence a Senate was proposed, to consist of the heads of Catholic colleges and representatives of the laity and clergy, representing an ecclesiastical 'mirror' to the University of London. The proposed Senate would grant prizes and scholarships and institute a team of examiners. The idea of an examining body was Manning's first step in the creation of a Catholic university. Casartelli however, voiced his disapproval of the scheme to a member of the staff of Ushaw College:

> Spoke with Mr. Newton about Arch. Manning's violent objections to the London University system, and (he) would like an examining body resembling it in shape, but Catholic. But where would be the good? It could not grant degrees.[42]

A new Catholic college was to be opened at Kensington as an alternative to London University. It was hoped that the 'Old Catholic' families (i.e. recusant) would be attracted to Kensington, a fashionable area of London, and that Catholic youths of the middle class, for whom the provision was also intended, would soon follow. The head of the College was to be Mgr. Capel: 'the bishops were impressed by Capel's record ... they thought that in securing him for the headship of the new College they were demonstrating to the gentry that the institution would have a distinct life of its own.'[43]

Casartelli was not impressed with this scheme either. His doubts arose from the influence of Newman's idea of what a university ought to be. Casartelli had begun to read Newman's work on university education in September 1872.[44] The Kensington model was not of the type envisaged by Newman because it did not constitute a *communitas* i.e. a body of resident students. Casartelli's doubts were compounded when he, 'Made acquaintance of Dr. Rohling, the famous architect. He has been in America, and lately accepted the tutorship of German at Kensington University College; but finding it so much below his expectations, resigned it.'[45]

In later life he described the Kensington venture as 'an ill-fated fiasco' and explained how he had 'narrowly escaped by declining a chair offered by Mgr. Capel.'[46]

Casartelli's own sympathies in the way of university education lay with the idea of bringing the Catholic Church once more into some contact with the national universities, as he believed this would be beneficial to the Church in general and for Catholic education in particular. He described the movement to bring this about as a 'stirring of the waters.'[47] The ensuing debate between Newman, Manning, and Ward[48] – centred on the participation of Catholics at the university of Oxford – Casartelli later described as a 'hurricane.' He had lived through a similar storm when a student at Ushaw College. Here we have an example of Casartelli who, as the author of 'John Pearl's Lay Sermons' followed Manning and Vaughan, now showing evidence of independent opinions and expressing them firmly and persuasively. In relation to Vaughan and Manning *vis-à-vis* education, Casartelli was no cipher.

The key change of policy, overturning the Roman rescript of 1865, came about after the death of Cardinal Manning in 1892 and the succession of Herbert Vaughan to the See of Westminster. Edward Norman has highlighted evidence that shows that Manning himself, shortly before his death, had changed his mind and thought the ban ought to be lifted.[49] A petition, containing Casartelli's name along with those of other sympathetic priests and religious, former students of Oxford and Cambridge, and members of the Catholic aristocracy, seeking the reversal of the rescript was drawn up in 1894. This was presented to the hierarchy, with a memorandum stating the gist of the petition's prayer and how 'the condition of the ancient Universities had changed radically, and that these institutions no longer constituted that threat to the faith and morals of English Catholics which had been the original cause of episcopal concern.'[50] The petition was addressed to the Roman authorities; the purpose of the memorandum to the English and Welsh bishops was to offer them the opportunity of taking the initiative, if they so wished, in discussing the removal of the ban with Rome. The bishops met on 4 January 1895. After discussing the petition, eight voted in favour of requesting Rome to suppress the rescript and six voted against. Casartelli's own bishop, John Bilsborrow, was among the six who opposed any change in policy.[51]

Casartelli claimed that Vaughan's change of heart had begun when he was Bishop of Salford and living at St Bede's College. Of the event Casartelli wrote,

> The almost violent opposition of Cardinal Manning and for a long time of his faithful disciple, Dr. Herbert Vaughan, – an opposition leading to the ill-fated fiasco of the projected Catholic University of Kensington – … seemed to shut out all hope of a reversal of the dominating policy. But with the end of the Manning régime the change came. The wonderful conversion of Herbert Vaughan on his succeeding to Westminster is excellently told by Mr. Snead-Cox in his *Life*, Vol. II. Such a volte-face surprised most people, shocked some. No doubt the famous petition of Catholic laymen and graduates played a great part in the conversion. But it was the result of no fickleness or instability. It had been gradually shaping itself. It is no small gratification to think that much of the conversion was going on within these walls before the successor of Manning had gone to Westminster. And I believe I am correct in stating that a large share of the credit was due to the influence and cogent reasoning of a singularly able member of our staff, now no longer in the diocese. Those of us who had spent 14 years in constant communication with Dr. Vaughan knew well that extraordinary honesty and humility of mind and character, which never refused to listen to the arguments of an opponent, or to acknowledge loyally mistakes of his own judgement when made clear to him.'[52]

McClelland has challenged those who have echoed this interpretation first put forward by Snead-Cox.[53] He believes it to be a mistaken assessment of the situation, and that Vaughan's decision was not ultimately due to the 'altered circumstances' at the universities, i.e. there being no longer any dangers to faith and morals, but due more to his having given way 'to the powerful pressure tactics of an exclusive social set' who drew up the petition asking for the ban on Catholics attending Oxford and Cambridge to be lifted.[54] However, Snead-Cox, before writing his biography of Vaughan, had consulted Casartelli on several occasions.[55] It is reasonable to conclude that his section recounting Vaughan's change of mind regarding the ban was based on Casartelli's recollections and was therefore accurate. If it were not, Casartelli would not have spoken of it as being 'excellently told.'

However, the part played by the petition must not be underplayed. As McClelland points out, Vaughan was susceptible to influence from the Duke of Norfolk who, along with Wilfrid Ward, co-opted the help of Friedrich von Hügel in trying to convince Vaughan that a change was necessary vis-à-vis the Universities question.[56] The pressure they sought to exert on Vaughan was enhanced by the fact that Friedrich von Hügel's mother-in-law, Lady Herbert of Lea, was one of Vaughan's closest friends. Vaughan's first reaction to the question was to try and establish a Catholic university, but he was dissuaded from this course of action. He also contemplated asking Rome for further and more stringent mandates to bolster the prescription. In the event, the petition organised by the Duke of Norfolk proved to be the tactical forcing of Vaughan's hand: if he refused to forward the petition to Rome, it would show a split between influential laity and the bishops. Given that the bishops were themselves divided on the issue there was a danger that the laity would achieve their aims in Rome. Vaughan was faced with a fait accompli. McClelland concludes that Vaughan gave in to the aristocracy under pressure and that his fellow bishops, who had voted against the petition's request, were annoyed by his claim that the Universities' question had been reopened by the request of the bishops.[57] McClelland quotes Vaughan's reaction to Anatole von Hügel[58] as evidence of his anger at the situation and that his hand had been forced: 'When Vaughan met Anatole von Hügel and told him that he would submit the lay petition to Rome, now that it had been endorsed by the act of the bishops, he added bitterly, 'it would be best if I took it and tore it and threw it in the fire.'[59]

However, it should be noted that evidence from the papers of the 15th Duke of Norfolk presents a somewhat different picture. Was Vaughan as resigned, and possibly as angry, as his comment to Anatole von Hügel suggested? After the bishops' meeting on 4 January 1895, Vaughan wrote to the Duke of Norfolk,

Be easy about the University question. I read you the Bishop's resolutions when we met. [One] provides for a Board or Senate of Bishops, Priests and *Laymen*. Nothing will be done *without you*: and I hope you really feel (now if not formerly) not only my deep affection for you but my complete trust in you, so that whatsoever I can tell you I will tell you, and whatsoever we can work together I shall feel myself not only strengthened but the happier. I super-abound in what you say as to the importance of winning the appreciation of the Universities and of avoiding a controversial and hostile attitude.[60]

Such comments suggest the attitude of a man who was quite at ease working alongside the Duke. There is no hint here of Vaughan wanting to retain information or control the situation; he treats the Duke as a colleague. Vaughan's second letter to the Duke, written after his meeting in Rome with Propaganda Fide, assured him that all went well, and he himself drew up the *ponenza* or case for the lifting of the ban – 'every point has been accepted, and strange to say, unanimously. It is seldom that such a thing happens at Prop. Fide.'[61] Rome granted the request, the only proviso being that a course of lectures on philosophy, history, and religion be given to the Catholic students.

Vaughan invited Norfolk to think over the composition of the Universities' Board and to make suggestions as to who should be invited to join: 'you, your nephew and W. Ward will naturally be on it.'[62] Vaughan seemed happy with the outcome and was willing to neutralise any adverse attempts by the bishops who were not in favour of the resolution – 'I shall be able, I think, to render Notts.[63] harmless or to neutralise his efforts.'[64] With Propaganda Fide's decision, Vaughan hoped that 'we have come to the end of our troubles on the Primrose bed.'[65]

In general, the evidence from the Duke of Norfolk's papers gives credence to both Casartelli's contemporary and McClelland's historical view that the lay petition did have the desired effect and that the Duke of Norfolk certainly had the advantage of having Vaughan's ear. It is also clear that Vaughan was co-operating more with the Duke of Norfolk than he was with some of his episcopal colleagues. This course of action would not have endeared itself to the bishops who were opposed to any change in the ban on Catholics attending Oxford or Cambridge. Bishop John Bilsborrow of Salford considered that the only advantage for Catholics would be social.[66] He was not alone in this opinion.[67] The way Vaughan had treated the dissenting bishops and had worked closely with the Duke of Norfolk, did not augur well for the near future, when Bilsborrow would be approached about the possibility of releasing Casartelli to be chaplain at Oxford.

Casartelli and university education for Catholics

With Catholic participation at Oxford and Cambridge on the way to becoming a reality, Casartelli wrote three significant review papers on the situation of the universities. The implicit target of his first paper was, once again, Gladstone, as he refuted his 'curious and ingenious contention ... that the universities of the early Middle Ages were the outcome of 'a great systematic effort of the lay mind to achieve self-assertion and emancipation', as against the predominance of ecclesiasticism.'[68] Casartelli acknowledged that the very earliest universities were called into existence before either papal or regal authority began to intervene; this, however, did not equate with an 'organised system of emancipation,' as Gladstone had claimed.[69] His purpose was 'to emphasise the essential Catholic character of our national Universities from their inception'[70] and how they were 'intimately bound up with all that was best and holiest in the English Church.'[71] Against the claim of the modern liberal for the freedom of universities in independence of the Church, Casartelli quoted Friedrich Paulson[72] who believed that: 'In the erection of the Universities there was formerly absolute liberty not outside of the Church, but inside the Church, and the Church blessed with equal affection both the good she did herself and the good which was done in her.'[73]

The Reformation had caused a rupture between the Church and the universities and was the catalyst of 'the sad history of the process by which these national universities were lost to the Catholic Church.'[74] The loss of the beautiful cathedrals was as nothing in comparison with the loss of the 'ancient seats of learning' and 'national schools of theology'.

Casartelli's second paper, 'Catholics and the Universities,' was tactical in its approach. He recalled how, at a recent meeting of the Heads of Catholic colleges, it had been acknowledged that the question of Catholics attending the Universities of Oxford and Cambridge was 'one of the most important topics of the hour.'[75] The London University system, as it stood, could not provide Catholics with a true education.[76] However, he sought to show what possibilities the opening up of the universities could present, in the hands of an active Catholic community. Since the reorganisation of secondary education was inextricably bound up with questions of university education, he urged those present not to be afraid of the opportunities now being offered to Catholics and to seize the advantage of a university education, thus to be better able to 'take their place in the full intellectual life of their country.'[77] He appealed for 'bridges of education' to link together the stages of primary, secondary, and tertiary education and concluded by repeating his belief that the removal of the ecclesiastical prohibition was 'nothing more than reverting to the state of things which prevailed in the Catholic England of the

Middle Ages. As such they could not but welcome the process.'[78] Casartelli
believed that the removal of civil disabilities in regard to Catholics, and their
admission to the universities, heralded a return to the medieval unity of faith
and learning. Extrapolating from his assertion that Oxford and Cambridge
were from their earliest days institutions 'intimately bound up with all that
was best and holiest in the English Church,'[79] he believed that the policies he
was advocating did indeed represent a restoration to the earlier ideal.

> These things being so, we are but acting in the very spirit of our Holy
> Mother the Church if we have a high appreciation of, and a great desire for
> the promotion of university education.[80]

Clearly, on this theme, Casartelli spoke with the voice of Newman. The
'training of the mind,' which he emphasised, was central to Newman's idea
of a university. A university, in this sense of the term, demanded the
presence of a resident community of students, who through their mutual
interaction would help educate one another. On these grounds, Casartelli
did not consider the London system to be a university in the true sense; for
that he looked to 'the great universities' of Oxford, Cambridge, and Louvain.
In a speech to the heads of Catholic colleges, Casartelli cited directly from
Newman's *The Idea of a University*:

> if I had to choose between a so-called university, which dispensed with
> residence and tutorial superintendence, and gave its degrees to any person
> who passed an examination in a wide range of subjects, and a university
> which had no professors or examinations at all, but merely brought a
> number of young men together for three or four years, and then sent them
> away, as the University of Oxford is said to have done some sixty years
> since, if I were asked which of these two methods was the better discipline
> of the intellect…was the more successful in training, moulding, enlarging
> the mind, which sent out men more fitted for their secular duties, which
> produced better public men … I have no hesitation in giving preference to
> that university which did nothing, over that which exacted of its members
> an acquaintance with every science under the sun.[81]

In this same paper, Casartelli spoke from the heart, as the convinced and
highly competent scholar-gentleman of a foremost European Catholic university. Through this formation, he had come to value Newman's model as
his own, and he stuck doggedly to this theme throughout his life. In 1923 he
claimed that the London University system was responsible for,

> The setting up of the examination – and worse still, of the written examin-
> ation – as a fetish, a tyrannous fetish, which dominated our whole
> educational system…and with it the estimation of the magic initials B.A.
> and M.A. as the hall-mark of all scholarship and the ever-to-be-sought-

after crown of an academic career. All idea of what we rightly term 'culture' (not the German variety) or true scholarship tended to disappear. Real teaching was giving way to cramming. The individual influence of the teacher in the formation of mind and taste was dying out before mere successful coaching.[82]

In general, however, his advocacy of an education at Oxford and Cambridge was part of his case for re-integrating Catholics into national life. This was something he was ever trying to achieve, whether by demonstrating the allegiance of Catholics to legitimate state authority or, later, by encouraging Catholics to play their full part in the First World War. Indeed, in the matter of education it can be said that, whilst he was an ardent advocate of Catholic schools, he was not 'denominational' in his outlook i.e. he did not advocate a separatist policy. He saw Catholic schools, and a Catholic philosophy of education, being for the good of society at large and not simply to provide schooling for Catholic pupils, hence his encouraging the Church to take its place on the 'ladder of education.' Neither did he see Catholic schools as a means of controlling the faithful. In this matter his views were at variance with Bilsborrow and the Salford Diocesan Chapter; in other words, Casartelli was atypical as far as many of the clergy of his diocese were concerned. This will be significant when we come to consider how Casartelli did not have a 'parochial' mentality.

To those who considered it unnecessary for Catholics to attend Oxford and Cambridge because, in their opinion, the existing Catholic colleges supplied all educational needs, Casartelli retorted: 'it is more than doubtful whether we, as a body, are keeping abreast of the remarkable intellectual developments of the day.'[83] In the past the Church had done well, considering the disadvantages under which it had had to labour, but circumstances were now different. Important intellectual developments were taking place in the national universities, in fields such as Oriental studies, philology, and textual criticism, but with the exception of a few scattered individuals, the Church was having little influence in these areas. This situation could not be allowed to rest. However, the opening up of the universities to Catholics also brought with it responsibility.[84] Slowly the Church was making its way from 'the penumbra of the penal times'[85] and coming to play its part in the public life of the nation.[86] This was a continuing and dynamic process; one in which the Church must constantly be engaged.

He foresaw that it would not only be the laity who stood to gain from attendance at the universities. The intellectual development of the clergy would also be greatly enhanced if they seized the possibilities now open to them. Casartelli was conscious of the need for an educated clergy to be an important part of the Church's agenda:

We shall need a learned clergy in that coming century as we had never needed it before; we shall need it for the defence and propagation of the truth, and we shall need it urgently for the work of education.[87]

In an address to a meeting of Ushaw College *alumni* in March 1898 he praised the college's efforts 'to be abreast of all that is best in the intellectual and religious life of the day' and warned them against the comforts to be had from playing the part of the *laudator temporis acti*:[88]

> it will not do for us – much less for a great institution like Ushaw – to be content with the *laudare tempus actum*. The Catholic Church in our country is face to face with a new England, a new century. Clergy and laity, we have both before us such opportunities, such duties as will require the utmost and best of all we possess in mind and soul.[89]

He urged the example of two former Ushaw men – John Lingard and Nicholas Wiseman – to be taken as patterns to follow. These men were 'men of the future', who, respectively, had pioneered the regeneration of English history and played an illustrious part in the resurrection of the Church in England.

Casartelli's third paper was dedicated to the encouragement of the clergy to take advantage of a university education.[90] The present state of higher education among the clergy was attributable to a variety of sources. The relatively small number of Catholics in England had prevented the existence of large seminaries able to provide an adequate education. Certain seminaries consisted of only two or three professors and a handful of students, so it was impossible to nurture 'eminent professors' and even the most gifted students were deprived of the opportunity of pursuing further studies. The policies of Cardinal Manning were partly to blame for this state of affairs. Manning had,

> believed his duty to be to establish in his own diocese, and to have other bishops establish in their respective dioceses, major seminaries ... However, we have forgotten one thing. The decrees of the Council of Trent were aimed at the great and powerful dioceses of Catholic countries which could provide not only material means, but also a great number of candidates to fill the places of diocesan seminaries and a choice of distinguished professors ... We can easily understand then that our small English dioceses are completely incapable of providing scholars in sufficient numbers so as to train so many professional bodies.[91]

Casartelli preferred the policy advocated by Vaughan, which was to concentrate the seminaries in order to improve ecclesiastical education and to lessen the burden on the Catholic community who were not in a position to finance a great number of diocesan seminaries.[92] Casartelli acknowledged that the shortage of priests meant that few could be spared from 'missionary work'. However, the English Church had not been completely devoid of erudite scholars of distinction. Two examples were Canon James Moyes, and the Benedictine Aidan Gasquet.[93] Without a 'following' these scholars remained isolated, unable to train disciples in their schools of thought. Casartelli saw this as 'the reason for our always remaining excluded from intellectual life, from the scientific movement in universities.'[94] In order for established scholarly schools to develop, it was necessary for clerics to take advantage of the opportunities recently offered to the laity. However, the English clergy were much too reticent about doing this:

> We worriedly ask ourselves what state our clergy will be in twenty-five years from now, not only in relation to the Anglican clergy, and even the clergy of the dissident sects, who are doing everything in order to make use of the advantages of higher education, but in relation to our laity who will be more educated and will have more cultivated minds than their priests.[95]

As a bishop Casartelli placed the education of his clergy high on his list of priorities.[96] The 'danger' of having a clergy who were less educated than the people they served was constantly pointed out in his appeals for donations to the ecclesiastical education fund.

One project he did support to the best of his ability in order to enhance the education of the clergy was that of St Edmund's House, Cambridge.[97] The 15th Duke of Norfolk and Baron Von Hügel had set up this institution in 1896 as a house of residence for Catholic clergymen. It was plagued by the serious problem of a shortage of students and the reluctance of many bishops to support the venture. Archbishop Thomas Whiteside of Liverpool pointed out that the bishops as a whole were not in favour of the scheme. The Northern bishops were positively opposed to it.[98] But Casartelli, ever the scholar with a wide European vision, was undeterred. He wrote to the secretary of the Association, expressing his concern for the foundation,

> in which I am so deeply interested. I am sorry to think that the support given to the House – whose continual existence seems to me so vital to the future education of our clergy, and especially of our clerical teachers – is so slender. It has been a great pleasure to me to be enabled to place one of my Church students at the House – I only wish I were able to send another. But to a poor diocese like ours, the cost is heavy when placed side by side with the expenses of an ordinary seminary.[99]

Casartelli became a member of its Council in 1904. In 1918 he was part of the discussions to launch a campaign to further the development of St Edmund's by securing wider interest and sympathetic support.

In all the campaigns he identified himself with for Catholics to be immersed in the world of tertiary education, Casartelli never desired the setting up of a Catholic university in England: 'The experiment has been tried in the past, and its woeful failure supplied a stern lesson for the future.'[100] Rather, it was to Germany he looked as an example of how things might work well. The situation and conditions there, *vis-à-vis* university education, were

> more or less similar to our own, and here we find the Catholic body taking its rightful share in the academic and intellectual life of the national universities. Indeed, the exigencies of the Catholic Church in the England of the twentieth century seem to involve the necessity of her taking her place fully and unreservedly in the highest and best work of the great universities.[101]

With the emergence of local universities in the early twentieth century he strongly urged that places should be sought there too, as only a few Catholics, apart from the members of wealthy families, could afford to attend Oxford or Cambridge. The provincial universities were also able to offer scholarships and bursaries and so widen the possibility of a university education for those who otherwise could not afford it. The opportunity to both benefit from, and contribute toward, the universities afforded the Church, 'a more favourable field than she has ever had before for exercising her influence upon the intellectual and moral life of the great centres of English thought and belief.'[102]

Casartelli's ideas on universities were not in harmony with those of Bishop Bilsborrow, during whose episcopate boys from his diocese were not granted permission to study at Oxford or Cambridge.[103] In his papers on the advantages of such an education and the reasons why Catholics ought to be able to attend, he was showing, whilst always docile to Church authority, he was capable of holding his own opinions in favour of intellectual freedom. It is ironic that one of the strongest episcopal opponents of the ancient Universities should have among the ranks of his clergy not only one of their strongest supporters but one who was among those approached to be the first chaplain to the Catholic students there.[104] This post had been created to fulfil the condition laid down by Propaganda Fide that Catholics attending Oxford and Cambridge should be provided with instruction in philosophy and theology from a Catholic standpoint. In the deliberations of who was to be appointed as chaplain, Casartelli's name was prominent.

Casartelli and the Oxford chaplaincy[105]

New evidence about the provision of a chaplain at the ancient Universities has come to light in the papers of Bishop John Cuthbert Hedley, Bishop of

Newport and Chairman of the Catholic Universities Board, recently deposited in the National Library of Wales.[106] The collection contains correspondence between the Bishop of Salford, John Bilsborrow, Casartelli, and Hedley. Bilsborrow strongly objected to Hedley's approaching Casartelli about becoming the chaplain at Oxford without first having consulted him in his capacity as diocesan bishop. The row that ensued illustrated Casartelli's preferred area of work, his wider vision, and his frustration at those who did not share the same.

Herbert Vaughan had nominated Canon James Moyes to the Council that was charged with the oversight of the implementation of the Roman directives of 1895. This became known as the 'Universities Catholic Education Board.' It met for the first time in June 1895.[107] Bishop Hedley was the chairman of a sub-committee, formed one week after the first general meeting, whose brief was, 'to investigate the feasibility and desirability of establishing at Oxford or at Cambridge, or at both, a house of resident priests with a view to further the spiritual interests of Catholic members of the Universities.'[108]

Bishop Hedley pursued the nomination of a Benedictine priest for the Cambridge chaplaincy and for the making over of the Cambridge parish to the Order's control. This proposal immediately met with the disapproval of the Bishop of Northampton, who did not want to see the post fall to a member of a religious Order. A similar conflict arose in Oxford, where the Duke of Norfolk did not want a Jesuit to fill the post of chaplain. Vaughan, who was a little less sceptical, nevertheless wrote to Hedley, saying,

> I also see a danger lest SJ should take possession of the whole Oxford position. I do not think we ought to allow this; it would be to deprive the hierarchy of their control and direction at Oxford. That they should be employed by the Bishops as any other person, well and good. But we must take care they do not snatch Oxford out of our hands.[109]

Accordingly, Canon Moyes, James Hope[110] and Wilfrid Ward[111] were appointed to draw up a list of suitable candidates. McClelland writes, 'At the June meeting [of the Universities' Board] there was a long discussion on the list of names for the office of chaplain at Oxford, but no decision was taken at that meeting, or, indeed, at the following two meetings of the Board on 13 October and 6 November 1896.'[112]

Various candidates had been approached but no definite decision had been reached as to who ought to be appointed. Two names mentioned were a secular priest named Canon Arthur Kennard and a Jesuit – Fr Joseph Rickaby. Kennard, who was first approached in January 1896 (when the original list of candidates was drawn up), was not keen to accept the offer as he was

disinclined to have to uproot himself; he was however, prepared to reconsider his refusal. McClelland summarises the protracted negotiations
between the supporters of the secular and regular: 'The negotiations with
Kennard and Rickaby dragged on throughout the summer, during which
time the supporters of the Jesuit cause were not idle.'[113] Neither were the
supporters of the seculars. On this issue the Hedley Papers reveal how close
Casartelli came to being appointed and the reasons why he declined.

A letter from the Bishop of Clifton[114] to Bishop Hedley, dated 25 June
1896, mentioned that a Fr A. S. McColl, from the diocese of Southwark, had
been approached in regard to the Oxford Chaplaincy but he had declined.
The Universities Board next sought the help of the Congregation of the
Oratory; they too felt unable to supply a suitable priest. It is at this point that
Casartelli's name was mentioned. The Bishop of Clifton wrote to Bishop
Hedley – 'We could not have a better man than Fr. Casartelli, if he will go to
Oxford. Please ask him.'[115] Hedley wrote to Casartelli on 27 August 1896.
Casartelli replied the following day, saying that he was grateful for the
honour paid him by the request to become the chaplain to Catholic students
at Oxford: 'Nothing could be more congenial to my tastes and aspirations
than work for Catholic Education in a University centre like Oxford.'[116] However, the description of the chaplain's duties i.e. 'religious lecturer', proved
too daunting. Therefore, 'before venturing upon a definite answer,' he asked
for a fuller description of what the task would entail, as he recognised that he
was neither a philosopher nor a theologian. If such a person was required, he
felt he could not adequately fulfil the post despite feeling 'great gratification
at the offer.' Casartelli in another letter to Hedley stated that '... the quotation from the Propaganda rescript considerably increases my embarrassment
in deciding upon the tempting offer made me by the University Board.'[117] His
understanding of the rescript was to the effect that it demanded the lecturer
to be widely read in modern schools of thought and adept in scholastic
philosophy. The lectures should be, according to Casartelli's understanding,
of a 'stimulating and convincing a character as to really influence and guide
the minds of the intelligent and keen young men.' In the light of this
Casartelli felt, 'I cannot conceal from myself the fact that I feel entirely unable to work up to such an ideal' and so 'fill with success the most tempting
post offered me.' As a matter of conscience he felt he must refuse. Two other
difficulties were significant. One was the importance of the work he was
engaged in at St Bede's, and secondly, 'the attitude of the Bishop of Salford
may be a very serious factor: he is very hostile to Oxford.' The latter fear
proved to be true; the whole affair gave Bilsborrow an opportunity to voice
his opposition to Catholics attending the ancient Universities.

Casartelli laid before Bilsborrow the offer Hedley had made him on behalf of the Universities' Board. In his initial letter, Hedley, according to Casartelli, 'adds many kind and encouraging words of his own, and assures me [Casartelli] that the selection meets with approval in very high and qualified quarters.'[118] Then followed the first of Hedley's mistakes; he had assumed that Bilsborrow would not object, and that Casartelli could continue as Rector of St Bede's. In Hedley's words,

> I am aware that the great obstacle to you going will be the importance of your present Diocesan duties. Your Bishop will, I am sure give the idea his most favourable consideration. At the most, residence at Oxford would only be for about half the year, and you would by no means be lost altogether to your diocese.[119]

Casartelli made no attempt to conceal from Bilsborrow the fact that life at Oxford would be for him a 'great attraction' and how 'congenial to [his] tastes and aspirations such a post would be.' He acknowledged being 'deeply attached' to St Bede's and that it would prove 'painful indeed' to be separated from the college. The Rescript from Propaganda made him feel, however, 'extreme diffidence in undertaking the lecture [sic] to young men on those subjects with any high hope of success.'[120]

Bishop Bilsborrow placed the whole matter, including Casartelli's letter, before the Diocesan Chapter of Canons on 2 September 1896. The minutes testify that Casartelli was willing to leave 'himself in the hands of the Bishop.'[121] The primary stumbling block was Hedley's 'assumed attitude' that the Bishop of Salford would not interpose any objection to one of his priests taking up the post at Oxford. This was further aggravated by his claim that 'there would be no necessity for the resignation of the position of Rector at St Bede's College, as the residence at the University would not be longer than six months in the year.'[122] Bilsborrow asked the Chapter's opinion on: '1. The fitness of the Rector for the proposed appointment. 2. As to the desirability considering the best interests of the Diocese, of the Bishop giving permission for the Rector to leave the Diocese.'[123]

As to the question of Casartelli's fitness 'and for the position generally, [and] as to [his] zeal, aptitude, influence and discipline and literary ability – there seemed to be unanimity of opinion.'[124] But it was agreed that it would be undesirable for the Rector of St Bede's to reside other than in the college; therefore, 'there was a general disposition to advise His Lordship to reply to Dr. Casartelli negative.' Furthermore, the Chapter wished it to be communicated to Casartelli 'that it was not canonical for a Bishop to approach a subject of another Bishop with such an offer without previous communication with the Ordinary.' The substance of a suitable reply was then drafted.[125] Casartelli copied the reply and forwarded it to Hedley. In a covering note he revealed his feelings of hurt and distress: 'It is really painful to me to transcribe a letter containing a judgement whose tone is so disobliging, not to say violent ... I feel much distressed that such intervention should have taken place.'[126]

In the meanwhile, Hedley, now aware of Casartelli's self-doubt regarding the duties of the chaplain, had sought the opinion of Herbert Vaughan. In response Vaughan commented on the preference of Fr Kennard to Casatelli, 'I should think he was the very man – at least to begin with – better than Casartelli.'[127] Later Vaughan added, 'Casartelli is certainly not philosophical – but he could give very good instruction of a religious and historical kind.'[128]

Casartelli vented his frustration at the Salford Chapter's lack of vision when he next wrote to Hedley: 'One looks in vain in them for a sense of interests wider and higher than mere diocesan ones, which perhaps, under the known circumstances is not to be wondered at.'[129] The attitude of Bilsborrow and the Chapter stood in stark contrast to that of Vaughan, who looked to the wider picture of the Church's needs. Casartelli shared this vision and would have been more at ease with Vaughan as bishop rather than Bilsborrow on this issue. However, Casartelli had the interests of St Bede's at heart and to leave it would be painful, yet,

> if I felt sure that I could serve the Church in England better by going to Oxford, I should not hesitate to go...If it were merely question of the charge of a house of residence for ecclesiastical students, as at Cambridge, or work of that kind, I should (as far as I am concerned) accept at once. It is the question of the lectureship which gives me pause.[130]

After Casartelli had taken the opportunity of seeking 'very good and valuable advice, especially from one whose opinion I esteem most highly,'[131] he sent Hedley his final decision: 'This has finally led me to make up my mind, and decline the lectureship at Oxford so kindly offered to me.' He felt that he could not put himself forward, as the person needed ought to be 'a thoroughly able specialist.' He still, however, entertained hope for the future, and showed where his interest would lie and the sort of work he would most like to be involved in:

> We know not what the future may bring; and should things develop and prosper, it may not be impossible that in the future I may have the privilege of lending my poor services in some other capacity at Oxford...My interest in the work is absolutely unchanged; and should a Catholic house of residence or hall ever grow up at Oxford, it is my firm wish and intention to bequeath to it my own library ...

The matter of the Oxford Chaplaincy and Casartelli was still not over, however. In October, Kennard, the favoured candidate, wrote to Hedley saying,

'I heartily re-echo the Council's wish that Dr. Casartelli should re-consider his refusal to go to Oxford – he would be so much more fitted for the post, and would make his mark there in a way that I could never hope to do.'[132]

A letter of Canon Moyes to Bishop Hedley suggests that Casartelli did in fact change his mind and was prepared to accept the post if it were offered to him a second time. Moyes wrote to Hedley as follows,

> His Eminence the Cardinal has asked me to write and to say that it has been suggested as a solution of the Oxford difficulty, that Dr. Casartelli should be asked to undertake the chaplaincy, and that Fr. Rickaby should be appointed to give the lectures.[133] This arrangement would meet the view of those who cannot consent to putting the post solely in the hands of a Jesuit, and also of those who wish to have a Jesuit lecturer. I have privately ascertained (at the suggestion of the Cardinal) from Dr. Casartelli his willingness to accept the post if offered him and the Cardinal is also able to say that in the event of the Board consenting, he will be able to arrange as to his transfer, with the Bishop of Salford.[134]

Bishop Hedley received a letter from Ampleforth, dated 25 November, saying that there was still no final decision about the chaplain and lecturer at Oxford. McClelland notes that 'Kennard was happy at the idea of such a division, [of the role of chaplain and lecturer] and he informed Wilfrid Ward that he would be willing to act as chaplain 'without a salary if only I get my house rent free.''[135] In the event Kennard was appointed on 10 December 1896.

Canon George Richardson, a member of the Salford Chapter who had known Casartelli since he was a boy, took it upon himself to write a private and confidential letter to Bishop Hedley on the matter of Casartelli's suitability. His was the only dissenting voice to express doubts about Casartelli being a suitable candidate for the post. He began by stating his intention in venturing to write to the Chairman of the Universities Board: 'I do this in all desire to aid you in your endeavours to find a suitable hand for the responsible office to be commenced at Oxford.'[136] Richardson understood that the type of person required was one who was not simply capable and good, 'but further still a man who can manage men, in so far as he will become the special advisor not only in question of every day philosophy etc., but in the more momentous questions of direction, a man, like Lacordaire or Newman as far as may be ...'

If such a priest were required Richardson's candid opinion was that Casartelli was not the man. He considered him to be pious, an admirable scholar and a walking polyglot and a good lecturer 'but no guide.' He criticised Casartelli for being 'a non-player' and for knowing nothing of the value of games. Richardson believed that, 'he has not been a great success as head of St Bede's as a guide to the staff nor advisor either to boys or parents and to my mind St Bede's would not lose much by Dr. Casartelli's resignation.' He added that it would neither be a favour, nor lead to his happiness, if he were to be appointed as chaplain to the students at Oxford. This was not – we may recall – how Casartelli's former pupils remembered him. One recalled that 'he was very keen on handball, and I enjoyed hundreds of games with him.'[137] Another recalled that his popularity was universal and well deserved.[138]

Casartelli's academic ability was not at issue. Richardson added yet more praise of him as 'a distinguished student, a man of many parts, a living specimen of scholarship and an excellent exponent of any subject, an object lesson of Catholic capability.'[139] Were these criticisms at all justified? No doubt Casartelli was a humble man who lacked self-confidence. His reaction to becoming chaplain was similar to his reaction at being asked to become a bishop – he feared failure. However, he was academically quite capable of the post at Oxford; even though he was not a specialist in theology and philosophy, he could have readily 'worked up' a course of lectures that would have been more than adequate. As for being a 'Lacordaire or a Newman', as Richardson understood the post to demand, Casartelli would not have been found wanting. Indeed, the 'special skill' of his ministry was his social grace and his ability to relate well with small groups and with individuals. Whilst not being an extrovert, his shyness was not crippling. Dealing with a relatively small, intelligent group of young men and having a position in the wider academic world of Oxford would have suited Casartelli and he would have made his mark. In view of this, the question remains as to why Richardson took it upon himself to write to Hedley and portray such a harsh and inaccurate picture of Casartelli? One reason could be that he was jealous of Casartelli and believed that he himself should have been appointed as the rector of St Bede's when it amalgamated with the Salford Grammar School.

Evidence in the Hedley Papers amply demonstrates Casartelli's interests and aspirations – an academic post near the universities of Oxford or Cambridge. Throughout the proceedings his absolute intellectual honesty is manifest:

> I have all my life disliked assuming the outward profession of teaching others what I feel in my own inner consciousness not to know well myself. Such work is all more or less of a sham, and as such must be found out in the end.[140]

Casartelli's hopes and aspirations of an academic post would be finally extinguished with the death of Bishop Bilsborrow in 1903 and his own name being put forward as the one to succeed him. However, it should be noted that in 1906 Casartelli became a member of the Catholic Universities' Board and its chairman *circa* 1916.

CASARTELLI: EDUCATIONAL PIONEER

Commercial education

The rise of technology and the progress of foreign competition were detrimental to Britain's foreign markets. This necessitated the development of a
more practical and technical approach to education in England. Conscious of
this, and following Henry Edward Manning's policy, Herbert Vaughan
decided upon the establishment of a commercial college for the Catholic
middle class of Manchester in order to provide an education commensurate
with the times and changed circumstances.[141] In Vaughan's own words:

> The new circumstances in modern life require a new provision in educa-
> tion. Experience daily proves that a considerable number of Catholic
> youth, whose social position rightly entitles them to a polite, refined, and
> liberal education, are no longer able to devote those years to the study of
> Greek and Latin literature[142]...many of our youth must hasten to acquire
> ... a thorough knowledge of their own mother tongue, and multiply
> themselves by a familiar acquaintance with modern languages, while
> strengthening and enlarging the faculties of the mind by the study of
> mathematics and science.[143]

In making provision for this want, Vaughan was acting in the spirit of the
First Provincial Synod of Westminster held in 1852, whose response to the
situation was: 'Where there is a sufficient Catholic population to warrant it,
we earnestly recommend the establishment of a middle school ... in which a
good commercial education shall be given to children of families in a better
worldly position.'[144]

A basic education was needed for the new trades, and in particular a knowledge of accountancy and foreign languages. Manning's policy as archbishop
was to provide an adequate education to serve the middle class.[145] This took
the form of a technical training for those who would earn their living in
industry. McClelland interprets this policy as

> [a] search for a 'via media' between scientific development and Christian-
> ity. Most of his educational policy as Archbishop can be attributed to his
> urgent desire to wean the Roman Catholic laity away from the traditional
> and classical branch of studies...towards the scientific and modern branch
> and thus he hoped to achieve a reconciliation between the claims of
> science and those of the Church.[146]

Herbert Vaughan had had experience of commercial education as it was
taught in America, Germany and France.[147] At the time he founded St Bede's
this type of education was largely unknown in England. The commercial and
technical programme to be carried out at St Bede's was based upon those

already in existence in foreign commercial establishments.[148] Casartelli's involvement since the earliest days of St Bede's, and his trips abroad to glean information from the long-established commercial colleges, are evidence of the part he played in the venture. It must not be assumed that he slavishly carried out Vaughan's wishes and simply put flesh on his ideas. Casartelli is to be seen as himself at the heart of the promotion and advancement of commercial education. His was a pioneering part in the furthering of the subject, both in regard to St Bede's, which had an above average department of geography, and in its acceptance in the field of education in general.

On 9 January 1876 Cardinal Manning officiated at the opening of the new College.[149] By 1880 as well as being Prefect of Studies, Casartelli was also undertaking the teaching of geography and 'commercial products' and also had charge of the college museum. He wrote his *Notes of a Course of Lectures on Commercial Geography* (J. B. Ledsham, London, 1884), after observing that no English textbook or syllabus existed for the course. The Preface describes it as, 'a set of brief notes upon commercial and industrial geography.'[150]

To appreciate Casartelli as a teacher of commercial education it is necessary to see him in the context of the Manchester Geographical Society. He was a member of the Society from its inception. Vaughan had been responsible, with a small group of others, for the foundation of the Society; at a meeting of the Manchester Chamber of Commerce in 1879, he referred to several commercial geographical societies that existed on the continent.[151] The purpose of the meeting was to discuss ways of defending British trade by acquiring knowledge of new markets. Characteristically, Vaughan introduced wider interests, 'envisaging the society spreading the knowledge of geography as there was such need of something or somebody to enlighten the ignorance of many, even educated persons, on the subject.'[152] Casartelli's specific contribution to the Society was in the improvement of the teaching of geography. In his history of the Society, T. Nigel L. Brown refers to Casartelli as being 'enlightened' in his views and to his teaching as being 'inspired' and 'advanced.'[153] Casartelli's work on the teaching of commercial geography began to receive national attention.[154]

It is significant that the first of Casartelli's papers on commercial education was given to the Manchester Statistical Society, an ideal forum for his arguments.[155] The interest of its membership in matters of education helped to place Manchester at the very forefront of discussion on the subject.[156] By his presence and his active involvement in the discussions at the Society's meetings Casartelli showed himself willing to engage with Manchester's wider society and contribute to current debate. On the occasion of his lecture on the 'Modern Languages Problem' in 1888, he expressed his appreciation as follows:

It is always with a feeling of encouragement and hopefulness that one addresses the Manchester Statistical Society upon an Educational subject. It has been several times mentioned, and I believe correctly, that the very first ventilation of the scheme of a national education, which eventually developed into our present educational system, was within the walls of this Society.[157]

Casartelli's definition of commercial education first appeared in a brief article in St Bede's College magazine.[158] The Mechanics' Institutes, founded 'with the object of giving special instruction to artisans engaged in trades' provided *technological* education.[159] The word *technical* was, on the other hand, commonly used in relation to science, art, or business, i.e. 'technical terms' in theology, law and science etc. From the distinction between 'technological' and 'technical' Casartelli concluded: 'In this sense we may fairly call any education which prepares for a special business or profession, a *technical* one.'[160] A more fitting name for this type of education was *commercial education*.

Casartelli considered that the great movement then underway in favour of technological education was vital for an industrial and commercial centre such as Manchester. In the early stages of the city's development, attention had been paid to advances in mechanics, machine construction, dyeing, printing, etc., but commercial education had been ignored or at best neglected. Although attempts had been made to remedy this situation he failed to see how 'the same interest has been extended to our purely mercantile pursuits – to the business-training of those young men who are to become clerks in our warehouses or banks, accountants, foreign correspondents or agents, and eventually the heads of our great firms.'[161]

Casartelli drew a comparison with Germany and other European countries where education was divided between the humanitarian and the practical. France had recognised the necessity of commercial education because many jobs within the country were being 'lost' to the Germans and the Swiss; as a result excellent commercial colleges were to be found in Paris and Rouen. In Germany commercial education had come under a developed curriculum involving book-keeping, commercial arithmetic, foreign correspondence in many languages, commercial history and geography and political economy. The task of teaching had been greatly aided by the vast amount of secondary literature upon which the teacher was able to draw.

A natural audience for Casartelli's argument was the Manchester Geographical Society. In a paper entitled 'Commercial Geography,'[162] he admitted that when he had first spoken on the matter of commercial education he had felt 'like one crying in the wilderness.'[163] Since then things had changed, but there still remained a prejudice to be overcome, and the need to eradicate the false view that commercial education was a mere branch of technological education.[164] The purpose of his address was to encourage the introduction of the subject, also called 'economic geography', into the education system not of every school but for specifically commercial schools.

Addressing a further task which was integral to this whole programme of education, Casartelli spoke on 'The Modern Languages Problem in Modern Education', to the Manchester Statistical Society in 1888. This subject-area was now fully accepted by the universities, and the Victoria University of Manchester had led the way with its provision of a Commercial Certificate.[165] University College, Liverpool, had been the first academic institution of higher rank to provide a two-year course in commercial education.[166] Since Europe showed no signs of homogeneity in matters of language, the future prospect was a need to learn more, not fewer, languages. Moreover, there was a distinct preference for business to be transacted in the native tongue of those concerned: Casartelli gave the example of the success of German businesses in Italy due to their ability to converse in Italian. For Britain to be competitive, it was necessary for her businessmen to preoccupy themselves with learning the language of the people with whom they wished to trade. He believed that modern languages and literatures, as an integral part of commercial education, could help fill the gap left by the diminution in the teaching of Classics.

Casartelli recognised the apparent incongruity of his addressing a professional body on a subject in which they enjoyed greater competence. The standpoint from which he addressed them was that of an 'educationalist with long and practical interest in educational matters.'[167] The study of continental methods in commercial education had, during the last ten years, helped to develop education along more practical lines. The benefits gained from this were to be seen in an increased skill in technical, scientific, and mercantile subjects. However, this had meant a lessening interest in the *litterae humaniores*. Casartelli did not deprecate the advances made in technical education, but he did observe how 'on the other hand, I cannot shut my eyes to the fact that the training of the pure intellect itself as a thinking instrument of keenness and precision, the formation of intellectual taste, the refinement of the imagination, are among the highest and most essential qualifications of a true education.'[168]

As it was not feasible to combine a classical and a commercial education, intellectual taste and the refinement of imagination had therefore to be supplied from another educative source. Casartelli demonstrated how commercial education could be this source of culture, given that it touched upon archaeology, philology, and literature. His synthesis of commercial education with the theory and purpose of cultivating the intellect showed how it could be simultaneously practical, and able to touch upon and develop the

'deeper' issues of education. He was thus able to pioneer a practical education imbued with a philosophy that did not reduce education to the merely
useful.

Casartelli not only advocated the learning of European languages. He
also thought that Oriental languages would be useful, both for trade with the
East, and because Britain 'held grave responsibilities towards ancient and
historical races with their teeming millions of population.'[169]

Casartelli: the orientalist

It was generally accepted that, for Casartelli, becoming a bishop seriously
curtailed his work as an Orientalist. For example, a former pupil wrote:

> When he was pressed to accept the Bishopric of Salford it was really a
> tragedy, because his life's work, for which he was eminently cut out, was
> brought to a premature close.[170]

Similarly, an obituary recalled how his 'knowledge and intelligence
would have called on him to train many more disciples, had it not been for
the absorbing responsibilities of the episcopacy which snatched him away
from his favourite studies.'[171]

Undoubtedly, for Casartelli there was painful truth in these observations.
However, another aspect to the matter is worth consideration. He noted
that in England the lack of scholars and scholarship among the diocesan
clergy reflected the lack of professors able to teach and train disciples. The
result of this was that the few scholars there were (Gasquet, Moyes, and
Ward) were unable to gather around themselves a circle of disciples thus
creating a 'school.' Had circumstances been different, allowing Casartelli to
develop his academic interests more fully, he would have found himself in
the same position – a professor with few or no pupils. Until he became a
bishop, his Oriental studies were done 'in exile', i.e. in Louvain. That university had a developing Oriental School, whereas at Manchester University no
such school yet existed. Given Bilsborrow's utter hostility to Oxford, there
was no chance of Casartelli teaching there either, even part-time. Thus,
paradoxically, it was within the limits of a bishopric and no longer able to go
to Louvain, that he made his greatest contribution to the academic life of the
city of Manchester, not least by being a founder member of its Faculty of
Theology and a founder-member of the Manchester Oriental and Egyptian
Societies. Other Catholic clerics had been members of some of the city's
learned societies, for example the Rev. Francis Gonne,[172] but none achieved
the prominence of Casartelli: none had become bishop, and none had his
qualities of intellect. Certainly his ability to dedicate more time to Oriental

Studies was curtailed by his appointment as bishop, but he nevertheless gave, and remains, a first class example of the 'scholarly, teaching bishop,' when teaching is understood in its widest sense, and not restricted to catechesis and the imparting of dogma. We may turn now to examine in more detail, one distinguished aspect of his teaching.

Casartelli dedicated his exceptional linguistic skills to one of the least approachable specialities in Oriental studies, that is the origins of Zoroastrianism and in particular Pahlevi. His particular interest was how it evidenced humanity's efforts to attain knowledge of the eternal.[173] Through his contact with the University of Manchester, Casartelli formed a friendship with James Hope Moulton, a fellow Orientalist and professor of Hellenistic Greek and Indo-European philology. After having given Casartelli a preview of his book *Early Zoroastrianism*, Moulton thanked him by saying, 'Bishop Casartelli, whom Manchester University is fortunate to claim as Lecturer in Iranian, has read the whole of my proofs, to my great profit.'[174] In reply Casartelli wrote, 'I must only deprecate the far too partial way in the way [sic] you refer to myself.'[175] Casartelli considered Moulton's scholarship to be 'a high-water level of up-to-date scholarship.'[176]

Casartelli was a founder member of both the Manchester Egyptian Society and the Manchester Oriental Society. By his membership of these societies he was able to pursue his passion for Oriental studies and contribute to the intellectual and cultural life of the city of Manchester and its university. The minute book of the Manchester Egyptian Society (founded 1906) shows that he often chaired the Society's meetings.[177] In 1908 he was elected President and re-elected to the same post the following year. In 1910 he became Vice-President. The minutes record his giving one paper, entitled, 'Egyptian and Ancient Persian Psychology: A Comparison'.[178] During his term of office as President, he appealed to fellow members for support of a scheme to re-house the Egyptian collection of the Manchester Museum.

The Manchester Oriental Society was founded in 1910 as a result of several meetings of University staff members who had an interest in Oriental studies. Casartelli, at the first meeting of the new society, was elected a member of its council and a Vice-President. The minutes again show him to have been a regularly attendee of the meetings. In October 1912 he read a paper entitled 'An Ancient Pyramid'.[179] When the two societies amalgamated in 1913, Casartelli was Vice-President of the new Manchester Oriental and Egyptian Society. In 1915 he proposed Moulton as the new President. In replying to the nomination Moulton said he had been 'much touched by the generous praise of his Hibbert Lectures by one who possessed a far wider knowledge of their subject than he could lay claim to himself. He had come that afternoon with the intention of making the far more appropriate proposal that the Bishop of Salford should himself be elected President, but the Bishop had rather stolen a march on him and he bowed to fate.'[180] During Moulton's absence in 1915, Casartelli was acting-President and succeeded him in the following year. Along with other Manchester scholars, Casartelli contributed to James Hastings' *Encyclopaedia of Religion and Ethics.*[181] As late as 1961, Casartelli's doctoral thesis was still deemed worthy of mention:

> (his) ... *Philosophy of the Mazdayasnian Religion under the Sassanids* (Bombay 1889) was unique in its time, and indeed still is, since it had never occurred to any of his contemporaries that the Zoroastrians of Sassanian times might have had a philosophy at all. Owing to the rudimentary state of Pahlevi studies in his time, the book is completely out of date but remains a challenge to Zoroastrian studies of the future to write the authoritative work Casartelli might have written had he been alive today.[182]

Even more recently Antonio Panaino has commented that Casartelli's doctoral thesis 'was for its time a remarkable synthesis of knowledge about Sassanian culture.'[183] As for his work on the medical conceptions found in Pahlavi texts, Panaino considers it still 'worth consulting as a monument in the history of Middle Iranian philology.'[184]

The late nineteenth and early twentieth centuries had seen the emergence, mostly in Germany, of the so-called 'History of Religions School'. This School, helped by advances in Mesopotamian and Egyptian studies in the fields of the Old and New Testaments, sought to elucidate the meaning of the Bible through the study of the religious conditions of the Hellenistic and Semitic worlds. Further stimulus came through the discipline of comparative Indo-European philology (Sanskrit, Avestan and other Indo-European languages). In his *Sketches in History*[185] Casartelli pointed out the usefulness of Oriental studies not only for Biblical exegesis but also, by means of Assyriology and Egyptology, its usefulness in defending Christianity against the 'newer kind of Orientalism' which was attacking Revelation itself. The then newer sciences of 'Comparative Mythology' and the 'History of Religions' were capable of being particularly hostile to Christianity. Casartelli wrote:

> In the teaching of those sciences both the religion of the Old Testament and the Christianity of the New are supposed to find their place as merely some out of the many phases of a mental and spiritual evolution in a primitive animism and fetish worship, to end in the Sermon on the Mount and the Epistles of St Paul.[186]

He urged, therefore, the involvement of Catholic scholars and the employment of their skills in the field of the Comparative History of Religions. To achieve this he called for 'an army of specialists' in the branches of mythology and folk-lore. Casartelli endeavoured to play his own part in this task through involvement with the Universities of Louvain and Manchester, and the Manchester Egyptian and Oriental Society. Manning himself had sought to evolve a similar response to the challenge posed by the new scientific liberalism. He appreciated that 'if the Church was to remain a vital force and not a mere sentiment, it must not ignore the new liberal thought. It must try to leaven it with the civilising influence of Christianity.'[187]

Casartelli's interest in Oriental languages was not confined to academic study alone. He saw them as a vital part of commercial education. In an article for the *Dublin Review*[188] he outlined the syllabus of the Berlin Seminary for Oriental Languages. This consisted of the teaching of 'the six principal living languages of the East.'[189] He advocated the establishment of a similar institution for an important commercial centre like Manchester; it would help to guard the country's Eastern markets since 'never before have there been such direct and intelligent efforts made to compete with us in these markets as are being made at present by Germany.'[190] This was dependent upon a change in the way Oriental studies were perceived. The tendency was that

> 'Oriental Studies' have hitherto been looked upon with a certain amount of good-humoured toleration, or of impatient contempt, as the case might be in this country. They were the hobby of amiable but musty antiquarians, or Scriptural enthusiasts, but of no earthly practical use, except when they had to be 'crammed' for an Indian Civil or Military Service Examination. The world is now wakening up to the fact that an acquaintance with the modes of speech and thought, the religions, philosophies, and literature, the history, and the social, political, and economical conditions of hundreds of Eastern races, and hundreds of millions of Eastern men, women, and children, whom we have either to rule and educate, or at least to trade with, is a matter of very practical utility, even from the lowest point of view – that of material interests.[191]

In a later pamphlet, entitled 'Eastward Ho! Or, Some Considerations on our Responsibilities in the East,' he pursued the commercial and practical applications of the ability to speak some of the Eastern languages and hoped for a demand to be created within Manchester for teachers of Hindustani, given the importance of its trade with India.[192] Casartelli also wanted to see at the University of Manchester the opportunity for students to study Oriental languages and literature, religions, philosophy and history. He himself became a lecturer in Persian languages at the University in 1903.

Characteristically Casartelli's interest was not restricted to the useful or financially expedient. He suggested the advancement of Oriental studies by quoting the German Orientalist, Max Müller, 'to conquer and rule Eastern nations is one thing, to understand them is quite another. In order to understand Eastern nations we must have their languages and their literature; we must, in a certain sense, become Orientalised, students of the East, lovers of the East. In this respect much remains to be done.'[193]

Improved knowledge of Eastern culture would not only help to improve trade, and so overcome German competition, it would also help to eliminate the ignorance, misconception and prejudice 'of the vast and complicated differences of every kind which go to build up our vast Eastern Empire.'[194]

Casartelli's prestige as an Oriental scholar was recognised in 1918 when he was elected as an Honorary Fellow of the Royal Asiatic Society[195] and again in 1924 when he was invited to give the Katrak Lecture, at the University of Oxford. His death prevented him delivering the lecture.[196]

CONCLUSION

Education was a vital contemporary issue for the Catholic Church as well as for the nation. From his early days as a priest and before, Casartelli was deeply immersed in the subject. This chapter has looked at his involvement in the varied rôles of advocate, promoter and pioneer of education in general, as well as Catholic education in particular. His achievements as a pioneer of commercial education were indirectly recognised, although not publicly acknowledged, by Frederick Hooper and James Graham who, in their *Commercial Education at Home and Abroad* (New York, 1901) copied wholesale from Casartelli's published papers on the subject![197]

Education, both in its elementary and technical form, was necessary, Casartelli urged, if the workforce was not to fall behind foreign competition. In pointing this out to the Manchester Statistical Society, he showed that his interest in and vision of education was not hampered by the confines of denominationalism. Rather, he saw education in a national perspective. However, the point where his vision differed from the majority of his audience was on the question of what education was for. The perspective of the Church was to see it in the light of eternity and as a religious question. When it came to a clash of interests between Church doctrine and party allegiance, Casartelli always advocated that Catholics choose the former. This cannot be taken to mean that he advocated isolating the Church in what is often, mistakenly, called a ghetto. He vehemently opposed the creation of an *imperium in imperio* that would have resulted if Catholics, as a body, had followed one political party. Manning had also opposed the withdrawal of Catholics from the public forum and civic duty. Casartelli saw Catholic schools not just from the point of view of the moral good of Catholics and denominationalism; these schools were, through their teaching and religious instruction, serving the common good and thus the whole nation. For the

Church to be more effective Casartelli believed that it was necessary for its various forces to act in concert. This belief in the importance of organisation, first seen in his support of the meeting of Catholic heads of colleges in 1896, he would carry over into his episcopate and make it his watchword.

Casartelli's abilities reached far beyond the demands that St Bede's College would have made on him had he remained a working teacher. All the evidence suggests that both by ability and desire, his ideal career would have lain in a higher and more academic field. His loyalties were thus deeply divided. He voiced his personal preference when the opportunity to become the chaplain to the Catholic students at Oxford arose, but he also gave evidence of his humility and his intellectual honesty, in his eventual refusal to accept this post. Casartelli therefore left a divided legacy. Had he been allowed to pursue his Oriental studies he would, without doubt, have made a still greater contribution to scholarship. In the event, however, as we have seen, he was able to turn his translation to good use, playing an important rôle in both the City and the University of Manchester in the years when both were establishing themselves on the international stage.

PART TWO

The Episcopal Years, 1903 to 1925

Louis Charles Casartelli, Bishop of Salford, 1903–1925
Note the Order of Leopold, granted to him in 1903; in 1919 he was promoted to Commander of the Order of Leopold in recognition of his work for Belgian refugees. Note also his pectoral cross. Casartelli commented in his diary: 'Bp. McIntyre called noon; has pectoral cross almost like my (Vaughan) [Herbert Vaughan, Bishop of Salford, 1872–1892] cross. It is pre-Reformation and belonged to last Abbot of Croyland. What can mine be I wonder'? (Casartelli Diaries, 2 June 1913, SDA.)

Chapter Four

The Making of a Bishop

Compared with the Nineteenth Century, and especially the years since 1850, British twentieth-century Catholicism has been strangely neglected by historians, as the dramatic achievements and charismatic personalities associated with Catholicism in the later nineteenth century gave way to administrative blandness and greater insularity after 1900. (Buchanan)[1]

'The leadership at the centre in these years was characterised by administrative skill and the encouragement of devotional practice rather than by the sort of scholarly enterprise to which many of the nineteenth-century bishops had been given. (Norman)[2]

Since Tom Buchanan made the first observation above, only Kester Aspden's PhD thesis, *The English Catholic Bishops and Politics, 1903–1943* (Cambridge, 1999), subsequently published as *Fortress Church* (Leominster, 2002), has begun to fill this historical lacuna. He maintains that it is inaccurate to regard the Church in this period 'as a ghetto or a fortress, inward-looking and defensive in its priorities,'[3] and 'characterised on the whole by a hide-bound conservatism.'[4] In support of this view, Aspden cites the example of Francis Bourne, who was always uncomfortable in his dealings with Rome, was suspected of Modernism, and 'was possessed of a healthy insouciance of Roman structures.'[5] Casartelli, too, was anxious for there not to be excessive intervention by the Vatican in the organisation of the Church in England. For example, he did not welcome the idea of an Apostolic Delegate to England, as his terse letter to Cardinal Gasquet showed: 'Is it true that we are threatened with an Apostolic delegate? [It] will not be popular.'[6] Aspden argues that 'a greater sense of commitment to the public realm developed amongst the episcopate.'[7] In a later article, he sees Casartelli as isolated from other bishops in this matter.[8] The chapters that follow present evidence that Casartelli set a high example in this area, as a bishop who looked to concerns wider than those of his diocese, and encouraged the laity to be involved in work for the commonweal.

Casartelli also set a high example as a scholar-bishop. No doubt – as Norman's observation reminds us – he was atypical in this regard. No doubt – given his personal preference for scholarly enterprise – he would have chosen such pursuits as his life's work, had circumstances, and opportunities allowed him. However, he succeeded, when in office, not only to continue with some scholarly work, but to combine this with encouraging personal devotion to the Eucharist, and with the exercise of his administrative responsibilities to good effect. As we shall see, Casartelli effectively combined the different characteristics of both nineteenth and twentieth century bishops, as Norman has distinguished them.

BISHOPS OF THE 20TH CENTURY – HUMDRUM MEN?

In his assessment of the 91 bishops who had governed the Church in England from 1850 to 1950, Philip Hughes pointed out that of these, 60 had come to the episcopate after a life of missionary (parish) work.[9] Of these bishops, 18 had been seminary rectors, and 3, including Casartelli, had been headmasters. Of these, only four had found a biographer: Vaughan, Bourne, Hedley, and Hinsley. Since this observation was made in 1950, further biographical work has again been sparse. Books have appeared on Amigo of Southwark, Griffin of Westminster, and Ilsley of Birmingham;[10] a doctoral thesis on Cardinal Hinsley[11] was subsequently published; an M.Phil thesis on Henshaw of Salford[12] by the present writer was presented in 1998; and Aspden's doctoral thesis examining the rôle of all the bishops in early twentieth century politics appeared in 1999.[13] Clearly there is ample scope and need for more research, in order to gain a more accurate understanding of English Catholicism in the twentieth century.

The case of Louis Charles Casartelli is particularly rewarding for such research. As Hughes tactfully recognised: 'there is a small handful of really outstanding personalities, and a few who survive as traditionally the 'great' bishop of the see they once occupied.'[14] He claimed that: 'the average bishop is very like the average man; finding 'the daily round, the common task' – the correspondence, the interview, the committees, the visitations of parishes, convents and schools, the conferences about money ... the social events, the annual meetings ... sufficiently occupying.'[15]

There had been exceptions: among the great preachers of the twentieth century Hughes included Keating of Northampton, McIntyre of Birmingham, and Burton of Clifton. As for bishops noted for their writing, Bishop Hedley of Newport is the exception who proves the rule that his contemporaries were not noted for scholarly enterprise.[16] But Hughes pointed out one more exception. He considered Casartelli to have been 'singularly free from the conventional narrowness of the Victorian cleric, a man of really cosmopolitan mind, with a breadth and variety of intellectual sympathies that recalled Wiseman, a bishop to whom the activities and the problems of the churches of continental Europe were as familiar as those which faced him in his native Lancashire.'[17]

What aspects of Casartelli's career justify seeing him as thus distinguished among his contemporaries?

Senior episcopal appointments at this time were being made – not without controversy – with a view to strong administrative abilities. In the case of Salford, when the hierarchy discussed the candidates submitted by the Diocesan Chapter they decided, given the importance of the diocese and the need for a good administrator, to add three more names to the *terna*. At Westminster, Bourne was similarly appointed in preference to intellectual figures. As Aspden has pointed out:

> Writing to the Sacred Congregation of Propaganda Fide in support of Francis Bourne's claims for the vacant see of Westminster, Bishop Cahill of Portsmouth urged the Holy See to eschew charismatic figures, great scholars, or brilliant public men; to opt for somebody who could concern himself exclusively with 'the more ordinary duties of a Bishop [...] a good organiser' who would put the diocese on a 'more certain basis' and consolidate the growth of the late nineteenth century.[18]

Accordingly the Archdiocese of Westminster got an efficient administrator, one who understood his responsibility to be specifically: 'the proper organization of the Cathedral, Archbishop's House, Clergy House and Curia; the reconstruction of St Edmund's College ... the Cathedral Choir School: the foundation of a secondary day-school.'[19]

In a period when administrative abilities were most sought after, a perusal of the entries in Brian Plumb's *From Arundel to Zabi*,[20] highlights the rare academic qualities Casartelli enjoyed among his contemporaries, and which singled him out from all but a tiny minority. Bishop Richard Collins (Hexham and Newcastle, 1909–1924) was recorded as having taken 'little interest in anything other than the needs of those committed to his care.'[21] Likewise, Bishop John Kiely (Plymouth, 1911 – 1928) was only interested in 'the pastoral care of his scattered flock.'[22] Bishop Joseph Cowgill (Leeds 1911 – 1936) was 'deemed solid rather than brilliant ... His initiative and skill at organisation were noticed early,'[23] whilst Bishop Hugh Singleton (Shrewsbury 1908 – 1934) 'was destined for an episcopate of 26 years, mostly times of consolidation rather than of much extension.'[24] Of Bishop Richard Lacy (Middlesborough 1879–1929) the opinion was that, 'although he was revered everywhere within his diocese he was hardly known outside it. He chose 'to plough the lonely furrow.'[25] The way these bishops have been remembered is symptomatic of the contemporary prerequisites deemed necessary for the episcopate.

Intellectual distinction did not appear high on the agenda. 'On hearing a rumour that a man of limited intellectual ability was about to be elected to the See of Northampton, Bishop Dunn of Nottingham reassured Bishop Amigo of Southwark: 'For subordinate positions give me, by all means men of exceptional intellectual development, but for Bishops let us have people (like you and me!) solid and good – if, perhaps, a bit old fashioned.'[26] Bishop Charles Graham of Plymouth summed up well the general approach of the bishops – 'he used to describe his career as humdrum.'[27]

Clearly, 'steadfast ordinariness' was the order of the day,[28] but the more applicable term for early twentieth century bishops is 'average men' rather than 'humdrum'. Casartelli did not conform to the model set out by Bishop Dunn. He was the most talented scholar among a hierarchy where scholarship was rare. What is even rarer about his scholarship is that it is still recognised today. As well as academic ability, Casartelli also had, an eye for detail, a well ordered mind, and the ability to delegate. It is significant that he himself stated that the watchword of his episcopate was 'organise.' He never grew tired of trying to instil this principle into his clergy and people.

In order that pastoral government be effective and efficient administration is vitally important. As Edward Norman has said, 'the earthly institutions which hold together the treasures of eternity still require effective stewardship and management.'[29] By the time Casartelli became bishop of Salford, the structures of the local Church were already in place – parishes, more accurately described as 'missions', elementary schools, parochial societies, confraternities, and sodalities, – and all these needed expanding. At the secondary level, schools had yet to be developed. Much work of consolidation and organisation lay ahead elsewhere. A network of Catholic schools was in existence, with the resulting duty imposed upon parents to ensure their children's attendance. Although he had inherited much, Casartelli astutely realised that the very strength of the Church's parochial structures was also the cause of one of its serious weaknesses. Parochialism had the effect of restricting vision and sense of duty to the immediate group pertaining to the parish church. He warned against the dangers of this myopic view when speaking of the provision of secondary schools. Replying to Revd A. Hinsley's paper 'The Place of Grammar Schools in a Scheme of Catholic Education in England,' Casartelli said: 'the greatest difficulty is Parochialism. The clergy as a body do not realise the importance of the questions. It is our business to form Catholic opinion among laity and clergy.'[30] On a later occasion, during the Diocesan Synod of 1915, he expressed this view more strongly:

> The Bishop made a strong and lengthy appeal to the Rectors to support him actively in the various Diocesan organisations, and expressed regret that in some cases he had experienced, not merely apathy, but even active

discouragement. In all such cases he believed that quite mistaken prejudices were at the bottom of such abstention or opposition. Such an attitude resulted in a narrow 'parochialism'.[31]

In the face of such difficulties, Casartelli sought to develop higher levels of organisation in his diocese.[32] In this strategy, a key body was to be the Catholic Federation: 'if well organised it will draw together all who are interested in Catholic affairs; it will, under due direction, cure the spirit of criticism and narrow-mindedness by leading Catholic men and women, to meet together for common counsel and organisation as Catholics and not as members of classes or parties, whether political or otherwise.'[33] However, many difficulties lay in his way. Henry Edward Manning had warned Casartelli's mentor, Herbert Vaughan, of one of the key sources of parochialism when he wrote, 'We are weak, and the Episcopate is weak, because our Bishops are parish priests. They must be broader and have a bird's eye view of the Church and the English people.'[34]

Herbert Vaughan took Manning's advice and avoided the prevailing parochial outlook. This was evident in the way that he strongly recommended Casartelli as *episcopabile*. When the hierarchy initially ignored his advice, he used stealth and political astuteness in his dealings with Rome to ensure that Casartelli remained the only viable candidate among the rest, including those whom the hierarchy had added to the original *terna*. Of Casartelli's qualities, Vaughan was at pains to draw attention to his scholarship, his breadth of vision that enabled him to take 'large and dispassionate views of public questions,' and his administrative skill. Vaughan was determined that the Diocese of Salford be guided by an administration of wide vision. To the detailed story of how this was achieved, we now turn.

CASARTELLI AND THE SALFORD TERNA

The See of Salford became vacant upon the death of the third bishop, John Bilsborrow, on 5 March 1903. Less than two weeks after the death of Bilsborrow, and before the diocesan Chapter of Canons had the opportunity to discuss suitable candidates to succeed him, speculation began as to who would be his successor; Casartelli's name featured amongst those mentioned. This disturbed him greatly. From Louvain he immediately wrote to Vaughan seeking his help in frustrating any possible plans to name him as a candidate:

I find to my great dismay, that rumours are flying about connecting my name with the succession to the vacant See of Salford. It may appear presumptuous on my part to take any notice of such absurd reports, yet I feel that 'fore-warned is fore-armed'. I venture to appeal to your Eminence on the matter, because you have known me so long and followed my whole career, and will therefore be able to appreciate the truth of what I say. And that is: my whole character, tastes, experience, career entirely unfit me for a bishopric in modern England.[35]

As reasons for his unsuitability for such responsibility Casartelli gave his lack of competence in matters of finance and ignorance of elementary education. Of elementary education he claimed: 'I know nothing and consequently feel little practical interest in it.' It would have been far more congenial for him to be either a university professor or a college rector; of being a bishop, 'the very thought of it would make me miserable.' Casartelli made no attempt to hide the strength of his feelings:

> ... I appeal to your conscience to exercise your all-powerful influence to save me from misfortune, and Salford from disaster ... Pray forgive me if I am imprudent or presumptuous in mentioning the matter; but it is to me a question of peace of mind and of conscience, and I cannot rest till I have done all I can to avert even remote danger. I trust in your Eminence as in a father and friend.

So strong was Casartelli's dread of becoming a bishop, that as well as writing to Vaughan, he made also a special journey to Rome and appealed in person at the office of Propaganda Fide requesting that his name should not even be mentioned for Salford.[36] The intensity of this fear is best appreciated when one considers that it was based only on the strength of rumour.

In accord with Church regulations, and under the chairmanship of the Bishop of Birmingham, the Diocesan Chapter met on 4 April 1903 to decide upon the *terna*, i.e. three names of suitable candidates to be forwarded to Rome for consideration. The result of the voting was: Louis Charles Casartelli, John Boulaye and Canon James Moyes.[37] This was not remotely an outcome which Casartelli privately desired. The results of the voting were then forwarded to Vaughan, whose hand in the consequent proceedings is readily apparent.

Although ill health prevented Vaughan from attending the April meeting of the hierarchy when the *terna* was discussed he wrote to Bishop Hedley asking him, as senior bishop, to make known his opinions and counsel. Casartelli's entreaties had left him unmoved. His opinions of the three candidates, whom he had known for nearly thirty years, were:

> **John Boulaye** ... A good second, but a bad first. Narrow, persistent, and almost, if not quite, a crank.
> **Moyes**, a good theologian. Roman in spirit, a good and incisive writer, a man of much piety. But in the sky and does not see what goes on around him ... I should not be willing to put him forward as a Bishop just now.

Casartelli. He is in terror of being named. He wrote to me to say that he knows nothing of finance or of Public Elementary Education ... I replied as old Mgr Newsham used to say that 'all the English Bishops were Bankers' – therefore I saw no harm in there being at least one who would employ one of the less inferior clergy to do his banking business for him! As to the Public Elementary Education – the first three Bishops of Salford knew nothing else, and it will be an advantage that the fourth should break forth in some other issue.

I believe he is the popular choice in Manchester. He is absolutely without ambition: always refused to be a Canon or anything beyond Rector of the College.

He has a mind that is very alert, seizes the position of things, very ready in writing and speaking – but prudent and cautious in action as well as in counsel. He is singularly pious and full of faith. He can take large and dispassionate views of public questions – is more inclined to yield to public opinion and to perhaps liberal opinions than I approve. But I think that even here responsibility as Bishop will modify the tendency.

I think he should be chosen, strongly recommended, and if need be urgently pressed to accept the nomination.[38]

The hierarchy met and discussed the Salford *terna* at Westminster on 21 April. The minutes for the meeting read, '[The Bishops] ... considering also the strength and vigour that were needed for the laborious and difficult administration of so large a Diocese, decided to add, in their report to the Holy See, three other names, *viz.* Rev. Thomas Smith (Hexham), Mgr Corbishley, and Rev. Peter Lonsdale.'[39]

By not endorsing Vaughan's opinions, the hierarchy failed to endorse his favoured candidate. The respective backgrounds of the bishops, already considered, give some clue as to why they were not disposed to accept Casartelli's nomination *carte blanche*. Of the twelve who met at Westminster, only three shared Casartelli's academic background. One was Bishop George Ambrose Burton of Clifton, who, as well as being an accomplished classical scholar, 'became a notable figure in the civic and ecclesiastical life of the West Country.'[40] The second was Bishop Cuthbert Hedley of Newport. The third was Bishop William Allen of Shrewsbury, who spoke Greek, Hebrew, Italian, and could write Latin fluently. He possessed a fine Egyptian antiquities library and was a member of the Shropshire Archaeological Society. Of the remaining nine, three of them had voted against the rescinding of the Roman rescript regarding the attendance of Catholics at the ancient Universities.[41] The rest of the bishops (six) were not distinguished for their academic achievements and could accurately be described as 'pastoral men.' Casartelli's high profile in the debate of 1894/5 and his ensuing articles in support of Catholics attending Oxford and Cambridge had probably not won him the sympathy of a significant proportion of the bench of bishops. Nor would his interest in Oriental languages have been an endearing qualification; the preference was for strong and vigorous administrators.

The addition of the extra names was a temporary setback for Vaughan's strategy of preserving the Salford diocese from too narrow a leadership. However, he was not the only one who was dismayed. Bishop Wilkinson of Hexham and Newcastle wrote to him expressing his disbelief at the inclusion of the three additional names. As regards Smith, he could not 'imagine under what respect he would be able to succeed in the episcopacy. To tell the truth I am really shocked on account of finding that name among the candidates. Will Your Eminence use every means in order that it may not be accepted by the Holy See'?[42] He considered Lonsdale as 'almost equally impossible ... and has shown himself to be of an overwhelmingly tyrannical nature and self-assertive.'[43] Corbishley was the only one of the three candidates, in Wilkinson's opinion, who had the necessary qualities for the episcopate.

Vaughan was probably aware of what had been said by the bishops at their meeting. He was now able to slant his further recommendation of Casartelli accordingly. Vaughan duly opened a further line of attack. He wrote a second letter to Cardinal Gotti of Propaganda Fide, expressing his concern at the hierarchy's decision to add three extra names; he considered the non-acceptance of the Chapter's *terna* as serious. The reason he gave for this further communication was the absence of 'some of the more important bishops' at the hierarchy's meeting.[44] He took the opportunity to weigh in strongly in favour of Casartelli, whom he considered to be 'of notable ability in every respect,' declaring that he 'enjoys the esteem equally of the English and of the Irish and of all the Catholics and Protestants of the region. His family is well known in Manchester where, as bishop, he would occupy a very good position in public and civic society.'

Vaughan also felt it necessary to qualify his original opinions as to Casartelli's lack of experience in financial matters and lack of interest in elementary education. In this way he skilfully neutralised any detrimental impact his earlier observations might have had. He now stated explicitly that education was within Casartelli's field of expertise, and that he was a skilled administrator. As an example, Vaughan cited St Bede's, 'which he has presided over with optimum success for more than ten years.' He affirmed that Casartelli was well up to the task of financial administration if he had a suitable assistant (for example, Lonsdale, whose name had appeared on the hierarchy's *terna*.) Even though Casartelli's specific expertise was in Oriental languages, Vaughan thought him 'an optimum and accomplished student in other matters, and very much interested in education.' Indeed, the previous ten years that Casartelli had spent as Rector of St Bede's College meant that he 'has acquired good experience of the needs and the methods of instruction. Such instruction would be useful for him as a bishop; his advice about the important question of education would be of great advantage to the other bishops.' Lastly, Vaughan wished to balance his comments about any suspicion of Casartelli being too liberal in educational matters:

> Whilst it is beyond doubt that he is very interested in this subject I am certain that he would not act in an independent way to the other bishops, but would walk in perfect harmony with them. I am of the opinion that the sense of episcopal responsibility would impose a brake upon his personal ideas without diminishing his own zeal.

Not only did Vaughan present a powerful case himself, but his arguments found additional support from other quarters. For the two other bishops who had been absent from the hierarchy's meeting also wrote to Rome. Bishop Bourne, from Southwark, agreed with Vaughan that 'the nomination of Smith would be deplorable.'[45] Bishop Wilkinson, from Hexham and Newcastle said that Smith would be 'absolutely impossible,' whilst Lonsdale was of an 'overwhelmingly tyrannical nature.' The opinion of another bishop, who remained anonymous, confirmed these comments. Vaughan forwarded the latter's explicit views to Rome, which stated: 'when I came to know the names chosen by the Chapter I was absolutely flabbergasted, I could not imagine for what motive such a *terna* was left ignored. It horrified me when the names chosen by the Bishops were considered to be preferable. Yet my sense of amazement and regret continues.'[46]

There was common agreement among the correspondents that any decision to ignore the *terna* of the Salford Chapter would create a bad impression, especially since one of those named was Casartelli. It was also pointed out that Casartelli, or Moyes, would have the respect of the people of the Diocese from the beginning; this could not be said of the additional candidates. Evidence suggests that these advisers wanted a bishop who could relate well to non-Catholics and who was acceptable to both English and Irish Catholics. Part of the strategy of Vaughan and his colleagues was to make Rome aware of how the hierarchy would be divided if the *terna* submitted by the Salford Chapter was ignored, and someone other than Casartelli was chosen. The decision to add the three extra names had not met with the approval of at least one third of the bishops; in such a small hierarchy this would have caused serious problems and a potential lack of unity. Clearly Vaughan spared no effort to ensure the appointment of his chosen candidate. The conclusion of his second letter contained a resounding affirmation:

With regard to the personal character of the Rev. Casartelli, I can assure Your Eminence that he is a man of outstanding piety, humble, docile and honest, and full of prudence and of the ecclesiastical spirit. With all that he is most tenacious of ideals; he would fittingly maintain the dignity of episcopal authority.[47]

CASARTELLI THE RELUCTANT BISHOP

Vaughan's campaign having succeeded, Casartelli was nominated as successor to Bilsborrow on 24 August 1903. He made no attempt to dissimulate his feelings of unease and apprehension about his future role. His choice of episcopal motto is succinct: *fiat voluntas tua*. In his letter to Cardinal Gotti he stated that he accepted the nomination out of obedience and because he saw it as the will of God:

> Your Eminence unfortunately knows from the conversation that I had with you in the audience which you deigned to accord me last April, how much I feel incapable and unworthy of such a dignity. Up until now my life has been dedicated exclusively to study and teaching the young, without any experience of administration or business. How much I fear then this formidable burden even for angels! Therefore, Eminence I do not say 'I accept' – but since this appears to be the will of God and His Vicar I say rather, 'I submit': *Fiat Voluntas Tua*.[48]

He had a letter published in the columns of the *Manchester Guardian* in which he thanked his friends and 'many of my non-Catholic fellow citizens' for their 'support and consolation in the ordeal which I have to go through,' and earnestly requested their consideration and prayers, 'at this trying time.'[49] On the day in which this letter was published, Casartelli also wrote privately to Abbot Gasquet. The letter showed Casartelli's humility and sense of obedience in the face of what had been asked of him. He confided to Gasquet:

> If the wish did not sound rather an impiety, I could almost desire that Cardinal Gotti might have held me 'suspect' of liberalism and other dreadful things, and so have spared me this most unwelcome burden. Is it not too bad to take off a student – and we have so few of them, and turn him into a very incompetent, perhaps unsuccessful, bishop? However, the *fiat* has gone forth, and one must humbly submit and obey.[50]

In his invitation to Gasquet to attend the ceremony at St John's Cathedral, Casartelli added a note of humour, 'the date of execution (– my pardon, consecration –) is fixed for September 21st. Will you honour me by being present and trying to cheer me up'?[51] On receiving Gasquet's acceptance Casartelli then invited him to preach the sermon. Gasquet originally declined the offer because of the adverse publicity he had received in the *Daily*

Chronicle in relation to the See of Westminster.[52] Casartelli rallied to his support and wished this to be known publicly. His letter to Gasquet made this clear and enunciated his hopes and intentions:

> Because these expressions have been cast upon you in a certain press, and I wish publicly to disassociate myself from them; because recent events have been contested in a manner offensive and perhaps painful to yourself, and I wish to make clear our friendship in a public manner; because you are our greatest Catholic scholar in England, and I myself though a very small one, wish from the outset to strike the note of devotion to scholarship and research; because you are the head of a great religious order, and I wish to strike a note of loyal and friendly co-operation between seculars and regular clergy: therefore I ask you earnestly to do me the favour of speaking at my consecration.[53]

Gasquet agreed to Casartelli's request.

The outcome of this reluctant appointment was quite other than had been feared. Unquestionably, Casartelli himself feared failure as a bishop because of his lack of experience. He saw his nomination as a potential loss to scholarship, an area in which he placed great importance and one in which he believed the Church ought to be more involved. In his first pastoral letter to his diocese he repeated his reservations and his unsuitability for the task,

> ... what must have been the astonishment of all concerned when a priest, whose previous life and experience seemed so very little suited to fit him for the episcopal office, was selected for the See of Salford! A life of books and study; an academic career devoted to education and literary pursuits; an entire ignorance of affairs and inexperience in administration; but slight acquaintance with parochial duties and none at all with financial matters; tastes far remote from the cares and duties of official life: such do not appear to form a likely preparation for a successful episcopate ... Hence the dismay and distress of mind occasioned by the announcement of a choice which seemed to him little less than an impossibility.[54]

Casartelli called upon his clergy and laity to support him in his difficult task: to unite forces and to join with him and one another in a spirit of co-operation. However, despite these heartfelt protestations of unsuitability at the time, there is ample evidence that the new bishop of Salford was a well-known and respected scholar who brought to the task a somewhat wider vision and appreciation of the work of the Church – and was to become in office far more successful than he had initially feared.

CASARTELLI AND THE ONUS EPISCOPALE

The duties of a bishop,' says the Consecrator, to the priest upon whom he is about to lay the *onus episcopale*, 'are to rule, to teach, to consecrate, to ordain, to offer [sacrifice], to baptise and to confirm.[55]

Unfortunately any correspondence between Vaughan and Casartelli regarding his nomination to the episcopate or what advice he might have offered to the distraught Casartelli has not survived. Something of what this correspondence might have contained, and what Vaughan had in mind when he spoke of it being an, 'advantage that the fourth [Bishop of Salford] break forth in some other issue,' i.e. other than finance and Public Elementary Education,[56] can be gleaned from the panegyric Canon Moyes preached at Casartelli's funeral. Moyes spoke of how Casartelli had

> as a priest and a bishop fulfilled to the utmost the behest of Bishop Vaughan that he should enter into the intellectual life of the city and community at large. Hence they found that he became the founder of the Dante Society and member of the Egyptian Association and Statistical Society, and that he held a lectureship at the Manchester University.[57]

We may surmise therefore, that Vaughan's advice to Casartelli was that he continue doing as a bishop what he was in fact already doing as a priest. Evidence of Casartelli's apostolate as a priest is to be found in the address given in his honour at the time of his consecration, where it was recognised that, 'not merely has Manchester been your place of residence; you have entered in the most intimate manner into the public life of the city and have given to your fellow-citizens a splendid example of civic virtues and zeal for public welfare.'[58]

Casartelli had witnessed a similar commitment and example in the person of Herbert Vaughan. In the sermon which Casartelli preached at Vaughan's funeral Mass at St John's Cathedral Salford he acknowledged how,

> Not only did Herbert Vaughan spend his energies for the Church but also for the citizens of Salford and Manchester. His work with the Manchester Chamber of Commerce helped to the development in 1903 of a faculty of Commerce at the University of Manchester. He was also one of the founders of the Geographical Society. Through such efforts Vaughan tried to bring 'the Kingdom of God to the souls of men.[59]

In the description of the duties of a bishop given above, the duty of ruling is placed before that of teaching. Casartelli's *forte* was as a teacher, and a teacher in the widest sense of the word because he possessed a broad understanding of education. Ruling was distasteful to him; teaching was not. Moreover, he understood his teaching rôle as a bishop not simply in terms of catechesis and formal religious instruction. Rather, his involvement in the learned societies of Manchester represented an application of his wider vision of the duty to teach and ultimately to preach. It was this vision that marked him out from the other bishops. It is this which constituted his particular and distinguished contribution to the life and history of the Diocese of Salford, and raised him above the level of 'humdrum.'

Amongst Casartelli's other duties were those which pertained to the realm of the sacraments, namely to consecrate, ordain, baptise, and confirm. His fulfilment of this rôle was hindered by his ill health. Throughout his life he was plagued by numerous ailments. During the winter months he suffered from bronchitis, and hay fever left him incapacitated for six weeks per year during the summer. In later years he complained of being 'badly crippled with lumbago and sciatica;'[60] his suffering was further compounded by what he described as 'prostate trouble.'[61] As a result of poor health, Casartelli often had to cancel engagements. By 1918, fifteen years after he had become the Bishop of Salford, he had fulfilled the liturgical duties of Holy Week on only seven occasions.[62] In 1909 he petitioned Rome for the help of an auxiliary bishop. He had wanted help of this kind soon after becoming a bishop, but the diocese could not afford a second episcopal *mensa*.[63] In the event, this latter problem was overcome when Casartelli was able to nominate a priest with private means.[64] A letter to John Stephen Vaughan reveals that perhaps Casartelli had secondary motives besides his health for seeking the assistance of an auxiliary: 'You would have a good deal of free time for study and writing and I should also gain in that respect.'[65] His primary motive was no doubt for assistance with his diocesan duties, but other advantages to be gained had obviously not escaped him. At heart he remained a scholar; writing was a means of solace whilst his shoulders were burdened by the episcopate.

For, in addition to his poor state of health was the fact that he found the *onus episcopale* a heavy and deadening responsibility. He regularly spent the weeks after Christmas at his sisters' house situated adjacent to St Bede's College. It was here that he was most at home and relaxed; clearly, by maintaining close links with his family, he was better able to face his uncongenial task. Further, Casartelli's favourite place in England was Bexhill-on-Sea, and it was here that he retreated for his summer holidays. In all, between staying at his sisters' house in Manchester, being incapacitated by ill health, and holidays in Bexhill, he was absent from the diocese for an average of sixteen weeks per year throughout the period of his episcopate.

Prolonged absence from the diocese, coupled with ill health and a reticent nature, and the general feeling of weariness as a bishop dictated how he fulfilled his duties. However, Casartelli was able to delegate, and he left much of the running of the Diocese to his Vicars General whom he met frequently on Tuesday mornings at Bishop's House, Salford, in order to discuss business. Many matters relating to the running of the diocese were forwarded (in specially pre-addressed envelopes) to the Vicar General's residence. Occasionally Casartelli might scribble in blue pencil what he considered to be the appropriate action to be taken. A letter to Mgr Boulaye, one of the Vicar Generals, shows how Casartelli respected his opinion and was unwilling to impose his own will: 'I should be better inclined to criticise you for too great deference and respect than the contrary. Besides what is the use of a VG unless he is perfectly frank and outspoken in criticism, as well as approval, in disagreeing as well as agreeing? A V.G. is supposed to be the Bishop's *alter ego*, or, like the Lord Chancellor, the "keeper of his conscience."'[66]

CASARTELLI'S PASTORAL GOVERNMENT

Casartelli did not rule his diocese with an iron fist nor was he autocratic. He was reluctant to take disciplinary measures.[67] He never personally involved himself, unless it was absolutely necessary, in cases of 'troublesome priests' where complaints or allegations had been made. If a specific case or issue demanded further investigation, his custom was to appoint another priest, or sometimes a panel of three, to act as his delegates in order to elicit more detail. An example of one of the rare occasions when he deemed involvement to be necessary was when Canon Lonsdale had failed to forward money collected for the Cathedral Fund. Casartelli's reaction betrayed his understanding of obedience. He had accepted the post of bishop in deference to Church authority; in like manner he expected the same reciprocal spirit from his clergy: 'To my old-fashioned way of thinking and understanding of the view of ecclesiastical authority in which I am trained, each rector was bound to carry out this general command of the bishop.'[68]

Casartelli, in fulfilling his duty of diocesan visitation was business-like and delegated two-thirds of the work to his two Vicars General. Evidence from his visitation register shows that he had an eye for detail and was eager that each mission be administered effectively. He made a careful note of the financial situation of each church he was visiting. For example, during his visitation to St Augustine's, Burnley, he noted that it was 'the least satisfactory mission I have visited ... Accounts 'cooked' to balance ... I spoke strongly to Fr Joyner on grave complaints of people and local clergy of his behaviour *re* cemetery; irascibility and offensive language even to public officials; imprudent exacting of fees etc., etc ... Warned him that the next move would be a curacy.'[69] He observed carefully whether his instructions on church music were being carried out; whether branches of the Protection and Rescue Society had been set up; and whether mixed-marriages had been agreed and contracted. He divided his comments between 'remarks,' 'personnel,' and *decreta;'* the latter were the instructions he gave to remedy any deficiencies, for example, if there was no crucifix in the confessionals, or if the rector had not suppressed the singing of solos by females. Ever the scholar and linguist, on occasions he commented on Latin grammatical errors made by the clergy when entering details in the parish registers. To some this must have appeared as pedantry.

In his diaries, there is little mention of his socialising with his priests. If they wanted to see him privately, the time and place to do so was at Bishop's House, Salford, on Tuesday mornings. As far as his priests were concerned, Casartelli was a distant figure. The rank and file clergy may well have held the view that he did not understand their problems because he had never served as a curate or as missionary rector. The very honest statements made in his first pastoral letter about his being ill equipped for the episcopate and his preference for 'a life of books', although admirable as an exercise in honesty, probably did not help to endear him to the clergy. Casartelli's preoccupation with diocesan-level organisation – especially the Catholic Federation –, 'the special work', of his episcopate would have further exaggerated this lack of endearment. Almost certainly, his dogged insistence on establishing and forwarding the Federation was a cause of division and resentment.[70]

CONCLUSION

It would be a mistake to assume that Casartelli was a cold, distant, inhuman figure. He preferred to mix in small circles of people. The strength of his apostolate lay more on a 'one to one basis' than in large audiences. His diaries carry innumerable references to individuals who came to seek his advice. Unfortunately, many of these names are obliterated. This was done presumably after Casartelli's death, perhaps by his successor, Thomas Henshaw. The interest he took in the individual person is well illustrated by the account he gave of a chance meeting with a soldier in a railway carriage. Casartelli took trouble to record the man's name, his rank (private), his army number and his attitude to the Boer War.[71] On another occasion he recorded the long conversation he had with the explorer Ernest Shackleton when they both attended a banquet of the Manchester Geographical Society.[72] The human side of Casartelli's character can be glimpsed from the following account, written by his nephew in 1972.

> He was certainly 'a man of many parts,' with considerable interests out-
> side his ecclesiastical duties. I well remember an extension of interest to

more worldly matters, for in the early twenties when I, with others of my generation, having been recently demobilised from the Forces, were full of the then craze for dancing, His Lordship summoned my wife-to-be and myself to give a demonstration of the 'modern' dancing for Episcopal information and, perhaps, approval. We, rather naturally, chose some of the more decorous dances, and I believe, met with approval. Another very human side was shown when, as I had become of the correct age for smoking, he introduced me to good cigars, and subsequently supplied me, at Christmas, with specimens of very choice (and, doubtless, expensive) brands.[73]

Casartelli never varied in his opinion of the episcopate as a burden. In 1921 when writing to congratulate the archbishop of Birmingham on his retirement he wrote,

> It must be, humanely speaking, a great relief to lay down the burden of the episcopate, one which I have myself often looked forward, without seeing the possibility of it.[74]

Casartelli was not insular. He understood that the Church existed for the benefit of the world, and that it was the instrument and means of leavening the stratum of society, culturally, academically, and spiritually. He feared failure as a bishop, yet this fear did not paralyse him. We now turn to see how he sought to implement his vision of the Church and his duties as a bishop.

Chapter Five

Casartelli as a Spiritual Leader

In his encouragement of, and provision for, the spiritual growth of the people of his diocese, Casartelli drew on the *motu proprio* on Church music[1] and the decree on frequent Communion[2] issued by Pope Pius X.[3] The Pope's motto was *instaurare omnia in Christo*;[4] if we take this and a description of Guiseppe Sarto as Bishop of Mantua and later as the Cardinal Patriarch of Venice into account, we may detect some similarities with that of Louis Charles Casartelli's:

> As bishop he tried to inspire his priests, especially in regard to instruction in the catechism, preaching, and frequent Communion, and he encouraged the laity to get involved as much as possible in ecclesiastical activities, insisting, however, that this collaboration was subject to the strict control of the clergy.[5]

Casartelli adopted a similar agenda in the leadership of his own diocese, although he interpreted 'clerical control' more in terms of due recognition of the hierarchy's authority. Despite the protestations he had made about his lack of parish experience contributing to his unsuitability as a bishop,[6] Casartelli demonstrated a clear awareness of the spiritual needs of his diocese. The pastoral measures with which he sought to meet these wants were not only appropriate, but were also forward-looking and 'radical' in the etymological sense of 'going to the root.' How was this so? Casartelli placed high on his priorities the reform of Church music within his diocese in order that its people might be re-introduced to the primary source of the Christian life, which was the liturgy. Pius X believed this would be achieved by means of 'an active participation in the mystery of worship and in the common and solemn prayers of the Church.'[7] J. D. Crichton has described this statement by Pius X as 'germinal.'[8] In essence, Casartelli was trying to promote a liturgical, rather than an individualistic, type of piety. He made this clear in his 'Message' for the *Catholic Federationist*:

the Holy Sacrifice of the Mass is *not* merely a quiet half hour in which to 'get in' one's daily prayers. It is an *act* which we ought to follow with the most careful attention and to *participate* in. The faithful attending Mass are true co-partners in its offering.[9]

In turn, Casartelli reasoned, the fruit of this participation would be a lessening in spiritual individualism and a commitment to the common good of one's neighbour and society in general. His understanding of the spiritual life was based on the theme of the two ends for which mankind was made, i.e. the temporal and the eternal, which he had first expounded in his articles for the *Catholic Opinion*.[10]

CASARTELLI'S UNDERSTANDING OF THE SPIRITUAL LIFE

Now, as the leader of an important diocese, Casartelli developed further the practical implications of the fundamentals of the spiritual life. In his pastoral letter for Lent 1910, 'What Shall it Profit a Man'? he drew a distinction between the Kingdom of Christ and 'the World'. The term the 'World' represented both 'the chosen object of [Christ's] loving mercy and compassion,'[11] and fallen Mankind, 'the enemy of Christ and his followers' which consisted of,

> the whole system of false principles, maxims and teachings, that had grown up in the minds and hearts of mankind, owing to the darkness and ignorance of the human intellect blinded by the corrupt inclinations and passions of fallen nature, misguided and deceived by the insidious suggestions and inspirations of the primeval Adversary, whose perfidious falsehood occasioned the Fall of our First parents in the Garden of Eden.[12]

These two opposing powers were in conflict on two levels – in history – that had witnessed the persecution of the Church and heresy – and in the soul of the individual.[13] In the case of individuals this tension characteristically manifested itself in the allurement of the senses, a love of material things, in the unruly passions of the heart, and in the false principles of the World. When faced with the temptations of such disorders, a fundamental choice had to be made: 'man is bound to sacrifice that which is temporal and secondary for the sake of that which is eternal.'[14] Earthly life was thus a time of 'probation' and of making choices. This probation would continue since human beings were endowed with free will. In this struggle the Christian was aided by divine grace, for although 'the malignity and dread spiritual power of the Evil One' was capable of continuing to act upon human actions until the end of time, it had been 'checked and greatly limited by the work of the Incarnation.'[15] Casartelli did not consider mankind therefore to be a *massa damnata*. Accordingly, his worldview was positive and free from the overtones of Jansenism.[16]

Given that Casartelli studied in what is now Belgium (then known as the Spanish Netherlands) where Jansenism originated, it would not have been surprising if he had become susceptible to its rigours and scruples, if only to a limited degree. Evidence that this heresy was still effective in Belgium at the time that he was living there, and that he was indeed free from its influence, is found in his diaries and letters. The first instance tells of his visit to a family living in Louvain: 'visited a family ... as we were speaking with regret of our 'merry Xmas' in England, it was said: ah, you see it would not do here, people go to Confession and Holy Communion at that time. (As if the Holy Sacraments were incompatible with amusement! Belgian idea that.)'[17] Secondly, in regard to the appointment of a chaplain to a convent he wrote: 'I feel that the chaplaincy ought to go to Fr De Pauw ... I am only anxious as to how he would get on with the Nuns and residents; would he be too stern and Jansenistic, esp., in the Confessional? He is Belgian ... and exceedingly pious and conscientious.'[18] Consonant with his non-Jansenistic views, Casartelli saw that, 'life on earth is God's gift; this earth itself with all it contains is good and beautiful and desirable and is also given to us by God for our use and temporal happiness.'[19] Therefore in the exercise of the natural faculties, as the means to secure reasonable well-being and comfort, human beings were not setting themselves against God. He outlined the correct principle governing the natural faculties: '[the] chief end and object of man's whole existence is to secure eternal happiness in that life which comes after his temporary sojourn in the present state of probation'.[20]

Casartelli evidently needed to find a balance between the good, present in the world as God's gift and creation, and man's inclination to sin due to the adverse effect of evil on his exercise of free will. He found this balance in the underlying principle that distinguished the teaching of Christ from the false principles of the World: 'What shall it profit a man if he gain the whole world and suffer the loss of his soul (Mk., 8.36.)?' This principle lay at the base of Casartelli's practical theology, his 'unpolitical politics,' and his critique of Socialism.

One of the specific pastoral and spiritual problems that Casartelli had to face was the potential lure Socialism might hold for Catholics, arising from the fact that,

> many of the individual reforms of social evils advocated by Socialism can be and are freely approved by the Church's social teaching, yet the danger of our people unconsciously absorbing the poison of a fundamentally false root-principle is perhaps the greatest that threatens the Faith of the rising generation.[21]

In order to avoid 'absorbing the poison of a false root-principle,' a process of discernment and an antidote were necessary. His approach to this problem was essentially intellectual in the sense that he perceived spiritual warfare to take place in the intellect, darkened and made ignorant as it was 'by the whole system of false principles, maxims and teachings, that had grown up in the minds and hearts of mankind.'[22] The most virulent of these systems was Socialism, which epitomised the doctrine of the world and which he saw as the new Paganism.[23] Materialist philosophy denied the existence of an afterlife and took as its chief end and object: 'Material well-being, health, prosperity, social advancement, education, intellectual culture, the progress of physical science, political and civic freedom, social and economic happiness, refinement, the pleasures of life.'[24] Casartelli warned how invidious and dangerous the new Paganism was because it came disguised 'under the outward forms and phraseology of Christianity, [and] was at the heart of much social and economic philosophy preached on platforms and in the press.'[25]

Casartelli gave two examples of the new Paganism – 'The John Bull League', which had recently been introduced into Manchester, and the ideas perpetrated by the Rev. J. Stitt Smith, known as the 'Californian Orator.'[26] Casartelli countered the ill effects of these assertions, and the corrupting effects of contemporary reading matter which, he claimed, was 'objectionable and anti-religious, or at least steeped in the spirit of worldliness,'[27] by suggesting means of sanctifying the intellect. Firstly, and in keeping with his intellectual understanding of the issue, he urged the nourishing of the mind and heart with sound spiritual doctrine by reading the Gospels, Thomas à Kempis' *The Imitation of Christ*, *The Spiritual Exercises* of St Ignatius, and St Francis de Sales' *Treatise on the Love of God*. Ideally a second type of spiritual reading followed, which Casartelli called 'Applied Christianity', such as the lives of saints who were appropriate examples of Christian living.

The limitation to this approach was that it presumed that all those susceptible to socialistic doctrines were literate, and it lacked the practicalities of a concept of social justice as expounded by the Dominican Fr Vincent McNabb.[28] Indeed, Casartelli referred to McNabb as 'a wild talker,' prone to 'such rash and dangerous things when he gets excited.' He deemed McNabb to be actually dangerous because of his 'socialist proclivities.'[29] However, Casartelli's concern for spiritual and moral well-being was not restricted to a reaction against Socialism, but was rooted in devotion to the Eucharist.

THE DEVOTIONAL LIFE

Casartelli had a profound personal devotion to the Eucharist. Evidence for this is found in his diaries[30] which he kept whilst he was living in Ardwick prior to his going to study in Louvain. During this time he frequently assisted at the Forty Hours' Exposition of the Blessed Sacrament in various churches in Manchester. This evidence is not only instructive about his own personal spirituality, it also enables us to revise a judgement that the devotion of *Quarant' Ore* or 'Forty Hours' was scarcely known outside of London.[31]

Historical overtones

In a paper entitled 'A Forgotten Chapter in the Second Spring,'[32] Casartelli wished to correct the internal self-understanding of the English Catholic Church by highlighting a phenomena in the period of its history known as the 'Second Spring.' John Henry Newman had used this term in his sermon to the bishops of England assembled at St Mary's College, Oscott, 13 July 1852, to describe the reawakening and growth in the Catholic faith that was taking place in England at the time. Commenting on how this growth was generally understood, Casartelli observed that:

> it is perhaps not too much to say that in the popular mind, and very likely in our own minds, the so-called 'Oxford Movement' is more or less identified with that other great spiritual phenomena … the Second Spring – that is to say, the marvellous revival, growth, and development of the Catholic Church in England during the last fifty years of our century.[33]

He considered this to be a misconception. Mary Heimann has recently argued that the description 'Second Spring' is itself inaccurate, misleading and a loaded term.[34] Casartelli was happy to use the term but not with the connotations with which John Bossy and Heimann use it.[35] According to Casartelli, the Oxford Movement, even though it had 'played an all-important – one is almost tempted to say a preponderating – part in the life of the Catholic Church in this country,' was not in itself the full story.[36] In fact, there was a 'forgotten chapter': the story of the popular missions given in England by Aloysius Gentili[37] and his companions in the years between 1843 – 1848, and especially those given in Manchester in 1846–7.

Casartelli described the Oxford Movement as representing the 'first chapter' of the Second Spring; it had given the Church in England 'our greatest leaders in Newman and Manning,' and it had revivified the intelligence and aided the emergence of modern Catholic English literature.[38] Nevertheless it remained an external influence – 'a movement [arising] primarily in the bosom of the Anglican Establishment.'[39] Casartelli identified the second chapter as being the stream of Irish immigrants to England who had played 'a very important share in the resuscitation of Catholic life and practice.'[40] There was another chapter however, which had not been given due attention. In contrast to the other two chapters, this was an internal movement and constituted 'the revival of Catholic faith and practice in the very midst of the Catholics of this country themselves; itself the effect of what, to borrow the pet phrase of a late Archbishop of Canterbury, was in truth literally an 'Italian Mission.''[41]

Casartelli's observations about the historical details of the 'forgotten chapter' shed light on the growth of Catholicism in nineteenth century Manchester, and the evidence of his diaries runs, in part, counter to recent scholarship.[42] By using data available in the *Catholic Directory* for the years 1850–1914, Heimann has concluded that 'arch-ultramontane devotions', such as *Quarant' Ore*, did not form part of general Catholic spirituality.[43] However Casartelli's paper 'The Forgotten Chapter' and his contemporary diaries tell a different story. He claimed that the year 1843 was significant in the devotional life of Catholics in England because it was from this date that the Italian missionaries, Gentili and companions, became free to pursue the rôle of itinerant missioners, going from cities and towns preaching and giving missions. With this change, Casartelli recorded, came,

> the introduction into our spiritual life, by the Fathers of Charity, of four great and potent factors which have done so much to vivify faith and piety. These four works were 1/the preaching of popular *Missions*; 2/the ceremony of *Renewal of Baptismal vows*; 3/the *Quarant' Ore*, or Forty Hours' Exposition of the Blessed Sacrament; and 4/the devotions of the *Month of May*.[44]

Elsewhere he writes,

> The month of May, frequent Benediction of the Blessed Sacrament, the *Quarant' Ore*, have actually passed into our tradition, and we can scarcely imagine a time when they were not ordinary phenomena of our religious life. It was far different in the early forties: the Fathers of Charity were real pioneers in all these works, and the very nature of them explains much of the enthusiasm they awakened, and of the profound impressions that they created in both the Catholic and Protestant public.[45]

That *Quarant' Ore* subsequently passed into the English spiritual tradition, and remained a vital part of it, we know from evidence from the diocese of Liverpool.[46] Bishop Goss of Liverpool 'urged *Quarant' Ore* ... [and] laid down careful rules for its celebration and ensured that the Liverpool missions kept up a continual rota of it, as far as possible, every Lent.'[47] He also ordered that the times and places be advertised in the local press so that as many people as possible could visit the churches whilst Exposition was taking place.[48] Indeed, the diocese of Liverpool produced a *Guide to the Catholic Church Services and Quarant' Ore in Liverpool for 1861.*[49] The general acceptance of *Quarant' Ore* in Manchester is evident in Casartelli's diaries for Lent 1874,[50] which tell of his assisting at the Forty Hours' Devotion in numerous churches throughout the city, and gives no suggestion that this was something extraordinary nor a response to a particular need or episcopal decree. Similarly, the *Acta* of the Bishop of Salford at this time, Herbert Vaughan, does not imply that *Quarant' Ore* was restricted to certain neighbourhoods, classes of people or churches pertaining to religious orders.[51] Vaughan had asked Rome for special permission for his diocese to have its own form of *Quarant' Ore*. In 'The Forgotten Chapter' Casartelli explained that 'the novelty of them [the devotions introduced by Gentili] explains much of the enthusiasm they awakened, and of the profound impression they created.'[52] They could not therefore have been imposed by Rome.

Heimann, although mistaken about *Quarant' Ore*, rightly argues that when describing and explaining the type of devotions preferred and the growth of Catholicism, it is more accurate to speak of 'a new piety,' 'enthusiasm,' and 'revival,' rather than using the terms 'Second Spring' or the 'triumph of Ultramontanism.'[53] Casartelli's contemporary account used the same vocabulary[54] and applied it to the missions preached by the religious orders, which encouraged 'conversion' among a great number of nominal Catholics through the Sacraments of Penance and the Eucharist.[55] The work of the missioners was revivalist in the sense of a 'stirring up of the mind and heart of the Catholics of England; and a gathering into the net of converts from Protestantism, on a scale which astonish us as we read of it at this distance of half a century.'[56]

Casartelli emphasised the efforts of Gentili, and doubted

> whether, without this internal revival, preparing the way for other and more external influences, even such a vital force as that of the Oxford Movement would have been able to produce the far-reaching effects which are attributed to it.[57]

Quoting a letter from his father, who had been present at a mission given in Liverpool, Casartelli described the scene:

> The mission created a great sensation at the time. Gentili was a square, mortified-looking man; he spoke broken English, rather difficult to understand till you got accustomed to it. The style of preaching was novel and very impressive. At times there was humour in it, especially when he spoke of dishonest dealings by trades people and various forms of cheating … The mission was very popular. Even at the five o'clock morning service I have seen the church crammed, whilst in the evening the people were actually standing on the broad window-ledges inside the church.[58]

Casartelli's 'A Forgotten Chapter' is an account of the Second Spring from the point of view of conversion, in the sense of returning to the practice of the duties of religion. For example, he recorded the number of hours the missioners spent hearing the confessions of penitents: at St Augustine's in 1846, fifteen confessors were needed; at St Wilfrid's, 'the penitents were so numerous that some waited for days in the church until their turn came to enter the confessionals … several confessors were engaged from six or seven in the morning till after twelve at night.'[59] Converts to Catholicism were numerous: Casartelli gives the figure as 398.[60] Gentili's influence was so great that in November 1846, when he had finished giving the last of his missions in Manchester, the local clergy presented him with a memorial in recognition of his work. Conversion is once again in the foreground in the contemporary record by the Manchester clergy,

> The immense multitude of degenerate Catholics who have been reclaimed, and the still more remarkable number of converts which have been received into the Church during the exercises which you have conducted, convince us that the hand of God is with you, that the practice of giving missions, which you have recently introduced into this country, is one of the greatest blessings which has occurred to religion in modern times.[61]

Heimann also sees the 'Second Spring' from the point of view of a revivalist movement that had a particular appeal to those who had already some link with the Catholic Church. It was, she claims,

> the conversion of large numbers of nominally Catholic Irish to an enthusiastic practice which gave the sense of a Second Spring; but converts from Protestantism, Old Catholics even Liberal Catholics were equally susceptible to its appeal.[62]

How does Casartelli's historiography of the Catholic revival compare with other accounts? Bernard Ward's *The Sequel to Catholic Emancipation* (London, 1915) recognised the vital rôle which the religious Orders played in the revival of the Catholic Church in England, without which, 'the Church could not have assumed its normal position in this country.'[63] He mentioned especially the work of Gentili in the reclaiming of many lapsed Catholics.[64] Ward also stated that the Irish immigrants 'in reality affected the future of Catholicism in this country more even than the Oxford Movement.'[65] Likewise, Denis Gwynn in his book *The Second Spring* (London, 1942) ascribed the great boost in the number of Catholics to the Irish immigrants. In his later work *Father Luigi Gentili and His Mission* (London 1951) Gywnn drew heavily on Casartelli's 'A Forgotten Chapter,' for the description of Gentili's missions in Manchester.[66] However, Gwynn, Ward, and Casartelli uncritically assumed that the Irish immigrants were practising Catholics, an assumption which has been shown to be inaccurate:

if the Irish were not yet practising Catholics at the time of the more modest moves to the mainland which preceded the great exodus of the 1840's, and even as late as the time of the Great Famine … then one should hardly cite them to support the contention that it was Irish immigrants who 'strengthened' or 'laid the seeds' of the English Catholic revival.[67]

Yet this is what Casartelli did by identifying the second chapter of the Second Spring with the influx of the Irish immigrants. For there to have been, as his contemporary evidence showed, the impressive number of conversions of sinners, an equally impressive number of lapsed Catholics was needed. Gwynn records that in Manchester in 1845 there were approximately 100,000 Catholics, many of whom were Irish. It follows that among the 'converts' the Irish must have figured very highly. Many of those who made up the 'forgotten chapter' must therefore have been the same people whom Casartelli described as belonging to the second chapter.

Casartelli was convinced of the insurmountable good that missions could achieve: for this reason he re-introduced 'General Missions' into the Salford Diocese when he became its Bishop. Within his lifetime Casartelli witnessed, and furthermore was instrumental in, a profound development in the understanding of the Eucharist. In simple terms this may be described as a shift from adoration to reception.

The Holy Eucharist

Casartelli wanted to deepen and enhance the spiritual life of the laity by a more participatory and prayerful rôle in the celebration of the liturgy, especially the Mass. He hoped to achieve this by implementing the reform of Church music as proposed by Pius X in *Inter Pastoralis Officii* (1903), and by putting into effect the decrees *Sacra Tridentina Synodus* (1905), and *Quam Singulari* (1910). Pius X had, in the second of these decrees, stated: 'It is the wish of the Church that all Christians should be daily nourished by the reception of the Sacrament of the Holy Eucharist.'[68] The decree resolved the theological discussion about the frequency of receiving Communion by declaring that the norm was to be: 'frequent and daily Communion should be open to all the faithful, that no one can be lawfully hindered therefore who is in a state of grace.'[69] During his allocution at the Diocesan Synod of 1906 Casartelli urged his priests to explain the instructions of the decree to the people in their care. By drawing his diocese into the rhythm of these changes, Casartelli was introducing it to one of the most profound and long-lasting pastoral innovations in Catholic sacramental practice.[70]

Pius X's other far-reaching decree on the Holy Eucharist, *Quam Singulari*, dealt with the question as to what was the appropriate age for children to receive the Eucharist for the first time. According to the decree, this was to be as soon as the age of discretion was reached. Casartelli pointed out that these changes did not constitute novelties, but were a return to the practice of the Early Church.[71] As regards *Quam Singulari*, modifications were needed in the preparation of children for their First Holy Communion and the continuing instruction that should follow. The Cenacle Convent in Manchester offered retreats which were deemed particularly appropriate for this purpose. Casartelli was a firm advocate of the retreat movement and keen for more adults to take advantage of the retreats being provided elsewhere in the diocese. His enthusiasm and promotion of the movement was recognised by Fr Charles Plater S.J., who requested that he write the preface to his own work *Retreats for the People*,[72] a work which specifically cited Casartelli's 1911 Pastoral Letter on the importance of retreats.[73]

A further display of Casartelli's wider vision of the Church's apostolate was his determination that a more frequent reception of the Eucharist should not remain purely an exercise of individual piety. In his pastoral letter for Lent 1908, 'Amare et Servire', he made a striking connection between the ideas of *Sacra Tridentina Synodus*, and a fundamental principle he had laid down in 'The Signs of the Times.' In the latter he had emphasised how the possession of civic rights and their unimpeded scope of action, brought with them the corresponding duty of exercising them for the commonweal.[74] In effect this meant that Catholics ought not to work solely for the good of the Church and its interests, but for the common good of all. In 'Amare et Servire' (the title being taken from Herbert Vaughan's episcopal motto when he was Bishop of Salford) Casartelli brought together the principle of frequent reception of the Eucharist with civic duty as a practical consequence. He thus connected spirituality and social responsibility. Crichton has noted how in this period it was generally understood that 'devotionalism meant individualism.'[75] With this observation in mind, we can appreciate how important and far-reaching Casartelli's views were. The antecedents to his change in focus were to be found in the way the Church, in face of 'the rapid development of the nervous system in the nations of the modern civilised world,' had made allowances in the forms of penance and fasting which it imposed upon its subjects.[76] Instead of the more rigorous and physical mortification of previous times, those of a 'more spiritual and intellectual kind' were now being encouraged.[77] Casartelli stressed that those related to the cult of the Blessed Sacrament were most important:

> Hence the multiplication in our times of Benediction and of the solemn Exposition of the Blessed Sacrament; hence above all the present action of the Holy See in encouraging the greater frequency of the reception of Holy Communion ... when possible, of daily Communion, not only

among her Clergy and religious but among the laity of all classes and conditions and even of her children.[78]

Casartelli took these developments a step further and incorporated them into his suggestions as to Lenten observance. The first practical suggestion was to receive Communion more frequently. He directed this especially to those

> excellent, devout and practical Catholics of the older generation [who] have been brought up in a different school so as to regard frequent Communion, at least if more frequent than weekly, as something hardly to be aspired to by the ordinary lay person, and daily Communion as the privilege only of saints and persons of extraordinary sanctity.[79]

To this 'older generation' his exhortation may well have appeared novel because it was their customary practice that Confession always preceded Communion. Casartelli was effectively encouraging them to receive Communion without having to go to Confession beforehand. Secondly, he emphasised how expressions of practical Christianity should flow from the Eucharist:

> True sanctification is effected by the love and service of our Blessed Lord – *Amare et Servire*. The love of Christ is primarily and chiefly maintained in and by the Holy Eucharist. From this Divine Love will overflow, of necessity, the supernatural love of our brethren ... From Love proceeds Service ... and the service of Christ is to be found, we may venture to say chiefly, in the service of our neighbour.[80]

In the Lenten religious programme that Casartelli was presenting, the chief source of spiritual nourishment was the liturgy. Here, as Crichton correctly observes, Casartelli was breaking new ground: 'most people [in that age] would have said that private prayer, devotions and other practices of piety were the chief source of that spirit.'[81] Casartelli used the decrees on the Eucharist as the means of encouraging both greater service and a more mature spirituality. Thus the St Vincent de Paul Society, which worked for the care of 'waifs and strays', was particularly commended as a worthy and appropriate cause. Similarly, the diocesan Protection and Rescue Society, which at the time wanted to open a shelter for the homeless, was another charity worthy of practical support. Casartelli had long dedicated himself to the realisation of the Society's hopes for such a home, having mentioned the SVP and the PRS in 'The Signs of the Times.' Now he expressed the wish that they not only be better known and appreciated, but more widely and generously supported.[82] His pastoral letter ended with reference to other diocesan works of charity such as the retreats organised by the Sisters of the Cenacle for women and for children about to make their First Holy

Communion. The various confraternities and guilds for young working women, teachers, nurses, and the Catholic Women's League were also strongly commended.

Casartelli's calling for a closer connection between reception of the Eucharist and a practical concern for the well-being of one's neighbour echoed a vital concern of his whole episcopate – a desire for unity and a unification of Catholic effort. There were two obstacles to this unity. One was the stumbling block of parochialism, which hindered the fostering of united effort. The other difficulty was a sense of individualism that pervaded the notion of the spiritual life. This had a double effect. It was an obstacle because it saw piety as unrelated to a concern for one's neighbour and the common good, and it prevented a greater participation in the liturgy because it viewed piety as essentially a private matter. To counter the second of these effects Casartelli recommended the use of missals: 'There is no better way of participating in the Great Sacrifice than by following step by step with the priest, joining with him in the words he utters ... no more beautiful and touching devotions can be found.'[83] This would imbue the individual with a true liturgical piety because it would be 'pre-eminently to think and feel and pray with the Church, whose voice they are.'[84] At the Eucharistic Congress in 1908, it was observed how such participation was at a low ebb.[85] Casartelli returned from the Congress to his diocese determined to rectify this.

The Eucharistic Congress 1908

The occasion of the Eucharistic Congress in London in 1908, was an opportunity for Casartelli to instruct his diocese further on the centrality of the Eucharist, which he described as: 'the vital centre of her love, her devotion, her entire spiritual life. Destroy this central dogma, and the Church's life, stricken in its very core, must disintegrate and perish.'[86]

To demonstrate this Casartelli referred to two salient changes that had happened in the religious life of the people of England during the Reformation, the rejection of Papal authority and 'the abolition of the Holy Sacrifice of the Mass.'[87] By drawing on Fr Hugh Benson's historical novel, *By What Authority?*,[88] Casartelli gave a brief exposition of the persecution of Catholics during the reigns of Edward VI and Elizabeth I. The lesson he wished to impart was, that to strike at the Eucharist was to strike at the very heart of the Church.

Following the Congress, Casartelli issued a letter to the diocese entitled 'The Eucharistic Congress and its Results'.[89] He explained that it had been an 'extraordinary, and almost unprecedented success,'[90] and an occasion marked with reverence, fervour, and devotion. Nevertheless, the proposed procession of the Blessed Sacrament had caused a political stir because some militant Protestants had seen it as an attempt to impose Catholicism on the country. In protest, Lord Ripon, a Catholic member of the cabinet, resigned his post as Lord Privy Seal because he was embarrassed by his government's action in cancelling the procession.[91] As a result of his mishandling of the situation, Herbert Gladstone, the Home Secretary, offered to resign and was sent by the Prime Minister, H. H. Asquith, to become governor-general of South Africa. Casartelli played down the furore:

> The sole discordant note, – the deplorable intervention of the Prime Minister to prevent the carrying in procession of the Blessed Sacrament and the wearing of sacerdotal vestments by the Bishops and Clergy, – has only added to the success of that unique demonstration itself.[92]

The effect of the ban on the carrying of the Blessed Sacrament was 'to raise to fever height the perfervid enthusiasm of the vast crowds ... and their deafening applause testified to their love of the Holy Eucharist and their loyalty to the Holy See.'[93] In response to the 'widespread and most deplorable neglect of Sunday Mass among our Catholics, especially in the great manu-facturing centres,'[94] Casartelli hoped that more people would join the Inter-national Archconfraternity of the Mass of Reparation. However, Casartelli's desire that congregations in all the churches of the diocese be trained to sing the responses to the Mass, was the most significant outcome of the Congress.

CHURCH MUSIC

Long before he became a bishop, Casartelli had developed an interest in liturgical celebration and its careful execution. His diaries occasionally refer to the poor state of liturgical music and the slovenly way in which the liturgy was celebrated.[95] In promoting Church music, Casartelli was laying out his understanding of the very heart of the Church's mission: the sanctification of the People of God. At the beginning of his episcopate, he expressed his desire 'that Ecclesiastical Musical Reform will be one of the chief features of the early Twentieth century, just as Ecclesiastical Architectural reform was of the early and middle nineteenth century ... We hope that this Diocese of Salford will be in the van of progress.'[96] He echoed Pius X's desire, uttered shortly after he became Pope, to 'produce good music.'[97] Casartelli lamented the state of much of contemporary Church music, which he considered, 'of such a *theatrical* style, unworthy of the House of God. High Mass and Bene-diction, especially on great feast-days, are too often turned into little better than concerts, where people go 'to hear music', and (as they admit) found it impossible to pray.'[98]

His criticisms were not only on the grounds of aesthetics and spirituality; many of the Mass settings were very long and Casartelli had in mind the well-being of the celebrant. He gave the example of priests who on Sundays had to rise early to say two Masses, and preach at the High Mass. Because of the rules on fasting, this meant an enforced abstaining from food from midnight until lunchtime the following day, and 'such a custom is a fruitful source of ill-health, and frequently leads to ultimate break-down of the health of the clergy.'[99]

The reform of Church music and frequent reception of the Eucharist were Casartelli's blueprint for achieving a greater participation in the celebration of the liturgy. This policy is a very important benchmark in assessing the success of his episcopate. The *motu proprio Inter Pastoralis Officii* (1903) was primarily concerned with participation and not only with music *per se*. Crichton has highlighted this fact, arguing that 'the emphasis on music in that document was certainly very strong, and at first few if any noticed the statement in it that active participation in the liturgy is the chief source of the Christian spirit.'[100] R. R. Terry[101] in a paper to the Catholic Truth Society's Conference at Preston in 1907,[102] emphasised the principles and commands of the document solely in terms of permissible music: Plainchant, Polyphony, and Modern music, on the lines of which Crichton has drawn attention. The only bishop, other than Casartelli, to comment upon the *motu proprio* was the Bishop of Clifton, whose response to it was in terms of obedience – 'music may be attractive, but obedience is still more so.'[103] The Bishop of Liverpool sent copies to each mission in his diocese in 1905. The Bishop of Birmingham encouraged his clergy to obey its spirit, whilst the Archdiocese of Westminster published a list of approved music in 1907.

In contrast to his episcopal colleagues, Casartelli took notice of the reference to participation, and made this the central point of his proposed reforms. In a 'Letter on Church Music' of 1906,[104] he quoted from the *motu proprio*: 'special efforts are to be made to restore the use of the Gregorian Chant by the people, so that the faithful may again take a more active part in the ecclesiastical offices [*sacrae liturgiae*], as in former times.'[105]

To enable 'a more active part' to be played, Casartelli ordered the introduction of simple devotional Mass settings aimed at assisting devotion instead of distracting from it. Moreover, his hope was for 'the gradual introduction into our churches of congregational singing, even of the Liturgy.'[106] The first practical step he took was to request that on all occasions when he was invited to assist at High Mass or Benediction in any church of the diocese, the intended programme of music was to be submitted to him one week beforehand for his approval. No music of which he disapproved was to be used; this included music performed by female soloists. This was not just a personal whim on Casartelli's part; in 'The Signs of the Times' he had referred to several of the Provincial and Diocesan Synods which had already forbidden such performances, along with the advertising of the names of soloists and other singers. To assist him in the proposed reform, he appointed a small consultative committee of experts made up of clergy and laity.

In May 1904, Casartelli, in preparation for the deliberations of the hierarchy at their June meeting when the matter of Church music would be discussed, circulated a questionnaire to his clergy soliciting information regarding the state of Church music in their parishes.[107] Casartelli was subsequently a member of the Bishops' Committee for Hymns, along with the bishops of Portsmouth, Birmingham, and Clifton. In August 1904, he sent two copies of Pius X's *Inter Pastoralis Officii* to each mission; one copy was for the missionary rector, the other was intended for the choirmaster. In all the larger churches of the diocese the document was to be put into effect without delay. The letter encouraged the training of boys' choirs to sing simple Gregorian settings for Mass and Benediction, thus allowing the congregation to participate more fully. Casartelli considered this to be the 'most excellent and convenient way of bringing about the necessary changes required by Pope Pius X.'[108] An official list of music, approved by the bishop's committee, accompanied the letter. This list was not meant to stifle genuine musical talent or initiative, nor was it meant to be definitive; local compositions of merit were welcomed.

By January 1906 Casartelli could congratulate the clergy and the people of the diocese for the way they had, on the whole, zealously taken up the challenge of musical reform. He commented that, 'already a very much more devotional and edifying style of music is to be heard in many of our churches.'[109] However, the diocesan regulations had not yet been universally carried out. Casartelli wanted to see the gradual restoration of the singing of the people's parts of the Mass. By reference to musical experts and the Tradition of the Church, notably the sermons of St Augustine, Casartelli showed that congregational singing, even of the Mass, was no novelty in the Church. In fact, he had many years earlier been deeply affected by Vaughan's efforts to introduce singing in the vernacular into the liturgy.[110]

In England the *motu proprio* received a poor reception, and in general there was little that could be described as a liturgical movement even in the early 1920s.[111] R. R. Terry wrote: 'looking back on the past four years, one is forced to admit that results have been exceedingly small ... Those who hailed the *motu proprio* as the beginning of a new era have sorrowfully modified their former optimistic tone.'[112]

One early sign of a liturgical movement however, was the use of bilingual missals. Crichton found the earliest example in this period to date from

1915.[113] Casartelli's promotion of these missals pre-dates this by two years. He was also leading the way in the introduction of the dialogue Mass at St Bede's College.[114] Monsignor William Brown[115] recorded his surprise when visiting St Bede's College *circa* 1916. He had been invited to celebrate the college Mass:

> I vested as quickly as possible and went to the altar. Then I got the surprise of my life. As soon as I said the first verse of the psalm, a full-throated united response came at me from behind like a volley and almost made me jump. This was my first introduction to the *Missa Dialogata*.[116]

It was not until 1922 that the Congregation of Rites officially introduced the dialogue Mass, and even then, according to Crichton, it was a further ten years before it was seen in England.[117] These two instances, when seen from a later perspective of liturgical renewal and reform, represent a forward-looking trend in Casartelli's liturgical thinking.

Were Casartelli's original hopes and ambitions for a reform of Church music within his diocese fulfilled, or did he modify his optimistic tone? In many ways, his attempts at reform mirror the general history of the *motu proprio*, which, as we have seen, was not universally well received nor implemented in England. He was able to summon an Episcopal Commission on Ecclesiastical Music, and he encouraged the laity to become active participants in the reform and to become patrons and members of the newly formed Guild of St Gregory and St Cecilia[118] and of the Catholic Philharmonic Society.[119] However, in 1916 he deemed it necessary to admonish the clergy in regard to Church music. To his distress he had found,

> In the course of Visitation ... a growing laxity in several Churches with regard to the observance of the Rules for Church Music. It must be clearly understood that no Masses may be sung in any of the Churches, secular or regular, of the Diocese, except those contained in the official Diocesan List and Supplement.[120]

Casartelli clearly expected his high standards to be met, and he found it 'difficult to understand how choirs and choirmasters can be ignorant of the mind of the Church in regard to sacred music and of the diocesan rules.'[121] He explained this partly due to the War having 'swept away the memory of all these disciplinary regulations.'[122] Secondly, he recognised how 'the terrible toll taken by the Moloch of War from our male population proved disastrous to this reform.'[123] The rules regarding male-only choirs were re-introduced in 1920, though the bishop duly acknowledged the part played by the female singers during the war years. Despite being 'gratified' by the way the reform in liturgical music had been maintained in 'many churches', he had clearly found that the reforms and regulations had not been fully introduced and applied. He once again reiterated the importance of music in the celebration of the Mass:

> the Mass music is not merely a kind of artistic accompaniment or embellishment to tickle the ears and meet the aesthetic taste of the hearers; it is an integral part of the Sacrificial rite, because it consists simply of the actual liturgical words of the Mass prayers rendered in musical form. That is why the Church is so jealous that the music should never be worldly, sensuous, theatrical, noisy, or boisterous.[124]

Whilst Casartelli's hopes for reforms and instructions *vis-à-vis* Church music did not come to full fruition in his lifetime, he never lost his optimistic tone. Given that any spirit of reform is always slow to take effect, his ambition to introduce liturgical reform should be recognised rather than dismissed as something that failed to happen. The quite remarkable nature of his attempts were in themselves an achievement, when it is recalled that Pius X in *Inter Pastoralis Officii* was the first to introduce such reforms for nearly three hundred and fifty years. The far-reaching importance of this document was correctly recognised by Aubert:

> Pius X played an important role in the rediscovery of the real position that the liturgy should take in Catholic life ... the first significant reforms in the area of liturgy since the Council of Trent were owed to Pius X. Under his pontificate and partially under his influence, the so-called 'liturgical movement', so far limited to a small elite and developing in the confinements of Benedictine abbeys, began to invade parishes.[125]

The failure of Casartelli's attempts at reform was, as already mentioned, partly due to choirs losing many of their male members during the War. Another factor was the rôle of the parish clergy, without whose willingness to co-operate, the reforms had little chance of success.[126] Casartelli had feared being a failure as a bishop because of his lack of experience and aptitude, yet his attempts at liturgical reform display a true pastoral mind. His linking together frequent reception of the Eucharist with expressions of practical Christianity show an understanding of his rôle as a bishop beyond the mere buttressing of diocesan structures and the encouraging of personal piety. Casartelli was aware of the need to enliven the faith of those who had lapsed and to encourage more fervour among practising Catholics. With an eye to both these responsibilities he re-introduced the idea of simultaneous General Missions.

GENERAL MISSIONS

A 'General Mission' signified the simultaneous preaching of missions in several parishes in a given area. It was the custom that this was done by members of religious Orders. Casartelli's decision in Lent 1905 to declare a 'General and Simultaneous Mission' in the Manchester and Salford areas followed 'the urgent advice of some of the more experienced and venerable of the Clergy.'[127] He had been impressed by the success of a similar mission that Vaughan had organised in 1875. In fact, Casartelli had used the effects of this Mission in his defence of the Church and its reaction to the two American evangelicals Moody and Sankey.[128] Casartelli's account of the missionary activity of Gentili, especially in Manchester, is further evidence of how he judged them to be a means of enkindling and reviving faith.

Casartelli noted how it was twenty-one years since the last General Mission had been given in the Diocese, and that 'a whole generation, we may say, has risen up since that date.'[129] The repetition of a well-tried and successful formula was his attempt at evangelising this new generation and to encourage the lapsed to return to the practice of their faith. In 1905, in both his letter *ad clerum* of Candlemas and in his Lenten Pastoral Letter, Casartelli quoted at length from the exhortation Vaughan had given back in 1875:

> Our Lord Jesus Christ holds out to you an extra-ordinary grace. In mercy and love He is bringing very many good and experienced Missioners of different Religious Orders and Congregations to spend three weeks among you, to labour for your salvation ... He is come to summon you to the Mission – to summon you to listen to the Divine Word, which is living and effectual and more piercing than any two-edged sword.[130]

At one level, this was reminiscent of an evangelical mission: the emphasis on salvation from one's sins and an invitation to form and ferment a relationship with a God that was personal and based on the heart of Jesus Christ.[131] However, the individual's conversion and new relationship with God was not to be thought of as a purely private affair with no ramifications for the wider circumstances of life. Casartelli repeated Vaughan's clear statement: 'Remember that you are bound to help your neighbour, if he needs you. You are bound to do so by charity, perhaps also by justice. Thousands of poor, blind, famished, and perishing souls will be eternally lost if their brethren do not help them.'[132]

To form an overview of the pastoral needs of the people in the Manchester and Salford districts, Casartelli asked the opinions of several rectors. Their assessment was for the need for more instruction in Christian doctrine and on the duties of Catholicism. In particular this meant the stressing of morning and night prayers, attendance at Mass, fasting, and the evil of drink. Furthermore, to ensure that enthusiasm might not wane once the Mission was over, they recommended that the clergy continue to visit the homes of their parishioners. Similarly, the setting up, or revival, of confraternities would also reap benefits. Casartelli quoted 'a distinguished and much esteemed member of the Chapter, whose opinion is also of great value':

> Find out what is the predominant sin of our people. I for one used to think it was *drink*, but later experience has shown me that, though drink is the most conspicuous, it is by no means the worst. The worst, and the one that is doing most damage to souls, and spreading most quickly, is parents' ignorance of, or total apathy regarding, the duties of their state of life.[133]

The practicalities and logistics of the Mission followed the pattern of 1875. It was to last for three weeks in each parish; in those where there was only one priest, this was reduced to two weeks. The first task was for rectors to take a 'complete and minute census of the Catholics of their district,' so that a *status animarum* of each parish was available.[134] As well as a means of gathering information, the house-to-house visiting would ensure that the Mission was well announced, and the people of each area, including the lapsed, would be better known to the clergy. Casartelli forwarded the advice he had solicited to the priests who would be doing the actual preaching.[135] Aware of his own lack of experience, he explained how he had no wish to interfere in the conduct of the Mission: 'lest I should myself err, through my own inexperience, in venturing upon any suggestions of the kind, I have sought the advice of some of the more experienced and zealous of the clergy.'[136]

A questionnaire was circulated to the thirty-eight parishes that had taken part to ascertain the effects.[137] Similar missions were held in 1905 in the Blackburn and Darwen area of the Diocese,[138] and in Oldham and Rochdale district in 1907.[139] They were repeated as part of an attempt at post-war reconstruction in Manchester and Salford in 1921; Blackburn and Burnley in 1922; and in the deaneries of Oldham, Rochdale, Bury, and Bolton in 1923. All followed to the letter the format laid down in the 1905 General Mission; Casartelli repeated *verbatim*, as he had done for the earlier Missions, Vaughan's exhortation of 1875.

The spirit of these General Missions, like those preached by Gentili and Vaughan, was revivalist. The appeal of the missions to those who were already Catholic, whether nominally or practising, can be seen by comparing the number of confessions heard and people confirmed with the relatively small number of converts.

EDUCATION AND FORMATION OF THE CLERGY

Casartelli considered that his 'greatest and most onerous task' was to provide his diocese with an adequate supply of priests. He cited Herbert Vaughan's *The Young Priest* (London, 1904) to this effect:

> The distinctive work of the episcopate ... is to produce and multiply a holy priesthood ... [the Bishop] is bound not only to give it birth, but to feed, train, and perfect it on the model of Christ and His Apostles. The Bishop has no more important and vital work than this.[140]

One of the problems associated with this duty was the continual lack of funds. Casartelli constantly appealed to the clergy and people of the diocese to financially assist him in this task. He fully recognised the debt of gratitude that was owed to the former bishop, John Bilsborrow, for the way in which he had raised the profile of the annual collection for ecclesiastical education and made it 'the most important and successful in the Diocese.'[141] Despite an increase in donations, which enabled more students to be accepted for seminary training, the perennial problem of raising sufficient funds to educate an adequate supply of candidates for the priesthood still remained.

Casartelli did not simply want to have the seminaries full of students, regardless of their aptitude or ability; he desired a zealous, well-educated, and well-trained *corpus* of priests fitted to meet the educational, missionary, and social needs of the diocese.[142] As far back as 1896 he had recognised how, 'we shall need a learned clergy in that coming century as we had never needed it before; we shall need it for the defence and propagation of the truth, and we shall need it urgently for the work of education.'[143]

He was well experienced in the discerning of vocations; from 1875 until his death in 1925, he lived at St Bede's College which, as well as being a commercial college, was also the Junior Seminary for the diocese. In his pastoral letter 'The Making of a Priest,' written in April 1909, Casartelli set out his ideas of a valid 'vocation' and warned of some of the associated misconceptions:

> it is dangerous to try and suggest or inspire a Vocation, and often leads to serious mistakes and unhappiness ... it has very frequently proved that the supposed 'Vocation' was really the outcome of the too great desire of a pious and affectionate mother.[144]

In another pastoral letter, he reflected upon his long experience of teaching and the benefits that had flowed from his personal knowledge of the priests of the diocese:

> if we may be allowed a personal observation, we cannot conceal our satisfaction at the fact that so many of our Clergy have been in the past our

CASARTELLI AS A SPIRITUAL LEADER

own pupils and under our own immediate care, when we engaged in the work of education at St Bede's College. The relations existing between a Bishop and those priests who have stood in this intimate relation with him in their early life must necessarily be very special and quite different in the way to other relations however sacred.[145]

As a result Casartelli knew the strengths and weaknesses of many of his priests. This was a great advantage to both bishop and clergy, particularly when it came to their future deployment. In order that a similar relationship might exist between himself and those he had not taught, he requested that every ecclesiastical student should write to him twice a year. These letters were 'to be perfectly frank and confidential ... an account of each Student's studies, progress, success, and difficulties of any kind.'[146] Casartelli recognised another important advantage of St Bede's and a reason why he wanted to see it on a sound financial footing: it was a place where future priests and laity studied together and became friends. This would produce fruit when, in later life, 'they will have to stand in friendly relationship and co-operation.'[147] This mutual friendship aided strength and unity among Catholics.[148]

Casartelli believed that 'without a well-educated and intellectually gifted Clergy the Church's battle in the twentieth century will be irretrievably lost.'[149] This issue was related to his earlier argument for Catholics in general to benefit from a university education. At the time of the University Question he had written:

we worriedly ask ourselves what state our clergy will be in twenty-five years from now, not only in relation to the Anglican clergy, and even the clergy of the dissident sects, who are doing everything in order to make use of the advantages of higher education, but in relation to our laity who will be more educated and will have more cultivated minds than their priests.[150]

Therefore he committed himself to ensuring every affordable means and opportunity for Church students to obtain the very best that could be offered in the way of education in both sacred and secular subjects. This was partly 'to fit them to hold their own side by side with the ministers of so many denominations' and to help them 'uphold the cause of the Church and of religion in an age that is rapidly becoming both more cultured and less Christian.'[151] In his pastoral letter of 1909, he reflected upon how the Anglican Clergy no longer enjoyed a near monopoly of higher and university education: 'of late years the ministers of the Nonconformist bodies have entered more and more fully into these educational advantages and have became rivals in intellectual and cultural equipment of the Clergy of the Establishment.'[152] He wanted the Catholic clergy to enjoy these advantages and so play their own part in the cultural and intellectual sphere. He considered it a

127

suicidal policy for us to neglect to do all in our power, despite our poverty, our lack of endowments, and the many claims upon our very limited resources, to train a Clergy who shall be fitted to hold their own in the intellectual arena, to teach the flock and instruct seekers after truth, to defend the Church's doctrines against her assailants in the name of science or history, and to take their proper place, as her Clergy have done in all ages, in the advancement of true Science and the spread of real Christian culture.[153]

Such a hope and desire was a key theme in the way he sought to live out his apostolate as both a priest and a bishop. He wished his priests to receive an excellent training, not only for the good of the Church and its people, but so that 'the greater will be the benign influence of the Catholic Church in England ... and as regards the non-Catholic world in which we live.'[154] His ideal of 'a perfect scholastic career for any Church candidate' was 'a University Honours Degree course at St Edmund's House, Cambridge, followed by the Theological Degree course in Rome.'[155] But the lack of funding often prevented this.[156]

Despite Casartelli's un-wearying promotion of Catholics, both lay and clerical, taking advantage of a university education at Oxford and Cambridge, he strongly opposed Bourne's plan for a 'Catholic Faculty of Theology and Philosophy' at one of these institutions.[157] He explained the reasons for his hostility to the Archbishop of Liverpool: 'the loss would be very great to the English Church; and besides there would be the danger of increased insularity, as against the 'widening' influence of the Centre of Christianity.'[158]

Another reason for Casartelli's unease at Bourne's suggestion, was the potential harm it could cause the English College in Rome. He feared that bishops might no longer send students there if a theology faculty was established in England. To press home his argument, Casartelli therefore wrote to Cardinal Gasquet, in his capacity as the Protector of the English College, and pointed out the disadvantages of the scheme, about which Bourne, characteristically, had not consulted the other bishops; it was rather, in Casartelli's words: 'suddenly sprung upon us.'[159]

Casartelli wanted his clergy to have 'wide minds'; therefore intellectual pursuits were not seen as something extraneous, but rather as integral, to the ministry of the priest. After ordination, and as part of their apostolate, Casartelli encouraged priests to continue studying, and to contribute to the moral, cultural, and intellectual climate of society. This brought together his love of learning and his eagerness to see the press used as an organ for teaching and apologetics. The report of the Diocesan Synod of 1907 recorded that:

the Bishop took the opportunity of urging especially upon the younger Clergy the great importance and desirability of reading and study, especially in Theological, Historical, and kindred subjects, urging them to endeavour to specialise in one or other department of learning for which they might feel special taste and aptitude. A few of the elder Clergy had for many years done conspicuous service for the Church by their writing for the public press. It seemed desirable that some, at least among the younger Clergy who were fitted for it, should be preparing themselves to take the place of the former when no longer able to continue.[160]

Casartelli ensured that at all Deanery conferences two of the questions to be discussed would always relate to contemporary issues, such as Socialism, Spiritualism, and Modernism. Evidence shows that he took this continuing formation very seriously; for example, when commenting upon the conference cases submitted during 1906, he observed that,

with one or two exceptions, there is a lack of finish about the literary style. In some cases English is handled as if it were a foreign language. In the majority of cases the writers would seem to have written about a subject they had tried to make their own by a few day's study, rather than about a subject they had lived with. A minority show a real first-hand acquaintance with the latest products of Biblical scholarship.[161]

Since 1911, the Diocese of Salford was self-supporting in its supply of priests.[162] What of Casartelli's hopes for a university education of his clergy? The diocese was able to maintain a presence of at least one student at Cambridge, more or less consistently, from 1905 until 1924. In 1910, Casartelli reported that three students had taken their degrees at Cambridge; three at Durham; two in Rome; and one in Paris. Other students, never more than two in number, sporadically studied at universities in Rome, Fribourg, Bonn, Angers, Munich, Louvain, and Lyon.

CONCLUSION

As a spiritual leader Casartelli gave a serious amount of time and encouragement to liturgical renewal within his diocese. He did this by advocating frequent reception of Holy Communion and through the reform of Church music. In this respect he mirrored the hopes and aspirations of Pope Pius X. What has been said of the latter's attempts in this regard can fittingly be applied to Casartelli:

From the perspective of the second Vatican Council, they may seem rather modest, but they required a certain measure of courage and, in any case, provided the first, not insignificant guidelines for the great liturgical awakenings of the twentieth century.[163]

From the individual's receiving of Holy Communion, Casartelli's implicit spiritual theology led him to speak of a 'practical Christianity,' i.e. the application of Faith to charitable causes and concern for the common good of others. In this way he was able to demonstrate and maintain a consequential link between spirituality and daily living.

Casartelli's efforts were not restricted to the sacramental life alone; he recognised that every generation needed to be evangelised and not just 'sacramentalised.' When he first advocated a General Mission he recognised that since the last one a whole new generation had grown up that needed to be evangelised. He was aware that lapsation or 'leakage' was a problem that had to be tackled, especially in the period of reconstruction after the war. He therefore reintroduced the preaching of simultaneous General Missions to revive faith, encourage the lapsed, and to ensure that the clergy were known to the people of the parishes they served.

The education of the clergy, particularly at university level, was of special concern to him. He wanted a *corpus* of priests who would not only be intelligent spiritual leaders of their people, but who could also act as a benign presence amid the wider society, especially in the work of education. Casartelli's understanding of the apostolate of the priesthood reflected his own academic background and his vision of the Church as the leaven of society that sanctified the intellect through the pursuit of true science and Christian culture. He looked not only to supplying the needs of his own diocese nor concentrated solely on Catholic interests, his concern included the common good and he envisaged ways in which the Church as preacher and teacher, in the widest sense of the terms, could contribute to this. To achieve these aims he considered the rôle of the educated clergy to be central. This is reminiscent of the spirit Casartelli had first encountered in the person of Herbert Vaughan, who had once written to him:

> I wish to provide for the children of my own flock in the first place, but at the same time I cannot fail to bear in mind that a bishop ought, as St Alphonso somewhere says, to be interested in and to work for objects which extend far beyond his own diocese. He who is of the Apostolic line ought to have the universal spirit of an Apostle.[164]

The great test of Casartelli as a spiritual leader came with the advent of the First World War. It is this issue, and to the general upheaval caused, that we now turn.

Chapter Six

Casartelli and the Great War

It cannot be repeated too often, that Louis Charles Casartelli was a European. His family roots were in Italy; he had mastered several European languages; he counted among his personal friends numerous people from the Continent, and the happiest days of his life had been spent in Belgium, his spiritual home. In a letter to his godson, written in 1913, he spoke of the destructive nature of ill-feeling between nations: 'The strong feeling against Germany is a dark spot in European relations and I firmly hope may pass away eventually in France and also in England. International hatred is a deadly disease.'[1] The weight of responsibility upon Casartelli's shoulders increased immeasurably when Great Britain entered into conflict with Germany in August 1914.[2] To see Europe torn apart by warfare was exceptionally painful for him because it signified a rupture among Catholics fighting in opposing armies. This meant that the Church's unity was weakened. Casartelli was deeply conscious of the need for unity in order to be strong; anything that caused disunion he saw as disastrous for the Church and its mission.[3] In addition to this was the grief he felt when news reached him that the library at Louvain had been burnt down by the German army.[4]

Casartelli's grief was not only personal; he had the task of being a spiritual leader in one of the numerically largest dioceses in the country. During the war he appears to have been a person torn by what was going on around him. He was undoubtedly patriotic and encouraged Catholics to 'play their part' as much as any section of the community. At the same time he was conscious of the number of 'aliens' who were living in Manchester and was eager that they should not be subjected to abuse.[5]

The First World War provided an opportunity for Catholics in England to show their loyalty and patriotism. No one was more aware of this than Casartelli, but this opportunity was also a cause of tension. For he also wished to be loyal to Pope Benedict XV, who was often criticised by Britain and her allies for being pro-German. Whilst wanting to be seen to be supporting the war effort, Casartelli nevertheless had to strike a balance between patriotism and fidelity to Rome. In the end, and for the only time in his life, there is evidence that he felt compelled to compromise when Benedict issued his controversial Peace Note in August 1917. In a letter to the *Manchester Guardian* he distanced the Catholic population of Britain from the Pope's call for peace.[6]

Casartelli considered the war to be one that was justified, that Britain had entered into it as the innocent party, and that it was a crusade against evil. He 'explained' the war in terms of a scourge sent by God to purify the nation of its sins. Although patriotic, he avoided falling into the narrow outlook of jingoism, for which the sole efforts of the British Empire would make the world a better place. While fully supportive of the British army and her allies, Casartelli tried to raise the hearts and minds of his people toward God rather than merely to bolster confidence in the superiority of the country's moral rôle in the conflict.

In the months leading up to the war, Casartelli was the only English bishop to speak about the issue of peace and the danger of war; he did this in his pastoral letter for Lent 1914, 'Pax Christi'.[7] The letter contains a synopsis of his views on what true peace consists of, the 'just war' theory, and the role of the Church in arbitration. Throughout the years 1914–1918 he often returned to the themes first laid out in this letter and developed them.

CASARTELLI'S ATTITUDE TO WAR: 'PAX CHRISTI'

Casartelli wrote 'Pax Christi' against a background of mounting political tension in Ireland, where civil war was perceived as a distinct possibility. He freely acknowledged that in writing it he owed much to the works of the 'learned Austrian ecclesiastic' Mgr Alexander Giesswein.[8] Casartelli made no boast of providing any new insights into the traditional teaching of the Church on the principle of the 'just war,' nor did he attempt to apply this tradition to actual situations. He gave a standard summary of the just war theory as found in the works of St Thomas Aquinas and St Augustine of Hippo. The novelty of the letter lay in the fact that Casartelli was the only Catholic bishop in England and Wales to dedicate his Lenten pastoral for that year to the idea of peace.[9] The pastoral was reproduced in *The Tablet* without comment.[10]

Why did Casartelli choose to write the pastoral from this particular angle? The letter is an example of his ability to look beyond the immediate confines of his diocese and to assess what was happening on the broader political and cultural front. The fact that he could read German enabled him to refer to similar statements by other European bishops. The German Bishops had issued a joint pastoral letter along similar lines in early spring of

1914. Casartelli described this letter as 'a most impressive and solemn warning against the evils to which their nation was becoming prey.'[11] The bitter rivalry between Britain and Germany had caused Casartelli concern since at least 1911 when he had encouraged the readers of the *Catholic Federationist* to 'pray very earnestly and constantly for Peace and good-will between the two great nations. Secondly, we shall do all we can to discourage sentiments of mutual suspicion and hatred, and to encourage mutual knowledge, understanding, and good-will.'[12]

The simultaneous threat of civil upheaval in Ireland was also very significant, since a large portion of his people were Irish and any conflict there would resonate in his diocese.

Casartelli firmly placed peace within a theological context and interpreted it as 'one of the chief results of the Incarnation of our Lord and Saviour Jesus Christ,' whose purpose was 'the bringing of a universal peace among all nations, and the eventual substitution of international peace for war.'[13] He used the term 'peace' in its scriptural sense.[14] It is primarily a relationship between the Creator and the whole of mankind. Following from this is peace between God and the individual, and finally peace between all members of the human family, reaching its plenitude in International Peace. The various ways in which attempts had been made by numerous individuals and bodies to make this a universal reality were then charted. These included the success of international arbitration, and the Church's teaching on the 'just war' when this was deemed a necessary and justified means of achieving peace.

Warfare was clearly opposed to God's plan as expressed in the Incarnation. Casartelli carefully distinguished between justified warfare and aggressive military attack and explained how the reality of war ought 'to be reckoned as one of those ills like the plague and the scourge of famine ... from which the Church bids us pray for deliverance.'[15] In support of his argument, he involved the Tradition of the Church, and especially the teachings of St Augustine[16] and St Thomas Aquinas. Paraphrasing the words of St Augustine in *The City of God*, Casartelli wrote:

> ... war, though itself an evil, is permitted by Divine Providence as a scourge for the wicked and a trial for the good. There are indeed justifiable wars to chastise injustices, but wars for mere cupidity or lust for power, for the oppression and conquest of peaceful nations, can only be called robberies on a large scale.[17]

Justified wars were only to be 'undertaken in defence of a nation's existence or welfare, or some high interest, like those of the Church, or the poor and oppressed.'[18] Even then there had to be certain checks and balances, as it could 'only be tolerated ... when it is the lesser of two inevitable evils.'[19] He warned that, even in cases where war was justified, no group or nation was free from the danger of falling into excessive aggression once an armed conflict had begun. In this regard, his argument overlapped with that developed by Randall Davidson, Archbishop of Canterbury, in February 1916.[20]

The keeping of armies, and the military profession remained justifiable.[21] Casartelli, again citing Augustine, recognised the gallantry of the men who joined the army: 'Great without doubt and famous are men of war, not only on account of their valour, but what is more praiseworthy because they truly fulfil their duties. They brave fatigue and danger, in order ... to chastise a rebellious foe or to restore peace and order.'[22]

Within the space of a few months Casartelli moved from simply quoting such authority to a stance where he actively encouraged the young men of his diocese, and his Church students who were not in major orders (i.e. subdeacon, deacon or priest) to volunteer for the army. In so doing they were fulfilling a duty of which the Church, and Casartelli, approved.

The third part of the pastoral, 'The Action of the Church', pre-empted a question which Casartelli and other bishops were later forced to ask: 'How is it that nineteen centuries after the coming of the Prince of Peace and the preaching of this Gospel of Peace by Himself and His Church, wars should still prevail'?[23] To answer this challenge Casartelli argued from the fact that humanity was endowed with free will. If human beings did not enjoy this freedom and were instead 'a mere automaton or machine, the Divine purpose would be accomplished automatically, mechanically, and immediately.'[24] Since this is not the case mankind was called to co-operate freely with the will of the Creator; God works on the mind and will of creatures through moral influence, not by force or coercion. Christ's teaching becomes effective in nature as 'leaven, which, though often slowly, gradually permeates the human mind and conscience.'[25]

To demonstrate that the hope of peace was not Utopian, Casartelli listed a number of events, under the title 'The Peace Movement', as signs that true progress had been made in the substitution of arbitration for war.[26] In the spirit of a European Catholic statesman, Casartelli reminded his readers of the Peace Conferences held at The Hague. From these, the Hague Tribunal had resulted, whose purpose it was to settle international disputes by peaceful means. Casartelli saw this as representing the 'higher tribunal' advocated by St Thomas Aquinas; the lack of which, according to Aquinas: 'was the cause of wars since States and rulers have no higher tribunal, from which they may receive decisions in matters of dispute.'[27] The Hague Tribunal potentially supplied the want, created by the breakup of Christendom and the subsequent loss of the Apostolic See, as the international court of arbitration: 'over and over again in the history of those times we find the Popes successfully acting as mediators and peacemakers.'[28] In the same vein, Casartelli referred to the attempts at closer and friendlier relations between Great Britain and Germany. National jealousy and dislike on the part of these two great nations had constituted one of the gravest menaces to international peace. Much had been done to obviate these dangers.[29] He considered it 'a mere justice' to recognise the large share which the German Emperor, William II had played in the maintenance of peace between Britain and Germany and Europe in general.[30]

The final part of the Pastoral Letter was devoted to 'The Duty of Catholics'. This duty consisted firstly in not standing aloof from the affairs of the world but to seek to become heralds of peace. Secondly, Casartelli repeated a previous plea for the necessity of Catholics to act beyond the interests of party politics:

> as citizens, each individual Catholic is entirely free to maintain such political views as appeal to his judgement. As Catholics, we are bound to judge all those higher interests which transcend mere Party from the standpoint of the teaching of the Church.[31]

In the context of the threat to peace, he warned his hearers about the need to avoid two extremes – excessive and unpatriotic anti-militarism, since the military profession was necessary, and an exaggerated and unhealthy militarism, since 'we are obliged to regard war as an evil to be avoided by all means in our power.'[32] Finally he encouraged his people to do all within their power and influence, by word or pen, to encourage peace and the elimination of war.

'Pax Christi' set out a summary of the arguments that Casartelli was to develop during the course of the forthcoming war. Repeatedly he urged that Britain had entered the war in order to pursue peace and that since she was not the aggressor, the war was therefore justified. He warned against the temptation of retribution and the dangers of unnecessary aggression; he continually called for prayers for peace and for the nation to turn away from the sinfulness that had warranted such an awful scourge. He believed profoundly in the unity of European culture. In the post-war period he supported the unfashionable cause of German-language teaching. In this way he continued to hold the balanced view of the German race which he had set out in 'Pax Christi':

From Casartelli's observations it may be concluded that his Pastoral Letter was well received:

> I was literally astonished at the response my Pastoral elicited even and perhaps chiefly in Germany. I received congratulations from societies and

organisations I had never heard of, both Catholic and non-Catholic. The Pastoral was translated into German and later into French. It was summarised and praised in very many newspapers and reviews.'[33]

It is significant that Casartelli's words were deemed worthy of translation by German authorities. One can conclude further that he enjoyed a certain regard among members of the German Church. Further evidence of the significance of the pastoral is the invitation he received to take part in the *Conference de la Ligue Internationale des Catholiques pour la Paix* to be held in Liège, on 10–14 August 1914.[34] No other English bishop had mentioned the threat to peace until war was declared in August 1914. Casartelli's awareness of the international situation and interest in wider European Church matters enabled him to take a lead among his episcopal brethren. The position he adopted in relation to other bishops is seen in his development of 'Pax Christi.'

DEVELOPMENT OF THEMES IN 'PAX CHRISTI'

On the day following the outbreak of war on 4 August 1914, Casartelli addressed the following measured response to the clergy of his diocese:

> In spite of the persevering and unwearied efforts of our Government on behalf of Peace, our Country has been forced into taking part in the deplorable War upon the Continent of Europe ... Encourage your flock to pray earnestly for the speedy return of Peace.[35]

Three days later he referred to the War as a 'dreadful scourge.'[36] This and the constant call for prayer[37] for peace were recurring themes in Casartelli's statements throughout the conflict.[38] As for the cause of the war, he discerned that 'the neglect of God and of his Divine Law is at the root of the evil that we now see rampant.'[39] The Lenten Pastoral Letters which he issued throughout the years 1915–1918 represented a series of repeated calls for penance in reparation for the evils of society which had merited such a dreadful scourge.[40] In the face of Britain's entry into the war, to exonerate her from any immediate cause, and no doubt to exhibit both loyalty and support of the Government's decision, he tried to reassure the people of the diocese by speaking of 'the conscientious satisfaction that we have been drawn into the great struggle through no desire of our own, through no lust for conquest or domination, but by a strict sense of duty, in the sacred cause of truth, justice, and loyalty to our sworn obligations, and the defence of the weak and oppressed.'[41] In Casartelli's own words the war was a 'crusade for right.'[42] It was so in a double sense. Firstly, it was a fight against the evils of militarism and therefore a national crusade. Secondly, it was a crusade against the personal evils that had corrupted society.

CASARTELLI AMONG HIS FELLOW BISHOPS

If we compare the number of pastoral letters, eight in total, that Casartelli wrote on the theological significance and the issues raised by the war, we find that he dedicated more attention in this regard than did the Archbishops of Westminster, Birmingham, and Liverpool. Where did he stand in this spectrum of Catholic episcopal reactions to the conflict? The evidence may be found in the Pastoral Letters of fellow bishops.

Archbishop Bourne mentioned the war in five of his pastorals, none of which was solely dedicated to the war. On the outbreak of war he called for prayers 'in time of war' and described the conflict as 'the greatest material evil' and a 'reminder of sin, for without the sin of individuals and of nations enmities and consequent hostilities would not exist.' [43] Significantly, he saw the war as justified and those who took part did so as though in 'a crusade.'[44]

Bourne recognised that 'God will surely give light and grace in proportion to [the] generosity' of those of other faiths who had enlisted with a less conscious offering of themselves than that displayed by Catholics.[45] Lack of consciousness was due to the former not having received the same religious formation. This attitude was redolent of the idea of martyrdom being a 'substitution' for baptism. The Bishop of Northampton, Frederick William Keating, openly espoused this idea in a letter to *The Tablet* in December 1914.[46] Moreover, there was a tendency in Bourne's patriotism to assign to the British Empire a divinely appointed rôle and mission.[47]

Casartelli never identified so strongly with England or the Empire as to see them in this light. Bourne's attitudes were closer to English sensibilities. After the war, he had a sharper eye for, and a more reconciliatory attitude, toward the 'signs of the times', especially when it came to accepting the rise of the Labour Party with its desire for social justice. However, Casartelli, unlike Bourne, was not given to patriotic outbursts. Thus, on the same day that Bourne was telling a parade of troops that there would be no question about whether the war was justified or not, Casartelli was attending a joint public meeting with the Mayor of Manchester where he advocated sympathetic treatment of the aliens living in Manchester and refraining from demonstrations against them.[48] Similarly, Casartelli remained unimpressed with Bourne's much publicised visit to the Western Front. He would have preferred the Cardinal to have remained at home and drawn up 'a statesman-like letter for us all to sign laying down for all men to know the principles on which we have our claims and our hostility to many clauses of the Fisher[49] [Education] Bill ... instead of donning a gas-helmet at the front.'[50]

What of the other bishops? The Archbishop of Birmingham[51] dedicated only two pastoral letters to the war. In 'Christian Patriotism' (Lent 1916) he wrote: 'Patriotism is part of our very religion. It is a duty which is second only to that which we owe to God Himself.'[52] Ilsley took the usual line of interpreting the war as a justified scourge which could have beneficent results by helping to reform the nation: 'If the war has come upon us to make us lay aside our sinful habits, the true way of ending the war is by ending our offences against God.'[53] Thomas Whiteside, the Archbishop of Liverpool,[54] in pastoral letters for Advent 1914 and Lent 1915, equally denounced pacifism and aggressive militarism[55] by demonstrating the case of the 'just war'. Bishop Hedley of Newport,[56] described by Casartelli as 'the doyen of our episcopal bench,'[57] spoke of the war as a universal chastisement: 'It is no matter that the innocent suffer with the guilty. It is intended that the guilty shall be awakened to their guilt, and the innocent shall be purified the more.'[58] He believed that if conscription became law, 'anyone who neglects to help when he can help, violates the cardinal precept of justice, and is, to a greater or lesser degree, guilty in the sight of God.'[59] Casartelli consulted Hedley before he made any statement on the moral duty of enlistment. Evidently then Casartelli did not differ radically from the rest of the bishops. Like their Anglican counterparts, the Catholic bishops hoped that out of the trials of war a more godly Church and a more just nation might arise.[60] However, unlike his counterparts, Casartelli showed signs of heart-searching and of wrestling with the ethical issues at stake. For example, on the occasion of a Zeppelin raid on the Lancashire town of Bolton he wrote to the rector Canon Holmes asking him

> to accept for your self and for your people the expression of my profound grief and heartfelt sympathy on the occasion of the hideous cruelty of the wicked raid which sent so many of your flock to a sudden death. We must all feel that those innocent victims of barbarity have laid down their lives for a sacred cause, like our heroes who have faced and met death in the field.[61]

On points where the conflict touched his own European roots, such as the burning of the library of Louvain, his *alma mater*, he experienced particular pain. On hearing the news he wrote, 'The most awful news yet received from the War: the German barbarians have *destroyed* Louvain and all its buildings ... It is a nightmare. Correspondents of the *Catholic Times* and *Manchester Guardian* called to ask me to give some statement to their paper on this diabolical outrage on humanity.'[62] The action was to him wanton vandalism against the epitome of Catholic learning and culture. Indeed, we can perhaps speak of the war with Germany as causing him 'intellectual pain' to a level near bereavement. Sensing the risk of Britain isolating itself from German scholarship, he insisted upon the necessity of not abandoning the learning of the German language; that really would be to allow the cultural and intellectual links to Europe die.

Casartelli's heart-searching was not only provoked by the actual trials of war. He believed it to be 'still more important to secure by all means in our power that the causes of such evils should be removed from our sick and degenerate Christendom and the world restored to a state of normal health.'[63] Those evils were represented by 'the substitution for the Charity of Jesus Christ of the anti-Christian principle of race hatred; the loss of respect for authority; the ravages of a false philosophy.'[64] The decadence of the world was further manifest in three areas that represented arenas where he had fought many battles – Socialism, Education as understood from only a secular basis, and the rôle of the Press. His concern was that 'the unbounded cult of only material welfare and prosperity in this life, with forgetfulness of the life to come, is really the root evil which has been fostered by various agencies, such as a godless education and an evil press.'[65]

Added to these ills was the increase in birth control and the class-war. All together they had 'for many long years merited God's chastisement.'[66] Such materialism had found 'its ultimate expression in all-absorbing aggressive militarism.'[67] This judgement, he characteristically extended to a diagnosis of the situation in Europe as a whole. Was it possible, he asked, to draw a distinction between Great Britain and Belgium on one side and Germany on the other in regard to the particular conflict in which they were engaged?[68] England and Belgium had not actually started the present war; nevertheless, it was impossible to deny that all countries shared in a corporate guilt of having rejected God.[69] So he asked: 'can we be surprised that a spiritually and morally decadent Europe should be smitten with a terrible chastisement'?[70] Could the horrors of the war, and in particular the invasion of Belgium, not be used to question the apparent failure of Christianity? No, for warfare was not only a chastisement of the guilty it was also a means of purification of the innocent.[71]

Casartelli's identification with Belgium and his beloved Louvain comes through in his wartime writings. To reinforce his argument, Casartelli cited Cardinal Mercier of Malines, and also the pastoral letter of the German Catholic bishops. Indeed, his pastoral letter of Lent 1915 to the Diocese of Salford was largely a summary of Mercier's own pastoral letter. Casartelli called attention to the fact that:

> nor does the Cardinal suggest that this neglect of Almighty God and consequent spread of evil principles was confined to the hostile nation at whose hands Belgium is suffering her martyrdom. No, he humbly admits that even his own people have merited the Divine chastisement that has fallen upon them, because they too have been tainted by the evil rampant in our decadent Christendom.[72]

It should also be realised, he pointed out, that the German bishops had 'spoken trumpet-tongued of their own people's share in the religious and moral corruption of the modern world.'[73] Britain was not free from similar guilt; 'we are bound to admit that, as a nation, in a greater or less degree ... we have merited our share of the scourge, our portion of the chastisement.'[74]

Casartelli thus found common ground between the bishops of England and Wales, Cardinal Mercier of Belgium, and to some degree the bishops of Germany, who agreed that the sins of 'the whole nation as a corporate entity ... call for general and corporate repentance and national acceptance of the scourge laid upon us by a justly offended God.'[75] This interpretation of the war as the means and an opportunity for the reform of the lives of individuals and the life of the nation allowed Casartelli and his fellow bishops to be patriotic, without going as far as Bourne in bellicosity. In this way they could offer both spiritual help and a plausible explanation of the terrible massacres that were being suffered by both sides.

LOYALTY AND THE CATHOLIC RESPONSE TO RECRUITMENT

The First World War and its 'rush to the colours' provided an opportunity for the Catholic community in England to prove its loyalty to the Crown and the Empire. Bishops and civic leaders with strong national sympathies held that their co-religionists had a sense of loyalty beyond the call of civic duty.[76] Thus Cardinal Bourne spoke of how such loyalty had helped remove the prejudice against Catholics and that they in turn, by sharing fully in the conflict, had overcome their former 'shyness and isolation.'[77] The Catholic Mayor of Manchester, Daniel McCabe, strongly encouraged recruitment. This earned him acclaim at the end of his mayoral year, at a thanksgiving service held at St Mary's Mulberry Street.[78]

Casartelli in a letter to his godson declared that: 'I cannot say that I regret or disapprove in any way of your joining the Forces in the Good Cause. But I am obliged to say plainly that you did very wrong in going off as you did without a word to your parents ... I hope you will do credit in every way – religiously, morally, professionally – to your holy Faith, to your home and to your upbringing ... Go on, do your duty, and get the V.C.'![79]

Again, when a nephew reached his 'military coming of age,' Casartelli and his sisters held a dinner party in honour of the occasion.[80] Thus in his public *persona* he was clearly as anxious as any other bishop to ensure that the Catholics under his care would do honour to their Faith by volunteering for the armed forces. He encouraged them to play their part in the 'crusade for right' and openly supported the efforts of Mayor McCabe:

One of the activities in which the Lord Mayor has done conspicuous good service for the common cause has been in encouraging and promoting the formation of several battalions of volunteers from the city and neighbourhood for service in defence of King and Country. We are glad to believe that our Catholic people have been in no way behind-hand in the generosity of their response to the appeal made to their loyal and public spirit in this all-important and even vital movement.[81]

However, Casartelli never addressed assembled troops nor recruitment meetings as Bourne and Whiteside did, and he exercised caution before offering an opinion on volunteering as a duty. He asked: 'Is the call [to arms] more than a matter of honour? Is it a matter of duty'?[82] Taking this issue of moral responsibility very seriously, he consulted the opinions of other bishops before giving his own answer. Bishops Hedley, Keating, and Singleton, were all in favour of it being a moral duty, and Casartelli duly published their opinions in the January 1915 edition of the *Catholic Federationist*. Hedley held that: 'A good Catholic is therefore bound to help and support the civil state, be it kingdom, empire, or republic ... The great duty that everyone owes to the country when the country is at war, is to help it to success and victory'.[83]

Moreover, Hedley said that 'anyone who neglects to help when he can help, violates the cardinal precept of Justice, and is, to a greater or lesser degree, guilty in the light of God.'[84] Casartelli remained hesitant, giving no clear personal judgement. He simply presented what the other bishops had said for 'the careful and serious attention of those young men who are not otherwise disqualified or impeded from following the example of the many thousands who have already gone forth to fulfil their duty,' and listed extenuating circumstances, such as certain types of work necessary for the 'war effort;' dependent families, education and care of the sick.[85] The public duties of the Diocese remained important, nevertheless. Rectors of missions were asked to send in to Bishop's House details of the number of men from their respective parishes in order to ascertain how many were serving in the ranks, and a register of names was to be kept in each parish.[86] In the case of those rectors who had not replied to the request, Casartelli rather sternly noted:

I am greatly surprised that, in spite of two requests, there are still a number of rectors who have not sent in their 'Roll of Honour' of men who have joined the colours ... The delay is very unfair to the Diocese, as it prevents one from publishing the complete lists of our gallant men and youths who have so volunteered.[87]

Providing a list of names of volunteers was important as a factual way of stating the loyalty of Roman Catholics during the war.

By the time Casartelli issued his letter *Ad Clerum*, on 18 December 1914, the number of Catholics who had enlisted had already reached 12, 585 in the 97 missions (out of a total of 158) which had replied to his appeal for statistics to be included in the Diocesan Almanac. Thus he felt he had 'good reason to think that when the complete statistics are available they will do credit to the patriotism and public spirit of our men and youths.'[88] We may detect here some element of the self-congratulatory propaganda which other religious bodies indulged in. As Alan Wilkinson puts it: 'in the autumn of 1914, Welsh Baptists were annoyed by Anglican claims that most of the recruits were coming from the Established Church. The Baptists refuted such claims, and pointed proudly to the numbers of Nonconformists who were enlisting.'[89] Somewhat similarly, by January 1915, Casartelli observed, 'If it were possible to ascertain the number ... of military age, our proportion would be found to be very large, probably much larger than of any other section of the community.'[90] By July 1915, he was able to write: 'at least some 25, 000 of our Diocese have gallantly answered the call of duty.'[91]

To some Catholic leaders, such as Bishop Cowgill of Leeds, the contribution of Catholics to the war effort was a way of demonstrating loyalty and overcoming the latent anti-Catholic prejudice still lurking in early twentieth-century England.[92] In comparison, Casartelli's patriotism was measured. We have noted already the caution with which he dealt with the question of volunteering as a duty. On the other hand there is no evidence of Casartelli himself defending conscientious objection or pacifism; he supported the posting of 'Rolls of Honour' in churches. When the Organising Secretary of the Catholic Federation, T. F. Burns, stated in its monthly newspaper that the Catholic population of Manchester and Salford 'has not provided a single conscientious objector, while it has sent a full quota to the Front',[93] he did so with the tacit approval of Casartelli, who closely scrutinised its contents. Certainly he was not always happy with the format of the *Catholic Federationist*, nor of the quality of what it contained;[94] nonetheless on the sensitive issue of volunteering he seemed comfortable in taking a low profile and letting others voice their opinions whilst he himself remained silent. In this, he stood in marked contrast to colleagues such as George Ambrose Burton, the Bishop of Clifton, who spoke in 1915 of 'the Prussians as a blonde beast' and described 'a certain body of men going about the country, or writing, and spouting' who wanted peace at any price, as 'peace cranks.'[95] Simultaneously, Archbishop Bourne felt no need to issue an appeal to encourage Catholics to volunteer, believing that 'the inspiration of their own conscience, and their love of country and hatred of oppression have made a wholly sufficing appeal.'[96]

The war offered other opportunities for Catholics to show their loyalty.

They took part in national days of intercession instigated by the King.[97] They co-operated with the observance of the 'black-out'; all evening services were brought forward from 6.30p.m. to 3.30p.m. In those churches where there was insufficient means to ensure that no light from within was visible on the outside, divine service was suspended.[98] The people of the diocese, in line with the King's appeal, were encouraged to limit their consumption of foodstuffs.[99] Thus, the years from 1914–1918 proved to be a time when Catholics entered more fully into national life, and when latent prejudices lessened.

In spite of the demonstration of patriotism, once the war was over and peace declared, pre-war conditions of marginality resumed. The causes were largely internal. Thus Catholic ex-servicemen were prohibited from attending Armistice Day Services; an *Ad Clerum* for January 1922 carried the following 'reminder':

> Kindly urge all ex-Service men that they should attend [the] service [in their local Catholic church] and remind them that it is not lawful to attend joint services with those of other religions. In other places [i.e. not in the Manchester district] where Catholics are asked to participate in joint services, a Catholic service should be arranged for the same hour.[100]

The *Catholic Herald* criticised the Cenotaph in Whitehall as 'nothing more or less than a pagan memorial which was a disgrace in a so-called Christian land at which Atheist, Mohammedan, Buddhist, Jew, men of any religion or none could offer homage, as if God and his Christ were mere superstition.'[101] Such utterances were not simply an attempt by the Church to make veterans see themselves as Catholics first and as veterans second, as Gregory has suggested.[102] Rather, the root of the prohibition was the theological problem of Catholics attending and actively taking part in a religious service that was not Catholic. The internal principles set by Canon Law prohibited this – but the consequences could easily be read as a snub to servicemen of other denominations. Some historians have failed to appreciate how fundamental this point was. Thus Aspden accuses Casartelli of snubbing Bishop Knox of Manchester when the latter invited him to share a public platform against immorality.[103] A close reading of the letter quoted by Aspden reveals that Casartelli actually refused to take part, (only after consulting some of his clergy) because 'a mixed assembly of various denominations [would] almost certainly lead to divergence of opinion and expression,' which 'would weaken the good effects of our co-operation.'[104] No social discourtesy was intended: the issue was purely one of doctrinal consistency. Thus Casartelli thanked the Bishop for his 'kind invitation' and expressed his 'full and warm sympathy' for the objects of the meeting. But in support, he chose to offer a series of sermons to be preached in his own Salford Cathedral on similar themes. In this way, Catholic theological integrity would be maintained, while showing willingness to use 'his pen or voice in the common cause, after hearing or reading the resolutions of your [the Bishop's] meeting.' Casartelli, ever cautious, was not willing to stray away from the rigid canonical line, but with equal care he avoided 'snubbing' the Bishop of Manchester.

Practical evidence of Casartelli's concern to preserve the integrity of Catholicism in wartime is widespread. Thus to help in caring for the spiritual needs of Catholic soldiers, he took advantage of an Army Council Instruction[105] that made provision for any conscripted male of Irish nationality to be asked if he wished to join an Irish regiment. This was desirable because 'Catholic lads should, as far as possible, be attached to regiments which are largely, or in some cases, predominantly Catholic, as is the case in the various Irish regiments.'[106] The benefits to be gained from enlisting in the Irish regiments were the 'advantage of Catholic comrades and better facilities for [their] religious duties' since these regiments had a higher proportion of Catholic chaplains.[107] Casartelli also sought to maintain a good level of support by Catholic forces chaplains. Eventually, the diocese provided in total 29 chaplains, 7 of whom were awarded the Military Cross.[108] To meet the pressing need, Casartelli on occasions sought the early ordination to the priesthood of men who were already deacons; this enabled others involved in parish work to volunteer as chaplains.[109] This policy was not in conflict with his general caution over the call to volunteer for military service. In a letter to letter to the President of Ushaw College, he wrote:

> Having had applications for direction from several of my students I think it desirable to ask you to inform all my subjects that, after careful thought and discussion, I have come to the conclusion that all under philosophy who are of military age should offer their services to the country at once without waiting for compunction to be applied.[110]

Moreover, this would result in their becoming non-combative aides, not active soldiers. In later correspondence, Casartelli is open about this point: 'It is generally felt that those below philosophy would do best to volunteer at once and so get better choice (i.e. non-combatant service). Otherwise they will be taken without choice left.'[111] Casartelli was supportive of the priests who volunteered as army chaplains.[112]

Further concern with the coherence of Catholics when at war, is evident in the support given to the work of the chaplains by the Catholic Women's League, which organised canteens, popularly called 'Catholic Huts'. These were used as recreation centres and as temporary chaplaincies. Casartelli encouraged the people of his diocese to be generous in their response to the appeal for financial help for these 'huts'. He thought it 'highly desirable that our Catholic men should have their own Catholic Huts. It is good for them spiritually and morally that they should associate together.'[113]

BENEDICT XV AND THE WAR

In face of the general patriotism of the Roman Catholic community and its eager expression by laity and bishops, the position taken by Pope Benedict XV caused a degree of embarrassment, since he was criticised by sections of English society, including the Church of England, for not coming down on the side of Great Britain and her allies.[114] This criticism was an issue which the Catholic Church in England had to face in order to demonstrate both solidarity with the Papacy and at the same time show themselves to be as patriotic as any other group. This must have caused the hierarchy some difficulty if, as John F. Pollard has said, 'Under Benedict and Gasparri the Vatican was, not ... a totally disinterested observer during the First World War.'[115] Evidence of a pro-German Stance was obvious to Cardinal Aidan Gasquet and no doubt this would have been fed back to his colleagues in England.[116] Cardinal Mercier, Casartelli's contemporary and friend at Louvain and Primate of Belgium, was not nearly so impartial as Benedict XV.[117]

Casartelli's support for the Pope was clear from the beginning, and continued throughout the war. In Advent 1914, he wrote: 'it is our duty to re-echo the exhortations of the Apostolic See and bid you ... lift up your hands and voices to the throne of God's mercy.'[118] When Benedict's first encyclical letter appeared,[119] it was described by the Press as 'mere repetition of pious platitudes and failed to come to grips with the urgent problems of the moment.'[120] The major cause of this overtly nationalistic criticism was Benedict's apparent failure to condemn the crimes committed by the German army. Casartelli defended the Pope: such critics misapprehended the position of the Holy See.[121] 'As Supreme Pontiff, [he] has laid down in unmistakable terms those great fundamental principles of the Christian law, of which he is the authoritative exponent to the world ... he leaves the application of those principles to the conscience of nations and individuals.'[122] Further, to fend off its critics, Casartelli gave a detailed elucidation of the arguments of the encyclical.

The Vicar of Christ had taught that there are two camps, each flying its own standard: one the standard of Love, the other the standard of Hatred. Therefore his readers were faced with a serious question: 'do you realise the full force of this fundamental distinction? In order to do so you have only to ask on which side of the present international conflict has the standard of Hate been raised?'[123] It was in Germany that the 'Hate Hymn of England' was being sung. So – Casartelli felt – 'no need to labour the conclusion. On which side of the battlefield floats the standard erected in the name of his Master, by Pope Benedict XV?'[124] Benedict's pronouncements on the war, spoken as the 'common father of all,' were a voice and an aspiration with which Casartelli strongly identified.

Casartelli's own position as a Catholic internationalist was further defined as the war proceeded. When the Bryce Report[125] on German atrocities was published in May 1915, the Archbishop of Canterbury accepted it unquestioningly.[126] By contrast Casartelli's letter of the following month, 'To the Clergy and Faithful of the Diocese', made no mention of it; instead, he pointedly cited the Pope's letter to the Cardinal Dean of the Sacred College, dated 23 May 1915, in which Benedict XV 'in no uncertain terms condemns the fact that 'both on sea and land methods of attack contrary to both the laws of humanity and to international law' are being resorted to.'[127] Casartelli clearly indicated that he agreed with the position of the Pope, who was appalled by the sinking of the Lusitania on 7 May 1915. In the light of such action Casartelli invited the laity and clergy of the diocese to take part in a 'strict ecclesiastical fast'. But he was simultaneously careful to avoid sanctioning the stance of Germany. Although Casartelli encouraged the Catholic Federation to support the Pope, he was watchful. To the Organising Secretary, T. F. Burns, he wrote:

> I am told that the *Daily Dispatch* … contained a virulent and calumnious attack on Pope Benedict XV accusing him of neo-Germanism, asserting that he justified the sinking of the 'Lusitania', etc. etc. If so, the matter is urgent and ought to be taken up at once in the columns of the *Catholic Federationist* as well as in the *Daily Dispatch* itself.[128]

When Benedict issued his Peace Note[129] in August 1917 Casartelli was faced with a dilemma. Here the Pope moved from general principles to more concrete and practical proposals for the cessation of war, such as the establishment of arbitration, disarmament, and the diminution of arms. It was this, more than any previous pronouncements by the Pope, which caused the greatest difficulty for Catholics and drew the most criticism. An editorial in *The Tablet* respectfully disagreed with the sentiments of the Peace Note: 'We conclude therefore by expressing our confident belief that the hopes of the Holy Father are identical with the aims of the Allies. But while in Rome the prospects of the struggle seem doubtful and uncertain, here the confidence in victory was never so high or so robust. And London is nearer to the War.'[130] The *Tablet* arrived at this conclusion after assuming the Peace Note to be based upon the impossibility of an Allied victory; to this the editorial replied – 'that opinion is not shared by the British people, and certainly not by anyone concerned with this journal.'[131] The *Manchester Guardian* described the Note as a 'well-meaning but highly ineffective document' and further a 'singularly flabby, uninspiring, and unilluminated document.'[132]

Casartelli felt it his duty to abandon his aversion to taking part in newspaper controversy and to protest publicly in the *Manchester Guardian* at this dismissal of Benedict's efforts and to correct the newspaper's assertion when it claimed 'Austro-German influences to have been behind the Pope's appeal.'[133] What is most unusual about Casartelli's letter is the recognition that 'it is quite open for us, even for Catholics, to maintain that the Pope's proposals are inadequate, or unacceptable as being too favourable to our adversaries.'[134] This is the only instance when he publicly admitted to the possibility of a legitimate difference of opinion between the Pope and the rest of the Church. Theologically he must have accepted this because infallibility was restricted to matters of faith and morals. Nevertheless, given Casartelli's strong desire for unity of opinion and approach, this marks a radical digression from his usual stance *vis-à-vis* Church authority. Neither Casartelli nor any English bishop made reference to the Peace Note in a pastoral letter or letter *ad clerum*. Casartelli was not alone in interpreting the Note as he did. The Bishop of Northampton wrote:

> The words of His Holiness were addressed, not to the Church, but to the secular powers. They were not to be regarded as a doctrinal exposition, but as a diplomatic effort. An English Catholic, therefore, was free to form his own opinion without any violation of his obedience.[135]

THE WAR AND A RELIGIOUS REVIVAL

Casartelli along with other Church leaders believed that if heed were paid to the scourge of war, then a religious revival would follow and the nation would be more just. He wrote:

> But there is this hope: that the very magnitude and horror of the scourge may turn men's minds and hearts back to God; and what is more, that the more terrible this War be and the more widespread the misery and desolation it may cause, the greater will be the reaction when it shall please God to bring it to an end, and the more powerful, the more irresistible, the movement in favour of the abolition of war and the substitution of arbitration.[136]

Evidence and examples of such a revival of war as a salutary chastisement could be seen in the way that France had undergone a revival of faith,[137] and in the 'outpouring of truly Christian charity' of the people of Salford Diocese in their response to the appeal for help with the Belgian refugees and the

National Distress Fund.[138] There was particular interest in such a revival in France. By the expulsion of religious teaching from schools and greater State control of the Church in an attempt to create a purely secular environment, Casartelli had feared France was running the risk of becoming godless. It was therefore important for him to show that such evil was being overcome thanks to the scourge of war.

In March 1916 the *Manchester Guardian* reported Casartelli as claiming that: 'One of the outstanding features of the war has been the large number of conversions among both officers and men in the various armies of those outside the pale of the Catholic faith to the Catholic Church, and also conversions of either lapsed Catholics who had in many cases abandoned for years the practice of their faith or else of others who had been professedly anti-Christian or anti-clerical.'[139]

The war, he claimed, had taught people the virtue of unselfishness, as could be seen in the response to volunteer to help with the Red Cross and munitions work. Casartelli gave the specific example of the 'womankind of the nation' … 'especially in the well-to-do and leisured classes' who once were leading 'practically selfish lives … And now, with rare exceptions they are devoting their time, their energy and their physical and mental powers to unselfish work for their country.'[140]

Other Catholic bishops spoke in a similar vein to Casartelli. The Archbishop of Liverpool claimed that church attendance had increased by 200,000 and the number of communicants had risen by 390,000.[141] The Archbishop of Birmingham noted that 'reports from the front have made known that large numbers of men are now thinking deeply of religious questions who, before the war, had never given much heed to such questions.'[142] Bourne's observations were more practical and therefore possibly more valid. He noted how the circumstances of the war had brought many people into contact with the Catholic Church and that certain Catholic practices had been adopted, for example the carrying of rosaries, wayside crosses, prayers for the dead. At another level, and in the post war period, there was the desire for social reform which echoed Catholic social doctrine: the value of the human person, human rights and the need for brotherhood.[143]

No doubt there were many cases of individuals coming to a greater spiritual awareness, but there are grounds for questioning the occurrence of a general religious revival.[144] In 1919 *The Army and Religion* asked three basic questions: What are the men thinking about Religion, Morality, and Society? Has the war made men more open to a religious appeal or has it created new difficulties for belief? What proportion of the men are vitally connected to any of the Churches, and what do they think of the Churches? To this we may add the Preface of Plater's *Catholic Soldiers*[145] which asked: How has the religion of Catholic soldiers in the British Empire stood the test of the war? These contemporary documents, although they generally spoke well of soldiers' faith, contained elements that must have given reason for concern. For example, one chaplain replied: 'A solid, practical Catholic before the war became a very earnest one during it ... the habitually neglectful Catholic in peace time did not improve at the front ... neglectful Catholics ... drifted rather than went wrong.'[146]

Despite some evidence of a revival of faith and morals Casartelli's general argument is also diminished by the fact that he had to remonstrate with his people for the increase in drunkenness and licentious behaviour. The war may have caused an increase in Church membership but it had also broken down many taboos and social mores, a fact to which Casartelli himself was not oblivious.[147] In retrospect, we may best concur with Wilkinson, who notes that, 'It was widely asserted by churchmen that the war would stem the tide of secularism and revive religion by recovering the spirit of self-denial and self-sacrifice and by facing people with the ultimate reality of death ... But no religious revival occurred.'[148]

PASTORAL ISSUES OF THE WAR

One of the important issues that the Salford diocese had to face was the need for assistance to the great number of Belgian refugees who were flooding into the area.[149] To assist them spiritually, Casartelli appointed two priests to act as chaplains.[150] He himself became a patron of the Belgian Refugees Committee, along with the Anglican Bishop of Manchester.[151] He visited those refugees who had been hospitalised and also, according to a rather telling phrase in his diary, held an 'at Home' at Bishop's House, Salford, for Belgian refugees of [a] better class'.[152]

The upheaval of war very soon effected changes in the consumption of alcohol and the way people viewed morality, particularly sexual mores.[153] Casartelli in his pastoral letter for Advent 1915, 'Dark Days', set himself in the role of prophet, criticising the root evils whereby mankind had turned away from God.[154] The increase in drunkenness was not restricted to men alone; according to reports Casartelli had received from the rectors in some of the larger towns, it was actually worse among women.[155] The greatest moral horror was, however, artificial birth control, or, as it was termed, 'race suicide'. Casartelli agreed with the Anglican Bishop of Manchester (Dr Knox) when the latter spoke of 'the great national sins of impurity and of race suicide.'[156]

Casartelli claimed that the Catholic body had, on the whole, so far been saved from adverse effects of the decline in moral standards. This was due to the Sacraments and the religious education received in schools at an early age. Nonetheless, what Casartelli called 'national sins' were capable of contaminating the whole of society including the Catholic body. The call for a general and corporate repentance was imperative before even worse scourges befell the nation.[157] The moral decline was aided and abetted by what he termed 'secret forces' i. e. 'godless education', and an 'evil press'.

Young people were exposed to moral danger through myriad forms of entertainment and novelties such as immoral literature, papers, pictures, 'suggestive films'; as a result of 'contamination of immoral sources', Casartelli wrote, 'the intercourse between the sexes is freeing itself from the prudent restraints and safeguards of a preceding generation.'[158]

As to the question of fatalities suffered by countless servicemen, Casartelli dedicated his Lenten pastoral letter for 1917 to the theme of death.[159] Here he presented death as 'God's messenger', recalling Mankind from sin and to preparation for the account to be given at life's end. One good effect of the scourge of war had been the enabling of 'thousand and tens of thousands' of people, especially young men, to meet their death in a 'state of grace, and so [to] have saved their immortal souls, who quite possibly, had they lived as in times of peace and died under other circumstances, might not have secured their eternal salvation.'[160] In response to the potential impending danger of death, membership of the 'Association of a Happy Death' was encouraged.[161] In his chapter, 'Death, Bereavement, and the Supernatural', Wilkinson writes, 'The pressures of bereavement drove some mourners to spiritualism, and seances were resorted to by an increasing number of people.'[162] In February 1919, Casartelli invited Bernard Vaughan SJ to deliver a public lecture at the Free Trade Hall, Manchester, on the theme 'The Menace of Spiritualism', which he, Casartelli, considered to be 'surely one of the most burning questions of the day'.[163]

In the matter of praying for the dead, Casartelli saw the resurgence of this tradition among non-Catholics as a further example of how God was using the war 'to draw men's minds and hearts back to the Truth and the traditional teachings of the Church.'[164] Wilkinson notes that 'In 1914 public prayer for the dead was uncommon in the Church of England; by the end of the war it had become widespread ... bereavement was sweeping away the latent Protestantism of the English people in this matter.'[165] When two Anglican archbishops issued prayers for the dead, the Bishop of Manchester forbade their use; however, the Dean of Manchester, Bishop Welldon, defied the ban and continued to use the prayers.[166] Casartelli quoted the opinion of 'Artifex',[167] who had written in the *Manchester Guardian*,

> When a mother has prayed morning and evening, and perhaps many
> times a day, for a quarter-of-a century for her boy, from the first moment
> when he lay on her breast till she heard of his death, can religion really bid

her take his name out of her prayers to his Father and Son? I cannot think so.'

On the 5 August 1915, to mark the first anniversary of the outbreak of war, Casartelli sang Pontifical High Mass at the Cathedral in Salford for the deceased soldiers and sailors of the diocese. In instigating this event and inviting rectors to send the names of the fallen from their respective missions, to be hung by the catafalque, Casartelli showed his feelings and understanding of the war that had been entered 'under the compelling sense of an obligation of right and justice.'[168] 25,000 men of the diocese 'have gallantly answered the call of duty [and] have gone to take their share in this great crusade for the rights of humanity and the principles of Christianity and the Divine Law.'[169] The parents and relatives of the deceased were invited to be present.

CASARTELLI'S ATTITUDE TO GERMANY DURING THE WAR

As we have seen, not only was Casartelli not a jingoist, he carefully resisted a narrowly nationalistic attitude. His cultural outlook we may describe as principled, intellectual Catholic internationalism. He strongly opposed the widespread abandonment of the teaching of German in schools as a consequence of the war, as 'dangerous' and 'suicidal.' Undoubtedly, at the moment, it was 'natural that people should abhor everything savouring of Teutonism, and that the very name 'German' should stink in their nostrils. But it is a fatal mistake to imagine that therefore we should give up the knowledge of the language.'[170] There was a practical, as well as a religious, basis to Casartelli's internationalism. Knowledge of the German language would better equip the country to stand against German influence in the political, commercial, and social order, he argued. 'The first step to conquer a people' was to learn its language.'[171] Here the advocate of commercial education spoke: languages would be especially important in the field of commerce – 'The Teutons filched many fields of trade from ourselves because their commercial agents were masters of (the) languages ... when too often our representatives were handicapped by the want of such knowledge.'[172] Casartelli hoped that *The Tablet* would support him in his attitude to the learning of German, but in this instance his hope was in vain. Writing to the Editor, J. S. Milburn, about another matter, he concluded:

> I hope you won't treat this matter with the contempt with which you treated my 'Message' in the *Catholic Federationist* on the study of German, of which I took the trouble to send you an advanced proof and of which the *Tablet* never condescended to take the least notice, – though the question in my opinion is an urgent one.[173]

Only rarely was Casartelli guilty of bellicosity, and any mention of the war was a rare occurrence in his diaries. Two exceptions were: 'Good News! The "Emden" sunk and the "Königsberg?"'[174] The second was: 'Splendid news of naval victory at Falkland Islands!'[175] Such outbursts, although rare indeed even in private, never showed themselves in the public domain. He used the pages of the *Catholic Federationist* to condemn the glorification of war, especially from church pulpits, 'I have read reports in the newspapers of sermons – delivered not only in non-Catholic, but also in Catholic pulpits – that have given me (and others) the impression of a glorification of war in itself, as something almost commendable for its own sake. Probably the preachers hardly meant that, but it is unfortunate that the impression should be caused.'[176]

However, as prophet of internationalism, he received little honour at home. Shortly after the publication of this letter, Alderman McCabe,[177] in a speech given at a garden party, was reported as having said, 'We have heard a great deal too much from the pulpits of the country and from the public platforms about the virtues of the Germans, We have heard a great deal about the Germans being our cousins in blood and our co-religionists ... I think there will be a different mind in this country in future.'[178] Since Casartelli regarded McCabe as the model Catholic layman, there is little reason to conclude that the Mayor's words were aimed directly at the Bishop of Salford. However, it is interesting that McCabe should be so forthright. This was clearly an implied criticism of some of the Catholic clergy.[179]

As in so many other ways Casartelli is to be found occupying the middle ground in episcopal opinion. He did not distinguish himself by his attitude toward Britain's enemies. He avoided the extreme language of the Bishop of Clifton who, as we have seen, spoke of Germans as the 'blonde beast,' and how Britain was 'warring against the unspeakable Turk ... who never had any business to be in Europe, who can have no part in its creed, or its civilisation, or polity, since the very principle of their existence pledges them to barbarism.'[180] The bishop finished his tirade by concluding: 'the time seems to have at last come when the Turks ... are to be expelled from Europe.' Casartelli referred to the Turks as the 'hereditary foe' of Christianity.[181] This gave certain weight to the idea that the then present conflict was also a crusade as Christian forces were once again engaged against their ancient foe.

In no public statement does Casartelli mention praying for the dead of all armies. Throughout the war years only one reference was made to such a gesture. The bishop in question was Francis Mostyn, the Bishop of Menevia.[182]

CONCLUSION

Casartelli pre-empted his fellow bishops' attitude to war and peace by his pastoral letter of Lent 1914, 'Pax Christi'. In doing so, he might be compared favourably with some of the Anglican bishops who, in pre-war days, had visited Germany in order to foster greater mutual understanding and tolerance between the two countries.

Another way in which Casartelli's stance was comparable to that of the Anglican bishops was the way in which he saw war with Germany as a cultural disaster in terms of the loss of scholarship, technical ability, and 'know how.' It was for this reason that he spoke out about the ever-greater need to learn German. The loss of the Louvain University Library represented for him a real 'intellectual bereavement.' The invasion of Belgium was, furthermore, not just the violation of his spiritual home but the attempted destruction of 'the ideal Catholic State' and thus an attack on what he held so dear.[183] In a revealing phrase, he wrote that here the invasion had reached its depth. 'The foulest of all the outrages which have marked the invasion has been the infamous destruction of Belgium's University city, the intellectual HQ, we may say without exaggeration, of Catholicism in Europe.'[184]

Throughout the duration of the war Casartelli repeatedly described the war as a scourge. This was essentially a brave stance, because it avoided the temptation to court popularity by adopting a more bellicose and jingoistic approach as adopted by some other Church leaders. We may ask whether, by this language, was Casartelli spiritually idealising the war? The title of one of his pastorals, 'Sursum Corda', reminds the reader of the idea of sacrifice and a basically hopeful attitude. However, nowhere in his letters to the people of the diocese did he mention the Suffering Christ who had known the pain of suffering and death. This task was effectively left to poets such as Siegfried Sassoon and Wilfrid Owen. However, in Casartelli's defence it must be said that never before had there been such mass destruction of human life by such effective weapons. The language he relied upon was taken from the Church's Tradition and liturgies that long pre-dated the horrors of the Somme and Passchendaele. There was not yet an adequate theological language to symbolise the appalling experiences encountered.

As a war time leader, Casartelli presented himself, albeit in a non-self-conscious way, in the role of the prophet:

> The mission of the prophets ... was to recall both the chosen people and their oppressors ... to the law of duty; they invariably declared to them they would find in ruin and bloodshed both their chastisement and the principle of their regeneration.[185]

To what degree his people found his pastorals consoling is open to question. The sheer carnage of the battles, such as the Somme, and the resulting suffering, bereavement and misery would surely have reduced the effect of what he had to say about war as a scourge. Casartelli had found his rôle as Prefect of Studies at St Bede's an ordeal; the task of being a leader during wartime must have been agony. He responded in the best way he could, and his actions stand well in comparison with other bishops. The peace Casartelli longed for would be achieved not only by the obvious cessation of hostilities, but also by a return to the *status quo*, for he was conservative by nature. He could not see the post-war social upheaval, with its profound social questioning and the rise of the Labour Party, in the positive light with which Bourne saw them in his pastoral letter of 1917 'The Nation's Crisis.' After the war Casartelli was a tired man, and the burden of the episcopate was ever increasing as legislation on education once again came to be a major issue of the day.

Chapter Seven

Casartelli's Episcopal *Praxis* in relation to Questions of Church and Society

From the beginning of his episcopate, Casartelli endeavoured to instil into the hearts and minds of the people of his diocese a greater awareness of their spiritual and temporal citizenship. As we have seen, during the Great War, he readily seized the opportunity to demonstrate how the Catholic community was fulfilling its temporal duty with patriotism and unalloyed citizenship.[1] Casartelli did not see the political and civic liberties enjoyed by Catholics in terms of a privilege; they were rather rights owed to every citizen and as such carried with them 'a corresponding duty of exercising them for the commonweal.'[2] Good citizenship was like charity:

> If it begins at home, [it] does not end at home. It should go forth to all the interests of the commonwealth of which we are part. Apart from mere party politics, there are vast fields of action for the general good, in matters social, municipal, philanthropic, educational, artistic, literary, in which we may exercise the powers we enjoy.[3]

In his first pastoral letter, 'The Signs of the Times', Casartelli encouraged his co-religionists to take an active part in a wide compass of committees that served the public good in various ways. These included city, borough, urban, and parish councils, as well as boards of guardians, and education and hospital committees. Other bodies on which Catholics might exercise their citizenship were those governing museums, libraries, and art galleries.[4] It was essentially an appeal to a middle-class audience and the assumption made, unconsciously, by Casartelli was that those to whom the pastoral letter was addressed were literate. Nevertheless, this should not detract from the fact that it had a potentially wider appeal. For example, it encouraged efforts to be made in aid of the foreign missions. In calling for 'lessons in citizenship' to be given to young people, Casartelli's exhortation carries a contemporary ring: 'It would perhaps be well if during the education of our youth of both sexes some effort were made to direct attention to their social and civic responsibilities, and so prepare them for the service they may render later on in life.'[5]

This evident desire for the Catholic community to adapt to and support the ethos of the country was apparent in a contemporary article by Frances Zanetti, who made still more explicit Casartelli's wish that Catholics be good citizens by asking: 'why seek suffrages as Catholics rather than as citizens concerned in the general welfare? ... We should make up our minds to be citizens, associating ourselves with every movement for the improvement of social conditions, not restricting our attention purely to Catholic affairs.'[6]

It has been shown already that the temporal and the spiritual spheres of human life were fundamental in shaping Casartelli's theology and his understanding of man as God's creation. At the root of his thinking, linking together the eternal and the temporal, was an understanding of human nature that was positive rather than pessimistic:

> There is a wondrous creature of God, who stands midway between the spiritual world and the material world. This creature is Man. Man is most justly defined as a spirit or soul endowed with a material body; and the complete man consists of the two in intimate and necessary union.[7]

The practical implications of this belief, as seen in Casartelli's response to the Education Bills, Socialism, and the rise of the Labour Party, are the subject of this and the following chapter. His belief in the eternal world was the foundation of his philosophy of education, which saw education as the development of the whole person, body and soul. In the field of education, the temporal and spiritual converged. It is therefore a perfect vantage point from which to discern Casartelli's commitment to both spheres.

It is not surprising that education was a key issue in Casartelli's episcopate. As Kester Aspden puts it: 'the first decade of the century saw the bishops above all concerned with the maintenance and defence of the Catholic schools. Indeed, throughout the period under consideration [1903 – 1935] the schools question constituted the single most important public issue for Catholics.'[8] Casartelli was more than a mere defender of Catholic schools. As a teacher and writer on commercial education he had shown himself to be an enlightened pioneer. As an educationalist, particularly on the University Question, his ideas were advanced. Spending the whole of his earlier adult life at St Bede's College had given him an invaluable experience of the problems and concerns of educational establishments.

Just as he had wanted Catholics to support the 'war effort,' so he was no less eager that they support developments in education. He perceived that 'the chief work which lies to the hand of the Catholic Church in this country will for a long time be that of Education.'[9] Therefore he encouraged Catholics to 'feel a lively and practical interest in the whole question ... and strive to do our share in perfecting our national systems which are so necessary for the well-being of the empire to which we belong.'[10] Part of the 'perfecting of [the] national system' was the safeguarding and expansion of Catholic education because this represented a positive contribution to the nation's educational system in general. Casartelli believed that the substitution of the Cowper-Temple model in place of Catholic denominational education would be a disservice to the country.[11] However, expansion of school provision was a difficult task. In 1911 Casartelli reported that, with the exception of Manchester, not one of the large industrial centres within the diocese possessed a secondary school for boys; on the other hand the diocese 'was fairly well off as regards secondary schools for girls' run by orders of nuns.[12] The major problem was shortage of funds to build new schools. Part of the solution he saw as coming from teaching orders of religious brothers establishing schools within the diocese. In 1921, with the promise of the Salesians opening a secondary school within the diocese for boys, Casartelli felt sufficiently confident to write: 'I see a bright outlook for the Secondary Education of Boys in Britain.'[13] By the time of Casartelli's death, there had been established four new secondary schools for boys: Blackburn (Marist); Pendleton (de la Salle); Bolton (Salesian); St Gregory's, Manchester; and one for girls: Accrington (Sisters of Mercy).

When matters political were intrinsically linked to the teaching of the Church, i.e. 'mixed-questions,' Casartelli believed that Catholics ought to put to one side personal political preferences, loyalty to party, and nationalist sympathies, and act as members of the Church. This was easier to hold in theory than it was to put into effect. The strength of feeling of Irish Nationalism within the diocese of Salford clashed with Casartelli's principle of how Catholics ought to adopt a stance of 'un-political politics.' During the elections of 1908 and 1910, Irish Catholic voters found the Liberal Party more acceptable because of its support for Home Rule for Ireland. Yet the Liberals failed to support Church schools. For the Conservative Party the reverse was true. In fact, Casartelli's attempts at promoting unity through the advocacy of 'un-political politics' aggravated the division between the United Irish League[14] and the Catholic Federation. The irony is that the latter was meant to unite Catholics and so overcome political differences on mixed-questions.

The question of education and denominational schools reflected Casartelli's relations with Francis Bourne, the Archbishop of Westminster. For instance, Casartelli viewed with foreboding the encroachment of the nascent Labour Party upon the field of education by its advocacy of a secular educational curriculum. He was also dissatisfied with the Liberal Party because of their stance on denominational schools. During the course of the long campaign to defend Church schools, he had begun to grow dissatisfied with Bourne's style of leadership. At times this disagreement put the two men at odds with each other. As we shall see, a feature of this period of Catholic Church history was the antagonism between Bourne and the rest of the hierarchy.[15] Bourne thwarted Casartelli, and the other bishops, because he prevented them making public statements regarding Catholic education in the light of the various Education Bills tabled between 1906 to 1921. Furthermore, he refused to consult them on the issue. As a result of the bishops' silence, certain individuals and lay groups had assumed the rôle of speaking on behalf of the Church. Casartelli thought this a usurpation of episcopal authority. Casartelli and Bourne also differed as to whether the Labour Party was to be considered as a socialist party, although on this issue Casartelli was to find himself out of step with his episcopal colleagues. In spite of an anxiety for a united Catholic front and a public portrayal of such unity, Casartelli's copy letters show that there was in practice a high degree of tension between the hierarchy and Bourne.[16] Casartelli aided and abetted his fellow bishops in mounting opposition against Bourne and often accused him of gagging them. At this juncture in his episcopal career Casartelli gained new self-confidence. Although he delegated many of the day-to-day diocesan tasks to his Vicar Generals, he was prepared to exercise his authority on the education question when he thought it necessary, and felt frustrated when Bourne prevented this.

Not only was Casartelli an inspired educationalist, he saw the twentieth century as 'the century of the laity' and therefore encouraged the lay apostolate, always with the *proviso* that it was under the aegis and command of the Bishops. For a united phalanx of laity to exist and function as it ought, he thought it necessary that the hierarchy give strong, clear leadership. He held a firm and unremitting belief that this leadership was the preserve and duty of the episcopate. If he detected any threat to this position, he was quick to condemn it and, when possible, to eliminate it. Casartelli's strong remarks of criticism when certain members of the 'Irish party',[17] and of the Catholic Teachers' Guild, presumed to act as spokesmen on behalf of the Church on matters of education, can lead to the impression that his 'control' of the laity amounted to domination. In this regard Aspden has described him as 'ineluctably clericalist' with a 'deep mistrust of independent lay initiative.'[18] This view is seemingly reinforced when one considers that the Modernist crisis of the early years of the century meant that 'clerical and hierarchical control were an inherent feature of any lay group.'[19] However, despite the temptation to conclude that Casartelli was at all times excessive in his desire to see the laity 'controlled,' it must be recognised, yet again, that in this matter, as in others, he represented a paradox. For, in the very midst of the Modernist crisis, Casartelli encouraged the founding of the lay Catenian Association, or 'Chums', as they were originally called, and suggested that the clergy be excluded from membership.[20]

Casartelli did not perceive Modernism, in its intellectual and doctrinal manifestations, to be a problem within his diocese. This can be adduced from his apparent lack of urgency in setting up a Vigilance Committee in accord with the encyclical *Pascendi* (September 1907).[21] Once set up, the Committee met on just one occasion; the meeting lasted for only thirty minutes.[22] Further evidence is contained in the *Relatio*[23] submitted by him to Rome prior to his visit *ad limina*,[24] in which Casartelli reported there were no errors of doctrine among either the clergy or the laity.[25] Other sources tell of only one occasion when he had direct dealings with 'intellectual' Modernism; this was the occasion when Maude Petre[26] sent him a manuscript of her book, hoping for his comments. Casartelli returned the parcel unopened, claiming that lack of time and the fact that he was not her bishop were the reasons why he had not read the material. He further added:

> I am bound in conscience as a Catholic priest to say that as long as you hold that you could not take an anti-Modernist oath, I deeply regret your position, and can only remember your case in prayer, in the hope that God may send you His light.[27]

Casartelli was grateful to Pius X and the 'clear-sighted outlook' of *Pascendi*, even though he recognised that at the time 'the unflinching severity of [its] disciplinary measures ... startled even many good Catholics.'[28] Whilst there may be a hint of sympathy for some academics who might have suffered unduly under the measures of *Pascendi*, understandable from the point of view that Casartelli himself had worked in a very difficult field of academic research,[29] he was unbending in his rejection of 'social' Modernism. He registered his gratitude to Pius X for his pronouncement against those ideas which stated

> that it was impossible to subordinate the temporal to the spiritual, and to concede to the Church the position of Queen and Mistress in mixed questions; that the Catholic must be separated from the citizen, and that every Catholic, from the fact that he was also a citizen, had the right and the duty to work for the common good in the way that he thought best, without troubling himself about the authority of the Church ... and that it was an abuse of authority against which one was bound to protest with all one's might, for the Church to trace out and prescribe for the citizen any line of action in any pretext whatsoever. These propositions received their condemnation in the encyclical letter on 'The Doctrines of the Modernists.'[30]

Undoubtedly Casartelli saw due deference to authority as the *sine qua non* of any lay initiative. However, the statements that have led him to be dubbed 'ineluctably clericalist' must be read and understood as reaction to

Bourne's actions or, as Casartelli saw it, lack of action and silence. The framework within which these statements were made was triangular: the issue in question (always education), the silence of the bishops due to Bourne, and certain laity acting as unofficial spokesmen. A brief overview of what was essentially objectionable, from the Catholic point of view, about the various education Bills between 1906 to 1921, will clarify what the education component of this framework was. The other aspects, namely Bourne's rôle and that of certain members of the laity will follow.

THE EDUCATION BILLS OF 1906, 1908, 1917 & 1921

J. H. Newman was the source of Casartelli's understanding of what constituted a university. From H. E. Manning he understood the ramifications of a Christian understanding of education, i.e. the different, but complementary, rôles of parents, State, and Church. The unacceptable common denominator of the Education Bills between 1906–1921 was, in Casartelli's words, 'the complete ruining of the supernatural side of teaching; [and] the effect which must follow, *viz.*, the paganising of the country.'[31] The 1902 Balfour Education Act had placed on the Local Education Authorities the responsibility of maintaining, by rate-aid, any Catholic elementary school in their area which was recognised as necessary by the Board of Education. Catholic schools had obtained a share of the rates thanks to this Act. As McClelland puts it: 'Anglicans and Catholics were on the whole well-satisfied with the Act of 1902 for 'they were now assured of a form of aid which would be automatically adjusted to changing costs and which would be available for any new school which they might build in the future'.'[32] The Church saw this as a compromise rather than a permanent solution to the heavy financial burdens demanded of them. Subsequent Bills tried to change this funding or to seek more control over voluntary-aided schools.

Although there was much about the Education Bills that he found unacceptable, Casartelli thought it imperative that any criticism by the Church should not be, nor seen to be, an attack on legitimate advances in teaching and school provision. In harmony with this, he pointed out:

> Now let it clearly be understood that we Catholics have always been keenly anxious for the promotion of all that could further and benefit the education of the children of the nation, our own included. All that can be done to make education more solid and useful, for opening up new avenues for our children to the higher walks of life, for carrying on that education to a later period ... all these ends and aims ... have our full and earnest sympathy.[33]

As a committed pioneering educationalist, he saw the provision of Catholic secondary schools and the bringing of primary schools into line with them as 'a vital question of our very existence.'[34] It is little wonder that any attempts by the State to wrestle power and control whether financial, managerial, or moral, out of the Church's hands was seen in the gravest and darkest terms. When such threats were on the horizon, he once again proved to be an outspoken defender of Catholic schools:

> During the eighteen years of my Episcopate, we have time and again had to face and fight Education Bills which threatened the rights of our Catholic schools, and, thank God, we have had the satisfaction of seeing Bill after Bill fail, and one Education Minister after another disappear.[35]

In expressing his misgivings and suggested courses of action in regard to the Education Bills, Casartelli drew upon the concepts and principles he had first worked out many years earlier in his 'Lay Sermons'.[36] His Pastoral Letters vis-à-vis education contained two basic tenets: firstly, education must be of the whole person, body and soul, 'not only to qualify him for excellent citizenship in this life, but also and still more for celestial citizenship in the next life.'[37] Secondly, the Catholic Church was not bound to any political party and 'she is represented by many of her most devoted children in each and all of the groups of our legislators; she can live under every form of Government, and is loyal and favourable to each and all.'[38] This did not amount to an apolitical stance. Catholics were encouraged to vote, and to use education as a measure of a party's acceptability or not. The main weapon of the Church in defence of its schools was the ballot box; hence the need to have a laity united in mind and action according to the principles of 'un-political politics.' Casartelli looked to the example of France to highlight the danger of how a lack of unity had facilitated the State's confiscation of a massive number of Church schools. From there he drew two fundamental lessons – that French Catholics had not been organised, and this had prevented them from using to the full the 'supreme weapon' of the ballot box.[39]

The Liberal Party's decision in 1906 to radically change the financial and managerial treatment of Church schools and to modify educational legislation caused a sense of alarm and hostility among Catholics. The heart of the problem lay in the intended alteration of the 1902 Education Act, under which Catholic schools were operating. A Bill introduced into Parliament by Augustine Birrell[40] sought to secure full public control of all rate-aided schools and the appointment of teachers regardless of their religious beliefs. All voluntary-aided schools were to be deprived of funding from the rates unless they agreed to become Council schools. In these schools denominational religious teaching was to be radically curtailed and replaced by a uniform system of 'undogmatic religious teaching.' Casartelli saw this as the state trying to supersede the rôle of the parents and trespassing upon their freedom to educate their children according to the light of conscience. In response, Casartelli, along with other bishops, marshalled the laity in order that politicians might hear their voice. The first of a number of protest meetings was held in the Free Trade Hall, Manchester, on 5 March 1906.[41] The theme of the meeting was: 'Catholic teaching by Catholic teachers, for Catholic children in Catholic schools in England, under Catholic Management.'[42] The laity responded so overwhelmingly that an 'over-spill' meeting was held simultaneously in the neighbouring Theatre Royal. In his address to the mass meeting, Casartelli stressed that Catholics were wedded to no political party. He criticised both the Liberal Party, for whom the 'vast bulk of the Catholic vote in this country went in favour,'[43] and the Tory Party. With a mixture of a hint of warning and political astuteness, knowing that what he said would be reported in the press, Casartelli took the opportunity to tell his audience:

> It should be remembered that English Catholics in the bulk were a working population. It would be a matter for the serious and conscientious consternation of Catholic working people as to how far they should continue to co-operate with a party that made an irreligious scheme of education one of the planks of its platform.[44]

The decision of the hierarchy to publish a joint pastoral letter on the Education crisis along with the resolutions of the Catholic Education Council condemning the Bill, must have pleased him greatly.[45] Casartelli liked this kind of statement because it manifested a strong leadership by legitimate authority – the bishops. In subsequent 'battles' when this was not the case he became very annoyed with Bourne for 'gagging' the rest of the hierarchy and preventing it from similar action.

The united response on the part of Catholics, witnessed at the Free Trade Hall, filled Casartelli with confidence and hope for the future and was a confirmation of his belief: *l'union fait la force*. It was the laity who provided the 'foot soldiers' in the campaign. Although promoted by the bishop and the clergy the protest against the 1906 Bill was, above all, a manifestation of the united forces of the Catholic laity. Casartelli wrote in his diary: 'Tonight 7.45 – 10.30 *magnificent* mass meetings of Catholics in Free Trade Hall (and overflow in Grand [*sic*] Theatre) – both densely packed – on education crisis: all speakers, except self, laymen. Extra-ordinary enthusiasm – no such Catholic gathering ever held before in Manchester! D.G.'[46]

The Free Trade Hall demonstration was followed by yet another, this time that organised by the newly-founded Catholic Federation, its first ever event, at Belle Vue, Manchester, on 13 October 1906. Casartelli rejoiced in this further 'demonstration of Catholic Faith and unity.'[47] This unity was enhanced by the support of John Redmond, the Leader of the 'Irish party,' and by Canon Patrick Lynch, of St Wilfrid's, Hulme. Both these men, as representatives of the Irish community, would play a very different rôle in later political debates when the Catholic body was not nearly so united. In spite of the passing of the Bill by a comfortable majority in the Commons, it was defeated in the Lords and withdrawn on 20 December 1906. The demonstrations against the 1906 Bill represented a high water mark for Casartelli and his desire for united Catholic action and for the laying aside of party preferences in favour of principle. This reaction to the Birrell Bill was the only experience he was to have of such unanimity; on no other issue was it so demonstrated.[48]

However, the political machinations that preceded the defeat of the Bill were to have repercussions in the diocese of Salford. Casartelli noted in his diary how, at the 'meeting of Bishops on the Education Question [it was] agreed to follow strong advice of Irish members and *not* support attempt to 'wreck' the Bill, but press amendments.'[49] The Duke of Norfolk and the Catholic peers surprisingly voted against the Bill at its third reading, despite its containing the amendments they previously secured.[50] As a result the Irish Members blamed them for the Bill's failure and the subsequent potential risk to church schools. Casartelli's assessment of the matter was that the

> attacks made upon the Catholic Peers by some of the Catholic members in the Lower House had a disastrous effect in causing at least apparent disunion in our hitherto so serried ranks, and will cause still more disastrous embarrassment in the near future. If we have an election here (now almost certain) owing to the promotion of Mr. Churchill, I foresee the danger of a serious scission owing to this censure.[51]

Casartelli felt 'considerable sympathy for the Duke of Norfolk',[52] and the Catholic Peers in general, against whom Bourne, he thought, had implied blame for wrecking the Bill.[53] Casartelli also felt that 'the Irish members have been making too much out of our approval of a certain line of conduct on their part in endeavouring to secure substantial amendments rather than 'wreck' the late Bill.'[54] Casartelli put the true reason for the Bill's withdrawal down to the direct 'action of the Government not the Conservative Party, owing to the pressure of the Nonconformists at the eleventh hour.'[55] In the forthcoming election Casartelli feared that the Irish Party would join with the Liberals in directing Irish Catholics to vote for Churchill, 'and our Federation will have to work on the opposite side.'[56] Casartelli's words were truly prophetic.[57] The split came in the face of the McKenna Bill of 1908.[58]

The Bill envisaged that Catholic schools would no longer be an integral part of the national system of education. As a consequence they would receive no rate aid. As we shall see later, the events surrounding the election showed the lack of unanimity among the Catholics of Manchester.

In 1917, H. A. L. Fisher[59] introduced an education Bill which, in Casartelli's opinion, represented a major step forward by the secular educationalists. Furthermore, he was dismayed by the disunifying consequences of 'unauthorised public utterances' by Catholics.

> A small number among our own people have been unfortunately led to judge of the effects of the Bill, rather by the fair promises and friendly professions of its promoters, than by careful study of the actual bearing of the dangerous clauses to which we are bound to take exception.[60]

He referred here to the Catholic Teachers' Guild who had spoken in favour of Fisher saying that, 'it gave them [the teachers] a chance of doing more for the Catholic child educationally and socially than in the past.'[61] The Hierarchy meanwhile remained silent.

Casartelli understood the 1921 Education Bill in the same way as he had seen the others – in terms of confiscation. He wrote to Bourne asking for a show of episcopal strength, as he believed 'the Catholic body can and will do nothing without a lead from the Hierarchy.'[62] When Bourne declined to act, Casartelli admitted to being very discouraged. He felt that the position of the bishops was untenable because of Bourne's manipulation of the hierarchy. Given that the Archbishop of Westminster did not provide the necessary lead, Casartelli took it upon himself to condemn the Bill in his Advent pastoral letter of 1921.

Bourne's blocking of the hierarchy made Casartelli feel angry and resentful, as it was a hindrance of his *praxis* in regard to educational matters. In effect, Bourne was preventing Casartelli exercising an authority that was well grounded in both ability and experience. In his reply to the education question, Casartelli responded as expected; his response did not differ in any large measure from those of his episcopal colleagues. What is informative is the way Casartelli's reaction illustrates the relations between Bourne and the rest of the bishops, which was at times uneasy and fraught with tension and suspicion.

THE EDUCATION CRISIS AS ILLUSTRATIVE OF THE RELATIONS BETWEEN BOURNE AND THE HIERARCHY

Casartelli strove for an ideal of internal unity manifesting itself in united public action. He considered anything that militated against this to be *anathema* and to be avoided at all costs. However, public displays of lack of disunity among Catholics were a spectre that haunted him during the 1908 and 1910 elections. Casartelli described as the most painful incident in his whole episcopate when one of his priests made public in the *Manchester Guardian* a disagreement between the Catholic Federation and the United Irish League.[63] Despite the determination to present an appearance of agreement and unanimity, he was not averse to expressing privately a virulent criticism of the Archbishop of Westminster, whom several times he accused of having 'gagged' the other bishops.[64] It was only fear of causing scandal and disunity that prevented Casartelli from publicly acting in defiance of Bourne and making public statements about Church policy regarding the education question.

Relations were strained between the two bishops partly because of their different characters and their preferred ways of doing things. Bourne was more reserved and given to quieter, more diplomatic methods when it came to questions concerning education and negotiations with Whitehall.[65] Casartelli wanted strong public leadership from the hierarchy in the form of statements that clearly stated the Catholic standpoint and at the same time showed that the Bishops alone held legitimate authority to speak on behalf of the Church. Since Bourne was disinclined to act in this way, and the bishops could not act without him, Casartelli thought that he made the other bishops play the rôle of 'dumb dogs.'[66] Another contributing factor to the poor state of their relationship was the fact that Casartelli had wanted Francis Aidan Gasquet to succeed Herbert Vaughan as Archbishop of Westminster. When events turned out differently Casartelli did not hide his disappointment. In a letter to Gasquet he wrote of how he had considered him to be 'the one man in England to up the grand tradition.'[67] Bourne was painfully aware that his nomination to Westminster had been accompanied by ill-feeling and speculation, thus giving him what his biographer called a 'poor start.'[68] A bishop such as Casartelli with his academic background and formidable intelligence might well have proved a threat to Bourne, who was younger and less academically capable. This added to Bourne's need to assert his authority both among the bishops and in the face of the leading Catholic aristocracy, some of whom he considered to have been against him.[69]

Casartelli further complained of Bourne's lack of consultation – 'There is a great deal too much of this recent work *inconsultis episcopis*. Everything is now practically done over our heads, not only without seeking our opinion or advice, but even without our knowing anything is being mooted.'[70] The Papal Bull, *Si Qua Est*, issued in October 1911, gave Bourne and his successors as Archbishop of Westminster the position of *praeses perpetuus* among the bishops of England and Wales. As the 'perpetual president' of the episcopal meetings it was his responsibility and prerogative to call meetings of the bishops and to preside over them. *Si Qua Est* defined this task as: 'to represent before the supreme civil authority the entire body of Bishops of England and Wales, always, however, after having consulted all the Bishops, the opinion of the majority of whom he is always to follow.'[71] Although the Archbishop of Westminster was considered to be the spokesman for the Church by the Government and the general Catholic population, he would 'not necessarily [be] so regarded by his brother ordinaries or provincials for his office was not primatial.'[72] This generated difficulties in two areas especially – education and the multiplication of dioceses.

The differences between Casartelli and Bourne come into relief because of their differing approaches to the education question. As we have seen, tension over this issue led to disunity among the Catholic laity, and the evidence shows that it led to fragmentation among the hierarchy also. Thus, for example, in March 1912, Bourne received from Casartelli an impassioned plea to summon a meeting of the bishops of England and Wales in order that they might issue an authoritative pronouncement on the 'Single Area Schools' Bill' introduced by Sir George Marks.[73] Casartelli's fears were two-fold. Firstly, he believed that the Bill represented a 'serious and fateful crisis' regarding the future of Catholic schools and the potential loss of some three hundred primary schools.[74] Secondly, and more importantly, John Dillon,[75] a Nationalist Member of Parliament, had claimed to accept the Bill on behalf of the Catholic Church. As a result of Dillon having spoken in favour of the Bill, some sixty Irish MPs had duly voted for it. Had they voted against, the Bill would have been defeated. Casartelli told Bourne that the hierarchy's silence had led people to ask: 'Has the Hierarchy abdicated its position as sole judge and authoritative exponent of Catholic principles and policy'?[76] He feared that the hierarchy would, if it remained silent, lose its moral authority not only among Catholics but also in the country in general. At the proposed meeting Casartelli wished the following principle to be made clear: 'no politician and no political party, but the hierarchy alone, has the power and right to speak in the name of the Catholic body.'[77] Casartelli wrote not only on his own behalf, but also for everyone who wanted such a statement to be made.[78] Since no statement was made, he was tempted to denounce Dillon's actions publicly. He felt confident that if he did so he would have the backing of his clergy and laity, but he feared the consequences: a show of potential disunity, exposing a weak flank to the enemies of Catholic schools.[79] He was disinclined to do personally what ought to have been done by the whole hierarchy. Had he spoken out against John Dillon he would have run the risk of further isolating the supporters of the Irish Nationalist. His reference to 'no politician and no political party, but the Hierarchy alone, has the power and right to speak in the name of the Catholic body'[80] was an oblique allusion to the Nationalist Party who he feared might assume the rôle that belonged to the bishops if the latter remained silent. If Dillon was allowed to go unchecked Casartelli feared that the bishops would 'for ever lose their position ... as the guides and directors of Catholic policy and action.'[81]

Bourne's refusal to convene a meeting filled Casartelli with despair and resentment. He commented to the Archbishop of Liverpool: 'To my mind it is little less than an insult to the whole bench of Bishops. We are practically told, like troublesome children, to keep quiet and not interfere.'[82] In the same letter he wrote: 'It is a crisis in our history; the most serious since the days of Milner [...] As much as I dislike Milner, I feel constrained to say 'O for an hour of John Milner!''[83] Aspden has taken this reference to Milner to be indicative of Casartelli's 'deep mistrust of lay initiative'[84] and a desire to see the laity put in their place.[85] However, the issue calls for closer attention to be paid to the details of Casartelli's remark.

The invocation of Milner was, I suggest, born not out of any wish to suppress lay initiative but as a response, *a cri de coeur*, against Bourne who was, in Casartelli's view, ignoring the voice of the bishops. The danger foreseen by Casartelli was that Bourne's stance left the field open for other individuals, such as politicians – in this case the Irish Party – to make statements about Church policy. Even though Milner was not, for Casartelli, an ideal rôle model, he recalled him wistfully as a way of expressing a desire for the hierarchy to fulfil its rôle as spokesmen for the Church. Likewise, when in a similar dispute he wrote of a desire 'for an Ullathorne!'[86] and, 'We want Ullathorne today!', his admiration was because Ullathorne refused to be manipulated by Manning, the then Cardinal Archbishop of Westminster.[87] Casartelli evidently believed that Bourne was manipulating the bishops. The task of issuing statements on the principles of Catholic education and what the Church considered acceptable and unacceptable was, according to Casartelli, the distinct rôle and prerogative of the bishops alone: 'nobody but the hierarchy has the right (and duty) to speak for the Catholics of the country.'[88]

The whole incident demonstrates, I suggest, the conscientious way in which Casartelli fulfilled his duties as a bishop. Given his preference to be relieved of tedious administration, he might then have chosen to hide behind Bourne's silence, instead he spoke out strongly. The incident is indicative of the hold that Bourne had upon the hierarchy. Casartelli's question to the Archbishop of Liverpool about Bourne's behaviour struck at the very heart of his authority – 'has his Eminence an absolutely free hand to settle the whole matter *inconsultis episcopis*'?[89] He emphasised how he wanted to speak out – 'I *must* be allowed to do so *in my own way*.' He was very uneasy about the whole matter and his clergy and people were pressing for a pronouncement – 'And yet I feel sorely on my conscience my duty as a Catholic bishop to my flock, to the interests of Catholic education, and to the episcopal order. Are we even *justified* in abdicating the rights and responsibilities we have inherited'?[90] We have here another example of Casartelli's sure-footed and confident style, challenging Bourne's behaviour relentlessly. When Bourne did finally speak out,[91] his action won him the profound respect and gratitude of Casartelli, who wrote to thank him for his 'clear and outspoken pronouncement on the schools question ... You have given us exactly the lead that was needed, and, I believe, saved the situation.'[92] In a letter to be read to a meeting of the Catholic Federation, Casartelli clearly stated the principle over which he had been battling:

> *No* politician or layman, of whatever party, and no political party, *can be* the spokesman or spokesmen of the Catholic body on such a purely religious subject as Catholic Education: that duty belongs to the Bishops of the country alone; they cannot in conscience abdicate it – only if directly *commissioned* by the Hierarchy can a politician speak in the name of the Catholic body.
>
> It is not a question of nationality, or percentage of nationality. The Bishops of the country are Bishops of the *entire flock*, whether English, Irish, or Scotch, whether German, Italian or Polish.[93]

The inference was clear: episcopal authority transcended any sectional interests and was the basis of Catholicity. Similar instances of differences with Bourne were to follow, and Casartelli remained afraid of being accused of abdicating responsibility. In 1920 Casartelli returned to the theme of the loss of authority: 'it is painful to be told by our clergy ... that we Bishops have abdicated our leadership and let it go by default to the school-masters.'[94] On this occasion it was a group of teachers who were presuming to speak on behalf of the Church. Casartelli wrote to the Archbishop of Liverpool: 'the Teachers have seized the reins that the Hierarchy have let drop. And our clergy are losing, or have lost, their respect for and their confidence in the Bishops.'[95]

Casartelli presented his view of Bourne's behaviour by reference to an earlier period of the English Catholic Church. Reflecting on his recent reading of Bernard Ward's *The Sequel to Catholic Emancipation*,[96] he spoke in glowing terms of the Vicars Apostolic who had been the forerunners of the diocesan bishops prior to the restoration of the hierarchy in 1850. Casartelli noted one exception – John Milner: 'Learned he was, sincerely pious too, and zealous almost to excess. But he was a born fighter, a ruthless adversary in discussion. In his opinion, we may say, he was always right and championed the right cause ... but he was merciless, so violent and abusive in his language, so persistent in his apparent enmity.'[97] The Vicars Apostolic had to assert their rights in the face of a vocal and powerful laity, some of whom made up the Cisalpine Club.[98] From this episode of English Church history Casartelli drew the following warning:

> There are weighty lessons to be gathered from the drama of the English Catholics. Nothing was more unfortunate during that distressful period than the frequent and deplorable dissensions between the Bishops and the Catholic laity. That 'laity' was made up exclusively of the 'noblemen and gentlemen' – staunch and devoted upholders of the Faith and often brave sufferers for it ... but dangerously Erastian ... in their views, intolerant of episcopal authority, too prone to compromise the cause of ecclesiastical liberty.[99]

Despite Casartelli's criticism of Bourne for his silence and the way he controlled the hierarchy, it ought to be remembered that he too was struggling at times to assert his authority with the Duke of Norfolk and other leading aristocratic Catholic families, for example over the issue of the 1906 Education Bill.

The incidents outlined above form the context in which Casartelli was driven to utter the phrase 'Much as I dislike Milner, I feel constrained to say: 'O for an hour of John Milner!' For him, the issue was not a simple matter of bishops exerting their power. It involved the more fundamental question of the exercise of legitimate authority and the theological question of how the individual bishops stood in relation to the *praeses perpetuus*. The episode was also coloured by the need of not isolating the Irish Party whilst at the same time preventing them from assuming an authority that was not theirs. Clearly Casartelli saw the Irish Nationalists and the Catholic Teachers' Guild as types of a contemporary 'Cisalpine Club.'

1917: AN ANNUS TERRIBILIS

In January 1917 Bourne was nominated to the Consistorial Congregation, the Vatican body responsible for the erection of dioceses and the election of bishops. Several of the English and Welsh bishops were alarmed at this and hoped that it would 'not mean mischief ahead!'[100] However, the year ahead saw relations between Bourne and the hierarchy become increasingly strained due to the proposed multiplication and division of dioceses in England. Casartelli was doubly concerned by the suggestion regarding the increase in the number of dioceses and with the way Bourne reacted to the Fisher Education Bill.

The Fisher Education Bill

The Fisher Education Bill of 1917 provoked serious problems, both as regards education *per se*, and because it fuelled the already existent internal dissension among the hierarchy. The education problem involved the same difficulties as before: Bourne's failure to consult his fellow bishops and preventing them making a statement, and an unofficial body, this time the Catholic Teachers' Guild, acting as spokesman for the Church. Casartelli saw the action of the Teachers as especially grave because it might lead to a rift between the teachers and the bishops.[101]

The bishops met on 25 September 1917 and were unanimous in condemning the Bill and wanted to issue a pronouncement to this effect, but they were prevented from doing so by Bourne who, in Casartelli's words, 'insisted on his own private negotiations with Fisher.'[102] This of course met with Casartelli's disapproval as it meant that the Bishops were forced to stand, 'like dumb dogs, stultified before the Teachers, and our clergy and people.'[103] He made his own pronouncement on the Fisher Bill in a sermon at St Thomas of Canterbury's, Salford, on 21 October 1917. Since the sermon received no newspaper coverage Casartelli published it privately in order for it to be distributed.[104] He reiterated his belief

> that we Catholics have always been keenly anxious for the promotion of all that could further and benefit the education of the children of the Nation, our own included. All that can be done to make education more solid and useful, for opening up new avenues for our children to the higher walks of life, for carrying on the education to a later period ... all these ends and aims ... have our full and earnest sympathy.[105]

He pointed out how Catholics had at first given the Bill a sympathetic hearing. However, on closer inspection it had been found to be a 'bad Bill ... containing a number of clauses which must eventually spell the ruin of our Catholic Elementary Schools and the loss from them of our Catholic teachers.'[106] The most offensive clause was one which made provision for the 'setting up the Board of Education as an absolute autocracy, from which there will be no right of appeal.'[107]

Amid mounting pressure for the hierarchy to make a pronouncement, Casartelli admitted that he too shared the thoughts and feelings of his clergy and people – impatience, suspicion, and resentment.[108] He informed Bourne of the widespread feeling of unrest in Salford Diocese and how everybody was expecting a lead from the Bishops. The situation was further aggravated by the Catholic Education Council[109] being prevented, again by Bourne, from making public the resolutions they had drawn up in regard to the Fisher Bill.

Casartelli believed that this would 'have a very bad effect and increase the atmosphere of suspicion.'[110] An example of the pressure Casartelli was under is seen in his letters to Canon O'Kelly and T. F. Burns, of the Catholic Federation.[111] Casartelli resented the way they were 'hammering away' at him, asking for the Bishops to make a pronouncement. He replied that he had not been idle and that he was doing all he could to procure a public statement, thus implying that Bourne was prevaricating.[112]

The burden of the episcopate must have been an extremely bitter one for Casartelli at this time. He was frustrated by Bourne, whom he blamed for the worsening situation regarding education,[113] and was under pressure from his own senior clergy and laity. In a rare show of feelings, he acknowledged to the Archbishop of Liverpool that he felt

> bitterness and dismay to find ourselves throttled by Westminster … Why is His Eminence, instead of donning a gas-helmet at the front and scheming for a third (!) Auxiliary, not drawing up a statesmanlike letter for us all to sign laying down for all men to know the principles on which we have our claims and our hostility to many clauses of the Fisher Bill?[114]

Casartelli's feelings of frustration were not entirely personal. They reflected the general atmosphere of the episcopal bench, which lacked leadership and therefore ran the risk of losing the confidence of the laity. He lamented that 'for the last few years, our hierarchical system has gone to pieces. Our Westminster meetings are a farce. We are gagged, and everything is decided and done without us or in spite of us. I am not the only bishop who feels like this.'[115] Casartelli's sense of dissatisfaction at the state of the bishops' meetings, because of the stranglehold Bourne exercised over them, is seen in a detailed letter to Cardinal Gasquet in which he fully explained the situation.[116] Judging from the letter he was not the only bishop to think as he did.[117] One bishop felt that it was a waste of time attending the bishops' meetings because Bourne continually over-ruled from the Chair.[118]

Much of what Casartelli said in relation to the Catholic Teachers' Guild must be read in the light of the above. The Guild had no real objection to the Bill and the silence of the bishops gave them the opportunity to speak in its favour. Casartelli vehemently disapproved of this and described a speech made by one of the Teachers' leaders as outrageous.[119] He was especially angered by the final sentence of the speech in which the speaker had hoped, 'that Catholics would not unnecessarily raise the religious question which the Bill and the good sense of the country in the present had avoided.'[120] Once again Casartelli was on a collision course with a lay group, whom he thought disloyal and self-seeking.[121] Moreover, he suspected that the high profile given to the speech in *The Tablet* was due to Bourne's influence.[122] His worst fears about the bishops' silence were now confirmed – 'the Teachers have the field to themselves and a handful of them are left practically to act as official spokesmen of the Catholic body.'[123] Casartelli saw the whole situation as just as dangerous as that in the days of the Cisalpine Club, with the hierarchy in danger of losing their authority.[124]

Casartelli reacted to the action of the Guild by demanding that the prefix 'Salford Diocesan' be removed from its name, i.e. 'Salford Diocesan Catholic Teachers' Guild.' In retaliation the Teachers withdrew from the Salford Diocesan Catholic Federation, claiming that its actions in condemning the Fisher Bill were 'over-hasty, injudicious, and dangerous.'[125] Casartelli replied that the Catholic Federation had acted in accord with his opinions and reminded the Guild:

> that the determination of Catholic policy as regards Catholic education is a matter of episcopal jurisdiction, and that no sectional body of Catholics has the right to formulate a policy, or enter into negotiations, or make any pronouncements on the subject without the sanction of ecclesiastical authority, much less in opposition to the known and declared judgement of such authority.[126]

Casartelli, nevertheless, sought to defend the action of the Catholic Federation, yet the truth was it had not helped the matter. When the Fisher Bill was introduced (10 August 1917), Casartelli had declined to offer an opinion until there had been time for reflection. The Catholic Teachers' Guild also declined to comment. Notwithstanding, within two weeks the Catholic Federationist had called for the defeat of the Bill.[127] This gave the argument of the Teachers' Guild a firm ground. In reply to Casartelli, T. Meehan, the Honorary Secretary to the Guild, said the Catholic Federation had been judged as 'over-hasty' in its calling for the defeat of Fisher because it had spoken before the hierarchy or the Catholic Education Council had done. This of course was accurate and was the central issue of Casartelli's complaints against Bourne. Meehan's retort was devastating: he stated, that 'other Catholic bodies having greater claims than the Federation to deal with educational matters' had so far remained silent.[128] Meehan offered assurances that the Guild accepted the authority of the hierarchy without question. The point at issue was the insistence by the Catholic teachers that,

> in matters of educational legislation vitally affecting our professional careers and prospects ... [they] are entitled to approach directly through their national organisations the authors of such actual or projected proposals, and to enunciate for their own body a considered plan of action, subject always to the final supreme authority of the Hierarchy.[129]

Casartelli had failed to grasp the fact that thanks to educational developments and the professionalisation of the teachers' rôle, they had the right to
ensure job security and adequate conditions of employment. Casartelli's idea
of the rôle of the laity seemingly did not take into consideration one effect
education would have on the Catholic middle-classes: it would enable them
to think for themselves.

The whole episode left Casartelli in despair and, along with his clergy,
disillusioned. 'Dangerous men' among the Teachers' Guild had gone over to
the enemy and were 'glorifying the Fisher Bill.'[130] The reason, according to
Casartelli, was the hierarchy maintaining its 'sphinx-like silence.'[131] By 1919
the burden of the episcopate and the way the hierarchy was being treated by
Bourne led Casartelli to admit:

> Frankly I am in despair. If I only had the means of living quietly and
> privately, I would send in my resignation to the Holy See this very day. I
> feel I am not able to grapple with the situation any longer. And what
> makes the position so painful is that I am forced to recognise in my own
> conscience that the complaints about the attitude of the Hierarchy are
> absolutely *true* and justified.[132]

I would suggest that Casartelli's comments about tendering his resignation
'this very day' are more a reflection of his feelings of despair rather than his
true intent. Because of the income which he would have received from the
family business of J. Casartelli & Son, he was probably in a financially secure
enough position to actually retire (the probate register records his having left
£4794 16^s 2^d.) The fact that he did not is a true reflection of his sense of duty
and commitment.

The proposed division of dioceses in England

Bourne's propensity to try and increase the number of dioceses in England
was the cause of further friction among the bishops. He began by trying to
bring under his control the diocese of Southwark.[133] Casartelli thought this an
'unjustifiable and preposterous scheme,' and 'firmly believed that the Roman
authorities don't understand our local English conditions one bit.'[134] Bourne's
presence in Rome in December 1916 created unease among the bishops who
thought that he might use the opportunity, as Casartelli put it:

> to press again on the Holy See the deplorable scheme of subdivision and
> multiplication of dioceses ... Many of us feel that it is a fatal policy; and
> personally I believe the splitting of us into 4 provinces is a dangerous source
> of weakness. We are already developing separate 'provincial' policies, and
> in some matters, e.g. Education, this process may become serious.[135]

Casartelli sought Cardinal Gasquet's 'powerful protection in face of such dangers.'[136] The whole issue was exacerbated by the fact that the bishops could not meet without Bourne's prior approval and they possessed no means of making their views known in Rome except *via* Bourne, whose voice was the only one listened to. To counter the fact that the bishops were inarticulate, Casartelli expressed a wish for 'some way by which the remaining 15 diocesans outside of Westminster can make themselves heard.'[137] In the absence of such means he suggested to Bishop Amigo that each bishop write to Gasquet as he had done.[138] This was one of the first stirrings that led to a meeting of the bishops at Oscott College, Birmingham, in March 1917.

In the first weeks of 1917, Bourne's plan to have Amigo removed to Birmingham became known. Casartelli thought that the bishops ought to write to Rome in support of Amigo and against his removal. News followed shortly that Bourne was also suggesting an 'Essex Vicariate.'[139] The feeling of inarticulateness among the bishops was now becoming acute. In the meanwhile, Casartelli was not idle and sought the views of other bishops. The Bishop of Clifton commented on the idea of an Essex Vicariate, 'Dio mio! Si retrogradisce!'[140] The Bishop of Leeds encouraged Casartelli to approach Archbishop Whiteside of Liverpool to call a provincial meeting prior to the Low Week meeting. It was thought that if nothing were said or done until Low Week, Bourne would have secured his aims and the bishops would be unable to lay their concerns before the Holy See.[141] However, Whiteside did not see his way to call the meeting.

It was left to the Archbishop of Birmingham to finally convene eleven bishops[142] at Oscott College on 15 March 1917 to discuss the subdivision and multiplication of dioceses. The meeting lasted for several days. Bourne was not present, since at the time he was in Rome. Casartelli described one day as being 'another of plain and strong speaking and much tension.'[143] His fellow bishops shared Casartelli's attitude toward Bourne. In his report to Gasquet[144] he commented on the unanimity and the strength of the bishops' feelings concerning the subdivision. The outcome of the meeting was a *memorandum* to the Pope containing the statistics of the Catholic community in England and Wales, comparing the number of dioceses and bishops with those of the United States, Belgium, Holland, and Italy. The conclusion from the comparison was that 'we are actually overstocked with dioceses and bishops in England compared with other countries.'[145]

Bourne was furious that the bishops had met in his absence. The Low Week meeting, which took place a month after Oscott, was described by Casartelli as 'rather painful; some very strong speaking; esp. by Card. B., Northampton and Southwark. Very strained feelings!'[146] It was suggested that a Standing Committee of bishops be created, but Bourne 'simply squashed the matter.'[147] Bourne excused his *modus agendi* by saying that the idea of subdivision and multiplication came from Rome and that he had been put under the *secretum pontificum*. Therefore his lips had been sealed. After obtaining permission from Rome to be released from his oath of secrecy, he explained to the assembly the history of the matter. Extracts from a document written by Bourne[148] show that his motives for multiplying the number of diocese were based on the growing influence of the Catholic Church in England at the time, and the fact that the erection of new dioceses had been envisaged by *Si Qua Est*. Bourne wrote, 'The War is causing a real religious awakening and men's minds are turning more than ever to the Catholic Church ... Unless the Catholic Church adopts a bold policy which will appeal to the popular imagination, an opportunity will be lost which is not likely to come again.'[149]

This 'bold policy' included more dioceses. According to Oldmeadow, Bourne thought the only objections his colleagues would have would be financial. The other bishops, including Casartelli, did not view it so and were angry that they had not been consulted. Casartelli, for his part, objected on the grounds that it would weaken the unity of Church policy. On 22 March 1917, the county of Essex, which had formerly formed part of the Archdiocese of Westminster, was made into the separate diocese of Brentwood. On 22 November 1924, the diocese of Lancaster was created.

When the proposal of a Standing Committee was squashed the bishops then suggested that two of their ranks proceed to Rome to present their case. This too was overruled by Bourne. Shortly after the Low Week meeting Casartelli wrote a full report of the proceedings to Cardinal Merry del Val,[150] in which he spoke of the bishops'

> Dutiful message to the Holy Father embodying our petition that no future development of a large policy regarding the whole country should be made without previous consultation of the whole Hierarchy, and no future modification of any particular diocese *inconsulto episcopo quidam*.' [And that] 'we wanted badly to delegate two of our number ... to proceed to Rome and represent our case. But H[is E[minence] fought hard against it.'[151]

In reply, Merry del Val suggested that two bishops should proceed to Rome anyway.[152] Casartelli forwarded Merry del Val's letter to the bishops of Northampton and Nottingham, and so played a very active part in engineering this move.[153]

In his letter to Merry del Val, Casartelli explained that the bishops had not acted earlier because Bourne inevitably failed to keep them abreast of developments and never took them into his confidence and that they suffered from a 'constitutional unfitness for the 'diplomatic' methods at which

His Eminence has shewn himself such an adept.' This was coupled with 'a natural shyness and diffidence at addressing the Holy See or the S. Congregation, based I suppose on an innate reverence for authority.'[154] He described the situation between Bourne and the other bishops as 'deplorable' and the meetings of the Hierarchy having 'become a farce, we can never decide anything, we are overruled from the Chair.'[155] Casartelli was not sparing in his criticism of Bourne, whom he accused of being autocratic and failing to give an adequate lead in educational matters: 'Meanwhile our 'Praeses', instead of leading us in defence of our schools, is at the Front lunching with General Haig or scheming to get a third (!) Auxiliary, after getting a part of his diocese (and presumably of his work) cut off!'[156]

By securing a third auxiliary bishop Casartelli claimed that Bourne had become, 'not a "King-maker", like Warwick, but a "bishop maker".'[157]

CONCLUSION

Casartelli did not want Catholics to be solely involved in the defence of Church interests alone, but to be no less committed and to take an equally active part in social, political, cultural, and especially educational spheres. It was in the field of education that the temporal and the spiritual met. Education, as understood according to the Church's philosophy of education and practical execution, was both a service to the individual and to the nation. This chapter has used the education question and the various education Bills as a means of viewing this and the relations between Bourne and Casartelli and the other bishops. It is clearly apparent that their styles of leadership and strategies differed. To obtain a full picture and understanding of the questions alluded to here, a thorough academic treatment of Francis Bourne's episcopate is needed. Bourne was not silent on education issues.[158] Whilst his fellow bishops, and particularly Casartelli, did not appreciate Bourne's reticence to speak out and 'lead from the front', his avoidance of undue episcopal interference in lay initiatives was welcomed by Wilfrid Ward whilst he was editor of the *Dublin Review*,[159] and by Margaret Fletcher of the Catholic Women's League.[160]

Adrian Hastings has observed that Bourne, 'often felt that others were conspiring in Rome behind his back, especially Cardinals Gasquet and Merry del Val.'[161] The evidence considered in this chapter, especially in relation to the multiplication of dioceses, shows that his suspicions were indeed justified and that Casartelli fed the conspiracy. The personal document drawn up by Bourne, and detailing the reasons for wanting an increase in the number of dioceses, is evidence that his intentions were to provide adequate provision for the future. This was based on his awareness of the growing influence of the Catholic Church. Had he been able to communicate better with his fellow bishops and share his thoughts and plans with them he might have overcome their hostility. Added to Bourne's natural shyness there was, no doubt, a fear founded on his suspicion of those who conspired behind his back, that these plans would be opposed. Even a bishop like Casartelli, who had the ability to look beyond his own diocese, was still zealous of being its ruler, and wanted not only to act, but moreover insisted, 'I *must* be allowed to do so *in my own way.*'[162] There are similarities between the difficulties that Casartelli had with the parish priests of the Salford diocese and those that Bourne experienced with his fellow bishops.[163]

It is tempting, and perhaps convenient, to conclude that Casartelli wanted a laity entirely subdued by ecclesiastical control and devoid of initiative. This was not so. He readily recognised that there was 'a very large area of most important work which lies outside and beyond the reach of any religious Orders, and which can only be undertaken by lay effort, organised and directed of course by the Authorities of the Church.'[164] He envisaged the rôle of the laity as one of influencing 'as a silent but potent leaven, the world in which they live.'[165] Despite a tendency to express his views in ways which could be interpreted as dictatorial in tone he believed that in the twentieth century the relationship between clergy and laity ought to be based on co-operation, as 'the old days of 'helping with a stick' were gone.'[166] He urged his clergy to recognise that the various organisations which made up parish life needed to be handled with great sympathy and concluded that 'the results of conflicts between clergy and lay organisations were deplorable, and such conflicts were often owing to want of tact.'[167] How successful was Casartelli in achieving this? To answer this we must look to his ideas on the laity and the organisations he proposed and supported within his own diocese.

Chapter Eight

The Lay Apostolate

The lay apostolate took root during the pontificate of Leo XIII[1] and was further nourished by Pius X. Casartelli was its ardent supporter and declared:

> It has been said that, in the history of the Church, the twentieth century will eventually be known as the century of the laity. And it must be admitted that probably at no preceding epoch have there been the same opportunity and need for the co-operation of the faithful laity in the defence of the Church, in the promotion of her interests and in the 'pacific penetration' by means of their example and intellectual influence, of the society in which they live.[2]

Casartelli was not alone in identifying the need for the involvement of the laity.[3] His encouragement of this apostolate was predated by a series of papers published by the Catholic Truth Society. Cuthbert Hedley advocated that Catholics organise themselves into uniform action.[4] Herbert Vaughan recognised the fact that 'the influence of the Catholic laity may be exercised in many ways – through literature, science, art, and the professions.'[5] The regeneration of the poor he stressed as being above all other social needs. John Norris[6] spoke of the 'many ways in which laymen can do good work for the Church;' he particularly advised a wise exercise of citizenship by the judicious use of the ballot box.[7] Casartelli's own views were an amalgam of the above with enlightened personal elements. His understanding of the apostolate followed the Catholic Action model of Pius X – 'the organised participation of the laity in the hierarchical apostolate of the Church.'

The Catholic Federation and the Catenian Association were the fruits of Casartelli's early vision for an organised and unified force of Catholic laity and clergy. He set out on this path utterly convinced that the adequate response to the supposedly malevolent and organised forces represented by Freemasonry and Socialism was to match them with an equally well-organised phalanx of Catholic forces.[8] Therefore, he saw no difficulty in the Catenian Association adopting certain features of Freemasonry to achieve this.[9] What was distinctive about Casartelli's understanding of the lay apostolate was the fact that he was the first bishop among the English Hierarchy to bring into being a structured organisation such as the Catholic Federation. He was also the episcopal patron of the Catenians, originally called the 'Manchester Chums.'

THE CATHOLIC FEDERATION: FEDERATIONISM V. PAROCHIALISM

Casartelli hoped that the Catholic Federation, which he considered 'the special work of [his] episcopate,'[10] would be 'a linking together of all Catholic energies in a phalanx of thinkers and workers, who shall watch over the interests of the Faith, and promote by every means co-operation, both social and religious, among the clergy and the laity of all classes in the Diocese.'[11]

The level of organisation that he had found among Catholics in Belgium and Germany[12] had impressed him. He regarded the lack of similar organisation among the Catholics of France, as a salutary lesson.[13] One may wonder whether his broader mind was ever truly appreciated in the Diocese of Salford.

T. Sharrock and T. Burns,[14] and more recently Peter Doyle,[15] have charted the history of the Salford Catholic Federation. Kester Aspden's view that the Federation in Salford diocese 'did not prove to be the agent of Catholic unity that Casartelli had envisaged,' also needs further explanation.[16]

The Federation was intended to engender a wider and more influential presence of the Church in the surrounding society and to reach beyond the divisions resulting from different political opinions and feelings of national sentiment. It was also meant to foster an interest in matters other than the purely parochial and to broaden the horizons of the laity and clergy.[17] Whilst he was still rector of St Bede's College Casartelli had spoken of how a narrowly parochial outlook was a serious obstacle to the creation of Catholic grammar schools.[18] The problem lay in the way that these schools were to be funded. Pupils would be drawn from various parishes and the responsibility of maintaining the grammar schools would be divided among these feeder parishes. However, parish priests would be less inclined to support them financially than if the schools belonged solely to their own parish.

Shortly after becoming a bishop Casartelli was pleased to witness a growing spirit of co-operation between parishes in the provision of secondary schools. He believed that 'this marked the beginning of a new era, the putting aside of the old-fashioned trammels of parochialism and the entrance upon a wider, and therefore more influential, sphere of Catholic life and activity.'[19] In spite of these positive signs of a more open-minded attitude, Sharrock later identified that parochialism was still one of the greatest obstacles to the Federation's progress. He commented:

One of the great obstacles to our progress in the past has been our failure to realise that we have been too parochial. Every Catholic will naturally take a proper pride in his own parish. To preach against that would be like preaching patriotism and forgetting to be patriotic to one's own hearth-stone. But pride in one's own parish is consistent with pride in the progress of the Church in another parish. We have acted as if we were oblivious of the existence and welfare of other parishes, and the Church has not gained by such action. Unity and the forces which make for unity, have been hampered and impeded by the narrowness of the parochial spirit.[20]

Any attempt to dismantle 'a parochial mentality,' or what Sharrock called the 'parochial spirit,' could have been misconstrued as an attack on the autonomy and authority of the clergy who had worked unceasingly in encouraging their people to finance the building and maintaining of churches and parish schools. Philip Hughes, a priest of the Diocese of Salford who knew Casartelli well, referred to how 'the Federation was not clerically controlled; it was autonomous vis-à-vis the clergy, but not autonomous vis-à-vis the bishop … What such a scheme needed absolutely, if it were to sur-mount prejudices and suspicions too evident to need description, was the active presidency of the bishop – the bishop active in the Federation, and seen to be active by all, at every turn.'[21]

The 'prejudices and suspicions too evident to mention' refer to the atti-tude of the clergy. Casartelli never ceased to hope that the Federation would take root in nearly every parish in the diocese.[22] Yet despite repeated appeals to the clergy to remedy the deficiencies in membership,[23] the actual number of members never rose above a small percentage of the total Catholic population. This did not escape Casartelli's notice: 'from an inspection of individual returns we are much disappointed to notice in both Manchester and Salford and other districts some large missions wherein the muster is either altogether disproportionate to the number of the faithful, or where the Federation is practically non-existent.'[24]

In 1915 Casartelli was still complaining of 'the apathy and lack of support in too many quarters.'[25] The result of this, he warned, would be that the diocese would never be able to 'look forward to a succession of laymen trained and qualified for every form of useful civic service.'[26] The clergy still remained hostile and uninterested in the Federation. The problem, Casartelli complained, was that 'quite mistaken prejudices were at the bottom of such abstention or opposition. Such an attitude resulted in narrow 'parochialism'.[27] During the Diocesan Synod of 1915 he made an impassioned plea for the clergy to support him and the Federation by cultivating a sense of *sentire cum episcopo*.[28] This would raise the minds of the clergy beyond the narrow horizon imposed by the limits of their parochial boundaries in proportion to their coming to share in his own wider vision. Nevertheless, several months later he noted in his diary the 'sad story of break up of the Catholic Federation at St Patrick's, always a storm centre.'[29] A series of recruitment campaigns began around the Diocese to engender an *esprit de corps* in the Federation. The first was held specifically for clergy in the Manchester and Salford district. Casartelli presided at the meeting at which twenty mission rectors attended, a fact that he found 'very satisfactory.'[30] Two weeks later he presided over a meeting of the laity at Bishop's House, Salford. He described it as 'a fine gathering ... chiefly women.'[31] A similar meeting for rectors took place in Bury, again attracting a 'good attendance, very favourable.'[32] A meeting in Blackburn attracted only fourteen or fifteen rectors. This was judged by Casartelli to have been only 'moderately successful.'[33] The twelve-week campaign in Manchester and Salford to stimulate renewed interest resulted in 10,000 new members.[34]

Was this a sufficient result to guarantee a more effective Federation? It would appear not, even though the clergy had shown their loyalty by attending the meetings. The Federation was still not given the support that Casartelli wanted. Toward the end of his episcopate the membership still remained ten times lower than it should have been for the situation to be considered satisfactory.[35] Financial troubles also blighted its life.[36] The greatest stumbling block had occurred in its earliest days with the accusation that, with the bishop's backing, it had tried to influence voting in the 1908 North-West Manchester by-election. To this issue we now turn: it provides good evidence in support of Aspden's judgement that the Federation 'did not prove to be the agent of Catholic unity that Casartelli had envisaged.'[37]

THE CATHOLIC FEDERATION AND THE 1908 BY-ELECTION IN NORTH-WEST MANCHESTER

In 'The Signs of the Times,' Casartelli had seen the Church as existing within the context of the liberal state and therefore 'bound to no political party.'[38] Likewise, in his conception, the Catholic Federation was to have no politics of its own and was meant to be the embodiment of un-political politics:

> Of its very nature it is and must be essentially non-political, for it must embrace men and women of every shade of political and economic belief, who must be left absolutely free to defend and carry out their political and economic principles, like all other citizens, except only when certain lines of action are opposed to Catholic principles, or to the vital interests of the Catholic Faith.[39]

The 1908 by-election demonstrated, however, that these high-sounding principles were not, in practice, sufficient to weld together the various factions of the Catholic community. The election was occasioned by the promotion of Winston Churchill, at that time a Liberal MP, to the Cabinet. The situation was aggravated by the fact that the McKenna Education Bill was then before Parliament. The Bill was unacceptable to Catholics because it posed a threat to Church schools. The dilemma was whether Catholics were to vote for Winston Churchill (and therefore Home Rule), or for the Tory candidate, William Joynson-Hicks,[40] who was sympathetic to the plight of Church schools. The Catholic Federation made the dilemma worse by being accused of favouring the Tory party. This accusation dogged the Federation for years to come. Peter Doyle says that the 'attempts to explain that it was not linked to any one political party occur so often that the accusation must have been common.'[41] Matters were further complicated by the fact that some members of the United Irish League[42] were opposed to the Catholic Federation. The misunderstanding and public wrangling that accompanied the by-election reflected a political split between the Catholics of Manchester. Casartelli's attempts to heal this rift by means of the Federation show him to have been aware of the weaknesses among his co-religionists.

With the approaching by-election, and aware of the distinct possibility of discord between the Catholic Federation and the United Irish League, an informal deputation of the Federation, led by its Chairman, Canon George Richardson, met members of the League. The hope was for a joint course of action and an agreed working policy. Much of the acrimony resulting from the 1908 fiasco may be traced to this meeting held on the 13 April 1908. Richardson told the assembly that he 'would not advise the Federation in any way to oppose itself as a Federation to Mr. Redmond[43] [...] so as not to show a divided front in Catholic politics,' when Redmond spoke with the full approval of the Archbishop of Westminster on matters concerning Education.[44] Richardson later claimed that this was his own suggested *modus vivendi* and was not meant as a pledge committing the Federation to follow any line of action taken by the Executive of the United Irish League in Manchester. The League however interpreted Richardson's statement differently. In essence they claimed to have understood that: 'in view of the recent speech by Mr. John Redmond M.P. at Manchester, in which he stated that the Irish party always acted on English Catholic Questions in accordance with the views of the English Catholic hierarchy, the Federation were agreed to leave the direction of the Catholic vote in Parliamentary elections ... to Mr. Redmond and the Irish party.'[45]

Why was this misapprehension not spotted earlier, before it gave rise to further misunderstandings? The truth is that neither side wished to give way as each claimed to be representative of the Church's best interests.[46]

Richardson claimed that 'much more has been made of the meeting than it conveyed,' because 'there has been read into that personal promise [of Richardson] powers which even [the] Bishop could not have given, viz.: – the right of the United Irish League to speak authoritatively on questions concerning faith and morals.'[47] This meeting was followed by an interview between a group from the Thomas Davis Branch[48] of the League and Churchill. The Davis Branch succeeded in drawing from Churchill verbal promises regarding the withdrawal of the McKenna Education Bill and due consideration of Home Rule for Ireland.[49] These concessions won for Churchill the support of the Irish voters. The Catholic Federation decided to take no action on the matter.

As well as the differences between the United Irish League and the Federation, members of Casartelli's senior clergy were of divided opinion. Richardson and the Revd T. Sharrock supported the Federation, but Canon Patrick Lynch of Hulme,[50] did not. Lynch wanted a deputation of Catholic laymen to approach Churchill and put to him certain questions on educational matters. Casartelli would not allow this and strongly resisted any action that was independent of the Federation.[51] However, Canon Tynan, with Casartelli's approval, organised a meeting of the priests in North-West Manchester. Richardson and Sharrock took this as a snub to the Federation.[52] In part, the purpose of the meeting was to get all the rectors to work with the Federation. The rectors in due course drew up a manifesto[53] and a course of action vis-à-vis the election. This amounted to opposition against Churchill and the Liberals. When John Redmond declared on 16 April that he could not ask Irishmen to vote for Churchill, the way looked open for the implementation of the action suggested by the clergy. At a meeting on Good Friday, 17 April, the United Irish League, in order to gain time for manoeuvre, asked the Federation not to declare a policy and to refrain from distributing the clergy manifesto. The Federation acquiesced. Arrangements were then made for a further meeting on Easter Sunday.

During all this time Casartelli had been ill and confined to his rooms since 7 April, but still able to hold meetings; on 17 April, he noted: 'several clergy re. N.W. Manchester elections: things in extraordinary confusion!'[54] The following day he wrote: 'Many visitors again re. Election – confusion more confused!'[55] The prevarication of the United Irish League spurred him to write to three of his senior clergy: 'we are being sold to the enemy by our friends of the League'[56] and: 'The Catholic Federation and myself have been working loyally with the Irish League representatives and I am beginning to fear that the latter (including some of the Clergy I regret to say) have not been playing fair.'[57] He was aware that, if the clergy manifesto in support of Joynson-Hicks were distributed, then a split in the Catholic community would be inevitable.[58] During one of the various meetings with the clergy, Casartelli handed Richardson a letter for him to use at his discretion. Despite wanting to remain impartial and above party politics, he felt it his duty to make his views known and to exercise his authority.

Meanwhile the United Irish League continued to prevaricate. The Easter Sunday meeting was adjourned until the following day when a further postponement was requested. The Catholic Federation felt unable to agree and decided to publish, as an expression of their views, Casartelli's letter. The Federation's reasons for acting as they did was to the effect that 'to have waited longer would have nullified any action which they might have thought it desirable to take, and that the Catholic vote would have been thrown away.'[59] Richardson explained that, 'The Executive of the Federation had never dreamt of asking his Lordship to interfere in any way. His letter was written at his own initiative and was a dignified, gentle, yet firm assertion that Catholics could vote for Mr. Joynson-Hicks, but not for Mr. Churchill on the Education question only.'[60]

In his letter Casartelli explained that the election *per se* did not concern Catholics as Catholics in its political, social or commercial aspects. However, the election did concern Catholics in its religious aspects i.e. the issue of Catholic schools. He felt that it was his 'duty to advise and direct our flock in the matter from the point of view of the sacred interest in Catholic education.'[61] After weighing the various views and opinions of the clergy, the Catholic Federation, and representatives of the Irish political party, he concluded that Mr. Joynson-Hicks had satisfactorily answered concerns about Catholic education. Mr. Winston Churchill had not. Therefore 'the Catholic Federation in the supreme interest of Catholic education are fully justified in casting their votes in his [Joynson-Hicks] favour.'[62] With masterly understatement, Casartelli wrote in his diary, 'Considerable excitement in town owing to publication of my letter to Federation on Election.'[63] The damage was done. Casartelli was seen to have spoken in favour of the Federation and against the United Irish League. Redmond, after having been assured that Home Rule would be considered in the next parliamentary session, withdrew his recommendation that the Irish vote should not go to Churchill. During an open-air meeting in Stevenson Square, Manchester, the United Irish League denounced the clergy of North-West Manchester and their manifesto as 'fanatics' and declared themselves to be the only trusted allies of the Bishops of England on the education question. These events showed that, despite the attempts at friendly overtures between the United Irish League and the Catholic Federation, the underlying reality was that the former was definitely aligned with political ends – Home Rule for Ireland. Therefore it did, in Casartelli's words, 'dally' with Churchill, hoping for a favourable response on the question of Home Rule, and was prepared to procrastinate in its dealing with the Federation in order to achieve this. In doing so it was simply acting according to its nature as a political body. Difficulties had arisen because the Federation was too idealistic in its hopes of securing definite assistance from the United Irish League. The whole episode shows the difficulty of acting in the political arena whilst trying to maintain a policy of 'un-political politics'. Realistically, the Catholic Federation could not have hoped to escape the censure of influencing the way Catholics were to vote. Churchill believed the result would have been very different 'but for those sulky Irish Catholics changing sides at the last moment under priestly pressure.'[64]

Casartelli's letter was a direct and public act of support for Joynson-Hicks. He hoped that the people of the diocese would pay heed to his voice, but the members of the United Irish League chose not to and even went as far to criticise him publicly. Opinion was split. Casartelli had actually said more than the Archbishop of Westminster, who had not issued any statement about the way Catholics were to vote. The *Catholic Herald* had urged Catholics to vote for Churchill, believing that he would best serve both Home Rule and Education.[65] Casartelli was manifestly over-reaching himself, by allowing his own opinions to assume an authority they did not have. By doing this he contributed, to a greater or lesser degree, to the divisions among the Catholics of the diocese. On the night of the election he wrote in his journal – 'The great election-day! Immense excitement. News received about 9.30 p.m. Joynson-Hicks elected, Churchill defeated. A great victory!'[66] Years later, in reply to a request for support from a would-be politician, Casartelli wrote: 'I have always on principle … avoided taking any active part in political elections, except on the rare occasion when it has meant a definite overt contest on behalf of our schools, as at the famous Churchill contest.'[67]

Within a short space of time the Federation was once again accused of acting politically by the Liberal-supporting Irish voters.

THE CATHOLIC FEDERATION AND THE 1910 GENERAL ELECTION

When Canon George Richardson died in 1909, Canon O'Kelly succeeded him as the Chairman of the Manchester and Salford District Committee. Casartelli looked to O'Kelly to heal the rift that had occurred during Richardson's tenure of office. He wrote to him saying, 'I believe *you* are the man to save the situation. You are a *persona grata* on all sides, and I feel a *rapprochement* with certain parties at present hostile is more likely under your chairmanship than under anybody else's – perhaps even than under Can. Richardson himself.'[68]

Unwittingly, O'Kelly's appointment as rector of St Augustine's, Granby Row, may have fuelled an attack upon the Catholic Federation by Canon Lynch, whose application for the post had not been successful. Lynch was rector of St Wilfrid's, Hulme, an area heavily populated by Irish Catholics and supporters of the United Irish League. Casartelli hesitated to appoint Lynch as he had 'the reputation of having played a hostile part toward the Federation, and having at least failed on several critical occasions to defend the policy of the Bishop when attacked by the United Irish League on public platforms.'[69]

Following a meeting of the bishops from the six northern dioceses,[70] Casartelli wrote to Bourne to acquaint him informally of the proceedings in regard to the forthcoming General Election and to make suggestions as to the wording of a possible joint pastoral letter.[71] The letter was duly published. Only one question on behalf of the Church was to be asked of every parliamentary candidate – to ascertain their willingness to 'secure just treatment for Catholic schools.'[72] In a covering letter Casartelli cautioned his clergy: 'I need hardly impress upon the Clergy the extreme importance of remaining both in word and act, wholly aloof from all purely party politics during the coming electoral contest.'[73]

He instructed that the question for the candidates was to be put by the Federation. If in a particular locality no branch existed then the task was to fall to the clergy. Answers received were to be posted at the church door and be read out, without comment, to the congregation at every Mass. Casartelli wrote to the Rev. T. Sharrock and urged that the Catholic Federation avoid anything that 'may be considered direct *political* action.'[74]

In spite of these clear instructions, the Catholic Federation, and by implication Casartelli, once again found itself bearing the brunt of severe criticism for meddling in politics. The point of contention was – exactly who among the Federation was meant to present the question? Canon Lynch was so incensed by the suggestion as to how the information was to be gathered that he wrote to the *Manchester Guardian*[75] claiming that a small group of officials of the Federation had taken the matter out of the hands of approximately 120,000 Catholics and 100 clergy by undertaking to address the candidates. Lynch argued that the local rectors, *via* members of the local committees of the Federation, should have done this. This objection by Lynch echoed the comment made by Mgr Boulaye to Casartelli when the idea of the Federation was first mooted – that it ignored the clergy.[76] Lynch considered such action to be degrading and humiliating as it gave the impression that only a select few of the Federation were the true guardians of the Faith. He complained that the answers to the question were withheld by the Federation and not distributed to the rectors. In the Hulme area of Manchester, where

Lynch was rector, the Liberal candidate, C. T. Needham, enjoyed the support of the United Irish League. Lynch pointed out that the behaviour of the Catholic Federation had caused Needham to appear in a bad light because of its claim that he had not replied to the question. Needham had in fact replied, but too late to prevent the Federation condemning him as not having done so. Casartelli was deeply pained by Lynch's public denouncement. He saw it as 'striking a blow of so serious a character at Catholic unity. No other incident in my episcopate has caused me such distress.'[77] A series of letters in the pages of the *Manchester Guardian* show how strong the feeling against the Catholic Federation was in certain quarters. Only one letter expressed any support for Casartelli and what he was trying to achieve by means of the Federation. One letter signed, 'A Priest of the People' (a pseudonym meant to convey the idea that the Bishop was out of touch?) claimed that only loyalty to the Bishop prevented 'some of the clergy and a great number of the faithful from breaking into open hostility.'[78] He described the Federation as a 'ghastly failure' whose membership was negligible and how the number of people present at many meetings could be counted on the figures of one hand. There was truth in this observation. Another complained of the 'domineering methods of the Catholic Federation' which caused the emphasising of strife and disunion between English and Irish Catholics.[79] The writer, signing himself or herself as 'J.M.', estimated that 'three fourths of the clergy and all the leading Irish laity' were of this opinion.

T. Sharrock and T. F. Burns replied to Lynch's letter stating that it had been the Federation's prerogative to decide whether it was to approach the candidates either by a committee or by district committees.[80] This does not sufficiently explain the reasons for the underlying groundswell against the Federation. Casartelli by his comments on the affair seemed equally oblivious to the sense of dissatisfaction and hostility toward the Federation. At the annual meeting of the Manchester and District Committee in 1910 he blamed the early timing of the elections in some parts of Manchester as the reason why some of the replies had not been supplied in time. He maintained that, if this had not been the case, then the critics of the Federation would have had no grounds for complaint.[81]

Why then did Casartelli continue to pursue the cause of the Catholic Federation in the face of such ill feeling, the widening of the division between the Irish and English members of the community, and the apathy of many clergy and laity? Casartelli did so, largely because he was too much of an idealist to see that in questions as emotive as Home Rule, compromise was necessary. The question of Home Rule was for Casartelli not a problem of nationalism, as it was for the Irish in his diocese, but a problem that caused disunity and friction within the Catholic community. Casartelli could not see this: his family background had left him emotionally removed from the Irish Question. Yet many in his diocese had close bonds with Ireland, and the question for them was too real to be put to one side in favour of 'un-political politics.' When he later wrote in his diary 'An historical day: today the Royal Assent was given to the Home Rule Bill for Ireland, D.G.!,'[82] it was not because of what Ireland hoped to gain, but because it meant the end of bitter strife and the removal of a serious obstacle to the organisation of Catholic forces in his diocese. The idea of 'un-political politics' thus remained 'a truth without a home,' the conviction of an uncompromising theoretician. His dogged attitude was not borne of stubbornness or a lack of willingness to try other means to forward the cause of the Church, although he never in fact did attempt any. He firmly believed in the principle of *'l'union fait la force'*; he never tried to force his clergy to support the Federation. He appealed to them to join with him in heart and mind and so see beyond the confines of single issues or parish boundaries. He tirelessly advocated a spirit of *sentire cum episcopo*, but he was nevertheless too inactive and removed from the Federation in its practical life and activity to achieve the effects he desired so strongly. Philip Hughes summed up the problem perfectly when he wrote: 'In nothing could the fallacy be more fatal that, whoever is commissioned in authority's name enjoys authority's prestige, and is as effective as authority's self.'[83]

After having had his fingers thus burned on two occasions, Casartelli wrote to T. F. Burns on the eve of the second General Election of 1910: 'As the forth-coming elections will turn purely and exclusively upon constitutional issues ... in which Catholics are free to hold any views, and Education will not enter into the contest, it is judged desirable that neither the Bishops nor their Federations should take any part in the contest.'[84]

Even if the Federation had refrained from meddling in the politics of the previous elections, it is still very unlikely that it would have proved more successful. The clergy were not in favour of the idea, as it appeared to by-pass them. The officials acted in a high-handed manner and tended to see everything from the perspective of the Federation. On one occasion Casartelli remonstrated with Sharrock, saying how he 'cannot let the Federation over-ride the government of the Diocese' neither could he 'suffer it to dictate a policy to me or my advisors.'[85] However, even when he admitted to being 'at the end of his tether'[86] with the financial mis-management of the Federation, and no longer in a position to fund it out of his own pocket, Casartelli failed to remove these people from their posts or to take a more firm hand in the running of the organisation.[87] He also found the *Catholic Federationist* to be too polemical and destructive.[88] This is symptomatic of Casartelli being a remote figure in relation to his diocese. He was happy to delegate tasks to his trusted priests and to the leaders of the Catholic Federation, especially T. F.

Burns. Yet the actions of these leaders, in particular Burns, won Casartelli criticism; for example, Bourne was very critical of Burns' methods and actions.[89]

THE CATENIAN ASSOCIATION

By the time of the 1908 by-election, a group of laity, among them members of the Thomas Davis Branch of the United Irish League, were already meeting informally and preparing the ground for another association of laymen distinct from the Catholic Federation.[90] This was the beginning of the Catenian Association, originally known as the 'Chums', with whom Casartelli's name was closely associated. Peter Lane comments that 'the Irish were an important part of the original "Chums"',[91] but dismisses the idea of one of the founding members, Frank Pendergast, that it was formed 'as a result of a split among Irish Nationalists and among Catholics with Irish sympathies as a result of the present Prime Minister (Mr Winston Churchill) being defeated by Mr Johnson [sic] Hicks at a by-election when Mr. Churchill took the Government side on the Education question.'[92] Lane bases this conclusion on a supposed insufficient time lapse between the 1908 election on 24 April, and the submission of a proposal for the Association reaching Casartelli's desk on 14 May. He argues that this would not have allowed time for a constitution and rules to be drawn up. However, Pendergast's opinion finds support in the fact that many of the Thomas Davis Branch of the United Irish League were businessmen and merchants, who would have feared repercussions in the form of loss of revenue as a result of ill-feeling engendered by the election campaign. Indeed, the founding members of the 'Chums' met with Casartelli to discuss the difficulties that they were facing as Catholic businessmen and the attraction felt by Catholics for Freemasonry, in order to overcome these disadvantages.[93]

Lane sees Casartelli as a 'bishop prepared to invite his people to act without priestly leadership, to learn to walk tall in their own right ... And when some of them endeavoured to do so – in the Federation – he gave them his full support, knowing, as he did, that their activity and the Federation was opposed by many priests, most active Irish voters and almost all the 'old' Catholics.'[94] Does this assessment represent the true reasons for the forming of the Catenian Association? There is no doubt that many clergy did not support, and in fact were hostile towards, the Catholic Federation. Nevertheless it is going too far to say that the foundation of the Catenians represented Casartelli's wishes for a Catholic middle-class laity independent of ecclesiastical control. His whole approach to the question of the lay apostolate contradicts such an interpretation. When he requested other bishops to allow the Association within their diocese he unfailingly stated that one of its primary purposes was either to prevent membership of, or to wean men away from, the Freemasons.[95] The founding of the Catenians was not related to a distinct apostolate nor did they set out to act on behalf of or represent the Church in any way, as did Catholic teachers for example. Casartelli therefore would have considered that strict ecclesiastical control was not as necessary as with other organisations that had a distinct apostolate.[96] The purpose of the Catenians was in Casartelli's words 'self-defence ... [and] common interests.'[97] Since many of his clergy had failed to support the Federation, their absence from its ranks would no doubt prove advantageous.[98] Many years later he wrote to Bishop Amigo: 'Many thanks. Your letter decides. I did not know that these Knights of Saint Columba were hostile to the Catenians. That being so, I won't have them in the diocese. The fact that the Catenians do not admit clergy into their ranks is to me in their favour.'[99]

Casartelli's inclination to support the proposal put to him by John O'Donnell[100] on 14 May 1908 on behalf of the 'Chums' was possibly heightened precisely because it embraced members of the United Irish League, and thus might prove to be a means of 'winning them over' and so heal divisions. On at least one occasion Casartelli attended a dinner with the leaders of the Davis Branch of the League. The party included Dan Boyle, M.P. for Co. Mayo and Daniel McCabe, the first Lord Mayor of Manchester whom Casartelli proposed as a Knight of St Gregory. This is evidence of one of Casartelli's strengths as a leader – a social ease that enabled him to act the part of the quiet diplomat, able to participate in social functions and reap the benefits of social intercourse. A further strength was his freedom from any feelings of ill will. McCabe had been one of the leading members of the Davis Branch who had publicly criticised Casartelli; this did not prevent Casartelli in later years writing in a pastoral letter: 'The hope has been repeatedly expressed in public that the example of Alderman McCabe may stimulate other Catholic laymen to take a more active part in public life and in working for the social welfare not only of our own body, but of the community at large.'[101]

McCabe was not a supporter of the Federation. T. F. Burns, reporting to Casartelli on the state of the Federation as at January 1917, wrote: 'The elevation to the Lord Mayoralty of Federation's chief opponent was, naturally, a blow to Federation, [sic] and he has consistently exerted his great influence, and his well-known anti-clerical sentiments to the detriment of Federation during his two years of office.'[102]

One other example of Casartelli's graciousness was his attitude toward Canon Lynch, whose letter to the *Manchester Guardian* had caused him great pain. On the day of Lynch's death, Casartelli recorded in his diary: 'the appalling news of the death of my old friend and colleague, Provost Lynch, ordained with me 10 September 1876. R.I.P.'[103]

CASARTELLI AND SOCIALISM

The Catholic Federation's withdrawal from direct political action subsequent to the 1908 and 1910 elections did not signal its total retreat from politics. Socialism and the emergence of the Labour Party represented an old and a new foe respectively. Casartelli's abhorrence of Socialism was another trait he had inherited from his mentor and former bishop, Herbert Vaughan, who had written:

> Satan no longer appeals to our fears, but to our pride, to our national desire for well being and material prosperity ... the doctrines of socialism are the outcome of his teaching, terrorism, incendiarism, violence and murder are lawful weapons, whenever it is judged that they will advance the cause of socialism.[104]

The reaction of Casartelli and his Federation, notably in the person of its organising secretary, T. F. Burns, against these two movements caused their isolation from the rest of the Catholic body.[105] Peter Doyle finds the roots of Casartelli's aversion to Socialism in his first-hand experience of anti-clericalism during the time he spent in Belgium.[106] However, before ever living in Belgium Casartelli had, in his 'John Pearl Lay Sermons,' already formulated his thoughts concerning the two spheres of human existence, i.e. the human and the divine. Socialism was a basic contradiction of this philosophy of life in that it failed to take into account the supernatural aspect of human existence. His repugnance towards Socialism was further compounded when he later saw it becoming an insidious threat among the working class of his diocese and having an adverse affect on the Labour Party.[107] When Socialism began to encroach upon the field of education Casartelli became alarmed. This was clearly a terrain in his view where such philosophies had no right to tread. During his Christmas homily in 1907 he warned of how 'Socialism had entered much more largely during the past twelve months into the controversy around religious education and religion generally. It had assumed a much more serious and aggressive attitude towards religion.'[108] The situation in France, which had witnessed the persecution of the Church by means of the Associations Laws and the confiscation of Church schools under Waldeck-Rousseau and Émile Combes,[109] served as a warning of what could happen in England if vigilance was not maintained.

The first time Casartelli's name is mentioned in the same breath as Socialism was after he had addressed the Manchester and Salford Co-operative Society, when, ironically, he earned the accusation of 'taking sides in a great economic protest' and that 'he was lending his countenance to a movement which was essentially socialistic in character.'[110] In his defence, he called upon the writings of Pope Leo XIII where he found that the Church not only failed to denounce, but positively supported, co-operativism: 'all unions and combinations of the working-class especially for legitimate objects were distinctly declared to be good and commendable.'[111] Sometime later, he addressed the Catholic Federation on the theme of 'the spiritual side of social work'; here he sought to clarify the antagonism between Catholicism and Socialism. Yet again his ideas drew adverse publicity, this time from the Catholic Socialist Society[112] which quoted him as a supporter and distributed a statement he had made in his lecture as a declaration in their favour! Casartelli replied that it was as 'inconsistent to speak of a 'Catholic Socialist Society' as it would be to speak of a 'Catholic Wesleyan Society'.'[113] He entirely disapproved of any Catholic joining a society that was in any way aligned with Socialism.

Casartelli has been perceived with justifiable reason as a virulent anti-Socialist.[114] Nevertheless, when all his statements and ideas on the subject are drawn together, it is possible to detect a more open attitude, one that in some ways is more akin to Bourne's readiness, expressed much later in his Pastoral Letter, 'The Nation's Crisis', (1918), to acknowledge 'certain features of the modern unrest which, though their expression may be crude and exaggerated, we recognise as the true lineaments of the Christian spirit.'[115]

Casartelli's approach to Socialism was characteristically intellectual and analytical. He saw that God had created Society and that the 'philosophy of the social' indicated what belonged to Society. It was permissible therefore to accept that part of Socialism that was Christian in its origins. The danger lay in the termination – *ism* which he took to signify that Social*ism* was identifiable with agnosticism and the denial of religious truth. He maintained that whilst Catholics could not accept a Socialistic programme, they could, and ought as a duty, to support certain social reforms which it contained such as: the rights of labour, the duty of capital toward labour, the right to a living wage, time for social, moral and physical improvement, and old-age pensions. Casartelli understood these to be essentially Christian aspirations. He did not frame the question in terms of whether a Catholic could become a Socialist or not, as though the two taught different things. What made Socialism unacceptable was an inherent error which invalidated 'much of the humanitarianism and philanthropy which directs the otherwise laudable efforts to ameliorate the lot of the poor toilers and the disinherited, not only because they [Socialists] proceed from a false principle, but because they set before those whom they materially benefit a false ideal and philosophy of life.'[116] He ventured to say that Catholicism not only taught many of the same things as Socialism, but that 'probably the majority of social reform advocated by Socialists could be, and were, equally advocated by Catholics, and were in complete harmony with Catholic teaching.'[117]

If Belgium was the place where he knew from personal experience the anti-clericalism associated with continental Socialism, it was also the country where he saw an integrated 'Socialistic policy'[118] in operation, having been established for twenty-four years. During a visit to Namur, he recorded in his diary a conversation about 'social questions' and how the 'Walloon work-people [were] excellent Catholics – even daily communicants – *and* Socialists!?'[119] He saw no difference between the practice of the Belgian Government and the policies advocated by the Socialist party in England. The difference lay in the divergent philosophy fundamental to the two systems of thought: 'It was not that Socialism advocated policies, legislation, or social reforms that were adverse to Catholicity, but it was that underlying the two systems was a different theory of life.'[120]

However, despite his experience of Belgian Catholics who claimed to be Socialists and Catholics, and the high regard he had for the 'Socialistic policy' of the Belgian government, he could not here in England distinguish between continental forms of Socialism and that espoused by the Labour Party. This failure would eventually lead to Casartelli and the Catholic Federation being isolated from the mainstream of Catholic thought and even to him receiving a rebuke from Bourne on more than one occasion. Problems mounted when Casartelli involved the Catholic Federation in the question of Socialism and the Labour Party. The Federation duly wrote an open letter to the Labour Party recognising 'the value of the work and appreciating the efforts it has made to improve the general condition of the working-classes.'[121] However, the letter was double-edged in that it sought clarification of Labour's educational policy and attitude toward religion and warned it that the latter was a potential danger, and a possible cause of loss of support. The Federation advised that these issues should not form the planks of Labour's election platform. Such advice was unwelcome: and from hereon the two bodies began to drift apart. Any attempts at mutual understanding became increasingly more difficult, due largely to the strident tones and unyielding criticism of T. F. Burns.

Casartelli's attitude to the Social Question was further prone to conflict also because his stance was theoretical and different from that of Fr Vincent McNabb OP, who favoured a social interpretation of Christianity. This divergence of outlook reflects an earlier difference of opinion between Manning and Vaughan. The latter's response to the challenge of Socialism, like Casartelli's, was in the form of Catholic charitable organisations, such as the Protection and Rescue Society (which Vaughan founded whilst Bishop of Salford). Manning on the other hand looked for more social reform. Casartelli's cerebral response is seen in his founding, in 1908, a 'School of Social Science,' based at St Bede's College, for the study and advancement of

Catholic social doctrine. Its aim was to 'train up a body of well-informed, earnest enquirers and students, who in their turn may become competent exponents of the true Christian principles underlying the solution of the great social problems which Church and State have to face.'[122] The School of Social Science eventually fell under the auspices of the Catholic Federation; but its ideas, like those of the Federation, were hard to propagate in Britain, and readily led to misunderstandings.

The influence of Charles Plater and the Catholic Social Guild, of which Casartelli was a supporter, is discernible in Casartelli's foundation of the School of Social Science. The Catholic Social Guild[123] arose from a meeting held during the 1909 Catholic Truth Society Conference in Manchester when it was decided to form an organisation which would 'endeavour to promote concerted social study.'[124] Casartelli announced its formation to the General meeting and 'throughout manifested his keen interest in the undertaking'.[125] There was a natural rapport between Charles Plater, the Jesuit priest and a central figure in the work of the Catholic Social Guild, and Casartelli. Marked by Continental contacts and experience, they both stressed the need for education at all levels and urged a proper and adequate rôle for the laity in the mission of the Church in order to counter the threat of organised Socialism. In fact, Casartelli was asked by Plater to write the prefaces for two of his books related to the Social Question and the education of the laity.[126]

CASARTELLI AND THE LABOUR PARTY

Patrick Doyle has outlined the varied responses of the Catholic Church to the emerging Labour Party.[127] He notes how on one side the Catholic Social Guild promoted a policy of 'permeation' whilst on the other the Catholic Federation and the National Conference of Catholic Trade Unionists preferred denunciation. Although Casartelli disagreed with the public wrangling between the Catholic Social Guild and the Catholic Federation, he ultimately identified himself with the opinion of the latter. This is an apparent contradiction in Casartelli's thinking. His general understanding of the rôle of the laity was that it ought to 'permeate' the surrounding society. Indeed he saw great opportunities for this, and had himself set an example in his contribution to the civic life of Manchester *via* several of its learned societies. As we have seen, his first pastoral letter was a plea for the Catholic laity to permeate at all levels various civic bodies and organisations. However, his complete inability to distinguish between Continental Socialism and the ideas of the Labour Party prevented argument for this same accommodating spirit being heeded. If this had not been so – given that the vast majority of the people of his diocese were of the working class – he could actually have made a positive and influential contribution to the question of Catholics joining the Labour Party. The way in which any such hopes were to remain unfilled, is shown in the history of the Catholic Trade Unionists. This organisation sprang up from different sections of the Salford Diocesan Catholic Federation being told by Casartelli that Catholic members of trades union ought to reconsider their position in the light of the Labour Party's position on Church schools and religious education.[128] Their purpose was to lobby union meetings and the Trades Union Congress against the donation of funds to the Labour Party as a protest at its wish to establish a system of education incompatible with the teachings of the Catholic Church. The Catholic Trade Unionists held their first meetings at St Bede's College and at Bishop's House, Salford in 1908. In 1910 it became the National Conference of Catholic Trade Unionists because the development of political agitation meant it was undesirable to act under the auspices of a sub-committee of the Catholic Federation. One of the protagonists in the organisation was T. F. Burns. Given his outspoken manner, it is not surprising that tension soon began to emerge. In July 1914 the National Conference of Catholic Trade Unionists asked the more progressive Catholic Social Guild to define its attitude towards Socialism and to reject the idea that 'Socialism is patient of Catholic interpretation.'[129] When the Catholic Social Guild refused to comply with the request, disagreement spilled over into a public dispute. Casartelli had once again to suffer the pain of seeing two Catholic organisations, one led by the Organising Secretary of his Catholic Federation, attacking one another in the pages of the press. Charles Plater wrote to Casartelli, whom he recognised as having been 'extremely kind to [him] in the past,' asking his advice and help in 'removing the unfortunate differences.'[130] Casartelli forwarded the letter to his Vicar General after having pencilled at the foot of the letter: 'I would like your opinion on this. I, too, deplore the public quarrelling.' He then tried to smooth over the rift by quiet diplomacy by writing to the two parties concerned – Mgr Parkinson, Chairman of the Catholic Social Guild, and to T. F. Burns, Secretary of the Conference of Catholic Trade Unionists. In his correspondence Casartelli stated his belief that the dispute would not have arisen if certain speakers of the CSG had not made such outspoken comments. These included 'Mr. Abretton Brock, a leading Fabian' and Fr. Vincent McNabb.[131] He considered the differences to have been due more to terminology rather than to a fundamental divergence of opinion. The letter to Burns was more forthright and demanded that the public disagreement cease.[132] Casartelli aligned himself with the views of the Catholic Trade Unionists as he explained to Mrs Virginia Crawford of the Catholic Social Guild. The Guild, he said, had weakened its campaign by certain of its members having 'coquetted with Socialism, and refused to join us in the categorical thesis that no form of Socialism is susceptible of a Catholic interpretation, and that no Catholic can belong to any Socialist organisation.'[133]

In 1918 the Labour Party by its 'Clause IV' formally adopted a Socialist agenda. This raised acutely the question whether Catholics could become members of the Labour Party. In a speech to the Catholic Women's League, Casartelli expressed his fear of the 'Labour Party becoming strangled by the Socialist Party' and how 'it would be disastrous for any Catholic Association to coquette with Socialism.'[134] The question of membership of the Labour Party was becoming a more important question because many more people had become enfranchised; among them many Catholics, who found the Labour Party appealing. In November of the same year the National Conference of Catholic Trade Unionists, through the offices of its secretary T. F. Burns, asked the hierarchy for a pronouncement on the question of whether a Catholic could join, render financial aid to, or accept the association of their trade union with, the Labour Party.[135] He felt that, if no such pronouncement were made, the Conference would then feel obliged to discontinue its contest with Socialism. Casartelli clarified his view on Catholics and Socialism in a letter to Burns:

> Catholics cannot become Socialists. But Catholics can *co-operate* with Socialists in any common measure or measures of which both parties approve, (e.g. the housing question) as they can co-operate with Anglicans, (e.g. in defence of religious education.) ... But I hold that a Catholic cannot support a Socialist *qua* Socialist and for the purpose of supporting Socialism.[136]

The hierarchy as a body made no comment on the matter. Bishop Keating of Northampton advised the people of his diocese who were members of the Labour Party to remain and to change it from within:

> Let them employ their voting strength and influence manfully, to dismiss from office and power those who misrepresent the true aims of trade unionism, and to replace them by honest men who will promote the interests of their own class without declaring an unjust war on every other class.[137]

This was a negation of the Conference's policy. Unperturbed, Burns continued his campaign by presenting the hierarchy, prior to their Low Week meeting, with a 'Statement of Facts in Connection with the National Conference of Catholic Trade Unionists and Socialists'[138] in which he openly criticised those, namely the Catholic Social Guild and by implication the Bishop of Northampton, who approved of 'permeation.' Such people, Burns claimed, had been deluded by priests and the Catholic press into believing that 'English Socialism is a kind of Socialism which has not been condemned and they will now believe that a Catholic may be a Socialist unless our hierarchy definitely pronounces to that effect.'[139]

Given the stridency of Burns' views, the days of the Catholic Trade Unionists as a formal group were numbered. At the national level, the bishops persisted with their silence in the face of Burns' attack. This tactic was effective. Soon afterwards Burns informed Casartelli that given such silence the time had come when the National Conference must consider disbanding. Casartelli, not knowing how to deal with this crisis, turned to Bourne for advice.[140] The damage was already done, Bourne's reply was icy and distant. Bourne blamed the *Federationist* for being an obstacle to united action. He thought Burns, in whom he no longer had confidence, a source of irritation and 'very unwise'.[141] The Archbishop had no intention of getting involved any further, and wished to distance himself from Burns and his ideas and irritating behaviour. His reply was also an oblique criticism of Casartelli for allowing Burns so much scope and for entrusting him with such a prominent position.

As a counter to the Labour Party and to the idea of permeation, T. F. Burns formed in September 1918 the Centre Labour Party, of which he was secretary. He wrote to Casartelli to inform him of his actions but did not seek his explicit approval because of its political nature.[142] The Centre Labour Party's objects were: to give political expression to Workers' requirements along the lines of Christian Democracy and not Socialist Democracy; to concentrate on wages, housing and land; to oppose State monopoly of teaching. The Centre Labour Party arose out of the perceived failure of the Trades Union Congress to protect non-Socialist trade unionists from the socialism of the Labour Party, which Burns claimed had become Socialist in 1918. The Centre Labour Party only ever had two branches, one in Manchester and one in Blackburn. It managed to field only one candidate in the municipal elections, Gorton North Ward, Manchester, who was easily defeated by Labour. The candidate in question was Miss Frances Zanetti. As a potential councillor she had sought and gained Casartelli's approval.[143] Bourne did not approve of the Centre Labour Party, nor Catholic parties in general,[144] and wrote to Casartelli voicing his concern about the way that Burns was behaving politically.[145]

Burns was not easily defeated, however, and contacted Rome. Soon, seeking information on the relation of the Labour Party to Socialism, Cardinal Gasparri, the Cardinal Secretary of State at the Vatican, wrote to Casartelli along with Amigo of Southwark and Keating of Northampton. Burn's correspondence behind the British scenes, copied to Rome, manifests strong alarm. In February 1919 he had written to Stuart Coates, a Conservative

Unionist and member of the Catholic Union of Great Britain: 'Unless Authority intervenes, there is nothing but chaos in front of us.'[146] Fr Michael Clifton says that Coates had tried his best to get Benedict XV to condemn the Labour Party in Great Britain as a Socialist party.[147] Burns was also able to continue his campaign with senior support for a while. Despite Bourne's rebuke of Burns, Casartelli still saw fit to delegate to him the task of drawing up a memorandum on the question.[148] Burn's contribution was entitled 'The Socialist Formula and the Labour Party'. However, this was not well received: Bishop Amigo of Southwark wrote in his letter to Gasparri:

> My own considered opinion after inquiry is that the Labour Party will probably be in power in a short time and that it is for us to try and work with them ... There is a small body of Catholics who have moved for the Pope to take action against the Labour Party on the grounds that it is socialist, but it would be a profound mistake if we were to condemn the Labour Party.[149]

Canon Moyes was not happy either with the Salford Catholic Federation's agitation against Labour. He feared that it was ' ... leading us into a calamitous war with the Labour Party, to which seven-tenths of our people belong ... It will mean that the Catholic labouring man will have his religion put into antagonism to his political and professional interests and sympathies, resulting either in alienation from the Faith, or ostracism in his Trade Union and the odium of disloyalty to his fellow workmen.'[150]

In the end, Rome chose not to condemn the Labour Party as Socialist. In 1924, Salford's opposition to the Labour Party was finally silenced when Bourne pronounced that he knew of nothing in the official programme of the Labour Party that was opposed to the Catholic Church. Furthermore, he 'had reason to believe that many of the Labour leaders in their revulsion from the non-Christian principles of what was once known as the 'Manchester School,' were unconsciously *approximating more and more to the views of the Catholic Church.*'[151] Casartelli referred to this as a 'tremendous announcement' and ordered T. F. Burns to make no reply for fear of scandal and consequent trouble.[152] He felt that Bourne's statement was aimed at Salford and was perhaps occasioned by the *Catholic Federationist* being too violent in its opinions. Casartelli requested therefore that the *Federationist* be more positive and constructive in future as at times it had been too destructive with a tendency to 'shout', or even 'yell', thus discrediting much of what it had to say. Thus did the Salford Catholic laity – along with their fellow church members nationally – flow into political channels quite different from those which Casartelli, their determined continental leader, had initially hoped for.

CONCLUSION

How far did Casartelli further the 'century of the laity'? We can certainly say that he was a pioneer in this area; the Catholic Federation was the first attempt in England to achieve structured organisation of the Catholic laity. The Federation sought to overcome political and class differences, thus nullifying the effects of Socialism and one cause of political disunity among Catholics. However, it was largely a middle-class organisation and was therefore out of tune with the vast majority of the people of the Salford diocese, who belonged to the working class. Furthermore, the clergy were more accustomed to dealing with the laity through the various parish sodalities, whose purpose it was to foster personal piety, rather than with extra-parochial organisations such as the Federation. Suspicion and hostility thus arose, and Casartelli's wider hopes were curtailed. Moreover, in the final analysis, Casartelli's 'practical Ultramontanism' i.e. 'un-political politics', which the Catholic Federation sought to foster, was perceived by its critics as disingenuous because of the way, in the By-Election of 1908, Casartelli had swayed the Catholic vote.

Only seven months before his death, Casartelli lamented the fact that, in the elections for membership of the Board of Guardians in the Manchester area, a number of Catholics had been defeated. He felt sufficiently dejected, because of the apathetic response of voters, to speak of people suffering from 'the sleepy sickness' and the 'Church dormant.'[153] He also admitted feeling humiliated by having read in a Catholic newspaper the headline: 'Manchester and Salford Elections. Apathetic Voters'.[154] He ascribed failure in the elections to the fact that people had not joined the various bodies whose aim it was to organise the Catholic laity, such as the Catholic Federation, the Catholic Women's League, and the Catholic Truth Society. These same organisations aptly illustrate the fact that it was largely the middle class Catholics who were the constituents of his idea of an active laity. For example, the protagonists of these groups, T. F. Burns, Daniel McCabe, Frances Zanetti, and John O'Donnell, were all white-collar workers. Moreover, his failure to see the Labour Party in other than socialistic terms distanced him from the working class of his diocese.

At the outset of his episcopate Casartelli had feared failure as a bishop. Reading the headline about the elections in a Catholic newspaper, so late in his episcopate, had humiliated him. Had his fears, his nightmare, come true? In the concluding review of his episcopate, this question will be addressed.

Conclusion

⤛ ⽥ ⤜

What must have been the astonishment of all concerned when a priest, whose previous life and experience seemed so very little suited to fit him for the episcopal office, was selected for the See of Salford! A life of books and study; an academic career devoted to education and literary pursuits; an entire ignorance of affairs and inexperience in administration; but light acquaintance with parochial duties and none at all with financial matters: such do not appear to form a likely preparation for a successful episcopate.[1]

Casartelli died on 18 January 1925, at St Bede's College – the place which had been his home since 1877. The cause of death was (1) bronchitis, (2) cardiac failure. On his deathbed he re-read Snead-Cox's *Life of Cardinal Vaughan*, which he had first read in 1910 when it was published. On that occasion he described it as: 'wonderful … as good as a retreat. What lessons for *me*: as for every priest and bishop. Would that it might convert me!'[2] To the clergy of the diocese, Casartelli issued a last message asking for forgiveness for any act of 'disedification as priest and Bishop.'[3] If Casartelli in the last weeks of his life had remonstrated with himself for not having replicated the ideal of Vaughan and if he had committed any such musings to his diary, they were lost forever when the pages for this period were removed.

Casartelli, because of the reasons stated in 'The Signs of the Times', quoted above, feared failure as a bishop. He clearly believed himself to be unsuitable for the task and eloquently expressed that concern. Yet the task of a bishop is not that of a parish priest. Edward Henry Manning recognised this, and lamented that too many bishops were parish priests in their outlook: 'we are weak and the Episcopate is weak, because our Bishops are parish priests. They must be broader and have a bird's eye view of the Church and the English people.'[4] Casartelli was a man of vision who brought to the diocese of Salford a universal spirit: he was European by culture and learning, he spoke several European languages and was thereby open to the intellectual currents in mainland Europe. He was not parochially minded, and had a deep commitment to the 'foreign missions'. In many ways he was a bishop in the spirit of a Manning or a Vaughan: he did not view the Church as an *imperium in imperio*.

In assessing Casartelli's episcopate the nature of the diocese of Salford must be taken into consideration. It was geographically small, but numerically large. Poverty amongst its working-class inhabitants was prevalent. Due to the large percentage of Irish Catholics, who were naturally sympathetic to the cause of Home Rule for Ireland, the diocese lacked political cohesion. This made the struggle for the cause of Catholic schools all the more difficult for reasons already made clear in chapters seven and eight. Casartelli made 'organise' the watchword of his episcopate and unfailingly encouraged Catholics to overcome divisions and to act in concerted effort when Church and political interests clashed. The various Catholic organisations to be found in other European countries, and of which he had knowledge, impressed him greatly;[5] he therefore tried to emulate their spirit through the Catholic Federation – *the* work of his episcopate. However, in Salford, this vision failed to achieve what he hoped it would, because it became entangled with the politics of Irish Home Rule, as in the 1908 and 1910 elections. Nor did this vision capture the imagination of the parish clergy, who remained somewhat entrenched in their parochialism and deaf to Casartelli's plea, '*sentire cum episcopo*'. This appeal reached far beyond the horizons of most of his fellow clergy. Casartelli, like his mentor, Herbert Vaughan, saw the Church's mission as being 'beneficial ... to the whole world'.[6] Margaret Fletcher[7] nicely sums up the parochial mentality, which she, like Casartelli, encountered, by describing each parish as 'a fortress to be captured'.[8] Casartelli knew the art of delegation and used it to good effect, but he lacked the necessary 'hands-on' approach that might have enabled the Federation to be accepted step by step in one parish, then another. Philip Hughes gave this as one of the reasons for the Federation's failure.[9] The idea of the Federation remained a middle-class preserve; the vast majority of the people of Salford diocese lacked interest in the movement or failed to see its relevance.[10] Indeed, most of the officials of the various other diocesan organisations lived, with the fewest of exceptions, in middle-class areas of Manchester and Salford.[11]

Casartelli suffered throughout his life from ill health, but despite this handicap he did not content himself with simply maintaining the local Church over which he had oversight. He encouraged growth and expansion and especially tried to inspire the laity and clergy with vision: educationally, liturgically, and pastorally.[12] Mary Heimann's observation that spirituality is an 'elusive phenomenon'[13] must be applied to any attempt to assess Casartelli's success as a spiritual leader. By its very nature the evidence is neither tangible nor easily quantifiable. However, evidence in the *Relationes* that

Casartelli submitted to the Holy See every four years shows that he was able to report that the decrees on Holy Communion (*Sacra Tridentina* and *Quam Singulari*) were proving fruitful, and that priests were encouraging daily communion.[14] By 1922 he reported on how the custom of receiving communion daily was growing.[15]

The Salford Diocese did not escape the effects of the First World War and the general move toward secularisation. Casartelli detected Socialism, Spiritualism, and drunkenness to be among the greatest evils that affected the people of the diocese. With regard to family life, birth control was becoming more prevalent and the number of mixed-marriages had risen sharply in the period after the war.[16] To counter these ill effects Casartelli called for a series of General Missions throughout the diocese.[17]

At the turn of the twentieth century the Catholic Church in England was entering more fully into national life. This penetration was accelerated by the full participation of Catholics during the Great War. The Church in Salford was fortunate in having Casartelli as a bishop at this time because he set an excellent example of good citizenship and encouraged Catholics to look to the common good and not just denominational issues; his leadership was an example of 'cometh the hour, cometh the man'. In his *Relatio* for his *ad limina* visit in 1912, Casartelli noted how the Church stood in good relations with the local civil authority. This was in no small measure due to the respect he had gained from his fellow citizens and the fruit of his good influence on civic life in general.[18] Here we may contrast Casartelli with Bourne. At the time of Bourne's death, *The Times* in a leading article, reflected on his having been 'intensely English,' and how this was 'the key to the steady, unsensational growth of his personal influence.' It concluded that, 'time has justified him, notably in those education controversies where his foresight and wisdom are now widely acknowledged.'[19] Casartelli had favoured a far different approach. As Bourne was 'intensely English', so Casartelli was 'intensely European'. Characteristically, Casartelli saw the exercise of authority as the means of securing unity. This had some negative consequences. A comparison between Casartelli's reaction to the Labour Party with Bourne's propensity to say as little as possible and to be in no hurry, allows us to speculate that if Casartelli had had his way on the schools question, and a more vociferous stance had been adopted, the Church would have been in a more disadvantageous position as a result. However, one of the greatest strengths that Casartelli the European thinker brought to the episcopate, was his Christian humanism which imbued his vision of life and philosophy of education. This enabled him to see Church schools as beneficial to the whole of society and not just to the denominations to which they belonged. Frances Zanetti alluded to this quality by a citation from Terence:

homo sum et humani a me nil alienum puto. His outlook anticipated that of the opening paragraph of the decree of the Second Vatican Council, 'The Constitution on the Church in the Modern World', where the phrase is used to describe the members of the Church in their relation to the world: 'nothing genuinely human fails to raise an echo in their hearts.'[20] It is notable that other Council documents treat of issues which were also dear to Casartelli: the rôle of the laity, the liturgy, and not least the place of the Church in the modern world, for he too recognised that the Church was 'truly and intimately linked with mankind and its history'.[21] Above all, Casartelli's work for education encapsulated this latter point.

In relation to the First Vatican Council, Jeffrey von Arx has very recently commented on how 'contemporary Roman Catholics have realised in the last thirty-five years that when an ecumenical council has concluded, it is far from over.'[22] Similarly, we may say of the intellectual ability, the spirit, and the pastoral vision of Louis Charles Casartelli, that when his life came to an end, it was far from over. In his lifetime, many of his pioneering ideas did not enjoy the success he had anticipated. Nevertheless, they were not disproved. Precursors as they were to similar themes developed in the Second Vatican Council, they still await fruition.

Appendices

Appendix One

_____

Newmaniana

ॐ ⚹ ॐ

'A DAY AT EGBASTON'[1]

'It was a fine morning. After breakfast slowly walked by New Street, Brown Street, and Hagley Road to Egbaston. I was much impressed with what I saw of Birmingham streets. It seems in some respects a finer place than Manchester; less grimy at least. The Town Hall is a splendid Greek building, fine composite columns on a lofty pediment of rough stone, like St. George's Hall, Liverpool. Hagley Road is very fine, and the whole suburb very like Kensington in London. The Oratory is a curious building, anything but like a Catholic establishment outside. It has a clock face on the road. You approach the church by an atrium. The whole church reminds you of the Catholic University chapel in Dublin. It is Roman or basilican in form. This is altogether very striking and made me study it attentively. I must say it is in excellent taste. The details are so good and so rich. The colouring is especially dainty. Was pleased with the tapering variegated columns by St. Joseph's altar. The massive candelabra are remarkable. The roof is the poorest part. As I got in Fr Caswall, a stout jolly looking man was finishing giving the children's' instructions and repeating their prayers.

At 11 High Mass began. Everything pure Roman. After the Gospel at last Fr Newman got into the pulpit! For a little before I felt quite agitated and nervous so highly was my expectation raised. I recognised him at once: my portrait of him is excellent. Only I was more struck by his fine nose and aristocratic mien. He seemed very old and even feeble. His voice quite like a woman's: (Worsley's remark). He read Epistle and Gospel in a low, weak voice: nicely, but not peculiarly. His pronunciation is not at all exaggerated or affected by mannerisms. Then he began a plain straight forward conference: utterly unlaboured and simple. He said: last time I spoke to you about the angels and their probation. 1/ It seems as if all rational creatures must have their trials: the angels had it in the beginning; men all life through. This trial of the angels happened perhaps millions of years ago. 2/ We may infer that one third of the angels fell. That must have been a great number. If we look at all the small insects and other animals that swarm on the earth, we get an idea of the infinitable lives made by God. Well, these angels were like swarms of flies or locusts. 3/ I said that the angels had originally two great natural excellencies: power and knowledge. To those who stood the trial was then given a third, or a supernatural gift: grace. Grace is like the soul's light in which what is natural grows and performs its functions. A second supernatural gift, beatitude or vision then added as a reward. The same for man. 4/ We learn that a struggle took place between the good and evil spirits. St. John calls is 'a war in heaven'. We don't exactly know what it was, but that is the nearest image to it. We are told that Michael and his hosts cast Lucifer out of heaven. But by the inscrutable mercy of God, he was allowed to occupy this world; and there the strife is continued. 5/ This world is really beautiful and good: (illegible) in man, in organisations of men, kingdoms, etc. But now it is also (illegible) with evil spirits; so as to be full of evil and temptations: 'situated in (illegible)' says St. John. Cf. locust plague: (reminiscent of Callista). Example of St Mary Magdalene (in whom seven devils), and the demoniac ('our name is legion': Roman Legion = 4000, also entered 2000 swine). 6/ This is the true philosophy of the great strife of good and evil taught us by the Holy Spirit. It tears away the veil. 7/ Therefore practically we must look out and try to turn all to our salvation. Pray.

I noticed an occasional cough, and a pretty pregnant hesitation in speaking, and sometimes a difficulty in getting a word. Several things he said struck me. He used the Bible a good deal: always called it 'Scripture' or the 'Bible'. He has no attempt at oratory: but I was greatly pleased.

After Mass called on Fr Neville at the house: a tall, thin, grey nice looking man. Nice features, quiet and very kind. He said Fr Newman was very tired and would I come to dinner at 5.00 and see him? So I lunched in the Refectory (somewhat like Mill Hill); and then saw Worsley, who is now quite settled here and likes it. After a chat, he took me over the school, which is not large. Dormitories are (illegible) with two or three beds. Strange study. Each prof. has a seat, and all his class sit round him (illegible) on a form: reminds you of Cicero. Worsley teaches III Form. Introduced me to Mr. Kelk and other professors: and we had a cigar in their smoke room. They are very nice intelligent men. Mr. Kelk is an ex-parson; pleasant grey-haired man, great traveller, knows all the world, just returned from (illegible); also scholar and linguist. W. admires him greatly. Mr. Aliquin (?) tall, hairy and half Breton. I suppose all except W. are Oxford men. Then W. and I had a walk in Birmingham: we saw the (illegible) art gallery in the Midland Institute; where there are a few good paintings. Also passed the fine grammar school, and saw exterior and interior of the very fine gothic parish church: old but quite renewed. Walked back. Chat in W's room; then down stairs to dinner at 5.00.

Met Newman suddenly in a corridor and at once he shook hands quite warmly. He is a small man, but his head is large. He wears spectacles; his hair always rough. He stoops greatly. His face very wrinkled and his throat emaciated. He took is into a parlour to wait dinner. He had a word for everybody: each professor and priest: so perfectly polite in his manner. We stood up talking. He said: 'I have just been reading with great interest the Duke of Wellington's Despatches, 1822. The position of Europe was about exactly similar to what it is now. There was the Spanish war, the Portuguese war, the Turkish war. Wellington lays down directions for acting in certain positions: they ought to be very useful to statesmen now'.

We then went into dinner. It is a curious refectory. All sit round, two and two at a small table. Mr. Kelk and I were together, and Fr Newman at my right. The meat is cut on a table by waiting brothers, and brought round on plates. During dinner someone read religious books and history (Edward III). Towards the end, one Father suddenly proposed two cases, one in moral and one in Scripture: 1/ if a son works for his father, is he entitled to a salary? 2/ We are told that Our Lord went up from Mt Olivet to heaven, and also that he took his disciples to Bethany and ascended. Fr Caswall (quite immediately) proposed a solution of 1/, so did some other Fathers. Each at the end touched his biretta saying: 'I speak under correction'. Newman took his turn and gave a solution to 2/, i.e. either Our Lord made a circuit discoursing through Bethany back to Olivet, or else Bethany is the name of a district, but it is difficult for [illegible] to be the name of a district.

After dinner back to parlour for dessert. Here W. sat with Caswall, and I sat to next Newman and had all the luxury of a long chat. We didn't get through much (illegible). Unfortunately I felt (sic) to use my power of 'drawing him out'. We spoke of Rev. Mother at Melle; I told him of the state of Belgium; he asked my opinion of the morals of the lay students at Louvain, as a friend wanted to send his son there. I wouldn't give him much encouragement.

Newman's avoidance of Gothic in his churches had puzzled both W. and myself. I asked him point-blank his reason. He said at the Oratory it was originally a pure matter of utility. Pugin wouldn't give a Gothic church with nave and sanctuary wide enough, and so Newman took the basilica. Generally, he thinks Gothic has not kept pace with the progress of thought in the Church, (having been violently broken off and extinguished by renaissance, etc.), and so is not suited to modern use: cf. the rood-screed is very awkward for the modern rite of benediction. Pugin ought to have been able to adapt the Gothic to our times; as it would naturally have developed itself, had it lived. Cf. half-Saxon and perpendicular: what a development! Seemed to take San Marco, Venice, as his ideal. 'I should like to lay it down as a principle: indeed it is a principle: that no place can be *devotional* but what is *small*'. So San Marco is a mass of small chapels, etc.

Praised tutor-system at Oxford, for moral effects. Fears it is dying out. Meanwhile a heavy thunderstorm came on, which lasted an hour or so. When we broke up, Newman going away hastily saying good-bye, Worsley took me to Fr Power's room. He is a jolly fellow, and thoroughly Ushaw. He has the complete management of the school, which seems in a very flourishing state. Our conversation turned mostly on schools, discipline, etc. Thinks Ushaw unique in the world for morals. Said a good thing: that rich Catholics will not and do not pay enough for their sons education. Hence they only send them to colleges where they pay like poor man's sons, and hence Catholic teachers are so wretchedly paid'.

19 OCTOBER 1875

Went to Meirzlbeke (?). "Saw Rev. Mother and delivered Fr Neville's parcel (MS. notes of Fr Newman's sermons). They were very kind and gave us a capital dinner. She said that the greatest treat was to hear Fr Newman instruct children, and that the children would sit with eyes open, hanging on his word".[2]

16 NOVEMBER 1875

"Newmaniana: when Rector of Catholic University, N. was once in a large hall which had to be measured then and there. They had no measures. N. at once lay down and measured it by his own length, getting his friend to mark the places. (Authority: Rev. Dan. Ryan, Thurles College.)"[3]

23 NOVEMBER 1875

'A charming letter from Fr Newman…after apologising for his delay, he has so much to write, he says: 'It has been very ungrateful in me, but I am sure you will pardon me, when I assure you your letter gave me real pleasure. And now I ask of you the further kindness of remembering in your prayers that I am very old and it cannot be many years before I shall have to give an account of a long life'.[4]

NOTES

1 Casartelli Diaries, 19 Sept. 1875, Salford Diocesan Archives.
2 Casartelli Diaries, 19 Oct. 1875, SDA.
3 Casartelli Diaries, 16 Nov. 1875, SDA.
4 Casartelli Diaries, 23 Nov. 1875, SDA.

Appendix Two

Extracts from Casartelli's Diary

JANUARY–MARCH 1905

Casartelli spent the greater part of the period from 2 January until 30 March 1905, at his sisters' home in Mayfield Road, adjacent to St. Bede's College. The following extracts are typical of those to be found throughout his diaries from 1905–1924. They show the wide range of his interests, the extent of his ill health, and his meetings with the Vicar General to discuss diocesan business.

2 January

Suffering from acute bronchitis, confined to bedroom and remained in doors until 10 January.

10 January

Met Vicar General at St Bede's. Attended Deanery Conference dinner and in the evening the annual dinner of the Catholic Truth Society.

11 January

Annual dinner of St. Bede's College. Appointed a new rector to St. Mary's, Burnley.

12 January

Confirmed a Mrs. Catherine Jane Bolton in his private chapel.

13 January

Able to go for a walk "for the first time" since his illness.

14 January

Appointed a new rural dean. Attended dinner at Italian Consul.

16 January

Farewell dinner at St Chad's, Manchester. Visited Convent of Sisters of Charity.

17 January

Attended Requiem Mass and appointed new rector in Blackburn. Attended Consular Dinner, Manchester.

18 January

Meeting with Vicar General at Salford Cathedral. Presided at Catholic Truth Society Meeting, Liverpool.

19 January

Appointed new rector to St. Patrick's, Manchester.

20 January

Spent day writing. 'Professor Rhys-Davis called to talk over his course of comparative religion at Manchester University.' In the evening attended concert at Midland Hotel.

21 January

Heard Confessions at Loreto Convent.

22 January

Attended Mass at Dominican church, Pendleton.

24 January

Interviewed candidates for position of canon penitentiary. Visited Good Shepherd Convent.

25 January

Meeting of Finance Board at Cathedral. Spent day writing correspondence.

26 January

Correspondence in the morning. Confirmed two soldiers in private chapel. Entertained to tea a Mrs. Kelly and her niece.

27 January

Writing all morning; paid social visits in the afternoon.

31 January

Said Mass at Salford Cathedral.

1 February

Attended conferring of freedom of the city at Manchester Town Hall. Later attended meeting of Zelators for St. Joseph's Foreign Mission Society.

2 February

Annual dinner of Xaverian College Old Boys, had 'very interesting conversation with Mr. Justice Walton.'

3 February

Opening of Exhibition of Antarctic objects and pictures at Athenaeum.

4 February

Heard Confessions. Spoke with John Snead-Cox about his proposed biography of Cardinal Vaughan.

6 February

Meeting of Ecclesiastical Education Council, Salford Cathedral.

7 February

Sent three names to Rome for vacant canon's stall. Meeting with Vicar General. Attended Lord Mayor's banquet.

8 February

Consecrated 42 altar stones at Bishop's House, 10.00a.m. – 2.00p.m., 'exceedingly fatiguing and exhausting service.'

9 February

Attended Requiem Mass for deceased priest.

10 February

Celebrated Requiem Mass at St Bede's. Visited convent of Sisters of St. Joseph. In the evening attended meeting of Classical Association at Ryland's Library.

11 February

Heard Confessions at Loreto Convent.

12 February

A quiet day at home.

13–18 February

Meeting of Hierarchy in London. Discussed new organisation of Catholic Schools Committee, reform of English College, Rome, and codification of Canon Law. Visited various convents; discussed with Mother General of the Sisters of Nazareth the possibility of their opening a convent in Salford Diocese.

20 February

Celebrated Mass at St Joseph's Convent, Manchester.

21 February

Meeting with Vicar General, Salford. Gave lecture to Catholic Truth Society on the life of St Bede.

22 February

Meeting of Finance Board. Attended annual Catholic Concert at the Free Trade Hall.

23 February

Meeting of Protection and Rescue Society.

24 February

Sat for portrait painting. Attended meeting at Pendlebury Children's Hospital. 'Wrote to give up post of Ordinary Confessor at Loreto nuns (held since 1891) owing to canonical objection. Sorry.'

25 February

Spoke with Mgr Nolan, [Master of St Edmund's House, Cambridge] about university education of secular clergy. 7.00 pm–10.00 pm, 'Inaugural meeting in my rooms of Roger Bacon Society (Catholic students of Manchester University.) Rules read and passed. Excellent address by Mgr Nolan on Roger Bacon.'

27 February

Went to Southport for short break until 6 March.

3 March

Returned to Manchester for opening of new laboratories at Girl's High School, Dover Street. Lord Mayor of Salford's Reception in evening. Returned to Southport.

6 March

Attended Catholic Truth Society Conference in Liverpool.

7 March

Professed two nuns.

8 March

Ash Wednesday. Said Mass in private chapel at Mayfield Road. Meeting of Ecclesiastical Education Council.

12 March

Attended Mass at St Chad's Manchester. Visited boarding house run by Third Order Franciscans for teachers. Tonight returned into residence at St. Bede's Lodge after absence since 21 December (at Mayfield Road.)

13 March

At home all day; visited convent in evening.

14 March

Meeting with Vicar General 11.00 am–12.30 pm. Attended Deanery Conference dinner. Attended lecture at Free Trade Hall on the 'Life of Our Lord' by Fr. Gallwey SJ

15 March

'Getting photographed at Ingram's and Lafayette's. Tedious!'

16 March

Meeting of Protection and Rescue Society.

17 March

Administered Confirmation at Royton.

18 March

Opening of new school in Rochdale.

19 March

Opening of new church in Nelson, spoke to St Vincent de Paul Society and to children.

20 March

Said Mass at St. Joseph's Cemetery on 5th anniversary of his "dear Father." Visited church, schools, and convent in Chorlton.

21 March

Meeting with Vicar General.

22 March

Walked to Withington, visited church and school. Answered a sick call to administer Extreme Unction at Loreto Convent. Attended lecture by Fr Gallwey at Free Trade Hall, 'immense crowd'.

23 March

Meeting of Protection and Rescue Society. 'Old Father Gallwey SJ (*aet.* 85) called this afternoon. Wonderful old man.'

24 March

4.30 pm tea with "Griffiths, the Egyptologist, very interesting."
5.30.pm visit by Mother General of Nazareth House, will set up house in Prestwich.
8.00 pm attended last lecture by Fr Gallwey, 'immense crowd. Said a few words.'

25 March

Attended funeral of Rev Mother of Loreto Convent, preached but 'did not go to cemetery owing to cold and loss of voice'.

28 March

Meeting with Vicar General. Prefect Apostolic of Borneo called. Presided at election of new Superior at Loreto Convent.

29 March

Finance Board meeting 10.30 am–1.00 pm. Benediction at St Chad's, Manchester. 'Long and interesting visit in afternoon from Rev. R. Eubank (Anglican): "not far from Kingdom of God".'

30 March

'Dined *chez* my brother, Withington.'

Appendix Three

Statistics of the Diocese of salford 1905–1924 Diocesan organisations 1903–1925

LENTEN RETURNS

Year	Confessions of communicants	Confessions of non-communicants	Converts
1905	119,715	16,171	687
1906	121,468	17,273	816
1907	117,360	17,312	698
1908	121,833	17,209	703
1909	118,126	15,621	699
1910	127,971	16,822	833
1911	137, 873	3,588*	854
1912	146,589	2,803	784
1913	147,213	2,317	803
1914	147,993	1,914	791
1915	143,967†	1,765	716
1916	140,601	2,024	754
1917	140,066	2,004	666
1918	148,125	1,642	820
1919	146,981	1,821	970
1920	146,229	2,082	1380
1921	182,809	2,222	1422
1922	184,245	1,837	1340
1923	191,302	1,667	1327
1924	182,768	1,579	1287

* Effect of Decree *Quam Singulari*

† 'No doubt largely owing to the war; almost certainly well over 20,000 of our young men have joined the ranks.' (Diocesan Synod, 1915, p. 186. Salford Diocesan Archives)

RECORD OF PROGRESS

24 new parishes; 2 male religious communities; 5 female religious communities; an increase of 90 priests to the ranks of the clergy; the foundation of 14 secondary and central schools; 2 new Rescue Homes.

1 Catholic Recorder; 2 Lord Mayors of Manchester; 2 Mayors; 6 County Magistrates (4); 35 Borough Magistrates (18); 35 Municipal Councillors (24); 18 District Councillors (15); 35 Poor Law Guardians (32); 51 members of Education Authorities (49); 5 members of Infirmary Boards(1)

(Figures in brackets represent records pre-1903)

DIOCESAN ORGANISATIONS & APPROX. YEAR OF INAUGURATION

1903 (organisations already)
Protection and Rescue Society
St. Peter's Brotherhood (to assist with ecclesiastical education)
Association of Ladies of Charity
St. Vincent de Paul Society
St. Joseph's Foreign Missionary Society

The following were begun whilst Casartelli was Bishop of Salford

1906
Catholic Federation

1908
Guild of St Gregory and St. Cecilia

1909
Catholic Needlework Guild

1910
Catholic Women's League
'Retreats for Men'
School of Social Science
Catholic Philharmonic Society

1911
Catholic Boys' Brigade

1913
Women's Night Shelter
Lancashire Catholic Players

1916
Catenian Association (3 Circles established in the diocese)
Association for the Propagation of Faith

1917
Catholic Crusade for the Promotion of Temperance

1918
Catholic Boys' Scouts
1 more Circle of Catenian Association established
Catholic Billiard League

1919
Catholic University Association

1922
Catholic Evidence Guild

1923
Stella Maris Association

1924
Apostleship of Prayer
Association of the Holy Childhood
Association of Our Lady of a Happy Death
Association of Perpetual Adoration and Work for Poor Churches
2 more Circles of Catenian association established
Catholic Girl Guides
Enthronement of the Sacred Heart
Priest's and People's Eucharistic League

Notes

INTRODUCTION

1 Frances Zanetti, 'The Late Bishop of Salford', in *The Harvest* April, 1925, p. 86. The quotation from Terence may be translated as: 'I am a man, I count nothing human foreign to me.'

2 See p. 2.

3 Frances Zanetti (1866–?), a recognised authority on infant life. In her capacity as such she gave evidence before the House of Commons for the amendment of the Infant Life Protection Act. Honorary Secretary of the Salford Diocesan Catholic Women's League. She promoted the duty of citizenship among Catholics, especially among women. See 'Our Duty as Citizens', in *The Harvest* Nov. 1905, pp. 256–257; and Jan. 1906, pp. 8–9.

4 Herbert Vaughan (1832–1903), the second bishop of Salford, 1872–1892. Archbishop of Westminster, 1892–1903.

5 See T. Nigel L. Brown, *The History of the Manchester Geographical Society: 1884–1950* (Manchester, 1971), p. 1.

6 See Edward Norman, *Anti-Catholicism in Victorian England* (London, 1967), p. 18.

7 *Manchester Guardian*, 19 Jan. 1925.

8 James Hope Moulton (1863–1917).

9 Despite this ability and willingness, Casartelli was not prepared to compromise his principles. He did not approve of the Malines Conversations, which took place from 1921–1925 between Roman Catholic and Anglican theologians, nor was he sympathetic toward the Conference on Christian Politics, Economics and Citizenship (COPEC). He expressed his antipathy to both in the following letter to Bishop Amigo of Southwark: 'It is interesting to see this 'reunion' question taken up by Frenchmen and Belgians and not a single Englishman in the conference (*tanto neglio!*) I should think Rome might feel that my old friend and fellow-student Cardinal Mercier has rather compromised himself and burnt his fingers. Hence the silence of the Vatican. Also I wonder what view they take in Rome of the 'COPEC' movement. I am strongly opposed to it and fear it may be dangerous, or at least misleading, – in spite of His Eminence's apparent approval.' Casartelli to Amigo, 15 Jan. 1924, Salford File, Archives of the Archdiocese of Southwark.

10 W. Fiddian Moulton, *James Hope Moulton* (London, 1919), p. 74.

11 *Ibid.* p. 79.

12 See 'Non-Catholic Societies', Box 182, Salford Diocesan Archives.

13 *Ibid.*, letter dated 13 July 1904.

14 Casartelli's preface to Charles Plater's, *Retreats for the People* (London, 1912), p. vii.

15 See Antonio Panaino's entry for 'Casartelli', in *Encyclopaedia Iranica* (California, 1992), Vol. 5.

16 Francis Bourne (1861–1935), coadjutor bishop of Southwark 1896, then bishop 1897–1903. Archbishop of Westminster 1903–1935.

17 Charles A. Bolton, *Salford Diocese and its Catholic Past* (Manchester, 1950), p. 132.

18 See Appendix Two for examples of the frequency of these meetings.

19 See Appendix Two.

20 For an example of the frequency and extent of his ill health, see Appendix Two.

21 Casartelli Diaries, 24 Dec. 1909, SDA.

22 Peter Doyle, 'The Catholic Federation', in W.J. Shiels and Diana Wood (eds), *Voluntary Religion*, (n.p. 1986), pp. 461–476.

23 Peter Lane, *The Catenian Association: 1908–1983* (London, 1982).

24 Philip Hughes, 'The Coming Century', in George Andrew Beck (ed.), *The English Catholics: 1850–1950* (London, 1950), p. 38.

25 Kester Aspden, 'The English Roman Catholic Bishops and the Social Order, 1918–1926', in *Recusant History* 25 (3) (2001), pp. 543–564.

26 In his report, or *relatio*, to the Holy See in 1917, Casartelli reported that among the clergy and laity of the diocese there were no cases of error of doctrine, i.e. Modernism. Vatican Secret Archives, Consistorial Congregation, Salford 705, 1917.

27 J. D. Holmes, 'Louis Charles Casartelli: Bishop of Salford 1903–1925', in *Ushaw Magazine* 243 (LXXXV) (1974), pp. 34–39.

CHAPTER ONE: THE FORMATIVE YEARS: 1852–1877

1 Asa Briggs, *Victorian Cities* (London, 1963), p. 88. For an overview of the importance of the cities of Manchester and Salford see F. A. Bruton, *A Short History of Manchester and Salford* (Manchester, 1914); A. Briggs, 'Manchester, Symbol of a New Age,' in *Victorian Cities*, pp. 88–139; Alan Kidd, *Manchester* (Keele, 1993); R. L. Greenall, *The Making of Victorian Salford* (Lancaster, 2000).

2 Greenall, *The Making of Victorian Salford*, p. 2.

3 For a description of the area, and of Roman Catholicism in the city at the time of Casartelli's birth see C. S. Ford, *Pastors and Polemicists* (Manchester, 2002); E. Hamer, *Elizabeth Prout 1820–1864* (Downside Abbey, 1994), pp. 33–57; J. O'Dea, *The Story of the Old Faith in Manchester* (Manchester, 1910); C. A. Bolton, *Salford Diocese and its Catholic Past* (Manchester, 1950).

4 M. O'Connor, 'Joseph Louis Casartelli,' in *The Harvest* XIII (152) (May 1900), p. 100. *The Harvest* was the diocesan monthly journal of the diocese of Salford.

5 Barbara Ronchetti observes of certain of the Italian *émigrés*, of whom Joseph Louis Casartelli was one, 'They had had to leave Italy usually because there were too many children in their families for one family household to support. Moreover, it was only natural that enterprising young men would want to seek their fortune in a country like England where progress in industry and trade was the watchword of the time.' Barbara Ronchetti, 'The Earliest Italian Immigrants in Manchester', in Antonio Rea, *Italians in Manchester* (n.p., 1990), p. 53.

6 J. T. Slugg, *Reminiscences of Manchester Fifty Years Ago* (Manchester, 1881), p. 98.

7 For details of Joseph Casartelli's meteorological reports, see Gordon Manley, 'Manchester Rainfall since 1765: Further Comments, Meteorological and Social', in *Memoirs and Proceedings of the Manchester Literary and Philosophical Society* 117 (1974–75), pp. 93–101.

8 See J. Wetton, *Scientific Instrument Making in Manchester 1790–1870* (Manchester, 1993).

9 An area of Manchester approximately one mile north-east of the city centre.

10 Paul de Felice, 'Reconstructing Manchester's Little Italy,' in *Manchester Region History Review* XII (1998), pp. 54–55.

11 Louis Charles, along with his brother and four sisters, maintained a financial interest in

the business throughout his life even when he was bishop of Salford. 'Joe [Joseph Casartelli jnr.] called to discuss change of firm's name owing to new legislation: we shall probably decide on 'J. Casartelli & Son, Ltd.', and change business into limited liability Co.,' and, 'Joe...again spent an hour here to go over draft of articles for turning business of Jos. Casartelli & Son into Limited Liability Co., all the shares among the six of us only (this owing to recent Trade Registration legislation.)' Casartelli Diaries, 4 and 17 Mar. 1917, Salford Diocesan Archives.

12 *Slater's Directory* (1855). Manchester Central Library, Microfilms Unit.

13 *Manchester of Today* (1888), p. 111. Central Library Manchester.

14 Joseph Casartelli, *A Short Discourse on the Structure of the Human Eye* (Manchester, 1868).

15 *Catalogue of Optical, Mining, Surveying, Meteorological, Drawing and Engineering Instruments etc. Manufactured and Sold by Joseph Casartelli, 43, Market Street, Manchester,* (Manchester, n.d.)

16 Asa Briggs, *Victorian Things* (London, 1988), p. 115. For an appreciation of the wider significance of Casartelli's involvement in the world of microscopes, cameras and spectacles, see Briggs, 'The Philosophy of the Eye, Spectacles, Cameras and the New Vision', in *Victorian Things*, pp. 103–142. The mention of 'the New Vision' in the title of the chapter is in reference to the convergence of nature and art, then being explored by the use of philosophical instruments and cameras.

17 O'Connor, 'Joseph Louis Casartelli,' p. 102. The paper was entitled, 'Rainfall at Longsight', in *Proceedings of the Manchester Literary and Philosophical Society* 2 (1862). A further entry in *Proceedings*, 3 (1862) p. 130, reports Casartelli having demonstrated a new registering barometer.

18 For further discussion on Manchester Man and his relation to the middle-class see Kidd, 'Manchester Men: Power and Prestige in the First Industrial City,' in *Manchester* second edition (Manchester 1996), pp. 63–81. For further discussion of this *milieu* see John Steed, 'Unitarianism, political economy and the antinomies of liberal culture in Manchester, 1830–50', in *Social History* 7 (1) (1982), pp. 1–25; Simon Gunn, 'The ministry, the middle class and the 'civilising mission' in Manchester, 1850–80', in *Social History* 21 (1) (1996), pp. 22–36.

19 Kidd, *Manchester*, p. 69.

20 *Ibid.*, p. 72.

21 O'Connor, 'Joseph Louis Casartelli,' p. 100.

22 *Ibid.*, p. 102.

23 Herbert Vaughan (1832–1903), consecrated Bishop of Salford 1872, became Archbishop of Westminster 1892.

24 John Cuthbert Hedley (1837–1915), Auxiliary Bishop (1873–1881) then Bishop of Newport and Menevia 1881–1915.

25 H. Vaughan to C. Hedley, April 1903, Hedley Papers, B.52, National Library of Wales, Aberystwyth.

26 L. C. Casartelli to his father, 14 Nov. 1867, Casartelli Letters, Ushaw College Archives.

27 Casartelli Diaries, 17 Jan. 1874, SDA.

28 *Ibid.*, 14 Mar. 1900.

29 *Ibid.*, 28 Aug. 1905.

30 One explanation could be the fact that Casartelli was only four and a half years of age when his mother gave birth to his sister, Frances Mary Cecilia; seventeen months later she gave birth to another child, Henrietta Agnes. Given that his mother had to attend to two very young children, it is possible that Louis Charles was denied, albeit unintentionally, maternal affection. Before attending the Salford Catholic Grammar School, he lived with his aunt, Elizabeth Ronchetti, who acted as a tutor to him and later to his sisters. In later years he would acknowledge her as one of two persons who inspired his vocation to the

priesthood; the other was Fr Peter Benoit.

31 William Turner (1799–1872), Bishop of Salford 1851–1872.

32 The Census Return for 1861 describes her 'Rank, Profession or Occupation' as: 'a lady'. Census Returns, 17 April 1861, Salford Local History Library. When he resumed keeping a diary in 1881, after not having done so since the previous year, Casartelli wrote: 'A dark shadow, – my first great loss has fallen on me since then. My dearest and earliest benefactor, who for so many years brought me up and educated me – teaching me to read and write, my Catechism, my first arithmetic, geography, who all through life was so passionately devoted to me, that I may honestly say she devoted her life to me – my aunt Elesa Ronchetti – died (and was buried) during my absence on the Continent, August 28. She had been ill (stroke perhaps) first at close of 1879. Recovered, spent Xmas with us. Returned to Southport, February 2. Soon after another stroke, and then a long painful illness of 6 or 7 month. I went down occasionally. It was a painful illness. For weeks she was unconscious. I left her (with great hope of seeing her again, as she was improving) to go to the passion-play at Oberammergau ... She told me she would never see me again! Alas! It was too true!' Casartelli Diaries, 26 Feb. 1881, SDA.

33 A. Carnoy, *Annuaire de L'Université de Louvain 1920–1926* p. XVIII. 'Un garçon soigneusement vêtu avec une belle figure italienne, pétillante d'espirit, une voix claire et une remarquable finesse de manières'.

34 L. C. Casartelli, ''Tis Fifty Years Since,' in *Baeda*, (1912), p. 187. *Baeda* was the school magazine for St Bede's College, Manchester. Casartelli wrote a short life of William Turner, entitled 'The First Bishop of Salford', in *The Harvest* XIV (166, 168, & 169) (1901).

35 L. C. Casartelli to his father, 14 July 1872, Casartelli Letters, UCA. Unfortunately the register containing the details of Casartelli's baptism is missing. It is not possible therefore to substantiate this interesting description.

36 *Ibid.* In his diary Casartelli wrote the following description of how he received the news of Turner's death and the affect it had upon him. 'Alas! This foulsome black day has made me almost an orphan, for today we received news of the death in Christ of our father. Our most beloved bishop died peacefully yesterday. He said Mass that morning as usual, and therefore what he had always foretold he fulfilled – that he would celebrate the most Holy Sacrifice until the last day of his life even if he had to be carried to the altar by the hands of others. At almost 12 noon he began to shiver with cold; the illness getting worse the doctor was summoned. Fr Benoit anointed him. Venerable father, unite yourself with Jesus and pray for us your deprived children. Like one falling asleep, he died peacefully in Christ. Even in this time I still owe him much. Grief has fallen on the whole diocese.' Casartelli Diaries, 14 July 1872, SDA.

37 See *The Harvest*, XIV (166) (July) 1901. See p. 10.

38 Canon Peter Benoit (1820–1892), one time secretary to Bishop Turner and his curate when Turner was rector of St Augustine's, Granby Row. Attended Vatican Council as Turner's theologian and advisor. In 1852 became Vicar General of Salford diocese; later made rector of Mill Hill when Vaughan came to Salford. (See R. O'Neil, *Cardinal Herbert Vaughan* (London, 1995).

39 On the anniversary of her death Casartelli wrote, 'Today is the anniversary of my dear Aunt Elesa and my 'spiritual father' Fr. Benoit, to both of whom, under God, I owe my vocation.' Casartelli Diaries, 28 Aug. 1915, SDA.

40 For a history of the college, see D. Milburn, *A History of Ushaw College* (Durham, 1964).

41 Casartelli to his sister Henrietta, [no date] Sept. 1867, Casartelli Letters, UCA.

42 'It is 5 years, to the day since I came to the college. How well I remember that wonderful day in my life! How frightened I was that every step I might be breaking your grave rule!' Casartelli Diaries, 21 Sept. 1875, SDA.

43 *The Ushaw Magazine*, 103 (Mar.) (1925), p. 31.

44 Casartelli Diaries, 16 Sept. 1872, SDA.

45 *The Ushaw Magazine*, 103 (Mar.) (1925), p. 32.

46 Casartelli to his father, 1 Dec. 1863, Casartelli Letters, UCA.

47 V. A. McClelland refers to the use of pedagogues at Ushaw as a 'unique institution.' The plan of education envisaged that 'Each student below the class of Poetry is placed under the care of a private tutor, who prepares him for the lessons of his Professor.' V. A. McClelland, *English Roman Catholics and Higher Education 1830–1903* (Oxford, 1973), p. 49. See Chapter IV 'Higher Studies at Ushaw', for an historical overview of its course of studies.

48 Casartelli to his father, 24 Nov. 1870, Casartelli Letters, UCA.

49 Casartelli to his father, 12 Jan. 1868, Casartelli Letters, UCA.

50 Casartelli presided at a meeting held on 13 September 1906 at the Grosvenor Hotel, Manchester, to discuss the founding of a Dante Society in the city; he subsequently became President.

51 Casartelli Diaries, 20 Sept. 1872, SDA.

52 Casartelli Diaries, 23 Nov. 1875, SDA.

53 See McClelland, *English Roman Catholics*, pp. 64–83.

54 President of Ushaw 1863–1876.

55 William George Ward, (1812–1882) a convert to Catholicism who taught moral philosophy at Old Hall and dogmatic theology at St Edmunds's. 'An uncompromising controversialist, a vigorous supporter of papal infallibility, opposed liberalism and modernism in the Church.' Delaney and Tobin, *Dictionary of Catholic Biography* (London, 1962), p. 1188.

56 McClelland, *English Roman Catholics*, pp. 65–66.

57 *Ibid.*, p. 70.

58 Prefect of Studies at Ushaw 1843–1858; President 1876–1877.

59 D. Milburn, *Ushaw College* (Durham, 1964), p. 280.

60 'Mr. Newton holds that all the London papers on moral philosophy could be answered by a simple knowledge of Scholastic Philosophy...Then why study Bain? To my mind Mr. N. is slightly exaggerated.' Casartelli Diaries, 27 Oct. 1872, SDA.

61 Ushaw College Diary, UCA.

62 Casartelli to his father, 12 Mar. 1871, Casartelli Letters, UCA.

63 Casartelli to his father, 14 Mar. 1871, Casartelli Letters, UCA.

64 Casartelli to his father, 26 Nov. 1871, Casartelli Letters, UCA.

65 Casartelli Diaries, 31 Oct. 1872, SDA.

66 See, *Baeda*, 3 (1941), pp. 8–9.

67 Casartelli Diaries, 21 Sept. 1872, SDA.

68 Casartelli, 'Des études supérieures dans le clergé catholique anglais,' *Revue Générale* (1896), p. 7. 'Ce régime, si différent de celui auquel on est habitué ailleurs, a été pour beaucoup, selon l'opinion de plusieurs, dans le développement remarquable de l'Église catholique en Angleterre dans notre siècle. Il a assuré aux laïques une éducation foncièrement réligieuse et les a formés à un esprit profondément catholique. Il a rattaché le clergé, par les liens si puissants d'une éducation commune, aux chefs laïques du parti, en lui donnant une influence très grande sur ces derniers'.

69 For Vaughan's opinion see chapter five, p. 127, n. 148.

70 Cited in, J. D. Holmes, 'English Ultramontanism and Clerical Education', *Clergy Review* (July 1977), p. 278.

71 See below pp. 23–27 & pp. 29–31.

72 In 1891 when the Salford Catholic Grammar School merged with St Bede's Commercial College, Casartelli wrote to the clergy of the diocese, 'The amalgamation of the two

Schools is an event of the first importance in the educational history of the Diocese. This Institution must necessarily become the chief recruiting ground of our Clergy and the School of our leading Laity. In its Classical department it will continue to be…what the old Grammar School has been for so many years – the *Petit Séminaire* for our ecclesiastical candidates, preparing them for Ushaw and other Colleges. In its Commercial department it ought to be the natural training school for all our promising laity, whose Catholic education and formation is of such vast importance to the future of the Church.' 30 July 1891, copy in St Bede's College Diary, New Series, (1) 1891–5, St Bede's College Archive, Manchester.

73 Holmes, 'English Ultramontanism,' p. 267.

74 J. D. Holmes, *More Roman Than Rome* (London, 1978.)

75 J. Von Arx, *Varieties of Ultramontanism* (Catholic University of America Press, 1998).

76 The point Von Arx makes about Ultramontanism being an opaque term is nicely seen by comparing how the word is defined in two editions of *The Catholic Encyclopaedia*. The first, published in 1912, defined it as: 'a term used to denote integral and active Catholicism, because it recognises as its spiritual head the pope, who, for the greater part of Europe, is a dweller beyond the mountains…that is, beyond the Alps.' *The Catholic Encyclopaedia* (New York, 1912), vol. XV, p. 125. A later version defined it thus: 'Ultramontanism, in the usage of modern Church history (17th, 18th, and 19th Centuries), is a strong emphasis on centralisation in the Church, or on papal authority, in matters of ecclesiastical government and doctrine.' *The New Catholic Encyclopaedia* (New York, 1967), vol. XIV, p. 380.

77 Holmes, 'English Ultramontanism,' p. 268. Ian Ker comments, 'The religious and theological movement called 'Ultramontanism' had begun as a protest against state control of the local church, but it is one of the great ironies of ecclesiastical history that its appeal to the external authority of Rome as a way of gaining religious freedom from the shackles of the state eventually led to an agitation to override local ecclesial autonomy by strictly curtailing the rights of the episcopate in favour of the centralising authority of the Holy See. As this kind of extreme Ultramontanism gathered force, so, in reaction, there grew up a recognizably liberalizing Catholicism, which included many, like Newman, who would have proudly claimed to be Ultramontanes in the original sense of the word'. Ian Ker, *Newman the Theologian* (London, 1990), p. 41.

78 Ian Ker, *John Henry Newman* (Oxford, 1988), p. 478.

79 Ker, *Newman The Theologian*, p. 43.

80 *Letters and Diaries of John Henry Newman*, ed. Charles Stephen Dessain, vols XI–XXII (London, 1961–1972), XIX, pp. 134–135.

81 See Ker, *John Henry Newman*, p. 561 re. Newman's *Apologia*: 'there was no doubt of the overwhelming support of most Catholic clergy (including even the redoubtable John Gillow of Ushaw);' and p. 588 re Newman's *A Letter to Pusey*: 'The Catholic clergy generally welcomed the pamphlet, including Bishop Brown and the redoubtable Dr Gillow.'

82 L. C. Casartelli, 'Catholic Secondary Schools and Our Universities', in *23rd Annual Conference of Catholic Colleges* (London, 1919), p. 19.

83 Bishop Brown had condemned 'On Consulting the Faithful' because it allegedly suggested that the Church, during the Arian heresy, had fallen into error. This led to a long lasting deep suspicion of Newman on the part of the Roman Curia. In his diary for 3 December 1906, Casartelli commented on his conversation with the bishop of Shrewsbury, 'Very long and interesting conversation with [Shrewsbury] over threatened new 'Syllabus – danger of condemnation of Newman! – need of English Bishops making their views felt in Rome'. Casartelli Diaries, 3 Dec. SDA.

84 Casartelli Diaries, 18 Sept. 1872, SDA.

85 Casartelli Diaries, 27 Sept. 1872, SDA. The dogma of papal infallibility was defined by the

First Vatican Council in 1870. 'Newman was an 'inopportunist': although he had accepted the essential doctrine as part of tradition when he became a Catholic, he thought that formally to define the dogma without a great deal more historical and theological study and to impose it as an article of faith on a Church that was not ready for it was premature'. Ker, *Newman*, p. 51.

86 C. S. Dessain and T. Gornall, eds., *The Letters and Diaries of John Henry Newman* (Oxford, 1975),Vol. XXVII, p. 336. See Appendix One for an account of their eventual meeting.

87 Casartelli, 'Catholic Schools and Our Universities,' p. 20.

88 A couple of days after Vaughan's consecration Casartelli wrote: 'An unknown person sent a copy of the *Catholic Times* which contains a lithographic portrait of Bp. Vaughan; a fine looking fellow, the very picture of Mrs. Lee. I have pinned him up on my wall, where he hangs over the piano opposite poor dear Dr. Turner, looking so young to my venerable bishop deceased. But he is beginning his work well and apostolically says Papa.' Casartelli Diaries, 3 Nov. 1872. SDA. Of his first pastoral letter he commented, 'It is well written, full of questions and shows a firm inflexible spirit.' Casartelli Diaries, 5 Nov. 1872, SDA.

89 'Ardwick was a suburban area of fine houses and picturesque gardens. The upper and middle classes lived there'. *1851 Census Surname Index* (10) Public Record Office, Ref. O107/2220. (Published by Manchester and Lancashire Family History Society, Manchester, 1986).

90 See Chapter Five, 'Historical Overtones.'

91 After having visited Southport, where he had hoped to see Casartelli's aunt, Vaughan wrote, 'I have learnt with pleasure that she also is gone to the University of Louvain, and is accompanying you through your course. If she does not become learned, I know she will take real care of you – and for this I thank her with all my heart.' Vaughan to Casartelli, 29 Dec. 1874, Box 179, SDA.

92 Quoted in, Cuthbert Butler, *The Life of Bishop Ullathorne*, 2 vols (London, 1926), I, p. 332.

93 Vaughan to Casartelli, 11 January 1876, Box 179, SDA. He was quite clear as to the type of priest he wanted: 'I am desirous of getting a few good young men, deacons or priests to form the first community of the new seminary. If you hear of three or four such, who desire to suit themselves to the English mission I shall be glad to know of them. And I am particularly anxious that they should not be of the low and dirty manners and negligent style with slip-shod habit which Germans sometimes have. Indeed it will be needful in order to counteract the natural prejudice against foreigners that they should conciliate by their presence rather than the reverse'. Vaughan to Casartelli, 30 May [1875?], Box 179, SDA.

94 See R. H. Oliver and P. Rafferty, 'The Jesuit College Manchester, 1875,' in *Recusant History*, 20 (2) (1990.)

95 R. O'Neil, *Cardinal Herbert Vaughan* (London, 1995), p. 219.

96 J. G. Snead-Cox, *Cardinal Vaughan*, 2 vols (London, 1910), I, p. 280.

97 For a description of the dispute see Snead-Cox, vol. 1, pp. 270–303.

98 For summary of the text of *Romanos Pontifices*, promulgated 8 May 1881 see Snead-Cox, vol. I pp. 350–352.

99 Vaughan to Casartelli, [no date] June 1876, Box 179, SDA.

100 Vaughan to Casartelli, 25 June 1877, Box 179, SDA.

101 H. Atkinson, 'September 1894 to July 1899', in *Baeda* XII (1) (1937), p.10.

102 Vaughan to Casartelli, 25 July 1883, Box 179, SDA.

103 Vaughan to Casartelli, 15 August [no year], Box 179, SDA.

104 Casartelli Diaries, 12 April 1874, SDA.

105 Casartelli Diaries, 8 May 1874, SDA.

106 Casartelli Diaries, April 20 1874, SDA.

107 Charles de Harlez (1832–1899). Casartelli described him as 'The greatest Orientalist the Catholic Church has produced during the present century; the foremost mind of the

Catholic University of Louvain [...] By his grammars and reading-books in Zend Avesta and Pahlevi de Harlez did a great deal to extend the study of the Eranian [sic] literatures far beyond Belgium, in France, Italy, America, and elsewhere.' L. C. Casartelli, 'Charles de Harlez: In Memoriam,' in *The Tablet*, 22 July 1899.

108 Casartelli Diaries, 10 Nov. 1875, SDA.

109 A commentary and translation into middle Persian vernacular (Zend) of the sacred writings of the Zoroastrians (Avesta.)

110 L. C. Casartelli, *The Philosophy of the Mazdayasnian Religion under the Sassanids* (Bombay, 1889.)

111 Obituary of de Harlez by Casartelli, *The Tablet*, 22 July 1899.

112 This interest in Oriental studies endured throughout his life. In 1876 he was elected a member of the German Oriental Society; in 1886 he was named an honorary member of the Société Orientale of Louvain; he became a member of the Royal Asiatic Society of Great Britain in 1889 and in 1891 a member of the Società per gli Studi Biblici of Rome. He became an Honorary Fellow of the Royal Asiatic Society in 1918.

113 Thomas Joseph Lamy (1827–1907), Orientalist and Biblical scholar.

114 Casartelli Diaries, 23 Mar. 1876, SDA.

115 Casartelli Diaries, 30 Mar. 1876, SDA.

116 Casartelli Diaries, 17 April 1876, SDA.

117 Vaughan to Casartelli, [no date] June 1876, Box 179, SDA.

118 Casartelli Diaries, 10 Sept. 1876, SDA.

119 Casartelli to his father, 29 Oct. 1876, Casartelli Letters, UCA.

120 Casartelli Diaries, 14 June 1877, SDA.

121 Casartelli Diaries, 20 Jan. 1879, SDA.

122 *Ibid.*

123 *Ibid.*, 15 Sept. 1887, SDA.

124 *Ibid.*, 19 Sept. 1887, SDA.

125 *Ibid.*, 21 Sept. 1887, SDA.

126 St Bede's College Diary, New Series, (1) 1891–1895, St Bede's College Archive. The entry is signed 'L. C. Casartelli'. This diary presumably contained evidence of the internal difficulties that Casartelli experienced and which made his life at the college so difficult. Fr William Hill was the keeper of the diary up to the time he destroyed it.

127 Richardson to Hedley, 14 September 1896, Hedley Papers, Box 53, National Library of Wales, Aberystwyth.

128 *Ibid.*

129 *Baeda*, XII (1) (1937), pp.1–19.

130 *Ibid.*, p. 8.

131 *Ibid.*, p. 10.

132 *Ibid.*, p. 14. This sentiment would seem to be the common assessment of his approach – 'Boys' hearts must be the most difficult to capture, but Dr. Casartelli captured ours. His popularity with the boys was universal, and was well deserved.' p. 17.

133 *Ibid.*, p. 40.

134 See above, pp. 25–26.

135 Casartelli Diaries, 16 Jan. 1884, UCA.

136 *Annuaire de L'Université Catholique de Louvain* (1885), p. 199.

137 *Baeda*, XII (1) (1937), p. 40.

138 Casartelli Diaries 21 Sept. 1872, SDA.

139 Casartelli Diaries, 24 Oct. 1875, SDA.

140 Casartelli to his father, 30 May 1875, Casartelli Letters, UCA.

141 P. Doyle, 'The Catholic Federation', in *Voluntary Religion*, W.J. Shiels and D. Woods,

(eds.), (London, 1986), p. 474.

142 After reading Wilfrid Ward's, *The Life of John Henry Cardinal Newman*, Casartelli noted in his diary: 'Finished W. Ward's very able life of Card. Newman: a fascinating, yet pathetic book. What a loveable character, and how misunderstood!' Casartelli Diaries, 21 Mar. 1912, SDA.

143 Established in 1867 and 'purchased by Dr. Vaughan, Bishop of Salford, to be brought out on Wednesdays in the same form as the *Tablet*, to which it was to be considered, in some sense, as a rider and supplement, with the intention of making it an educational record.' Joseph Gillow, *A Bibliographic Dictionary of the English Catholics* (London, n.d.), vol. IV, p. 300.

CHAPTER TWO: APOLOGIST AND WRITER

1 'I see I gave up keeping my often interrupted diary on July 6, 1877. I was partly prompted to give it up by the time and trouble it took; partly by the idea that it was perhaps an imperfection and a vanity to keep one...Re-reading my old diaries has filled me with deep regret that I ever omitted keeping my diary.' Casartelli Diaries, 20 Jan. 1879, Salford Diocesan Archives.

2 Casartelli Diaries, 11 Sept. 1872, SDA.

3 Casartelli Diaries, 15 June 1874, SDA.

4 See Bibliography.

5 Begun in 1867 and ceased circulation in February 1876 when it was incorporated into the *Catholic Times*. It was issued weekly on Saturday. It gave considerable amount of space to general questions and interests of popular education. Its format was a review of Catholic news, both home and foreign.

6 Casartelli noted in his diary that Vaughan had commented that 'John Pearl's Lay Sermons' were 'excellent.' Casartelli Diaries, 20 Dec. 1874, SDA.

7 See J. G. Snead-Cox, *The Life of Cardinal Vaughan*, 2 vols (London, 1910) I, chapter VIII, 'The Newspaper Apostolate.' In his prospectus for the *Tablet*, Vaughan wrote: 'The spread of education among all classes in England during the present century is a fact that no one can regard without some degree of national pride and yet with intense anxiety. In the very proportion that our working men are educated, their danger from infidel and nationalistic publication increases, and of such there is a deluge at this moment...But we Catholics have another enemy to contend with – the Tract Societies – which annually distribute fifty or sixty million publications...To counter this evil there is but one way: to meet them on their own ground: to make use of the same engine, the Press; that instrument so mighty for good or evil.' Quoted in Gerard Edwards, *The Catholic Truth Society in the Diocese of Salford* (Liverpool, 1992), p. 2.

8 For example, 'Entertained at supper in my dining-room our five Cambridge graduates (Gonne, McNulty, Morrisey, Ingram, Cooke) and spoke to them at length, urging them to work by writing and speaking for the cause of the Church, and to become members of various scientific and literary societies. Very well received. DG.' Casartelli Diaries, 3 Oct. 1917, SDA.

9 Kenelm Vaughan (1840–1909), a priest, and one time secretary to Cardinal Manning.

10 Casartelli noted in his diary: 'The liberal press are very (*illegible*) against us Catholics and our Bp. What for? For preferring the dictates of conscience to party spirit!' The following day he added, 'The Liberals are bitterly mad that Catholics are favourable to the Tories.' Casartelli Diaries, 2 and 3 Feb. 1874, SDA. See p. 40ff.

11 This controversy between Kenelm Vaughan and the Rev. William Unwick was carried out in the pages of the *Manchester Examiner and Times* between October 1873 and December 1873. During a speech at the British and Foreign Bible Society in Manchester, it

was asserted that the Catholic Church did not support the dissemination of Scripture and that the Church was moving away, day by day, from the Scriptures. The gist of Vaughan's reply was: the Catholic Church believes that the Divine Author of Scripture dwells in the Church as interpreter; the Church does not separate the Author from interpretation; the Church does not forbid her subjects to read the Bible. The whole controversy was subsequently printed as, *The Papacy and the Bible: A Controversy* (Alex. Ireland and Co., 1874, n.p.)

12 In Birmingham in 1867, a crowd addressed by William Murphy rioted and police used sabres to quell the demonstration, see Edward Norman, *The English Catholic Church in the Nineteenth Century* (Oxford, 1985), p. 204. Murphy, an itinerant preacher and lecturer, was a Protestant convert from Co. Limerick; see Walter L. Arnstein, 'The Murphy Riots: A Victorian Dilemma,' in *Victorian Studies*, XIX (1) (1975). For similar attacks on Catholic churches in the Salford diocese by Murphy, see John O'Dea, *The Story of the Old Faith in Manchester* (London, 1910), pp. 189–193. The Franciscan church in Gorton, Manchester, a place dear to Casartelli who was a Franciscan Tertiary, had to be defended day and night against Murphy and his mob. In 1868 rioters, again led by Murphy, destroyed St Anne's church in Ashton; thanks to the efforts of the parishioners the rioters failed in their attack on St Mary's, also in Ashton.

13 Casartelli mentions the sense of caution practised amongst Catholics resident in Manchester in the face of occasional hostility and the local political situation. For example, there was no mid-night Mass in 1867 at St Augustine's, Granby Row, as a 'precaution.' Casartelli to his father, 29 Dec. 1867, Casartelli Letters, Ushaw College Archives. This could possibly be because of the excitement caused by the execution on 23 November 1867 of five Irishmen for the murder of a policeman. See O'Dea, *The Story of the Old Faith*, pp. 177–184. There were further precautions in 1872 at the Holy Name church, Manchester, 'on account of the rows last year.' However it was celebrated in other churches and 'on account of due precautions, passed off very well.' Casartelli Diaries, no exact date but vol. dated 'September 1872– June 1874,' SDA.

14 See Walter L. Arnstein, *Protestant versus Catholic in Mid-Victorian England: Mr. Newdegate and the Nuns* (London, 1982).

15 Based at 53, Market Street, Manchester.

16 *Manchester Guardian*, 29 April 1874.

17 'This scene of the dispatch of sixteenth century Huguenots…was almost as familiar to the Victorians as the Bible itself…this representation of the Massacre of St Bartholomew, together with numerous other tableaux on similar themes, belonged to a tradition of anti-Catholicism whose wide acceptance and long endurance, among all classes in society, secured it an important place in Victorian civilisation.' Edward Norman, *Anti-Catholicism in Victorian England* (London, 1968), p. 1.

18 D. G. Paz, *Popular Anti-Catholicism in Mid-Victorian England* (California, 1992), p.1.

19 George Frederick Samuel Robinson, Marquis of Ripon (1827–1908), converted to Catholicism in 1874; Viceroy of India (1880–84); first Lord of the Admiralty (1886), Lord Privy Seal (1905–1908.)

20 Casartelli, 'John Pearl's Lay Sermons: Sermon IX, 'Forgotten Watchwords,' *Catholic Opinion*, 21 Nov. 1874. These articles have been collected in Casartelli Papers, Miscellanea vol. 1, SDA.

21 'The Syllabus of Condemned Errors' was issued on the same day (8 December 1864) as the encyclical letter of Pius IX *Quanta Cura*. The encyclical 'reviews some of the errors of the time on the relationship between Church and State. [It] stresses the Church's full independence from temporal powers and the divine origin of its authority.' J. Neuner and J. Dupuis, *The Christian Faith* (Dublin, 1976), p. 218. The Syllabus condemned all doctrines

which undermined religion and the relationship of Church and State.

22 Cited in H. Jedin, *Ecumenical Councils of the Catholic Church* (London, 1960), p. 194.

23 'Those types of philosophy which assert that the world can best be accounted for by means of the categories of the natural sciences (including biology and psychology) without recourse to the supernatural or transcendent as a means of explanation.' A. Richardson and J. Bowden, *A New Dictionary of Christian Theology* (London, 1983), p. 392.

24 'In the nineteenth century the term became equated with secularism, or atheism, or agnosticism, terms designating positions which base their rejection of religious belief on the use of human reason.' Richardson and Bowden, p. 485. See also Neuner and Dupuis, *The Christian Faith*, nos. 112/2–112/11.

25 See Neuner and Dupuis, *The Christian Faith*, nos. 113–117; 216–219.

26 Norman, *Anti-Catholicism*, p. 80.

27 See p. 37.

28 David Friedrich Strauss (1808–1874), wrote *The Life of Jesus* (1835).

29 Joseph Ernest Renan (1823–1892), wrote *Life of Jesus* (1863). Both this and the work by Strauss saw the person of Jesus as nothing more than a model of humanity to be admired.

30 H. Daniel-Rops, *The Church in the Age of Revolution* (London, 1965), p. 319.

31 'Had dispute with Dawson as to the date of the building of the pyramids. According to one theory they were built three hundred years after the Deluge. Now we are told two or three million men were employed at it. Is it possible for that race to have multiplied so since the Deluge from three sons, so that Egypt should supply some ten million...After dinner we argued on the universality of the Deluge (over the earth.) 'Where did the water go'? asked Dawson.' Casartelli Diaries, 17 Oct. 1872, SDA.

32 'Finished reading *Turkish Reading Book*, this excellent book I began about the end of 1870 or end of 1871, so it really felt like parting with an old friend.' Casartelli Diaries, 17 June 1874, SDA. He taught himself Russian. His diary for 1887 is mostly in Russian.

33 See Chapter One, p. 18.

34 See Chapter One, pp. 27–28.

35 Edward Joseph Butler (1858–1934), he took the name Cuthbert on his profession as a Benedictine monk of Downside Abbey where he was abbot in 1906 and 1914.

36 'Years ago I recognised that these things – Xtian origins, New Testament, History of Dogma, etc. – have been made impossible for a priest, except on the most narrow apologetic lines...When the Biblical Commission got under way, and the *Lamentabli* and *Pascendi* were issued, I deliberately turned away from all this work.' Cuthbert Butler to Baron von Hügel, cited in Adrian Hastings, *A History of English Christianity 1920–1990*, third edition (London, 1991), pp. 152–153.

37 *The Vatican Decrees in their Bearing on Civil Allegiance. A Political Expostulation* (1874).

38 *Pastor Aeternus*, issued during the fourth session of the Council in 1870. See *The Christian Faith*, nos. 818–840.

39 Jeffrey von Arx, 'Interpreting the Council: Archbishop Manning and the Vatican Decrees Controversy', in *Recusant History*, 26 (1) (2002) p. 229.

40 Norman, *Anti-Catholicism*, p. 81.

41 R. L. Greenall, *The Making of Victorian Salford* (Lancaster, 2000), p. 101.

42 John Bilsborrow (1836–1903), Bishop of Salford 1892–1903.

43 Cited in Greenall, *Victorian Salford*, p. 215.

44 Casartelli commented of de Harlez and his influence at Louvain: 'With a single exception of the great biologist Carnoy, there is no man whose intellectual power has so remodelled the higher studies in that University as de Harlez. What the one did for the natural sciences, the other did for the philological and historical ones; and it has been said, without much exaggeration, that de Harlez left Louvain on his death in 1899 a hundred

years ahead of what he found it on his arrival in 1874.' L. C. Casartelli, *Sketches in History* (London, 1906), p. 218.

45   This argument is typified by Max Muller's *Introduction to the Science of Religion* (published 1873). Eric J. Sharpe has called this work the 'foundation document' of the 'History of Religions School,' see his article 'Comparative Religion at the University of Manchester 1904–1979,' in David A. Pailin, *University of Manchester Faculty of Theology Seventy-Fifth Anniversary Papers* (University of Manchester, 1980), p. 26. Casartelli comments that according to the teaching of the 'History of Religions School,' 'both the religion of the Old Testament and the Christianity of the New are supposed to find their place as merely some out of the many phases of a mental and spiritual evolution.' Casartelli, *Sketches in History*, pp. 186–7.

46   See p. 227, n. 7.

47   *CO.*, 24 Feb. 1875.

48   'An empire with an empire,' see Chapter Three. Herbert Vaughan was ever eager to show that Catholics were good citizens and interested in the well-being of society. He set an example himself by involving himself in the task for improving the sanitary conditions of Manchester and Salford. Casartelli followed this example in other ways when he too became a bishop.

49   Daniel-Rops, *The Church in the Age of Revolution*, p. 259.

50   For titles in both series see Bibliography.

51   Casartelli, 'John Pearl's Lay Sermons': Sermon IX, 'Forgotten Watchwords,' *CO.*, 21 Oct. 1874.

52   At Herbert Vaughan's episcopal consecration a stir had been caused by 'a provincial alderman' who objected to the toast to the health of the Pope preceding that of the Queen. Sermon IX.

53   Sermon IX.

54   Charles Wentworth Dilke (1843–1911), an English radical politician and avowed Republican.

55   Sermon IX.

56   R. Jenkins, *Sir Charles Dilke: A Victorian Tragedy* (London, 1958), p. 69.

57   *Ibid.*, p. 70.

58   *Ibid.*, pp. 70–73.

59   Cited in Norman, *Anti-Catholicism*, p. 86

60   See Neuner and Dupuis, *The Christian Faith*, nos. 815–816; and E. Denzinger, *El Magisterio de la Iglesia* (Barcelona, 1963), nos. 1719–1720; 1724; 1739–1749; 1742.

61   Read before The Academia of the Catholic Religion and published in *The Tablet*, 3 Jan. 1874.

62   John Henry Newman, 'A Letter Addressed to His Grace the Duke of Norfolk on the Occasion of Mr. Gladstone's Recent Expostulation' in *Certain Difficulties Felt By Anglicans in Catholic Teaching*, vol. 2, (London, 1885).

63   Casartelli, 'John Pearl's Lay Sermons: Sermon IV 'Politics and Education,' *CO.*, 28 Jan. 1874.

64   Manning, *Caesarism*, p. 3. See also Jeffrey von Arx, 'Manning's Ultramontanism and the Catholic Church in British Politics', in *Recusant History*, 19 (3) (1989), pp. 332–347.

65   *Ibid.*, p. 2.

66   Casartelli, 'John Pearl's Lay Sermons: Sermon I, 'What the Bible Teaches About Itself and the Church,' *CO.*, 24 Dec. 1873.

67   *Ibid.*

68   *Ibid.*

69   Norman, *Anti-Catholicism*, p. 81.

70   Cited in Norman, *Anti-Catholicism*, p. 98.

71   *Manchester Guardian*, 4 Feb. 1874. Signed 'An Irish Catholic Elector.'

72 Manning, *Caesarism*, p. 2.

73 *Ibid.*, p. 2.

74 *CO.*, Sermon I, 24 Dec. 1873; Sermon II, 21 Dec. 1873; Sermon V 11 Feb. 1874; Sermon VI, 25 Feb. 1874.

75 Sermon I.

76 *Ibid.*

77 *Ibid.* 2 Peter 1.20; Acts 8.26; Mt.16.18; Acts 2.47; Eph. 5.25; Mt. 18.17; 1 Tim. 3.15.

78 *Ibid.* See, Neuner and Dupuis, *The Christian Faith*, no. 217: 'In matters of faith and morals, affecting the building up of Christian doctrine, that is to be held as the true sense of Holy Scripture which Holy Mother the Church has held and holds, to whom it belongs to judge of the true sense and interpretation of Holy Scriptures. Therefore no one is allowed to interpret the same sacred Scriptures contrary to this sense, or contrary to the unanimous consent of the Fathers.'

79 'Patrick Murphy' in his book entitled *Popery in Ireland*, published in 1865, described how a girl was rescued from a convent where she had been imprisoned for reading the Bible. The real name of the author was G. H. Whalley, M.P. for Peterborough.

80 Casartelli, 'John Pearl's Lay Sermons: Sermon II, 'The Bible and Conversion,' *CO.*, 31 Dec. 1873.

81 Casartelli, 'John Pearl's Lay Sermons: Sermon III, 'Unpolitical Politics,' *CO.*, 14 Jan. 1874. This discussion is further explored in the following chapter.

82 Casartelli, 'John Pearl's Lay Sermons: Sermon V, 'A Church and a Bible,' *CO.*, 11 Feb. 1874.

83 Casartelli mentions the Trinitarian Bible Society which was dedicated to this task.

84 Sermon V.

85 *Ibid.*

86 John Cassell (1817–1865), self-taught writer and publisher. He entered publishing for the purpose of achieving the moral and social well-being of the working-classes.

87 Simon Nowell-Smith, *The House of Cassell 1848–1958* (London, 1958), p. 29.

88 See Neuner and Dupuis, *The Christian Faith*, nos 218. The Vatican Council repeated Trent's teaching on which books were to be accepted as canonical: 'If anyone does not receive as sacred and canonical the books of Holy Scripture, entire and with all their parts, as the sacred Synod of Trent has enumerated them, or denies that they have been divinely inspired, *anathema sit.*'

89 Casartelli, 'John Pearl's Lay Sermons: Sermon VI, 'What is the Bible,' *CO.*, 15 Feb. 1874.

90 *Ibid.* Casartelli was here referring to the English Reformers such as Miles Coverdale (?1488–1569), Thomas Cranmer (1489–1556), Hugh Latimer (*c.* 1485–1555), Nicholas Ridley (*c.* 1500–1555).

91 *Ibid.*

92 Sermons III and IV.

93 Cited in A. V. McClelland and M. Hodgetts, *From Without the Flaminian Gate* (London, 1999), p. 353.

94 Herbert Vaughan to Lady Herbert, 11 February 1874, Shane Leslie, *Letters of Herbert Cardinal Vaughan to Lady Herbert of Lea 1867–1903* (London, 1942), p. 243.

95 *Manchester Guardian*, 4 Feb. 1874. Signed 'An English Catholic.'

96 *MG.*, 4 Feb. 1875. Signed 'Limerick.'

97 Sermon III.

98 *Ibid.*

99 *Ibid.*

100 *Ibid.*

101 *Ibid.*

102 *Ibid.*

103 *Ibid.*

104 *Ibid.*

105 *Ibid.*

106 Casartelli, 'John Pearl's Lay Sermons: Sermon X 'Mr. Gladstone and Our Loyalty', *CO.*, 9 Dec. 1874; Sermon XI, 'Mr. Gladstone's Mistake and Somebody Else's', *CO.*, 16 Dec.1874; Sermon XIII, 'Other Theories – Loyalty', *CO.*, 20 Jan. 1875; Sermon XIV, 'Before and After', *CO.*, 27 Jan. 1875.

107 Gladstone, *The Vatican Decrees in their Bearing on Civil Allegiance: A Political Expostulation* (1874) quoted in Sermon X.

108 Sermon X.

109 *Ibid.*

110 Sermon III.

111 Sermon X.

112 *Ibid.*

113 See 'John Pearl's Lay Sermons: Sermon XII 'Fixing the Limit', *CO.*, 23 Dec. 1874.

114 Sermon XI.

115 For a discussion of the replies by Newman and Manning see von Arx, 'Interpreting the Council'.

116 Sermon XI.

117 *Ibid.*

118 Newman, *Letter to the Duke of Norfolk*, p. 342,

119 Sermon XIV,

120 Casartelli, 'John Pearl's Lay Sermons: Sermon XVI 'Odd Difficulties', *CO.*, 17 Feb. 1875.

121 Newman, *Letter to the Duke of Norfolk* p. 256.

122 Casartelli, 'John Pearl's Lay Sermons: Sermon XV, 'Before and After (contd.),' *CO.*, 10 Feb. 1875.

123 Casartelli, 'John Pearl's Lay Sermons: Sermon XVI 'Odd Difficulties,' *CO.*, 17 Feb. 1875.

124 Newman, *Letter to the Duke of Norfolk*, p. 231.

125 *Ibid.*, p. 229.

126 Sermon XVI.

127 See chapter one, p. 22.

128 Yves Congar speaks of 'infallibility *in credendo*, in the order of believing, and of infallibility *in docendo*, in the order of teaching.' See his *Lay People and the Church* (London, 1965), p. 291.

129 See, Manning, *Caesarism.*

130 I Peter 2.17. (A.V.) Quoted in Sermon XVII.

131 *Ibid.*

132 Casartelli, 'Difficulties of the Day: 'Introduction,' *CO.*, 24 Nov. 1875.

133 'Difficulties of the Day: Conversion and the Peace of Families,' *CO.*, 22 Dec. 1875.

134 'Difficulties of the Day: Moody and Sankeyism,' *CO.*, 29 Dec. 1875.

135 *Ibid.*

136 *Ibid.*

137 Dwight Moody, 1837–1899. Ira Sankey 1840–1908. See Owen Chadwick, *The Victorian Church*, 2 vols, second edition (London 1987), II, pp. 286–7.

138 'Moody and Sankeyism,' *CO.*, 5 Jan. 1876.

139 *Ibid.*

140 'Moody and Sankeyism' contd., *CO.*, 19 Jan. 1876.

141 *Ibid.*

142 *Ibid.*

143 Casartelli, 'Difficulties of the Day: The Education of Women,' *Catholic Opinion & Times*, 16 Feb. 1876.

144 *Ibid.*

145 *Ibid.*

146 *Ibid.*

147 *Ibid.*

148 *Ibid.*

149 'The Education of Women' contd., *COT.*, 23 Feb. 1876.

150 *Ibid.*

151 'The Education of Women' concld., *COT.*, 1 March 1876.

152 *Ibid.*

153 *Ibid.*

154 'The Education of Women,' *COT.*, 16 Feb. 1876.

155 'This morning came a letter from Dr. Shewen of Gravesend enclosing a petition to Mr. Lowe asking him to introduce a bill allowing the universities to admit women to degrees. He asked for my signature; I declined and at same time told him my mind.' Casartelli Diaries, 11 Jan. 1874, SDA.

156 'Fr. Reichart called re projected hostel for women University students run by German nuns.' Casartelli Diaries, 7 May 1914, SDA. Casartelli later became chairman of the board of Governors of the Hall, in Victoria Park.

157 Casartelli wrote to Dean Rothwell, editor of the *Harvest* re the 'Catholic Women's Suffrage Society': I suspect they may want to get a report in the *Harvest*. I beg you to refuse to admit it. I hold that such a Society has no right to pose as a Catholic organisation. The question of votes for women is a *purely* political one, and such a Society has no more right to the name than a Catholic Tariff Reform Society or Catholic Free Trade Society, etc...I shall certainly not allow it into the Diocesan Almanac, and I mean to complain about its appearing in the Catholic Directory.' Casartelli to Rothwell, 19 April 1913, Casartelli Letters, 1901–2000, Box 159, SDA.

158 Newman, *A Letter to the Duke of Norfolk*, p. 240.

CHAPTER THREE: CASARTELLI AND EDUCATION: ADVOCATE, PROMOTER AND PIONEER

1 T. H. Huxley, cited in Marjorie Cruickshank, *Church and State in English Education* (London, 1964), p. 21.

2 See Sr. Dominic Savio Hamer's article, 'A Phase of the Struggle for Catholic Education: Manchester and Salford in the mid-Nineteenth-Century', in *Recusant History*, 23 (1) (1996), pp. 107–126.

3 Casartelli's name was among those who signed a petition in 1894 asking that the Roman Rescript preventing Catholics attending the Universities of Oxford and Cambridge be rescinded. He wrote three articles explaining why it was to the advantage of the Church that Catholics be allowed to attend the national universities. See pp. 62ff.

4 V. A. McClelland, *Cardinal Manning His Public Life and Influence 1865–1892* (London, 1962), p. 125.

5 L. C. Casartelli, *De l'Etat Actuel des Études Supérieures dans le Clergé Catholique Anglais* (Brussels, 1896).

6 In some cases the plea by Catholics to use the Douai version, instead of the King James, was rejected. For a history of this struggle in Manchester and Salford, see E. Hamer, *Elizabeth Prout 1820–1864* (Downside Abbey, 1994), p. 96 ff.

7 Sermon I, 'What the Bible Teaches about itself and the Church', *Catholic Opinion*, 24 Dec.1873; Sermon V, 'A Church and A Bible', *CO.*, 11 Feb. 1874; Sermon VI, 'What is the Bible'? *CO.*, 25 Feb. 1874. These articles are discussed in Chapter Two.

8 Cruickshank, *Church and State*, p. 8.

9 The grant included 10s. to 20s. per square feet towards provision of new schools and teachers' houses, two-thirds of outlay required for fittings, 9d. per child each three years for books and maps, and grants to certain teachers. Cardinal Wiseman in 1851 formed the Catholic Poor Schools Society. This Society dealt directly with the Government on the education question. It won the right to have Catholic school inspectors paid by the Government and to set up Reformatories and Industrial Schools. McClelland, *Cardinal Manning*, p. 29.

10 See M. Eaton, J. Longmore & A. Naylor, *Commitment to Diversity* (London, 2000), p. 2.

11 Cruickshank, *Church and State*, pp. 21–22.

12 Cited in V. A. McClelland and M. Hodgetts, *From Without the Flaminian Gate* (London, 1999), p. 219.

13 See McClelland, *Cardinal Manning*, p. 26ff.

14 The conflict reached a partial resolution through the 'dual system.' The Radicals of Birmingham had formed the National Education League to campaign for universal and unsectarian education. They were countered by a rival organisation formed in Manchester, the National Education Union, which enjoyed the support of Catholics. Both League and Union had a common aim – universal elementary education, but they differed in the means of attaining it: the Union wanted the absorption of denominational schools, whilst the League sought their future provision. The Forster Education Act of 1870 skirted round the problem. Cruickshank comments, 'Undoubtedly the establishment of the dual system in England was the most significant of all the decisions taken in 1870. In the future there were to be two types of school, different not only in the spirit of their religious teaching, but different also in their control and management. The gulf was enormous; and the tragic consequences was that churches and school boards, instead of being partners in the work of education, were to be rivals and competitors.' Cruickshank, *Church and State*, p. 33.

15 So called after W. F. Cowper-Temple, MP for South Hants, who introduced the amendment in 1870.

16 Cruickshank, *Church and State*, p. 36.

17 See McClelland, *Cardinal Manning*, p. 62ff.

18 A paper read by Manning to the 'Academia of the Catholic Religion' in 1873, reproduced in the *Tablet*, 3 Jan. 1874.

19 Sermon IV, 'Politics and Education,' *CO.*, 28 Jan. 1874.

20 Sermon IV.

21 *Ibid.*

22 See chapter one, 'Casartelli as a Member of Staff at St Bede's College.'

23 This is an oblique criticism of 'the simple Bible teaching without note or comment' favoured by the Radicals.

24 Sermon IV.

25 *Ibid.* Compare Manning, Pastoral Letter for 1868, cited in Whitehead 'View From the Bridge,' in McClelland and Hodgetts (eds.), *Flaminian Gate*, p. 230.

26 'A Catholic Head Masters' Meeting,' in *Downside Review*, 5 (1886), pp. 9–14.

27 In a letter to the *Tablet*, Casartelli had advocated better mutual communication: 'Our greater colleges at least ought to be brought into some organic connection with each other and a centre, say Kensington University College, so that none should fall below the general efficiency, and something like uniformity of system and correspondence of classes or years should obtain,' The *Tablet*, 29 Jan. 1878, p. 77.

28 L. C. Casartelli, 'A Catholic Head Masters' Meeting. 1. Further Considerations', in *Downside Review*, 5 (1886), p. 148.

29 *Ibid.*, p. 148. Many years later, when again he spoke of the limited advantages gained from

Catholic Colleges being associated with the examining system of the University, he did recognise its advantages: 'However, let us not be ungrateful, and let us acknowledge that the much maligned 'Stinkomalee,' as it was irreverently nicknamed, did open to us the portals and afford us some kind of academic distinction, at a time when other portals were locked to us both inside and out.' L. Casartelli, 'Catholic Secondary Schools and our Universities,' in *23rd Annual Conference of Catholic Colleges* (London, 1919), p. 22.

30 L. C. Casartelli, 'Our Silver Jubilee,' in *25th Annual Conference of Catholic Colleges* (London, 1921), p. 22.

31 See, T. A. Burge, 'Conference of Catholic Colleges', in *The Ampleforth Journal*, 1896 (July), pp. 39–47.

32 'Our chief sensation was probably a certain shyness and a realisation of the utter isolation in which we had all hitherto been living, an isolation which carried with it the further disadvantage of a certain amount of what I may call unfortunate jealousy among our various educational establishments.' Casartelli, 'Our Silver Jubilee,' p. 23.

33 Generally referred to as the 'Bryce Commission' after its chairman James Bryce.

34 T. A. Burge, 'Conference of Catholic Colleges', p. 40.

35 L. C. Casartelli, 'The English Universities and the Reformation,' in the *Dublin Review*, CXVII (16) (October) 1895, pp. 416–442.

36 Casartelli, 'Our Silver Jubilee,' p. 23.

37 R. L. Archer, *Secondary Education in the Nineteenth Century* (London, 1966), pp. 310–311.

38 Casartelli, 'Our Silver Jubilee,' p. 24.

39 H. O. Evennett, 'Catholics and the Universities, 1850–1950', in G. A. Beck, (ed.), *The English Catholics 1850–1950*, (London, 1950), p. 292. The repeal of the Test Acts in 1871 had opened the English universities to Roman Catholics.

40 The Prefect of Propaganda Fide, Cardinal Barnabo, wrote to Manning 19 September 1872 referring to the fact that 'the British Parliament has lately entirely abolished all profession of religious belief as a condition no longer to be required of the students at the Universities', and he declared that the Sacred Congregation now considered the dangers to faith and morals at these institutions to be immeasurably greater than ever before.' Cited in McClelland, *English Roman Catholics and Higher Education 1830–1903* (Oxford, 1973), p. 275.

41 McClelland, *English Roman Catholics*, p. 235.

42 Casartelli Diaries, 27 Oct. 1872, Salford Diocesan Archives.

43 McClelland, *English Roman Catholics*, p. 303.

44 'Received Dr. Newman's *Historical Sketches* (just out) the first steps towards a collection of J N's work I hope to make. The greater part of the vol., is his 'Universities' (office and work). It is very charming. Only what a contrast to London!' Casartelli Diaries, 18 Jan. 1872, SDA.

45 Casartelli Diaries, 14 Oct. 1875, SDA. When Casartelli met Mgr Capel at a garden party, held at his (Capel's) house, he noted in his diary: 'Talk about my being professor at Kensington new University. I think I should like it.' Casartelli Diaries, 19 July 1874, SDA.

46 Casartelli, 'Catholic Secondary Schools,' p. 22.

47 *Ibid.*, p. 19, see also same page where Casartelli refers to the 'controversy regarding Catholic participation in Oxford,' as being 'vividly described in W. Ward's admirable biography of Cardinal Newman.' Wilfrid Ward, *The Life of John Henry Newman*, vol. II (London, 1912).

48 William George Ward (1812–1882), a convert to Catholicism and a teacher of moral and dogmatic philosophy.

49 'Cardinal Manning, a year or two before his death, said to me that circumstances had changed, but that he was too old to change his attitude towards the Universities, but that the change would have to come after his death.' Vaughan to the Cardinal Prefect of

Propaganda Fide, 19 May 1896, Box 402, Archdiocesan Archives Westminster. Cited in Edward Norman, *The English Catholic Church in the Nineteenth Century* (Oxford, 1985), p. 367.

50 Memorandum 'de libertate Universitates adeundi Catholicis Anglicis concedenda' cited in McClelland, *English Roman Catholics*, p. 374. Casartelli himself used this 'altered circumstances' argument in an article demonstrating the Catholic roots of the Universities and how, in the 1890s, there was no longer any moral danger to young Catholics who attended Oxford and Cambridge: 'During the last twenty years, we are assured by unquestionable authority, the growth of earnestness and the spirit of work, the decline of luxury and frivolity, the greater simplicity of student life have made the Oxford and Cambridge of 1895 something very much unlike that even of the seventies.' L. C. Casartelli, 'The English Universities and the Reformation', in the *Dublin Review*, CXVII (16) (October) 1895, p. 442.

51 The other five were: Thomas Wilkinson, Hexham and Newcastle; William Gordon, Leeds; Richard Lacy, Middlesborough; Arthur Riddell, Northampton; Edward Bagshawe, Nottingham.

52 L. C. Casartelli, 'Catholic Secondary Schools', p. 22. Casartelli is here speaking of St Bede's College; the unnamed member of the College staff was presumably Canon James Moyes.

53 McClelland, *English Roman Catholics*, p. 371–372. In relation to this see Gordon Wheeler, 'The Archdiocese of Westminster', in G. A. Beck, (ed.), *The English Catholics, 1850–19950* (London, 1950), p. 167; and A. McCormack, *Cardinal Vaughan*, (London, 1966), p. 264.

54 *Ibid.*, p. 384. For a full account see part five, 'Classes, Coteries, and Family Alliances,' p. 369ff.

55 'John Snead-Cox (*Tablet*) called to talk over forthcoming life of Cardinal Vaughan.' Casartelli Diaries, 4 April 1905; and 'Cox came to my room and we talked reminiscences of Cardinal Vaughan (I consulted my old diaries for the purpose.)' Casartelli Diaries, 10 Feb. 1906, SDA.

56 McClelland, *English Roman Catholics*, pp. 369–375.

57 *Ibid.*, p. 384.

58 The brother of Friedrich von Hügel.

59 McClelland, *English Roman Catholics*, p. 384.

60 Vaughan to Duke of Norfolk, 19 Feb. 1895, 15th Duke of Norfolk's Papers, Arundel Castle Archives.

61 Vaughan to the Duke of Norfolk, 29 Mar. 1895. ACA.

62 *Ibid.*

63 Bishop Edward G. Bagshawe.

64 Vaughan to Duke of Norfolk, 29 Mar. 1985, ACA.

65 *Ibid.* By alluding to the 'primrose bed' Vaughan presumably was referring to 'the primrose path' of Shakespeare's Hamlet:

> Do not, as some ungracious pastors do,
> Show me the steep and thorny way to heaven,
> Whiles, like a puffed and reckless libertine,
> Himself the primrose path of dalliance treads,
> And recks not his own rede.' Hamlet act 1, sc., 3.

66 'His Lordship [Bilsborrow] declared emphatically that he had been of the opinion from the first that this scheme of university education would be disastrous to the faith and morals of our young men, nor had he been able to elicit from the advocates of the scheme any reasons for its adoption, or the knowledge of any benefits which were likely to accrue to our Catholic laity other than social.' Salford Diocesan Chapter Minutes (vol. 2), 2 Sept. 1896, Cathedral House, Salford

67 See McClelland, *English Roman Catholics*, p. 383.

68 W. E. Gladstone, *The Romanes Lecture 1892*, cited in L. C. Casartelli, 'The English Universities and the Reformation,' in *Dublin Review*, CXVII (16) (October) 1895, pp. 417–8.

69 Casartelli, 'The English Universities', p. 418.

70 *Ibid.*, p. 421. Cruickshank describes the Church of the Middle Ages as 'the great matrix of Christendom [that] founded and nourished educational institutions of all kinds.' Cruickshank, *Church and State*, p. XIII.

71 Casartelli, 'The English Universities', p. 419.

72 Friedrich Paulson (1846–1908), philosopher and educator (especially the history of education.)

73 Cited in Casartelli, 'The English Universities', pp. 418–419.

74 Casartelli, 'The English Universities', p. 417. Casartelli's 'Catholic retrospect' echoed the position taken by Manning, who in a sermon on the occasion of the opening of St Bede's College, 9 January 1876, referred to the England of St Bede's day: 'The Church was the mistress of science as she was the teacher of faith, and these two things were her undivided inheritance. But some may ask, is the Church in the lead of science now? In other lands I should not fear to say she is. But is the Church in the lead of science amongst us in England? I answer – Who robbed the Church of all her means of culture; who took away from her the universities which the Church had founded; who appropriated the schools which she had endowed…who spoiled the Church of all the means of culture?' 'St Bede: His Personal Life, Work, and Death. A Sermon. 9 January 1876.' A copy is to be found in 'St Bede's Calendar,' St Bede's College Archives.

75 *Catholic Times*, 6 Mar. 1896.

76 To those who observed that Roman Catholics had 'got the advantages of a university in the University of London' Casartelli's replied 'that it was not a university at all in the true sense of the word' as it lacked the constituent element, namely 'local habitation', a *vox viva*, the opportunity for original research. *CT.*, 6 Mar. 1896. Many years later Casartelli did however recognise the advantages gained from Catholic colleges being associated with the examining system of the University: 'However, let us not be ungrateful, and let us acknowledge that the much maligned 'Stinkomalee,' as it was irreverently nicknamed, did open to us the portals and afford us some kind academic distinction, at a time when other portals were locked to both inside and out.' Casartelli, 'The English Universities,' p. 22.

77 *CT.*, 6 Mar. 1896.

78 *Ibid.*

79 Casartelli, 'The English Universities', p. 419.

80 *CT.*, 6 Mar. 1896.

81 John Henry Newman, *The Idea of a University* (London, 1907), Discourse VI, p. 145 cited in Casartelli, 'The English Universities,' p. 21.

82 Casartelli, 'The English Universities,' p. 21. See I. Ker, *The Achievement of John Henry Newman* (London, 1990), p. 12.

83 *CT.*, 6 Mar. 1896.

84 *CT.*, 6 Mar. 1896.

85 *Ibid.*

86 To encourage this, Casartelli later founded the 'Roger Bacon Society' for Catholic students at the University of Manchester. At the inaugural meeting, which was held in Casartelli's rooms at St Bede's, about fifteen students attended. Casartelli Diaries, 25 Feb. 1905. Later still, in 1919, he was instrumental in establishing a Catholic Society at the University; forty students attended the first meeting. Casartelli Diaries, 20 Nov. 1919. Casartelli wrote to the Chairman of the Society: 'Catholic young men and women have nowadays, to an extent that a few years ago was absolutely impossible, immense opportunities for the

statement of Catholic principles among the great public of our fellow countrymen.'
Casartelli – Miss Mather, 7 Nov. 1923, Casartelli Letters, 6210–6300, Box 164, SDA.

87 *CT.*, 6 Mar. 1896.

88 Taken from Horace: 'one who praises the world as it was when he was a boy.'

89 *Ushaw Magazine*, 3 (March) 1898, p. 108.

90 L. C. Casartelli, *De l'Etat Actuel des Études Supérieures dans le Clergé Catholique Anglais* (Brussels, 1896).

91 *Ibid.*, p. 7.

92 For Vaughan's policy see Snead-Cox, *The Life of Cardinal Vaughan*, vol. 2, 'The Education of the Priest' pp. 34–69; see also Vaughan's Preface to, *Life of St John Baptist de Rossi* (London, 1883).

93 James Moyes (1851–1927), a priest of Salford Diocese, member of staff at St Bede's College 1876–1890, Canon Theologian of Salford Diocese. In 1892 went to Westminster with Herbert Vaughan. Member of the commission along with Aidan Gasquet set up by Vaughan to explore validity of Anglican orders. One time editor of *Dublin Review*. Aidan Gasquet (1846–1929), headmaster and prior of Downside Abbey, after resigning due to ill health, devoted himself to historical research. Became Vatican librarian in 1917 and archivist in 1920.

94 Casartelli, *Des Etudes Supérieures*, p.17. '*Cela tient à ce que nous restons toujours exclus de la vie intellectuelle, du mouvement scientifique des universités.*' Newman in *The Idea of a University* spoke of a university as having, 'a self-perpetuating tradition, or *genius loci* … which haunts the home where it has been born, and which imbues and forms, more or less, and one by one, every individual who is successively brought under its shadow.' Cited in Ker, *The Achievement of John Henry Newman*, p. 16.

95 *Ibid.*, p. 18. '*On se demande avec anxiété, dans quelle position se trouvera notre clergé d'ici à un quart de siècle, non seulement vis-à-vis du clergé anglican et même du clergé des dissidents, qui font tout pour participer aux avantages des hautes études, mais encore vis-à-vis de nos laïques qui seront plus instruits, qui auront l'espirit mieux cultivé que leurs prêtres.*'

96 See chapter four, 'Education and Formation of the Clergy'.

97 For a history of St Edmund's see M. Walsh, *St Edmund's College, Cambridge, 1896–1996* (St Edmund's College, 1996).

98 See Walsh, *St Edmund's College*, p. 34.

99 Casartelli to Charles Case, 6 Mar. 1905, Box 4, St Edmund's House Archives. In 1904 he recommended Francis Gonne, then studying at St Sulpice, as a possible recipient of a Cambridge scholarship. As a further sign of support he sent Thomas Fish to be a student there. Fish had, with Casartelli's encouragement, studied Hebrew at the University of Manchester (where he later became the first Catholic chaplain.)

100 *CT.*, 6 Mar. 1896. This included opposition to Bourne's suggestion in 1923 of a 'Catholic Faculty of Theology and Philosophy' at Oxford or Cambridge. See E. Oldmeadow, *Francis Cardinal Bourne*, 2 vol. (London, 1944), II, pp. 200–204; for Casartelli's reaction see below Chapter Five, p. 128.

101 *Ibid.*

102 *Ibid.*

103 See McClelland, *Cardinal Manning*, p. 124.

104 Among the others were: Canon Arthur Kennard, Clifton; Fr. Joseph Rickaby, S.J.; Fr. William Barry, Westminster; Fr. A. McColl, Southwark; the Congregation of the Oratory were also asked to consider the post.

105 The question of Roman Catholics attending the universities of Oxford and Cambridge has received detailed coverage in G. A. Beck (ed.), *The English Catholics 1850–1950* (London, 1950) and V. A. McClelland, *English Roman Catholics and Higher Education 1830–1903* (Oxford, 1973). The provision for the religious welfare of Catholic students at Oxford and

Cambridge has also been detailed by McClelland in 'The Universities' Catholic Educational Board and the Chaplains, 1895–1939', in *The Ampleforth Journal*, LXXVIII part. 1 (Spring) 1973, pp. 69–84. The Hedley Papers, now available, shed light on the issues.

106 Hedley Papers, Boxes 23 & 52–55, National Library of Wales, Aberystwyth.
107 See V. A. McClelland, 'The Universities' Catholic Education Board and the Chaplain, 1895–1939', in *The Ampleforth Journal*, pp. 69–84.
108 'Universities' Catholic Education Board: a Report of its Work from 1895 to 1897', quoted in V. A. McClelland, *English Roman Catholics*, p. 386.
109 Vaughan to Hedley, 25 June 1895, Hedley Papers, Box 53, NLW.
110 James Fitzalan Hope (1870–1949), nephew to the 15th Duke of Norfolk, later Lord Rankeillour.
111 Wilfrid Philip Ward (1856–1916), son of William George Ward.
112 McClelland, *English Roman Catholics*, p. 4.
113 *Ibid.*, p. 400.
114 William Robert Brownlow (1830–1901) Bishop of Clifton 1894–1901.
115 Bishop Brownlow to Hedley, 27 Aug. 1896, Hedley Papers, Box 53, NLW.
116 Casartelli to Hedley, 28 Aug. 1896, Hedley Papers, Box 53, NLW.
117 Casartelli to Hedley, 1 Sept. 1896, Hedley Papers, Box 53, NLW.
118 Salford Diocesan Chapter Minutes (SDCM), (vol. 2), 11 Sept. 1896, Salford Cathedral.
119 *Ibid.*
120 *Ibid.*
121 *Ibid.*
122 SDCM, 2 Sept. 1896.
123 *Ibid.* The Chapter's reply was summarised thus:
1. This was the second time the Bishop had been asked to release 'a valuable and learned priest.' [The other priest was presumably James Moyes who had accompanied Herbert Vaughan to Westminster.]
2. General opinion that it would be incompatible for the Rector of St Bede's to reside elsewhere.
3. 'That the Bishops had not been unanimous in their approval of the University Education Scheme for Catholic Young Men.'
4. 'That the concession granted by Propaganda – for the laity to attend the university lectures – and consequently for clerical students – was made reluctantly – and safeguarded by very stringent conditions.'
5. '… in deference to a request more in favour of the residence of clerical students…the same reluctance was even more strongly exhibited – no words of direct sanction were expressed' only the formula *tolerare potest* was used.
6. 'The question of the residence of the laity at the universities will now rest with parents – the question of the residence of clerical students will reside with the bishops. His Lordship declared that he had been of the opinion from the first that this scheme of university education would prove disastrous to the faith and morals of our young men – nor had he been able to elicit from the advocates of the scheme any reasons for its adoption, or the knowledge of any benefits which were likely to accrue to our Catholic laity other than social.'
124 *Ibid.*
125 Bilsborrow replied: 'Owing to its grave importance to the interests of this Diocese I submitted to my Chapter…the Bishop of Newport's offer to you of the post of 'religious Lecturer to the Catholic Students at Oxford. Their judgement and counsel, which were emphatic and universal, were as follows:
1. That such a request, considering your position and responsibility in the Diocese, was unreasonable;

2. That the duties of rector of St Bede's College and those of the proposed office at Oxford were incompatible;

3. That the Chairman of the Universities Board to make such a proposal to a priest and high official without the knowledge of his Ordinary was unbecoming and uncanonical.

I regret to say that my own opinion and conscience, as candour counsels me to admit, leave me no alternative but to endorse the deliberate convictions of my Chapter.' Copy of letter, Bilsborrow to Casartelli, 3 Sept. 1896, Hedley Papers, Box 53, NLW.

126 Casartelli to Hedley, 3 Sept. 1896, Hedley Papers, Box 53, NLW.

127 Vaughan to Hedley, 4 Sept. 1896, Hedley Papers, Box 53, NLW.

128 Vaughan to Hedley, 7 Sept. 1896, Hedley Papers, Box 53, NLW.

129 Casartelli to Hedley, 6 Sept. 1896, Hedley Papers, Box 53, NLW.

130 *Ibid.*

131 Casartelli to Hedley, 13 Sept. 1896, Hedley Papers, Box 53, NLW.

132 Kennard to Hedley, 19 Oct. 1896, Hedley Papers, Box 53, NLW.

133 This was the pattern chosen at Cambridge.

134 Moyes to Hedley, 17 Nov. 1896, Hedley Papers, Box 53, NLW.

135 McClelland, *English Roman Catholics*, p. 404.

136 Richardson to Hedley, 14 Sept. 1896, Hedley Papers, Box 53, NLW.

137 *Baeda*, XII (1) (1937), p. 8.

138 *Ibid.*, p. 17.

139 Richardson to Hedley, 14 Sept. 1896, Hedley Papers, Box 53, NLW.

140 Casartelli to Hedley, 1 Sept. 1896, Hedley Papers, Box 53, NLW.

141 The 'Prospectus and Description of the College', issued for the opening of St Bede's in January 1876, described the situation then pertaining and the *raison d' être* of the college: 'Whilst there exist [sic] in England many excellent Catholic Colleges, whose system of education is based mainly upon the classical and dead languages, the want is increasingly felt of a College which should afford a more direct and practical preparation for the Civil Service, and such professions as must be entered at an early age, by concentrating the attention of its scholars upon modern languages, and the more useful branches of science.' St Bede's College, Manchester, 1876.

142 It was not Vaughan's intention to ignore totally the Classical side of education. In a letter to Oswald Hunter Blair he stated: '*my* [St Bede's] college is destined for the sons of the commercial classes, to give a business training to our pupils such as no Catholic school imparts to-day. But don't think that we shall ignore or neglect the claims of 'humane letters', for they too will form an essential part of our curriculum.' Cited in *Baeda*, XII (I) (1937), p. 5.

143 The 'Prospectus and Description of the College'. St Bede's College, Manchester 1876.

144 Cited in McClelland and Hodgetts, *Flaminian Gate*, p. 219.

145 See McClelland, *Manning*, p. 12.

146 McClelland, *Manning*, pp. 13–14.

147 See Snead-Cox, *Cardinal Vaughan*, vol. I, p. 305.

148 'The Needs of Commercial Education', *Baeda*, 9 (1880), p. 130.

149 During his sermon, Manning summed up the work of the College, 'Also in this place an Academia, or scientific and literary association, founded for the defence of the Catholic faith, and for its justification against the perverted intellect of our times, will hold its sessions. The whole of this work, therefore, may be taken as one, the purpose and end of which is the same, namely, the sanctification of the intellect, the defence of truth, and the union of faith and intellectual culture.' 'St Bede. His Personal Life, Work, and Death. A Sermon.' St Bede's College, Manchester, 1887.

150 Other related works by Casartelli are *Commercial Education*, (Manchester, 1882); *The Teaching of Commercial Geography*, (Manchester, 1886); *The Modern Languages Problem. A*

Paper read to the Manchester Statistical Society, (London, 1888); *Commercial Geography*, (Manchester, 1889); *Eastward Ho! Or some Considerations on our Responsibilities in the East*, (London, 1893); *The Study of Commercial History*, (Manchester, 1897).

151 T. Nigel. L. Brown, *History of the Manchester Geographical Society: 1884–1950* (Manchester, 1971), p. 1.

152 *Ibid.*, p. 3.

153 *Ibid.*, pp. 13; 21; 27.

154 *Ibid.*, p. 21.

155 L. C. Casartelli, *Commercial Education* (Manchester, 1882).

156 Casartelli described the members of the Statistical Society as 'true educational pioneers.' L. C. Casartelli, *Commercial Geography* (Manchester, 1889), p. 3.

157 *The Modern Languages Problem in Modern Education* (Manchester, 1888), p.105.

158 L. C. Casartelli, 'Commercial and Technical Education in Manchester', in *Baeda*, 18 (1881), pp. 113–115.

159 *Ibid.*, p. 114.

160 *Ibid.*, p. 115.

161 Casartelli, *Commercial Education*, p. 71.

162 Casartelli repeated his claim for academic sanction of commercial subjects: 'Nor is there any reason why full academic honours should not be awarded to Commercial Geography, for it must be clearly understood that, though practical or utilitarian in its application, it must be based on the strictest scientific principles and deductions.' Casartelli, *Commercial Geography*, p. 6.

163 'The Teaching of Commercial Geography', *Journal of Manchester Geographical Society* 12 (1886), p. 329.

164 See Brown, *Manchester Geographical Society*, p. 11.

165 For a history of the study of commercial subjects in the University of Manchester see E. Fiddes, *History of Owens College and of Manchester University* (Manchester, 1937), pp. 147–155.

166 'Commercial Education is rapidly coming to the fore all the country over. The Manchester Chamber of Commerce has warmly taken it up, established an 'Education Committee', on which the Bishop of Salford and Dr. Casartelli have places, and formulated a scheme of examinations in commercial subjects to come into operation next July. The Owens College has established a Higher Commercial Course in its evening department, and the lecturer in Commerce and Commercial History will be Mr. C. T. Trevor, F.C.A., who since 1882 has been regularly delivering to our upper forms the admirable courses of Commercial Lectures so familiar to St Bede's students for six or seven generations.' 'St Bede's College Calendar 1890–91', p. 31. St Bede's College, Manchester.

167 Casartelli, *Commercial History*, p. 3.

168 *Ibid.*, p. 5.

169 L. C. Casartelli, 'A Problem of After-War Reconstruction: The Study of Foreign Languages,' in *Transactions of the Manchester Statistical Society*, 1918–19, p. 55.

170 *Baeda*, XII (1) (1937), p. 10.

171 A. Carnoy, 'Sa G. Monseigneur Louis-Charles Casartelli, Évéque de Salford, Professeur honoraire de la Faculté de Philosophie et Lettres,' in *Annuaire de L'Université de Louvain: 1920–1926*, pp. xvii-xxxiv.

172 Francis Gonne (1879–1938), Rector of St Bede's 1916–1938.

173 Casartelli was a part-time lecturer in Persian languages at the universities of Louvain and Manchester. Ronald H. Preston in his essay, 'The Faculty of Theology in the University of Manchester: the First Seventy-Five Years', recognises Casartelli as among those scholars who made the Faculty's existence possible. *University of Manchester Faculty of Theology Seventy-Fifth Anniversary Papers* (Faculty of Theology, Manchester, 1980), p. 3.

174   J. H. Moulton, *Early Zoroastrianism* (London, 1913), p. xii.

175   Casartelli to Moulton, 5 Dec. 1913, Moulton Papers, MA. MOU. II. 24. John Rylands Library Manchester.

176   Casartelli to Moulton, 4 May 1913, MA. MOU. II. 18. JRL

177   See Minute Book EOS/1/, John Ryland's Library: 24 Nov. 1906; 30 April 1907; 15 Nov. 1907; 8 Feb. 1908; 14 Jan. 1909; 24 Jan. 1909; 21 May 1909; 29 Oct. 1909; 18 Feb. 1910; 4 Mar. 1910; 3 Oct. 1910.

178   Minute Book, 1 May 1909.

179   EOS/2. JRL,

180   EOS/3/1, 15 Oct. 1915. JRL.

181   See Bibliography for a list of the articles he wrote.

182   R. C. Zaehner, *The Dawn and Twilight of Zoroastrianism* (London, 1961), p. 343. A review of Casartelli's thesis in the *Dublin Review* XIII (11) (1885), p. 464, concludes, 'We believe we have said enough to enable the reader to understand what important questions are mooted and often solved in the doctoral dissertation of Dr. Casartelli. Before concluding, we wish to bear testimony to the profound knowledge of authorities and thorough acquaintance with all that relates to the Eranian [*sic*] philology displayed on every page ... We are certain that all those who are interested in the study of languages and of ancient religions will desire that the author may continue to communicate to us the fruit of his researches on the language, literature, ceremonial, and religion of the votaries of Zoroaster.'

183   Antonio Panaino, 'Casartelli', in *Encyclopaedia Iranica*, (California, 1992), vol. 5, pp. 24–25.

184   *Ibid.*, p. 25.

185   L. C. Casartelli, *Sketches in History* (London, 1906).

186   *Ibid.*, p. 187.

187   McClelland, *Manning*, p. 111.

188   L. C. Casartelli, 'An Educational Lesson From Berlin', in *Dublin Review*, XIX (11) (April) 1888, pp. 294–304. The languages were: Turkish, Arabic, Persian, Japanese, Chinese, and Hindustani.

189   *Ibid.*, p. 294.

190   *Ibid.*, pp. 302–3.

191   *Ibid.*, pp. 303–4.

192   Hindustani 'has practically become a *lingua franca* in common use over well-nigh every portion of the Indian Empire.' L. C. Casartelli, *Eastward Ho! Or Some Considerations on our Responsibilities in the East*, (Manchester, 1893), p. 78.

193   *Ibid.*, p. 91.

194   Casartelli, 'An Educational Lesson', p. 92.

195   In his diary he described this as 'a most astonishing and unexpected honour.' Casartelli Diaries, 21 December 1918, SDA.

196   The Katrak Lectureship was founded in 1922 by Dr. Nanabhai Navrosji Katrak, who is described in the entry in the *Oxford University Calendar* as 'a Parsi gentleman of Bombay, Licentiate of Medicine and Surgery of the University of Bombay, a Justice of the Peace of the town and island of Bombay'. He endowed the lecture in memory of his late wife; its purpose was 'to promote the study of the religion of Zoroaster and of its later developments from a theological, philological, and historical point of view.' Letter to author from Archives Assistant, University of Oxford, 8 July 2000.

197   Compare Hooper and Graham's chapter 'The Modern Languages Course in Commercial Education' pp. 29–30 with Casartelli's *Modern Languages Problem* pp. 107 & 116; also 'The Study of Material Course' pp. 64–65, with Casartelli's *Commercial Geography* pp. 329–330 & p. 332. Hooper and Graham's chapter 'Commercial Education Abroad' pp. 81–134 is redolent of Casartelli's description of the commercial colleges of Germany, Holland, and France.

CHAPTER FOUR: THE MAKING OF A BISHOP

1 T. Buchanan and Martin Conway (eds.), 'Great Britain' in *Political Catholicism in Europe, 1918–1965* (Oxford, 1996), p. 249.

2 E. Norman, *Roman Catholicism in England* (Oxford, 1985), p.107.

3 Kester Aspden, *The English Catholic Bishops and Politics, 1903–1943* (PhD thesis University of Cambridge, 1999), p. 2.

4 Kester Aspden, 'The English Roman Catholic Bishops and Politics, 1903–1935.' A paper read to the Ecclesiastical History Seminar, University of London, 10 Jan. 2000. I am very grateful to Dr. Aspden for a copy of this paper.

5 Aspden, 'The English Roman Catholic Bishops and Politics, 1903–1935,' p. 4.

6 Casartelli to Gasquet, 23 May 1917, Casartelli Letters, 4201–4300, Box 161, Salford Diocesan Archives.

7 Aspden, *The English Catholic Bishops and Politics, 1903–1943*, Abstract.

8 Kester Aspden, 'The English Roman Catholic Bishops and The Social Order, 1918–26' in *Recusant History*, 25 (3) (2001), pp. 543–560.

9 Philip Hughes, 'The Bishops of the Century' in George Andrew Beck, (ed.), *The English Catholics 1850–1950* (London 1950), p. 187.

10 M. de la Bedoyere, *Cardinal Bernard Griffin* (London, 1955); M. Clifton, *Amigo Friend of the Poor* (Leominster, 1987). M. McInally, *Edward Ilsley Archbishop of Birmingham* (London, 2002.)

11 T. M. Maloney, 'The Public Ministry of Cardinal Hinsley 1935–1943', PhD thesis, University of London, 1981; subsequently published as *Westminster, Whitehall and the Vatican* (London, 1985).

12 M. J. Broadley, 'The Episcopate of Thomas Henshaw 1925–1938,' (unpublished MPhil., dissertation, University of Manchester, 1998.)

13 Kester Aspden, *The English Catholic Bishops and Politics, 1903–1943* (unpublished PhD thesis, University of Cambridge, 1999.)

14 Hughes, 'Bishops of the Century,' p. 191.

15 *Ibid.*, p. 191.

16 See 'Bishops of the Century', p. 193.

17 Philip Hughes, 'The Coming Century', in Beck, *The English Catholics 1850–1950*, p. 38.

18 Aspden, 'The English Roman Catholic Bishops and Politics, 1903–1935', p. 1.

19 Ernest Oldmeadow, *Francis Cardinal Bourne* 2 vols (London, 1944), II, p. 168.

20 Brian Plumb, *From Arundel to Zabi. A Biographical Dictionary of the Catholic Bishops of England and Wales (Deceased)* (Warrington, n.d.)

21 Plumb, *Arundel to Zabi.*

22 Ibid.

23 Ibid.

24 Ibid.

25 Ibid.

26 Aspden, 'The English Roman Catholic Bishops and Politics, 1903–1935,' p. 1. See also M. McInally, *Edward Ilsley Archbishop of Birmingham* (London, 2002), pp. 82–84, where she describes Ullathorne's recommendation of Ilsley as *episcopabile* to Propaganda Fide. Ullathorne described Ilsley thus: 'Firm of purpose, prudent in his actions, good at organising, humble in spirit, cautious in speech – he is the man to whom I would freely confide episcopal duties.' p. 84.

27 Plumb, *Arundel to Zabi.*

28 See Aspden, 'The English Roman Catholic Bishops and Politics, 1903–1935,' p. 1.

29 Cited in Aspden, 'The English Roman Catholic Bishops and Politics, 1903–1935,' p. 8.

30 *Annual Report of the 7th Conference of Catholic Head Masters' Meeting* (Ware, 1902), p. 36.

31 *Acta Salfordiensia Episcopi Quarti*, Anns. XII-XIII, 1914–1916, Synod 1915, SDA.

32 For the numerous diocesan organisations which originated during his episcopacy, see Appendix Three.

33 Casartelli, Pastoral Letter, Lent 1909, 'Faith and Works', ASEQ, An. II, 1908–9, SDA.

34 J. G. Snead Cox, *Life of Cardinal Vaughan* 2 vol. (London, 1910), I, p. 458.

35 Casartelli to Vaughan, 17 Mar. 1903, Box V.I/63, 1–259, Archdiocesan Archives Westminster.

36 See as evidence of this, Casartelli to Cardinal Gotti, 19 Sept. 1903, A. 1903, Rub. 102, p. 62, Propaganda Fide Archives, Rome.

37 Salford Diocesan Chapter Minutes, vol. 2, 4 April 1903, Cathedral House, Salford. John Galbois Boulaye became Vicar General of Salford Diocese in 1907.

38 Vaughan to Hedley, April 1903, Hedley Papers, Box 53, National Library of Wales, Aberystwyth.

39 Annual Meeting of Bishops, Westminster, 21 April 1903. Archdiocesan Archives Birmingham.

40 Plumb, *Arundel to Zabi.*

41 Bishop Arthur Riddell of Northampton, 'took a formidable stance against the admission of Catholics to the Universities;' Bishop William Gordon of Leeds – 'dogged, blunt in speech, single in purpose, a hard bargainer in business.' Brian Plumb, *Arundel to Zabi.*

42 Wilkinson to Vaughan, 25 April 1903, A.1903, vol. 259, Rub. 102, pp. 247–254, PFA.

43 *Ibid.*

44 Vaughan to Gotti, 13 June 1903, A. 1903, vol. 259, Rub. 102, pp. 247–254, PFA. The absent bishops were: Herbert Vaughan of Westminster, Francis Bourne of Southwark and Thomas Wilkinson of Hexham and Newcastle.

45 Bourne to Gotti, 20 June 1903, A. 1903, vol. 259, Rub. 102, pp. 247–254, PFA.

46 Anonymous letter marked, 'Confidential', from an English bishop to Gotti, no date, A. 1903, vol. 259, Rub. 102, pp. 247–254, PFA.

47 Vaughan to Gotti, 13 June 1903, A. 1903, vol. 259, Rub. 102, pp. 247–254, PFA.

48 Casartelli to Gotti, 19 Sept. 1903, A.1903, vol. 259, Rub. 102, pp. 247–254, PFA.

49 *Manchester Guardian*, 1 Sept. 1903, p. 6.

50 Casartelli to Gasquet, 1 Sept. 1903, Gasquet Papers 1885–1904, no. 938, Downside Abbey.

51 Casartelli to Gasquet, 6 Sept. 1903, Gasquet Papers 1885–1904, no. 938, DA.

52 The four names on the Westminster *terna* were Bourne, Hedley, Merry del Val and Gasquet. The newspaper had reported that 'two candidates on the *terna* had not shewn themselves free from tendencies of the Liberal Catholic party.' Quoted in Shane Leslie, *Cardinal Gasquet* (London, 1935), p. 82. This jibe was aimed at Hedley and Gasquet. Shane Leslie writes that, 'The *Chronicle* had hit him (sc. Gasquet) hard, for he was sensitive to Liberalism used as a taunt or taint when applied to his Catholicism.' p. 82. Gasquet's part in the issue of the succession to Westminster can be read in Chapter Five, 'The Succession to Westminster in 1903 and Gasquet's Memorandum', pp. 80–90. Casartelli in the second part of his letter wrote: 'I had fully expected that I should have had to write and congratulate you, or better the English Church, on your nomination to the Metropolitan See. I felt that you were the one man in England to take up the grand tradition and add lustre to it. *Dis aliter visum*. I cannot honestly deny my disappointment, and I venture to think it is pretty general'. Casartelli to Gasquet, 6 Sept. 1903, Gasquet Papers 1885–1904, no. 938, DA.

53 Casartelli to Gasquet, 12 Sep. 1903, Gasquet Papers 1885–1904, no. 938 DA.

54 Casartelli, Pastoral Letter, October 1904, 'The Signs of The Times,' ASEQ, An. I, 1903–4. SDA.

55 Philip Hughes, 'The Bishops of the Century,' pp. 189–190.

56 Vaughan to Hedley, April 1903, Hedley Papers, Box 53, NLW. See above p. 97.

57 *MG.*, 22 Jan. 1925.

58 *The Universe*, 23 Jan. 1925.

59 Robert O'Neil, *Cardinal Herbert Vaughan* (London, 1995), p. 483.

60 Casartelli Diaries, 21 Dec. 1919, SDA.

61 *Ibid.*, 7 Feb. 1921.

62 'I have thus once more performed all the Holy Week services, Sunday to Sunday, as in 1904, 1905, 1907, 1909, 1915, 1917, D.G.!' *Ibid.*, 31 Mar. 1918.

63 The annual allowance for the bishop's household.

64 John Stephen Vaughan (1853–1925), the youngest brother of Herbert Vaughan, consecrated auxiliary bishop of Salford, 15 August 1909.

65 Casartelli to J. S. Vaughan, 3 May 1909, Casartelli Letters, E401–500, Box 157, SDA.

66 Casartelli to Mgr. Boulaye, 25 Feb. 1910, Casartelli Letters, G601–700, Box 157, SDA.

67 See Casartelli to Mgr. Boulaye, 28 Feb. 1913, Casartelli Letters, 1901–2000, Box 159, SDA.

68 Casartelli to Canon Lonsdale, 21 Nov. 1910, Casartelli Letters, 801–900, Box 158, SDA.

69 Salford Visitation Register 1905–1921, p. 58, SDA.

70 See Chapter Seven, pp. 179–189.

71 Casartelli Diaries, 12 Feb. 1900, Ushaw College Archives.

72 Casartelli Diaries, 6 Nov. 1909, SDA (see p. 2).

73 Letter of Joseph D. Casartelli to Fr Derek Holmes, 11 Dec. 1972, Casartelli File, UCA.

74 Casartelli to Archbishop of Birmingham, 22 Jan. 1921, Illsley Papers, Archdiocesan Archives Birmingham.

CHAPTER FIVE: CASARTELLI AS A SPIRITUAL LEADER

1 *Inter Pastoralis Officii* (1903). An oft quoted passage from the Introduction is: 'Since we have very much at heart that the true Christian spirit be revived in all possible ways and that it be maintained among all the faithful, it is above all necessary to provide for the holiness and dignity of the sacred places where precisely the faithful gather to draw this spirit at its primary and indispensable source, that is, active participation in the sacred mysteries and in the public and solemn prayer of the Church.' J. Neuner & J. Dupuis, *The Christian Faith* (Dublin 1976), p. 322,

2 *Sacra Tridentina* (1905). 'By this Decree Pope Pius X allowed the practice of daily communion which he considered to be 'the desire of Christ and of the Church.' After a brief survey of the history of frequent communion and of the discussions regarding the necessary dispositions, the Pope lays down definite rules on the observance of which the fruit of the practice depends. Though partly conditioned by the theology of the time, this is a clear statement of the personal appropriation required from the recipient of the sacrament for its fruitful reception.' Neuner & Dupuis, *The Christian Faith*, p. 323.

3 Guiseppe Sarto (1835–1914), elected Pope 4 August 1903.

4 'A mystic phrase re-echoing St Paul's famous words: 'It is no longer I that live, but Christ who liveth in me'. To place Christ at the centre of all life, to rest everything upon His message, must be the aim of every Christian and *a fortiori a pope*. It was the purpose that dictated all the great decisions of Pius X in the spiritual sphere ... He himself took care to explain his ideas on this point. 'To restore all things in Christ is to strengthen not only what belongs to the divine mission of the Church, but also what derives from that mission; it is to promote a Christian society in all those fields'.' H. Daniel-Rops, *A Fight for God* (London, 1965), p. 55.

5 Roger Aubert, *History of the Church* vol. IX (London, 1981), p. 384.

6 See his Pastoral Letter 'The Signs of the Times,' *Acta Salfordiensia, Episcopi Quarti, An. 1. 1903–4*, Salford Diocesan Archives. (Will be cited as 'Signs'.)

7 Pius X, *Inter Pastoralis Officii*.

8 J. D. Crichton, and others, *English Catholic Worship: Liturgical Renewal in England since 1900* (London, 1979), p. X.
9 'The Bishop's Message', *The Catholic Federationist*, Jan. 1913.
10 For dates and titles see Bibliography. The core themes relating to spirituality are found in Sermon III, 'Unpolitical Politics' and Sermon XII 'Fixing the Limit,' where the whole doctrine of the relationship between the Church and the world revolves around the question, 'Who made me'? The answer to this question is 'God'. It follows that, 'If God made us, God has a perfect right to do with us what He pleases.' God made Man for a specific purpose, namely, 'to serve Him in this world and to be happy with Him in the next' according to the Catechism of Trent. Mankind is therefore made for two worlds – 'this temporal world' and the 'eternal world' of heaven. *The Catholic Opinion*, 23 Dec. 1874, Sermon XII, 'Fixing the Limit'.
11 Pastoral Letter, Lent 1910, 'What Shall it Profit a Man'? ASEQ, An. VII, 1909–10, SDA. (Will be cited as 'Lent 1910') Casartelli cites the following from Scripture: Jn., 1.29; 3.16; 4.42; 6.2; 8.12; 13.47; 2 Cor., 5.19.
12 'Lent 1910.' See Jn., 7.7; 8.23–24; 12.31; 14.17,27; 15.18–19; 16.11,33; 17.7,9; 18.36;
13 To illustrate that 'every man's soul is a battlefield' Casartelli refers to the meditation on 'The Two Standards' in the Spiritual Exercises of St Ignatius of Loyola: 'this great spiritual artist depicts Christ our Lord setting up His Standard of the Cross and preaching to men His Gospel, whose principles and maxims are diametrically opposed to those of the World; sending forth His Apostles to inspire men with indifference to riches, with humility, evangelical poverty, self-denial, and the other Christian virtues which the World cannot even understand. It is between these two standards that the Christian is called to make his choice.' 'Lent 1910.'
14 *Ibid.*
15 *Ibid.*
16 Jansenism: a rigorist presentation of Augustine's theology of grace which owes its name to Cornelius Otto Jansen (1585–1638), Bishop of Ypres. 'In sacramental discipline strict standards should be observed … and the moral life of the Christian must make no concessions to self (e.g. the theatre and luxury are condemned, charitable works are demanded.' Alan Richardson and John Bowden (eds.), *A New Dictionary of Christian Theology* (London, 1983), p. 305.
17 Casartelli Diaries, 9 Jan. 1876, SDA.
18 Casartelli to Canon Boulaye, 25 Sept. 1911, Casartelli Copy Letters, 1201–1300, Box 158, SDA.
19 'Lent 1910'. Casartelli applied this maxim during the War to the question of science: 'There is an old Latin proverb: *Corruptio optimi pessima* … the best things by being corrupted become the worst of all. Science in itself is good, it is one of God' best gifts to His creatures … the best of God's endowments of His creatures may be perverted and corrupted by the human will to be the worst of scourges for the punishment of the proud humanity that sets up those endowments like the Golden Calf, in the place of their maker.' 'The Bishop's Message', *CF.*, Sept. 1915.
20 'Lent 1910.'
21 *Ibid.*
22 *Ibid.*
23 *Ibid.*
24 *Ibid.*
25 *Ibid.*
26 'The John Bull League' was under the presidency of Horatio Bottomley M.P., and professed to be 'a religious body without a creed.' 'Instead of thinking so much about the next life, its members will make the most of this.' At the time of Casartelli's Pastoral Letter, the Rev. J. Stitt Smith had recently delivered a speech in Manchester, during

which he had spoken of 'What good is access to God if you have to belong to the army of unemployed? What good is access to heaven on the other side of the moon if you have not a change of shirt on this side of the moon?' *Ibid.*

27 *Ibid.*

28 1868–1943. Worked energetically for social reforms and for a 'back-to-the-land movement' known as 'Distributism.' See Chapter Eight, 'Casartelli and Socialism.'

29 Casartelli to Rev. W. Aspinall, 15 Sept. 1912, Casartelli Copy Letters, 1601–1800, Box 159, SDA. See also Kester Aspden, 'The English Catholic Bishops and the Social Order, 1818–19226', in *Recusant History*, 25 (3) (2001), p. 549.

30 This evidence is discussed below.

31 Mary Heimann, 'Devotional Stereotypes in English Catholicism, 1850–1914,' in F. Tallett and N. Atkin, (eds.), *Catholicism in Britain and France Since 1783* (London, 1996), p. 18.

32 L. C. Casartelli, (London 1903); later appeared in Casartelli's *Sketches in History* (New York, 1906), it is this version which will be referred to throughout.

33 L. C. Casartelli, *Sketches in History* (New York, 1906), pp. 238–239.

34 Mary Heimann in her *Catholic Devotion in Victorian England* (Oxford, 1995), claims that the growth which the Catholic Church underwent in this period cannot be accurately explained by the 'Second Spring' argument, i.e. the perceived idea that salient dates and events in the history of the Church enabled its members to express themselves in ways hitherto impossible because of legislation; the 1829 Emancipation Act and the Restoration of the Hierarchy in 1850 being central. Thanks to these events Catholics, according to the Second Spring argument, could be more demonstrative in their devotions and so tended to choose continental ones and those imported by the Irish immigrants. Likewise she dismisses another argument, again a perceived idea, which sees the change in devotional practice as a triumph for Ultramontanism, i.e. that Roman and continental devotions were imposed by the authority of Rome. For this latter argument see, J. D. Holmes, *More Roman Than Rome* (London, 1978).

35 See John Bossy, *The English Catholic Community 1570–1850* (London, 1975), p. 297, where he describes the idea of the Second Spring as a miraculous rebirth dating from *circa* 1840 as 'a piece of tendentious ecclesiastical propaganda.' See also Heimann, *Catholic Devotion*, pp. 5–10.

36 Casartelli, *Sketches*, p. 238.

37 Gentili was a member of the institute of Charity, a religious order founded in 1828 by Antonio Rosmini; hence the name 'Rosminians' given to its members. Casartelli was a great admirer of the Founder of the Order to which Gentili belonged. In the same year that 'A Forgotten Chapter' appeared in *Sketches in History*, he wrote the preface to G. B. Pagini's *The Life of Antonio Rosmini-Serbati* (London, 1906.) In 1910 Casartelli presented a paper to the Manchester Dante Society entitled, 'Dante and Rosmini,' where he praised the unity of philosophy and theology found in Rosmini's writings. See L. C. Casartelli, *Dante and Rosmini. A Lecture to the Dante Society Manchester*, (Market Weighton, 1910.)

38 Casartelli, *Sketches*, p. 239.

39 *Ibid.*, p. 239.

40 *Ibid.*, p. 240.

41 *Ibid.*, p. 240.

42 Heimann, *Catholic Devotion*, and 'Devotional Stereotypes.'

43 Heimann, 'Devotional Stereotypes.' The data for the diocese of Salford for this period reads: churches offering *Quarant' Ore*: 0; churches offering Exposition of the Blessed Sacrament: 1875:1; 1880:3; 1885:1; 1890:2; 1895:2.

44 Casartelli, *Sketches*, pp. 252–253.

45 *Ibid.*, p. 258.

46 P. Doyle, *The Episcopate of Alexander Goss of Liverpool, 1856–1872: Diocesan Organisation and Control After the Restoration of the Roman Catholic Hierarchy*, (unpublished PhD. thesis, University of London, 1981.)

47 Doyle, *Goss*, p.272.

48 *Ibid.*, p. 272.

49 Published in Liverpool 1861. See Doyle, *Goss* p. 272. Further insights into the popularity of parish missions and Exposition of the Blessed Sacrament can be found in E. Hamer's *Martha and Mary: A Study of Elizabeth Prout (1820–1864) in the Context of the Passionist Mission to England in the Working Classes of the Manchester Area*, PhD. thesis University of Manchester, 1992, pp.91–107. The National Newspaper Archive, Collindale, holds several years' editions of the *Catholic Opinion circa* 1874, in which *Quarant' Ore* was advertised for many city missions throughout England. The pattern seems to have been, as advocated by Goss, that the service was held in various missions on a rota basis.

50 Casartelli Diaries, vol. 1, 1872–1874, SDA.

18 February [Ash Wednesday] *Quarant' Ore* at Gorton Monastery. Benediction at Gesu.

21 February: *Quarant' Ore* at Cathedral Salford.

22 February: Compline, sermon and devotions of the Blessed Sacrament without Benediction at the Cathedral.

24 February: Visited Blessed Sacrament at St Alban's, John St, Ancoats.

1 March: St Austin's for Compline, litany, procession and Benediction of Blessed Sacrament.

4 March: High Mass at Gesu, procession of Blessed Sacrament to open *Quarant' Ore*. Visited St Chad's. 'Cissy and Fanny [Casartelli's younger sisters] and self loved our turn of watching at the church … back after tea … for devotions and Benediction.'

6 March: *Quarant' Ore* at Gesu, watched 6–6.30p.m.

8 March: '6.30 service at St Austin's. This is the most beautiful, really splendid illumination that we have seen. The service was likewise beautiful: the Rosary sung partly to *Stabat Mater* and the *Pater* and *Ave* to psalm-tones; a capital idea, a sort of English vespers. Everything was so devotional.'

9 March: Benediction at Gesu.

10 March: 'Went to St Anne's to visit Blessed Sacrament and to St Aloysius to prepare for tomorrow. I had the lion's share of the work to do I think. I put up the lace curtains behind the altar and arranged the candles.'

12 March: 8.00p.m. service at St Aloysius – 'very crowded and beautiful.'

13 March: Benediction at St Aloysius.

14 March: Visited Blessed Sacrament at St Wilfrid's.

17 March Visited Blessed Sacrament at St Joseph's and St Patrick's.

22 March: annual parish retreat began [St Augustine's.]

26 March: *Quarant' Ore* at Fairfield, 'this poor mission gave 33 shillings in buying candles' for *Quarant' Ore*.

51 *The Acta of Herbert Vaughan Second Bishop of Salford* (Salford Diocesan Archives, 1997).

52 Casartelli, *Sketches*, p. 258.

53 Heimann, *Catholic Devotion*, p. 38.

54 See Casartelli, *Sketches*, 'new' p. 258; 'revival' p. 240; 'enthusiasm' pp. 256 & 258.

55 For a description of the missions preached by the Redemptorists see, John Sharp, *Reapers of the Harvest. The Redemptorists in Great Britain and Ireland 1843–1898* (Dublin, 1978).

56 Casartelli, *Sketches*, pp. 253, 258, 240, 256.

57 *Ibid.*, p. 240.

58 Casartelli, *Sketches*, p. 256. Casartelli cited a further similar communication from Provost Robert Croskell, who witnessed the missions in Manchester: 'I cannot remember the exact date of the first mission given by Dr. Gentili at St Augustine's, Manchester. Being

the first mission given in that town, the excitement was great and the attendance overwhelming. The Doctor's discourses were reasoning [sic] and argumentative, and very greatly appreciated by the educated portion of the congregation.' *Ibid.*, p. 256.

59 *Ibid.*, p. 263.
60 Closely confirmed by C. R. Leetham in, *Luigi Gentili. A Sower for the Second Spring* (London, 1965), p. 264. The Rev. J. F. Whitaker of St Wilfrid's, writing to a colleague after the mission at St Augustine's, commented, 'What Dr. Gentili has done here is almost miraculous. Old sinners who had not been to church for thirty, forty and fifty years, left their factories and stood waiting at the sacristy door from early morning until midnight waiting their turn for confession ... All lay people are unanimous about this wonderful man and his worthy colleague. Apart from a few clergy, I have not heard anyone complain about the severity of the teaching.' *Ibid.*, pp. 242–243.
61 Casartelli, *Sketches*, p. 263.
62 Heimann, *Stereotypes*, p. 23.
63 B. Ward, *The Sequel to Catholic Emancipation* (London, 1915), p. 18.
64 *Ibid.*, p. 23.
65 *Ibid.*, p. 130.
66 D. Gwynn, *Father Luigi Gentili and His Mission* (London, 1951), pp. 214–220.
67 Heimann, *Catholic Devotion*, pp. 16–17.
68 The norm and practice of the Early Church was the daily reception of the Eucharist. This had ceased, according to the decree, because 'piety waned, Jansenism waxed, disputes arose, very few were considered worthy to communicate daily.' Casartelli's Allocution to the Salford Diocesan Synod 1906, ASEQ, An. III, 1905–6, V2.16, SDA.
69 *Ibid.*
70 Adrian Hastings has remarked in regard to the reign of Pius X, 'Perhaps when the consequences of most other events of his reign have faded away, this one great decision will stand, out of which so much has gown. The implications of these decrees [frequent communion and the receiving of Communion by children from the age of seven years] have hardly been fully appreciated. But they did begin the renewal of the sacramental centre of catholic life, stimulating the liturgical movement, and in a strong non-élitist direction.' Adrian Hastings, *A History of English Christianity 1920–1990* 3rd ed., (London, 1991), p. 151.
71 Casartelli, Pastoral Letter, 'The Pope of the Eucharist', Lent 1911, ASEQ, An. VII, 1909–10 SDA. Casartelli, whilst visiting Belgium, noted his 'interesting chat about recent Decree on First Communion' and how in Belgium there were 'grave apprehensions' about it. Casartelli Diaries, 29 Aug. 1910, SDA.
72 Charles Plater, *Retreats for the People* (London, 1911).
73 *Ibid.*, pp. 196–197.
74 'Signs'.
75 Crichton, '1920–1940: The Dawn of the Liturgical Movement' in, *English Catholic Worship*, p. 21.
76 Casartelli, Pastoral Letter, Lent 1908, 'Amare et Servire', ASEQ, An. V, 1907–8, SDA.
77 *Ibid.*
78 *Ibid.*
79 *Ibid.* This sense of unworthiness was borne out by a war-time Catholic chaplain, who in replying to Charles Plater's questionnaire regarding sacramental practice among the troops, wrote, 'Frequent Communion was on the whole rare, but the reason for that seemed to me – the difficulties of confession, and their training in the idea that it was necessary to be 'very good already' before daring to approach Holy Communion.' Charles Plater, *Catholic Soldiers* (London, 1917), p. 49.
80 *Ibid.*

81 Crichton, 'The Dawn of the Liturgical Movement', p. 40.

82 'Signs'.

83 *CF.*, Jan. 1913.

84 *Ibid.*

85 See M. Richards, 'Prelude: 1890s to 1920', in Crichton, *English Catholic Worship*, p. 9 n. 17.

86 Casartelli, Pastoral Letter, July 1908, 'The Eucharistic Congress and the Papal Jubilee,' ASEQ, An. V, 1907–8, SDA.

87 *Ibid.*

88 Published 1904.

89 14 Sept. 1908, ASEQ, V2.18, 1908–9, SDA.

90 *Ibid.*

91 For a discussion of the incident and its implications see G. I. T. Machin, 'The Liberal Government and the Eucharistic Procession of 1908', in *Journal of Ecclesiastical History*, 34 (4) (1983), pp. 559–583; Carol A. Devlin, 'The Eucharistic procession of 1908: The Dilemma of the Liberal Government', in *Church History*, 63 (1994), pp. 407–425; Thomas Horwood, 'Public Opinion and the 1908 Eucharistic Congress', in *Recusant History*, 25 (1) (2000), pp. 120–132.

92 'The Eucharistic Congress and its Results'.

93 *Ibid.*

94 *Ibid.*

95 For example, 'At 11 there was the 'Month's Mind' for Prof. Hubert ... The carelessness business-like way of doing things, if anything, more disgusting than ever. A Black Mass here is enough to turn anybody from the Catholic Church.' Casartelli Diaries, 4 April 1876, SDA. 'At 3 began the long and tedious office of the dead in S. Michel ... The affair was the most miserable I ever saw. The wretched singing, and the utter ignorance of all rubric, the careless disrespectful way of doing things, the benediction of B.S. with the altar and sanctuary all draped in black and a huge catafalque in front! – all this was disgusting.' Casartelli Diaries, 1 Nov. 1875, SDA.

96 'Signs'.

97 *Ibid.* According to Casartelli, 'His Holiness is credited with an intention to prosecute with vigour at no distant date the much-needed Reform of Sacred Music. This will be a day for which many, both Clergy and Laity, have long been anxiously looking.' Roger Aubert comments on Pius X's *Motu proprio, Inter Pastoralis Officii*: 'its significance by far extended this area [Church music] so that it is justified to speak of it as being the 'charter of the liturgical movement.' R. Aubert, 'The Reform Work of Pius X', in H. Jedin (ed.) *History of the Church* (London, 1981), vol. IX, p.407.

98 'Signs'.

99 *Ibid.*

100 Crichton, 'The Dawn of a Liturgical Movement', p. 40.

101 Richard Runciman Terry (1865–1938), Choirmaster of Westminster Cathedral.

102 *The Tablet*, 19 Oct. 1907, pp. 617–621.

103 *Ibid.*, 16 April 1904.

104 'A Letter on Church Music', 20 Jan. 1906, ASEQ, An. III, V2.16, 1906–6, SDA.

105 *Motu Proprio*, 22 Nov., 1903, para. 3. English translation in *The Tablet*, 2 Jan. 1904.

106 'A Letter on Church Music', 20 January 1906. SDA.

107 The questionnaire asked: how many Catholics lived in the mission? Was the *Motu proprio* of Pius X being carried out already? Was there a mens' and boys' choir or was the choir mixed (i.e. with female singers)? If there was a mixed choir, would it be easy to substitute a mens' and boys' choir? In regard to the latter question, if the answer was no, what were the chief difficulties?

108 *Ad Clerum*, 12 Aug. 1904, ASEQ, An. I, V2.14, 1903–4, SDA.
109 'A Letter on Church Music'.
110 Casartelli Diaries, 16 April 1876, SDA. See also Arthur McCormack, *Cardinal Vaughan* (London, 1966) pp. 179–180 on Vaughan's encouragement of services in English.
111 Crichton, 'The Dawn of a Liturgical Movement', p. 21.
112 R. R. Terry, 'Church Music and the 'Motu Proprio,' in *The Tablet*, 19 Oct. 1907, p. 617.
113 Crichton, 'The Dawn of a Liturgical Movement', p. 21.
114 'The dialogue Mass seems to have originated at the Abbey of Maredsous in Belgium about the year 1880, although the idea behind it comes from apostolic times.' 'Mass, Dialogue', in the *New Catholic Encyclopaedia*, vol. IX (Washington, 1967).
115 William Brown (1862–1951), titular bishop of Pella; auxiliary in Southwark 1924–1951.
116 William Francis Brown, *Through Windows of Memory* (London, 1946), p. 113.
117 Crichton, 'The Dawn of a Liturgical Movement', pp. 23 & 35.
118 The Guild of St Gregory and St Cecilia was introduced into the diocese in 1906 for the purpose of training men and boy singers in ecclesiastical music, both plainsong and polyphonic.
119 Pastoral Letter 'A Memorable Year', Advent 1911, ASEQ, Anns. VIII-XI, 1911–14, SDA.
120 *Ad clerum*, 25 Feb. 1916, An. XIII, V2.22, 1915–16, SDA.
121 Pastoral Letter, Advent 1920, 'Cantate Domino', ASEQ, Anns. XIV-XVIII, 1916–21, SDA.
122 *Ibid.*
123 *Ibid.*
124 *Ibid.*
125 Aubert, 'The Reform Work of Pius X', p. 407.
126 An example of this willingness is found in Fr James Callaway, rector of St Mary's, Oswaldtwistle. 'One of the first things that Fr Callaway did on his arrival was to start a male voice choir. In December 1912 he wrote in the Pulpit Notice book the following memo: 'I wish to record your thanks and mine to the members of the choir for the great and noble service they have rendered to the Church. It is only because it is the spirit of the Church that a male voice choir should be established.' M. J. Broadley, *A History of St Mary's Roman Catholic Church Oswaldtwistle* (Accrington, 1997), p. 29.
127 Pastoral Letter, 'Immaculata,' Advent 1904, ASEQ, An. II, 1904–5, SDA.
128 *CO.*, 19 Jan. 1875. (See Chapter Two, pp. 52–53.) The statistics for the Mission were: 116 000 people present at all the services on one particular Sunday; 53 000 approached the Sacraments of Confession and Communion and 5 000 were Confirmed and 330 converts received into the Church. Casartelli commented on the success of the mission, 'The wonderful success of that remarkable and soul-stirring event, and the astonishing out-pouring of divine grace of which it was the occasion, will yet be remembered by many of the older members of both the Clergy and Laity.' Casartelli, 'A Lenten Pastoral Letter,' Lent 1905, ASEQ, An. II, 1904–5, SDA.
129 'A Lenten Pastoral Letter,' 1905.
130 *Ibid.*
131 *Ibid.*
132 *Ibid.*
133 'Letter to the Missionary Fathers', 9 Mar. 1905, ASEQ, An. II, V.2.15, 1904–5, SDA. In a similar letter in 1921, when addressing the Missionary Fathers, Casartelli mentioned the following as topics of concern: 'wide spread evil of Mixed marriages', unpunctuality at Sunday Mass, the immodesty of female dress, and attendance at non-Catholic schools. Casartelli to the Missionary Fathers, Sexagesima Sunday, 1921, Casartelli Letters, 5801–5900, Box 164, SDA.
134 *Ad Clerum*, Candlemas 1905, ASEQ, An. II, V2.15, SDA.

135 'To the Missionary Fathers.'

136 *Ibid.*

137 Synod 1905, ASEQ, An. II, V.2.15, 1904–5, SDA. The statistics for the mission were:

Confessions heard	(58, 259)
Communions received:	(53, 000)
Persons Confirmed:	(170)
Converts made:	(98)
Converts under instruction:	(230)
Average attendance at Night Service:	(22, 775)

138 Synod 1906, ASEQ, An. III, V.2.16, 1905–6, SDA. The statistics for this Mission were:

Confessions heard:	(13, 794)
Communions received:	(11, 711)
Persons Confirmed:	(480)
Converts made:	(14)
Converts under instruction:	(25)
Average attendance at daily attendance:	(5, 080)

139 Synod 1907, ASEQ, An. IV, V.2.15, 1906–7, SDA. The statistics for this Mission were:

Confessions heard:	(15, 719)
Communions received:	(15, 146)
Persons Confirmed:	(1, 238)
Converts made:	(16)
Converts under instruction:	(66)
Average attendance at daily attendance:	(8, 267)

140 Pastoral Letter, 'The Distinctive Work of the Episcopate', May 1908, ASEQ, An. V, 1907–8.

141 Pastoral Letter, 'Education of our Future Clergy', April 1904, ASEQ, An. I, 1903–4.

142 See Pastoral Letters, 'Education of our Future Priests', 1904; 'Our Church Students', 1905; 'The Recruiting of the Clergy', 1906.

143 *Catholic Times*, 6 Mar. 1896.

144 Pastoral Letter, 'The Making of a Priest', April 1909, ASEQ, An. VI, 1908–9, SDA.

145 Pastoral Letter, 'The Clergy of the Future', April 1911, ASEQ, Anns. VIII-XI, 1911–14, SDA.

146 'A Letter to Church Students', 18 Oct. 1907, ASEQ, An. V, V2.18, 1907–8, SDA.

147 'The Clergy of the Future.'

148 Casartelli in this matter shared the mind of Herbert Vaughan who wrote, 'I am glad to learn from many witnesses that St Bede's College is doing a great work. The happy mixture of the clerical and lay element will be its strength. In this country, and especially now that the Church is entering into a new phase of contact with the people of England, it is more than ever important that the Catholic laity and clergy should know each other and work together in all that concerns their common religious interests. This happy combination and mutual confidence are fruits of early education in common. I am, therefore, always pleased when I hear that there is a large proportion of the lay as well as of the clerical element in our great diocesan colleges such as Ushaw, Old Hall, and St Bede's. The advantages of such a union are well divided, and each would be the poorer and the weaker without them.' Herbert Vaughan, *The Manchester Guardian circa* 29 Oct.1897, cited in *St Bede's College Diary*, New Series vol. II, 1897, p. 115, St Bede's College, Manchester

149 'The Making of a Priest.'

150 'De l'Etat Actuel des Études Supérieures dans le Clergé Anglais' in *Revue Générale*, April 1896, p. 18. '*On se demande avec anxiété, dans quelle position se trouvera notre clergé d'ici à un quart de siècle, non seulement vis-à-vis du clergé anglican et même du clergé des dissidents, qui font tout pour participer aux avantages des hautes études, mais encore vis-à-vis de nos laïques qui seront plus instruits, qui auront l'esprit mieux cultivé que leurs prêtres.*'

151 Pastoral Letter, 'The Progress of Ecclesiastical Education', April 1907, ASEQ, An. IV, 1906–7, SDA.

152 'The Making of a Priest.'

153 *Ibid.*

154 Pastoral Letter, 'The Future of Ecclesiastical Education', April 1923, ASEQ, Anns. XIV-XXII, 1922–25, SDA.

155 *Ibid.*

156 Pastoral Letter, 'Labourers for the Harvest', April 1910, ASEQ, An. VII, 1909–10, SDA. On occasions Casartelli himself met the cost of M.A. fees for his students; in 1914 he wrote to Rev. J. Rowntree to say: 'I cannot undertake the same burden in the future.' Casartelli to Rev. J. Rowntree, 29 May 1914, Casartelli Letters, 2301–2400, Box 159, SDA,

157 See Ernest Oldmeadow, *Francis Cardinal Bourne*, 2 vol. (London, 1944), II, pp. 199–204.

158 Casartelli to Archbishop of Liverpool, 24 Sept. 1923, Casartelli Letters, 6301–6400, Box 165, SDA.

159 Casartelli to Cardinal Gasquet, 24 Sept. 1923, Casartelli Letters, 6301–6400, Box 165, SDA.

160 Synod 1907, ASEQ, An. IV, V2.17, SDA. In his diary he wrote, 'Entertained at supper in my dining-room our five Cambridge graduates (Gonne, McNulty, Morrisey, Ingram, Cooke) and spoke to them at length, urging them to work by writing and speaking for the cause of the Church, and to become members of various scientific and literary societies. Very well received: D.G.' Casartelli Diaries, 3 Oct. 1917, SDA.

161 'Report on Conference Cases III & V', 3 Mar. 1906, ASEQ, An. III, 1905–6, SDA.

162 See Pastoral Letter, 'The Clergy of the Future', April 1911.

163 Aubert, 'The Reform Work of Pius X', p. 409.

164 Vaughan to Casartelli, 25 June [no year], Box 179, SDA.

CHAPTER SIX: CASARTELLI AND THE GREAT WAR

1 Casartelli to Louis McCulloch, 14 April 1913, Grieve Papers (private collection). I am indebted to Mrs M. Grieve for permission to cite this letter.

2 For example, he wrote in his diary: 'Today I complete my 41st year of priesthood and my 14th of episcopate ... what a dead weight of responsibility!' Casartelli Diaries, 10 Sept. 1917, Salford Diocesan Archives.

3 This breadth of vision is a marked characteristic of his personality and one that was fostered and encouraged during his years at Louvain. A significant example of this is found in Casartelli's call for closer links between Germany and Britain based on the common bond of faith and the work of St Boniface – the 'Apostle of Germany': 'God bless', wrote the present Vicar General of Cologne in my album many years ago, when we were fellow-students, 'England which gave St Boniface to Germany'. And another, now an eminent University professor, added these words: 'England gave to Germany her greatest benefactor, St Boniface. As in him both lands were united so may his intercession assist us that we may work in his spirit.' 'The Bishop's Message,' *Catholic Federationist*, Dec. 1911.

4 'The most awful news yet received from the War: the German barbarians have *destroyed* Louvain and all its buildings ... It is a nightmare! Correspondents of the Catholic Times and Manchester Guardian called me to give some statement to their papers on this diabolical outrage on humanity.' Casartelli Diaries, 29 Aug. 1914, Salford Diocesan Archives, SDA.

5 For example, see *Manchester Guardian*, 11 May 1915, and *Manchester Evening News*, 11 & 12 May 1915, for report of riots against aliens in Manchester and Salford.

6 *Manchester Guardian*, 20 Aug. 1917.

7 Pastoral Letter, 'Pax Christi', Feb. 1914, *Acta Salfordiensia Episcopi Quarti*, Anns. VIII-XI,

1911–14, SDA. (Will be cited as 'Pax Christi'.) The pastoral letter was later published as a separate pamphlet by the Catholic Truth Society.

8 Alexander Giesswein, *Der Friede Christi: Christentum und Friedensbewegung* (Wien, Kirsch, 1913).

9 *The Tablet*, 14 Aug. 1915.

10 *The Tablet* 14 Mar. 1914.

11 *The Tablet*, 14 Aug. 1915.

12 *CF.*, Dec. 1911.

13 'Pax Christi.'

14 References to Scripture are Is., 2.3–4; 9. 6,-7; Mich., 5. 3–4; Lk., 2,14; 14,36; Jn., 20.19; Eph., 6.23; 2.Pet., 5.14; 2 Jn., 14.27; 3. Jn., 14; Rom., 10,15; 15.33; 16.20; 2 Cor., 13.11; Phil., 4.9; 1 Thes., 5.23; Heb., 13.20;

15 'Pax Christi'. This is echoed in Casartelli's article in the *CF.*, September 1914: 'We must believe, according to the teachings of the Church, that War is indeed a grave evil, having its roots in the sins and passions of man. Secondly, both Holy Scripture and the Fathers and Liturgy of the Church teach us that, as with famine, pestilence and earthquake, Almighty God allows War as a scourge for the chastisement and healing of His sinful people.' *CF.*, September 1914. See also *CF.*, Nov. 1914.

16 See R. A. Markus, 'Saint Augustine on the Just War', in *The Church and War*, W. J.Shiels, (ed.), (Blackwell, 1983) pp. 1–15.

17 'Pax Christi'.

18 *Ibid.*

19 *Ibid.*

20 'In 1916, some were urging through the press a declared policy of air-reprisals on Germany in retaliation for Zeppelin raids on London … In February 1916 Archbishop Davidson [Archbishop of Canterbury 1903–28] … proposed this motion (drawing on the long Christian tradition of teaching about the 'Just War'), which was passed unanimously […] 'the principles of morality forbid a policy of reprisals which has, as a deliberate object the killing and wounding of non-combatants, and believes that the adoption of such a mode of retaliation, even for barbarous outrages, would permanently lower the standard of honourable conduct between nation and nation.' Alan Wilkinson, *The Church of England* (London, 1978), pp. 98–99. Davidson's stand only managed to convince a minority of churchmen. See Wilkinson, p. 101.

21 In 'Pax Christi' Casartelli cites Lk., 3.14; 7.2; Mt., 8. 5–13; Acts 10.

22 *Ibid.*, citing Augustine's Book Four of his *City of God*. On this, Wilkinson's commentary is pertinent: 'Two main views of the spiritual significance of the war were proclaimed by the clergy: the war was a solemn duty laid upon the nation by God; it was a divine punishment for a variety of national sins […] The failures or successes of the war were frequently explained in terms of divine punishments or rewards. As the war proceeded, and it became more difficult to present it as a crusade, clergy turned to expound it as human folly which God could use for his purposes, for example in order to rouse England from selfishness and complacency.' Wilkinson, *The Church of England*, pp. 9–10.

23 'Pax Christi'.

24 *Ibid.* The misuse of this freedom is seen in the case of science; Casartelli saw that one of the outcomes of the War had been the bankruptcy of science. Germany, 'which has furnished us for years with the best of our chemical products and apparatus, our instruments of precision, and even our very methods of scientific education … has dragged down the art of science of war to the degraded level of bloodshed, lust, pillage and deceit […] So true is it that the best of God's endowments of His creatures may be perverted and corrupted by the human will to be the worst of scourges for the punishment of the

proud humanity that sets up those endowments, like the Golden Calf, in the place of their Maker'! *CF.*, Sept. 1915.

25 'Pax Christi'.

26 The first Peace Society was founded in London in 1816. However, he considered 'The European Unity League', actively supported by Cardinal Manning and Lord Ripon, as more important. Popes Leo XIII and Pius X had written letters of sympathy to the Peace Congresses held in Budapest (1896) and Milan (1906). Other Congresses were held in Stockholm (1910) and Geneva (1912).

27 'Pax Christi'.

28 *Ibid.*

29 *Ibid.* Casartelli had earlier, in 1911, warned of the dangers of antagonism between Britain and Germany: 'There is one direction in which the Catholics of this country are surely called upon to labour in every way in this sacred cause: I mean in bringing about more friendly relations between our own and the German nation. There is no concealing the fact that a very serious state of tension subsists between at least the politicians of the two nations ... Commercial rivalry yes; but surely that ought to be a healthy rivalry ... I believe all these bitter jealousies, and even rumours of an impending 'war-cloud' are chiefly newspaper-made.' *CF.*, Dec. 1911.

30 *Ibid.* 'Leading statesmen on both sides, the clergy of all denominations, municipal representatives, the learned professions, and at least the saner and better part of the Press in both countries are still striving to bring about a better understanding.'

31 *Ibid.*

32 *Ibid.*

33 *CF.*, Sept. 1914.

34 Casartelli was unable to attend because of ill health. He asked Fr. Lomax to be his representative. See Casartelli to Fr. Lomax, 28 June 1914, Casartelli Letters, 2301–2400, Box 159, SDA.

35 'Special Prayers', 5 Aug. 1914, ASEQ, An. XI, 1913–14, V2.2, SDA.

36 *Ibid.*

37 A constant feature during the war was the celebration of Masses *in tempore belli*. The teachings contained in the prayers of this liturgy were: 1/ God is the Sovereign Lord and as such puts an end to all wars and grants victory. 2/ War is a scourge and a punishment for sin. 3/ War is a means of correcting vices if humanity are properly disposed to profit by it. 4/ Prayer for the end of war. See article on the presidential prayers of the Mass *in tempore belli* by the Abbot of Farnborough, *The Tablet*, 10 Oct. 1914, pp. 498–499.

38 Casartelli encouraged rectors to take part in 'A Day of Humble Prayer and Intercession' on 3 January 1915 (*Ad Clerum*, 18 Dec. 1914, ASEQ, Anns. XII-XIII, 1914–16, SDA.) Suitable services were to be arranged in keeping with the occasion and any alms taken were to be forwarded to the Fund for the Care of the Sick and Wounded administered by the Order of St John of Jerusalem and the British Red Cross. Further Days of Prayer were: 'Day of International Intercession' on 7 February 1915 (*Ad Clerum*, 25 Jan. 1915, 1914–16.) An invitation by Pope Benedict XV to take part in a strict ecclesiastical fast for three days (*Ad Clerum*, 6 June 1915, 1914–16.) 'At the opening of the Third year of the war, together with other Bishops, and at the suggestion of His Eminence the Cardinal Archbishop, I direct that on either Friday, 4th August, or Sunday 6th August ... there shall be Exposition of the Blessed Sacrament and some form of special devotions at the services to beg God's blessing on the allied Armies, and the speedy conclusion of a just and lasting peace.' (*Ad Clerum*, no date, 1914–1916.)

39 Pastoral Letter, Lent 1915, 'Lent and the World War,' ASEQ, Anns. XII-XIII, 1914–16, SDA.

40 See Casartelli's Pastoral Letters: Advent 1915, 'Dark Days'; Advent 1916, 'Sursum Corda'; Advent 1917, 'Watchmen, What of the Night'?

41 'The Terrible Year'. In the *Catholic Federationist*, he expressed his belief that, 'It must be our consolation that, as far as we can judge, our Government has up to the last moment persistently and unwearyingly done its best to prevent this great War ... and that only the genuine conviction, at last forced upon our rulers, that both our national existence and our sworn pledges in a cause of justice have rendered the momentous step inevitable, has finally decided them to unsheathe the Sword.' *CF.*, Sept. 1914.

42 Pastoral Letter, Advent 1914, 'The Terrible Year,' ASEQ, Anns. XII-XIII, 1914–16, SDA. (Will be cited as 'Terrible Year'.)

43 Francis Bourne, 'Letter on the War', 9 Aug. 1914, Bourne *Acta*, Brompton Oratory Library.

44 Ibid.

45 Bourne, Pastoral Letter, Lent 1915, Bourne *Acta*, BOL.

46 *The Tablet*, 19 Dec. 1914. A year later he seems to have modified his ideas on this point. He still maintained that 'a soldier's death in battle is beyond question the highest of natural virtues', but he described as 'over confident' the description of fallen soldiers as martyrs because in the theological sense this is not applicable.

47 Wilkinson notes among evangelical circles a similar attitude to Bourne's: 'it was widely believed that England had replaced the Jews as God's chosen people and instrument.' Wilkinson, *The Church of England*, p. 10.

48 *The Tablet*, 15 Aug. 1914.

49 H. A. L. Fisher (1865–1940), President of the Board of Education 1916–1926, introduced the Education Act 1918 which made education compulsory up to the age of 14.

50 Casartelli to Archbishop of Liverpool, 6 Nov. 1917, Casartelli Letters, 4501–4600, Box 163, SDA.

51 Edward Illsley (1838–1926), Bishop of Birmingham 1888–1911, Archbishop 1911–1926.

52 Pastoral Letter, Lent 1916, 'Christian Patriotism', Illsley *Acta*, Archdiocesan Archives Birmingham..

53 Pastoral Letter, Lent 1918, 'The War: The Scourge of God,' Illsley *Acta*, AAB.

54 Thomas Whiteside (1857–1921), Bishop of Liverpool 1894–1911, Archbishop 1911–1921.

55 Whiteside, Pastoral Letter Advent 1914, Whiteside *Acta*, Archdiocesan Archives Liverpool.

56 John Cuthbert Hedley (1837–1915), Bishop of Newport 1881–1915.

57 *CF.*, Jan. 1915.

58 Pastoral Letter, Advent 1914, cited in J. Anselm Wilson, *The Life of Bishop Hedley* (London, 1930), p. 361.

59 *Bishop Hedley*, p. 361.

60 The Anglican Bishop Gore of Oxford said of the war, 'Truly war is not a Christian weapon. It "cometh of the evil one" ... But he was convinced that British participation was right. It was a judgement of God and it had to be endured to the bitter end. "I feel as if we must be greatly chastised before we can be strengthened."' The Archbishop of York, Cosmo Gordon Lang, stressed that the quarrel was not with the people of Germany but with the nation's leaders. Wilkinson, *The Church of England*, p. 16.

61 Casartelli to Canon Holmes, 29 Sept. 1916, Casartelli Letters, 3901–4000, Box 161, SDA. For a description of the Zeppelin raid see Peter J. C. Smith, *Zeppelins Over Lancashire: the Story of the Air Raids on the County of Lancashire in 1916 and 1918* (Manchester, 1991).

62 Casartelli, Diaries, 29 Aug. 1914, SDA. See also 16 October 1914, where he wrote: 'Oh! What heartrending stories of fiendish German brutality and unexampled sufferings of Belgians! They make one almost ill.'

63 'The Terrible Year'.

64 Ibid.

65 'Lent and the World War'. In this Pastoral Letter Casartelli wrote: 'The neglect of God and of his Divine Law is at the root of the evil that we now see rampant.'

66 Ibid. 'Almighty God in His Wisdom allows from time to time such dreadful evils as War as a

salutary chastisement to bring back His erring people, and that even when, as strikingly in the present, the innocent have to suffer together with the guilty.' 'The Terrible Year'.

67 Casartelli thought this 'latter-day paganism has so far made no headway among ourselves … rather it has stimulated the best qualities of our race, not only in self-defence, but also in defence of these sacred and high ideals which this militarism is seeking to destroy.' 'The Terrible Year.'

68 *Re* the present war, 'We are firmly convinced that before Almighty God we stand with clean hands and clean consciences as regards the immediate responsibility for its outbreak.' 'The Terrible Year'.

69 Compare this attitude with Watts-Ditchfield, the Evangelical Bishop of Chelmsford: Sermon for Holy Week, 1916, 'Had not the allies much to answer for in the past – Russia for her treatment of the Jews, Belgium for the Congo atrocities, France for overthrow of God and religion … We should look on our own sins – the opium traffic on China, our refusal to interfere when Armenians were massacred, the neglect of Sunday, the prevalence of intemperance and impurity, the hastening to be rich, the division among the classes and the masses, the unhealthy public spirit as shown in the press, the neglect of the housing question, the begrudging for old-age pensions, and removal of slums.' Wilkinson describes the sermon as having been 'much discussed.' Wilkinson, *The Church if England*, p. 248.

70 *CF.*, Sept. 1914.

71 'Now I can understand one of the weaker brethren finding in all this a serious stone of scandal. How is it possible … that Divine providence can allow this chosen portion of Christ's Kingdom, this model Catholic nation, to be singled out for cruel ruin and devastation? […] Do you not realise how God is permitting the Evil One, as a supreme trial to inflict these terrible calamities upon a people which, both by its religious excellence and its material prosperity, seems typified in the patriarch Job … So it is that God suffers His just ones to be tried in the fiery furnace of tribulation, from which they come forth only confirmed in their fidelity and humble submission to His Divine Will.' Casartelli in his 'Bishop's Message', *CF.*, Sept. 1915.

72 'Lent and the World War'.

73 *Ibid.* For example, 'Among us also secret forces have been working for a separation of Church and State, for the greatest possible exclusion of Christian spirit and Christian principles from the education of youth, from public life; their ideal is a maximum of freedom even for the most dangerous tendencies of the time, but the closest restriction and tutelage for the Church and religious movements.' Quoted in 'Lent and the World War'.

74 *Ibid.*

75 Pastoral Letter, Advent 1915, 'Dark Days,' ASEQ, Anns. XII–XIII, 1914–16, SDA. See also Casartelli's Pastoral Letter for Lent 1916, 'Auxilium Christianorum' *re* the war having been 'inflicted upon us by the just anger of almighty God.'

76 The Bishop of Northampton, when speaking of the patriotism of British Catholics, claimed that, 'Over and above the common motives of loyalty, based upon attachment to our ancient institutions and the greatest of our Empire, which we share with our fellow countrymen, we Catholics clearly recognise a strict obligation of conscience, which is perhaps hardly recognised in the same degree in others.' Advent Pastoral Letter 1916, cited in *The Tablet*, 30 December 1916. The Bishop of Clifton wrote: 'It cannot surely but be that one of the effects of this war will be to disarm, if not to destroy, much of the old prejudice against us, especially since all realise with what devotion to duty Catholics have paid their fair contribution in blood, nay, more than their fair contribution, to the general weal.' Pastoral Letter, Lent 1916, cited in *The Tablet*, 25 Mar. 1916.

77 Bourne, Pastoral Letter, Lent 1918, Bourne *Acta*, BOL.

78 During the sermon Fr Fitzjames SJ mentioned how 'the past year has been marked by much good work done for the city he loves, and for which he has been ready to make so many sacrifices, by the removal of many prejudices against the Catholic Church.' *The Tablet*, 28 Nov. 1914.

79 Casartelli to Louis McCulloch, 16 Oct. 1915, GP.

80 Casartelli Diaries, 8 Feb. 1917, SDA.

81 'The Terrible Year.'

82 *CF.*, Jan. 1914.

83 *CF.*, January 1915.

84 *Ibid*. In the same article Bishop Keating of Northampton is cited as saying, 'Resistance to the external aggressor is a religious as well as patriotic duty ... Under such circumstances, national Service in some form or other becomes an obligation in conscience, and the faithful fulfilment of our duty, not merely a natural, but a supernatural virtue. No man or woman can shirk the work which falls to them without sin.'

85 *Ibid*.

86 Casartelli said that 'such a list is rightly called a 'Roll of Honour'; for indeed, nothing can be more honourable than to go forth to face hardship, danger, perhaps death itself, in the sacred cause of Fatherland, and, as in this war, of Justice and Truth.' *Ibid*.

87 *Ad Clerum*, 18 Dec. 1914, ASEQ, Anns. XII-XIII, 1914–15, SDA.

88 'Dark Days.'

89 Wilkinson, *The Church of England*, p. 30.

90 *Ad Clerum*, 14 Jan. 1915, ASEQ, Anns. XII-XIII, 1914–16, SDA.

91 *Ad Clerum*, 22 July 1915, ASEQ, Anns. XII-XIII, 1914–16, SDA.

92 J. M. Hagerty, 'The Diocese of Leeds During the First World War', in *Northern Catholic History*, 337 (1996), p. 39.

93 *CF.*, April 1916.

94 See Casartelli to Canon O'Kelly, 27 Jan. 1917, Casartelli Letters, 3601–3700, Box 161; Casartelli to T. F. Burns, 28 June 1923, Casartelli Letters, 6210–6300, Box 164; Casartelli to Rev. Sharrock, 22 Aug. 1924, 6401–6500, Box 164, SDA.

95 *The Tablet*, 11 Dec. 1915.

96 Bourne, Pastoral Letter, Advent 1915, Bourne *Acta*, BOL.

97 *The Tablet* commented on the occasion of one such day of prayer, 'The Patriotism of the Catholic body evinced in these acts of religion has been everywhere fervent and wholehearted.' 9 Jan. 1915.

98 *Ad Clerum*, 2 Mar. 1915, ASEQ, Anns. XII-XIII, 1914–16, SDA.

99 *Ad Clerum*, 5 April 1917, ASEQ, Anns. XV-XVIII, 1916–21, SDA.

100 *Ad Clerum*, 2 Nov. 1922, ASEQ, Anns. XIX-XX, 1922–25, SDA.

101 Cited in Adrian Gregory, *The Silence of Memory. Armistice Day 1919–1946* (Oxford, 1994), p. 199. On the Cenotaph see also Wilkinson, *The Church of England*, p. 300.

102 Gregory, *The Silence of Memory*, p. 198.

103 Kester Aspden, 'The English Roman Catholic Bishops and the Social Order', in *Recusant History*, 25 (3) (2001), p. 548.

104 Casartelli to Bishop Knox, 9 Feb. 1917, Casartelli Letters, 3601–3700, Box 161, SDA.

105 *Army Council Instruction* No. 688. 13. 'Any man called up from Class B, Army Reserve, who is of Irish nationality and classified in category A should be asked whether he wishes to join an Irish Regiment, and will, if he so desires, be sent to the Depot of the Irish Regiment he wishes to join and will then be appointed to that regiment.' See *CF.*, Aug. 1917.

106 *CF.*, Aug. 1917.

107 *Ibid*.

108 These were Revs. Arthur O'Connor, William Leighton, Robert McGuiness, Vincent

O'Shaughnessy, Michael P. Moran, John O'Riordan Browne, and John Delaney. For a discussion on the role and how the Anglican chaplains were received and perceived, and for details of particular chaplains, see Wilkinson, *The Church of England*, chapters 5 & 6. For the work of Catholic chaplains see J. Hagerty and T. Johnstone, *The Cross on the Sword: Catholic Chaplains in the Forces* (London, 1996).

109 'The two priests whom I am allowing to offer their services as C. F. for the war are Rev. John Birch [and] Rev. Joseph Rees. They are two excellent priests, of whom I can speak most highly.' Casartelli to Cardinal Bourne, 1 Feb. 1916, Casartelli Letters, 3401–3500, Box 161, SDA.

110 Casartelli to the President of Ushaw, 17 Nov. 1915, Casartelli Letters, 3301–2400, Box 161 SDA.

111 Casartelli to Rev. J. Rowntree, 9 Feb. 1916, Casartelli Letters, 3401–3500, Box 161, SDA. See also Casartelli, Pastoral Letter, 'The Call of the King,' April 1915. Conscription in Britain only became compulsory in January 1916. Wilkinson comments that, 'The Derby Scheme of October 1915 was a half-way house. It involved a personal canvass of all men between eighteen and forty who were invited to attest their willingness to serve.' Wilkinson, *The Church of England*, p. 32. In encouraging service to the nation, and in this instance pre-empting the Derby Scheme, Casartelli was joined by the voices of the Archbishops of Canterbury and York, as well as other religious and civic leaders, including the Vice-Chancellor of the University of Manchester.

112 J. Brodie Brosnan dedicated his book, *The Sacrifice of the New Law* (London, 1926) to the memory of Casartelli and acknowledged the latter's 'interest and concern for his chaplains during the war, to whom he ever made it his concern to write consolingly and encouragingly.' p. i

113 *CF.*, May 1917. On 'Hut Sunday', 2 May 1917, the diocese raised £1047–10-8. £500 had, on a previous occasion, already been taken for a hut in Richmond.

114 J. D. Holmes, in reference to Benedict XV, quotes the following, 'Alone among those in authority, in any Christian sect, he seemed to think that peace remained, even in war time, the leading doctrine of His Master. For that he received the scorn and abuse of all the warring nations.' *The Papacy in the Modern World* (London, 1981), p. 1. Casartelli wrote on the occasion of Benedict's death, 'The unworthy suspicions and unmerited accusations and reproaches of the dark years of the Great War and its sad aftermath, the charges of secret partiality or overt neglect of duty, that had been brought against him from both of the two opposing camps, had died out and men of all parties had come at last to realise the splendid impartiality and truly Christian charity, which had dictated [his] words and deeds.' Casartelli, Pastoral Letter, Lent 1922, 'The Holy See, the World and the Church', ASEQ, Anns. XIX-XXII, 1922–25, SDA. See also John F. Pollard, *The Unknown Pope: Benedict XV and the Pursuit of Peace* (London, 1999), chapters 4 & 5.

115 Pollard, *The Unknown Pope*, p. 91.

116 Pollard observes that, 'Cardinal Aidan Gasquet, Britain's only curial cardinal in 1914, was appalled by the pro-German atmosphere which he found in the Roman Curia, and among the Italian Catholic clergy and laity in general.' *Ibid.*, p. 87.

117 He has been described as ultra-patriotic, and was constantly involved in disagreements with the occupying German forces that caused embarrassment for the Vatican; the Pope suspected him of wanting to be a martyr. Mercier's stance made him a very popular figure among the allied countries; numerous times the English bishops, especially Casartelli, quoted him in their own pastorals. *Ibid.*, p. 95.

118 'Terrible Year.'

119 *Ad Beatissimi Apostolorum*, 1 Nov. 1914.

120 *CF.*, Mar. 1915.

121 'The Pope has no jurisdiction as a judge of specific issues between nations.' And, 'Quite apart from its religious functions, the world-wide influence of the Vatican as a moral force in the present crisis cannot be over-estimated, since every Catholic, of whatever nationality, looks to the Vatican for guidance in moral principles and responds to any appeal from the Pope.' *CF.*, Mar. 1915.

122 *CF.*, Mar. 1915.

123 *Ibid.*

124 *CF.*, Mar. 1915.

125 The Bryce Report helped to create an intense anti-German feeling in Britain.

126 See Wilkinson, *The Church of England*, p. 214.

127 *ASEQ*, Anns. XII-XIII, 1914–16. 6 June 1915, SDA.

128 Casartelli to T.F. Burns, 30 Nov. 1915, Casartelli Letters, 3301–2400, Box 161, SDA. In his reply Burns made the point that Catholics represented 'more than one-fifth of the population of Manchester and Salford. It is a fifth that has not provided a single conscientious objector, while it has sent its full quota to the front.' *CF.*, April 1916. In a further letter to the Editor of the *Manchester Guardian*, March 1916, the Revs. L. J. Kelly, T. Sharrock, and Mr. T. Burns asked, 'Why this anxiety on the part of Bishop Welldon to prove that the Catholic Church is on the side of our enemies?' The reason they gave as to why the Vatican had not been forthcoming in a direct condemnation was because it was not in full possession of the facts of the matters in question, i.e. the invasion of Belgium, the sinking of the Lusitania and the use of gas, *MG*, 14 Mar. 1916.

129 A full text of the Peace Note is to be found in *The Tablet*, 18 Aug. 1917.

130 *The Tablet*, 18 Aug. 1917.

131 *Ibid.*

132 Reported in *The Tablet*, 25 Aug. 1917.

133 *MG.*, 20 Aug. 1917.

134 *Ibid.*

135 *The Tablet*, 22 Sept. 1917.

136 *CF.*, Sept. 1914.

137 Feliz Klein, *Diary of a French Army Chaplain* (London, 1915), pp. 110 & 129.

138 See 'Terrible Year'. Compare this with Wilkinson's comment, 'If by the end of the war anyone was still under the illusion that a religious revival had taken place or was about to take place, he would soon have had his wishful thinking dispelled by two symposia: *The Army and Religion* (1919) published by an inter-denominational group, and *The Church in the Furnace* (1917) a symposium of Anglican chaplains.' Wilkinson, *The Church of England*, p. 160. .

139 *MG.*, 1 Mar. 1916. This optimistic opinion can be questioned by Charles Plater's survey, *Sixty Catholic Chaplains* (London, 1919). *The Tablet* estimated in 1918 that 40,000 had converted to the Catholic Faith on the Western Front, see Johnstone and Hagerty, *The Cross on the Sword*, p. 175.

140 *CF.*, Aug. 1916.

141 Pastoral Letter, Advent, 1915, Whiteside *Acta*, AAL.

142 Pastoral Letter, Pentecost 1917, Illsley *Acta*, AAB.

143 See Bourne, Pastoral Letter, Lent 1918, Bourne *Acta*, BOL.

144 See Wilkinson, *The Church of England*, p. 160, where he discusses *The Army and Religion* (1919); *The Church in the Furnace* (1917).

145 Charles Plater S. J., *Catholic Soldiers* (London, 1919).

146 *Catholic Soldiers*, p. 144. Michael Snape has observed of *Catholic Soldiers*: 'Upon publication, *Catholic Soldiers* was instantly seized upon by the Catholic press as a means of belabouring the Protestant churches[...]No doubt because of its mixed findings,

Catholic Soldiers soon began to be viewed more circumspectly by Catholic commentators. Writing only three years after its publication, Plater's biographer, Fr Cyril Martindale S.J., announced his deep misgivings as to the whole project: 'I cannot pretend I ever thought this a wise plan', he wrote, 'nor do I think it was successfully carried out.' I am indebted to Dr. Snape for allowing me sight of his unpublished article, 'British Catholicism and the British Army in the First World War,' from which the above is taken. Subsequently published as 'British Catholicism in the British Army in the First World War', *Recusant History*, vol. 26, no. 2, Oct. 2002.

147 Compare Casartelli's view with that of E. A. Burroughs, bishop of Ripon 1926–34, who saw the first two months of the war as a means to shock both nation and Church into a new way of life. 'But the mood soon cooled. Strikes, selfishness in capital and labour, drunkenness, brothels, desecration of Sunday, gambling ... all indicated the tragic fact that the nation was failing to realise how decisive the hour was.' Wilkinson, *The Church of England*, p. 73.

148 A. Wilkinson, *Dissent or Conform?* (London, 1986), p. 45.

149 'Belgian refugees poured into this country. Large parties came to Manchester at intervals, their arrival at the stations being watched by large and sympathetic crowds; these were housed and cared for by the Belgian Refugees Committee, and a special Belgian fund realised in Manchester over £14,000,and in Salford over £7,000 ... The number of Belgian Refugees assisted in Manchester is given as 3,500; similarly, Salford made itself responsible for 115 families.' F. A. Bruton, *A Short History of Manchester and Salford* (Manchester, 1924), p. 285.

150 *Ad Clerum*, 14 Oct. 1914, ASEQ, Anns. XII-XIII, 1914–16, SDA.

151 Despite an extensive search in the archives of the Belgian Refugee Committee at the Local Studies Unit, Central Reference Library, Manchester, (ref. M138) no relevant material was found concerning Casartelli and the work of the BRC. However, in 1919 Casartelli was awarded the Commandership of the Order of Leopold. This was presumably in recognition for his work for the Belgian Refugees. He put his own house, 'Italian Villa,' at the disposal of Belgian refugees, see *The Harvest* (Nov. 1914), p. 312.

152 Casartelli Diaries, 11 Nov. 1914, SDA.

153 'Inevitably the war made sexual relationships more casual; by 1918, the illegitimacy rate had increased 30 per cent compared with before the war.' Wilkinson, *The Church of England*, p. 104.

154 Speaking of the prophets he wrote, 'the inspired writers ... had a great mission to accomplish, and that was to convince God's people that their miseries were the wages of sin, a terrible scourge, inflicted indeed by the hands of wicked men and enemies of God, but permitted by His all-seeing Providence to punish their violation of His Divine Law, but also to bring them back to Him.' 'Dark Days.'

155 *Ibid.* 'Before the war, public houses in London were allowed to open from 5 a.m. to 12.30a.m. on weekdays; in other areas the hours were only slightly shorter.' Wilkinson, *The Church of England*, p.102; for discussion on the varied reaction of Anglican churchmen see pp. 102–104.

156 Casartelli to Canon Sharrock, 9 Feb. 1917, Casartelli Letters, 3601–3700, Box 161, SDA.

157 'We, too, in this country must in sackcloth and ashes cry *mea culpa* and, as a nation, turn back to God if we are to have any reasonable hope of the cessation of the scourge.' 'Dark Days'.

158 'Dark Days'.

159 Pastoral Letter, Feb. 1917, 'Our Lady of a Happy Death,' ASEQ, An. XIV-XVIII, 1916–21, SDA.

160 *Ibid.* For attitude to religion by Catholic servicemen cf. Charles Plater, *Catholic Soldiers*; also Wilkinson, *The Church of England*, chapter 7, 'The Army and Religion'. 'During the

first world war I was a chaplain with the army, and was able to see how completely the catechism, learned parrot-fashion in childhood, had disappeared from the minds of our Catholic men; though they still remembered the practical part of their religion, even when they had long abandoned its practice.' F. H. Drinkwater, *Educational Essays* (London, 1951), p. 96.

161 'Membership' was not a formal agreement between an individual and the Church authorities, nor was subscription necessary. The purpose of the Association was to pray to meet one's death in a 'state of grace', i.e. being free from mortal sin. Casartelli wrote the preface to R. H. Benson's book, *Vexilla Regis* (London, 1914), a collection of prayers for use during war-time. It was a book he strongly recommended to the people of the diocese.

162 Wilkinson, *The Church of England*, p. 179.

163 Pastoral Letter, Nov. 1919, 'Queen of Peace,' Anns. XIV-XVIII, 1916–21, SDA. See also Jennifer Hazelgrove, 'Spiritualism After the Great War', in *Twentieth British History*, 10 (4) (1999).

164 *CF.*, Sept. 1917.

165 Wilkinson, *The Church of England*, pp. 176–178.

166 *CF.*, Sept. 1917.

167 Peter Green (1871–1961), Rector of Sacred Trinity, Salford, 1901–11; wrote as *Artifex* in the *Manchester Guardian* from 1910; Rector of St Philip's, Salford 1911–51.

168 *Ad Clerum*, 22 July 1915, Anns. XII-XIII, 1914–16, SDA.

169 *Ibid.*

170 *CF.*, April 1918.

171 *Ibid.*

172 *Ibid.* See also Chapter Three, 'Commercial Education'. Casartelli commented – 'so vast an amount of the best scientific work in every branch of human research is embedded in German books and periodicals that wilfully to deprive ourselves of the advantages to be derived from these sources would be no less than an educational and cultural suicide.' 'A Problem of After-War Reconstruction: the Study of Foreign Languages', *Transactions of the Manchester Statistical Society*, 1915–1916, p.65.

173 Casartelli to J. B. Milburn, 3 May 1918, Casartelli Letters, 4901–5000, Box 162, SDA.

174 Casartelli Diaries, 10 Nov. 1914, SDA.

175 *Ibid.*, 10 Dec. 1914.

176 *CF.*, Nov. 1914.

177 Daniel McCabe (1852–1919), first Catholic Lord Mayor of Manchester.

178 *MG.*, 21 June 1915.

179 T. F. Burns, the Organising Secretary of the Catholic Federation, countered by accusing McCabe of harbouring 'anti-clerical sentiments'. 'Report of Organising Secretary,' File 2, Box 182, SDA.

180 *The Tablet*, 25 Mar. 1916.

181 Pastoral Letter, Feb. 1916, 'Auxilium Christianorum,' ASEQ, Anns. XII-XIII, 1915–16, SDA.

182 Francis Mostyn (1860–1939), Bishop of Menevia 1898–1921. In his pastoral letter for Advent 1914 he remarked: 'Indeed, our charity in this regard should extend not merely to those who have fought in the ranks of the Allies, but it should also extend to those who have fought under the enemy's flag. For all who are in purgatory belong to the Church of Christ.' *The Tablet* 5 Dec. 1914.

183 *CF.*, Oct. 1914.

184 *Ibid.*

185 Pastoral Letter, Nov. 1916, 'Sursum Corda,' ASEQ, Anns. XIV-XVIII, 1916–21, SDA.

CHAPTER SEVEN: CASARTELL'S EPISCOPAL PRAXIS IN RELATION TO QUESTIONS OF CHURCH AND SOCIETY

1 The First World War has, in Michael Snape's words, 'often been regarded by non-Catholics as a 'good' war for British Catholicism, an outcome reflected in a widening diffusion of Catholic influences on British religious life.' Michael Snape, 'British Catholicism in the British Army in the First World War' (unpublished article), p. 1.

2 Pastoral Letter, 'The Signs of the Times,' October, 1903, *Acta Salfordiensia, Episcopi Quarti*, An. I. 1903–4, Salford Diocesan Archives. (Will be cited as 'Signs'.)

3 *Ibid.*

4 *Ibid.*

5 *Ibid.*

6 Frances Zanetti, 'Our Duty as Catholics', in *The Harvest*, 218 (XVIII) (1905), p. 256.

7 Pastoral Letter, Lent 1921, 'The Acceptable Time,' ASEQ, Anns. XIV-XVIII, 1916–21, SDA.

8 Kester Aspden, 'The English Roman Catholic Bishops and Politics, 1903–1935', a paper read to the Ecclesiastical History Seminar, University of London 10 Jan. 2000.

9 'Signs.'

10 *Ibid.*

11 'And we do not believe for a moment that the sacrifice need be made. We believe that the two trainings, that of the intellect and that of the soul and heart, go safely and surely hand in hand, so as to produce the best type of man and citizen for both here and hereafter.' Pastoral Letter, Lent 1906, 'The Crisis in Catholic Education,' ASEQ, An. III, 1905–6, SDA.

12 'Bishop's Message', *The Catholic Federationist*, April 1911.

13 Casartelli – 'Very Rev. Canon' [no name given] 22 Mar. 1921, Casartelli Letters, 6001–6100, Box 164, SDA.

14 Formed in 1900, the United Irish League sought to mobilise the Irish voters in England in order to achieve Home Rule for Ireland. It expected its members to vote for candidates who won its approval. In 1910 there were 1,500 members in Manchester and district. S. Fielding, *Class and Ethnicity Irish Catholics in England, 1880–1939* (Buckingham, 1993), pp. 80–81.

15 See below, pp. 164–169.

16 See the following in Casartelli Letters in the Salford Diocesan Archives: Casartelli to Bishop of Southwark, 2 Jan. 1912, 1301–1400, Box 158; Casartelli to Archbishop of Liverpool, 13 Mar. 1912, 1401–1500, Box 158; Casartelli to Bishop Hedley, 8 Dec. 1912, 1801–1900, Box 159; Casartelli to Cardinal Gasquet, 6 Dec. 1916, 4001–4100, Box 161; Casartelli to Bishop of Southwark, 8 Dec. 1916, 4001–4100, Box 161; Casartelli to Bishop of Northampton, 22 April 1917, 4201–4300, Box 161; Casartelli to Bishop of Southwark, 22 April 1917, 4201–4300, Box 161; Casartelli to Cardinal Merry del Val, 22 April 1917, 4201–4300, Box 161; Casartelli to Bishop of Northampton, 25 April 1917, 4201–4300, Box 161; Casartelli to Archbishop of Liverpool, 27 Oct. 1917, 4501–4600, Box 162; Casartelli to Archbishop of Liverpool, 6 Nov. 1917, 4501–4600, Box 162; Casartelli to Cardinal Gasquet, 10 Nov. 1917, 4601–4700, Box 162; Casartelli to Archbishop of Liverpool, 17 Nov. 1917, 4601–4700, Box 162; Casartelli to Mgr Browne, 17 Nov. 1917, 4601–4700, Box 162; Casartelli to Bishop of Northampton, 18 Nov. 1917, 4601–4700, Box 162; Casartelli to Bishop of Plymouth 4 Feb. 1918, 4701–4800, Box 162; Casartelli to Archbishop of Liverpool, 1 Dec. 1919, 5601–5700, Box 162; Casartelli to Archbishop of Liverpool, 19 April 1920, 5701–5800, Box 164; Casartelli to Bishop of Middlesborough, Good Friday 1921, 6001–6100, Box 164; Casartelli to Bishop of Southwark, Good Friday, 1921, 6001–6100, Box 164.

17 The 'Irish party' consisted of Irish MPs who sought Home Rule for Ireland; by 1906 they were united behind John Redmond MP.

18 Kester Aspden, 'The English Roman Catholic Bishops and the Social Order, 1918–26,' in *Recusant History* 25 (3) (2001), p. 546.

19 Paula M. Kane, "The Willing Captive of Home?' The English Catholic Women's League, 1906–1920,' in *Church History*, 60 (3) (1991), p. 333.

20 Casartelli wrote to Bishop Amigo, 'The fact that the Catenians do not admit clergy into their ranks is to me in their favour.' Casartelli to Amigo 7 May 1924, Salford File, Archdiocesan Archives Southwark.

21 Casartelli wrote to the auxiliary bishop of Westminster, William Anthony Johnson (1832–1909), enquiring if such a committee had already been established in Westminster. In the case of his own diocese, Casartelli noted, 'I suppose it is time to do so.' Casartelli to Bishop of Arindela, 21 May 1908, Casartelli Letters, D301–400, Box 157, SDA.

22 Casartelli Diaries, 10 April 1912, SDA.

23 A report submitted every four years to Rome by the bishops on the spiritual and material state of their diocese. The report was written using a detailed questionnaire.

24 A bishop's four-yearly visit to Rome to submit a report (*Relatio*) on his diocese.

25 Vatican Secret Archives, Consistorial Congregation, Salford 705, 1912; 1917; 1921.

26 Maude Petre (1863–1942), friend of George Tyrell (1861–1909) who was expelled from the Jesuits because of his Modernism and finally excommunicated for criticising *Pascendi*. See Clyde F. Crews, *English Catholic Modernism. Maude Petre's Way of Faith* (Burns and Oates, London 1984.)

27 Casartelli to Maud Petre, 22 Sept. 1922, Casartelli Letters, 6210–6300, Box 164, SDA.

28 Pastoral Letter, Aug. 1914, 'Pius X, and the Life of the Church', ASEQ, Anns. VIII-XI, 1911–14, SDA.

29 An obituary in *Baeda* acknowledged that Casartelli had 'studied in a field where many had made shipwreck of the faith.' *Baeda*, 1925 (April), p. 86.

30 'Bishop's Message' *CF.*, Sept. 1914.

31 'Mr. McKenna's Education Bill, 1908', ASEQ, An. V, 1907–8, SDA.

32 V.A. McClelland, 'Bourne, Norfolk and the Irish Parliamentarians: Roman Catholics and the Education Bill of 1906', in *Recusant History*, 23 (2) (1996), p. 230.

33 L. C. Casartelli, 'Reconstruction and Defence: A Sermon Preached at St Thomas of Canterbury's, Higher Broughton,' unmarked file, SDA. (Later published as a pamphlet by J. McGrane, Manchester.)

34 'Signs.'

35 'Bishop's Message', *CF.*, Dec. 1921.

36 See Chapter Three, pp. 56–62.

37 'Bishop's Message', *CF.*, July 1914.

38 'Crisis in Catholic Education.'

39 'Bishop's Message', *CF.*, Aug. 1914.

40 Augustine Birrell (1850–1933), Liberal MP for Fife and later for North Bristol; one-time Minister of Education.

41 See M. Fanning, 'The 1906 Liberal Education Bill and the Roman Catholic Reaction of the Diocese of Salford', (undergraduate dissertation, Exeter College, University of Oxford, 1996).

42 'Catholic Parents' Demonstration', ASEQ, An. III, 1905–6, SDA.

43 *Manchester Guardian*, 6 Mar. 1906.

44 *Ibid.*

45 'The Education Bill 1906. Declaration of the Archbishop and Bishops of the Province of Westminster, and Resolutions of the Catholic Education Council.' ASEQ, An. III, 1905–1906, SDA.

46 Casartelli Diaries, 5 Mar. 1906, SDA,

47 'A Letter to the Clergy and Laity,' ASEQ, An. IV, 1906–07, SDA.

48 'Mr Birrell has done for us what probably no other agency could have done so simply and so completely. The threatened attack has had a wonderful effect in drawing together our

ranks, in stirring up throughout the length and breadth of the land quite a new spirit of militant loyalty and unity, in infusing new life and energy into all sections of our community and obliterating unfortunate causes of divisions ... Here we see Catholics of all social classes and every political party united on one and the same platform, and above all, English and Irish Catholics banded together in defence of their common faith and forgetting differences that never ought to have existed.' In 'A Letter to the Clergy and Laity', Whit Sunday 1906, ASEQ, An. III, 1905–6, SDA.

49 Casartelli Diaries, 4 Dec. 1906, SDA.
50 The details of the complicated event can be read in McClelland, 'Bourne, Norfolk and the Irish Parliamentarians', pp. 228–256.
51 Casartelli to Bourne, 6 Jan. 1907, Bo., 1/178, Archdiocesan Archives Westminster.
52 Ibid.
53 Casartelli to Bishop Whiteside, 6 Jan. 1907, Whiteside Papers, Archdiocesan Archives Liverpool.
54 Ibid.
55 Ibid. Casartelli based this on a report in the Daily Dispatch, 3 Jan. 1907, and which he understood had not been 'disproved' at the time of his writing to Whiteside and Bourne.
56 Ibid.
57 When Churchill was promoted to the Cabinet as President of the Board of Trade, he had, according to the then procedure, to seek re-election in his constituency. This was not until 1908. From 1905 until 1908 he was Under-Secretary of State for the Colonies. Yet Casartelli speaks of the 'promotion of Mr. Churchill.' Was he getting confused with Reginald McKenna who was promoted to the cabinet as President of the Board of Education in 1907? Whatever be the explanation, the fact of Churchill's later promotion to Cabinet office did cause havoc in the 1908 North West Manchester by-election. See Chapter Eight, 'The Catholic Federation and the 1908 By-Election in North-West Manchester.'
58 Reginald McKenna (1863–1943), Liberal MP for North Monmouthshire 1895–1918.
59 H(erbert) A(lbert) L(aurens) Fisher (1865–1940), President of the Board of Education 1916–26.
60 Pastoral Letter, Advent 1917, 'Watchman, What of the Night'? ASEQ, Anns. XIV-XVIII, 1916–21, SDA.
61 The Tablet, 17 Jan. 1917, p. 634.
62 Casartelli to Bourne, 16 Nov. 1921, Casartelli Letters, 6101–6200, Box 164, SDA.
63 See Chapter Eight, pp. 185–189.
64 See Casartelli Letters: Casartelli to Archbishop of Liverpool, 27 Oct. 1917, 4501–4600, Box 162; Casartelli to Archbishop of Liverpool, 6 Nov. 1917, 5401–4600, Box 162; Casartelli to Cardinal Gasquet (for Archbishop of Liverpool's views), 10 Nov. 1917, 4601–4700, Box 162; Casartelli to Bishop of Middlesborough, Good Friday 1921, 6001–6100, Box 164; Casartelli to Bishop of Southwark, Good Friday, 1921, 6001–6100, Box 164; SDA.
65 In its appreciation of Bourne, The Times considered him to have been 'statesmanlike' in his work for and support of religious education. The Times, 2 Jan. 1935.
66 Casartelli to Archbishop of Liverpool, 3 Oct. 1917, Casartelli Letters, 4301–4400, Box 162, SDA.
67 Casartelli to Gasquet, 1 Sept. 1903, Letters to Gasquet 1885–1904, No.938, Gasquet Papers, Downside Abbey Archives.
68 Ernest Oldmeadow, Francis Cardinal Bourne, 2 vol. (London, 1940), I, p. 208.
69 See McClelland, 'Bourne, Norfolk and the Irish Parliamentarians,' p. 249.
70 Casartelli to Amigo, 2 Jan. 1912, Casartelli Letters, 1301–1400, Box 158, SDA.
71 Quoted in Oldmeadow, Bourne, vol. II, p. 84.
72 T. M. Maloney, 'The Public Ministry of Cardinal Hinsley', (PhD thesis, University of London 1981), p. 369.

73 George Croydon Marks (1858–1938), Liberal MP for Launceston division of Cornwall 1906–1918.

74 Casartelli to Bourne, 12 Mar. 1912, Casartelli Letters, 1401–1500, Box 158, SDA.

75 John Dillon (1851–1927), Irish nationalist and strong supporter of Home Rule for Ireland.

76 Casartelli to Bourne 12 Mar. 1912.

77 *Ibid.*

78 'I can assure your Eminence that the feeling here is very intense on this crisis and everybody is looking for an authoritative pronouncement.' *Ibid.*

79 'It would be easy enough for me to make a strong and outspoken protest and a disavowal of Mr. Dillon and I should have enthusiastic backing among my clergy and Laity. But I feel it would be almost disastrous for an individual bishop to step forward and endeavour to do what the whole Hierarchy ought to do.' *Ibid.*

80 *Ibid.*

81 *Ibid.*

82 Casartelli to Archbishop of Liverpool, 14 Mar. 1912, Casartelli Letters, 1401–1500, Box 158.

83 John Milner (1752–1826), one of the English Vicars Apostolic. 'He was an ardent defender of the papacy, became embroiled in controversy with the sizeable body of Catholics (some of whom organised the Catholic Committee in 1872, later known as the Cisalpine Club).' *Dictionary of Catholic Biography*, (London, 1962).

84 Kester Aspden, 'The English Roman Catholic Bishops and the Social Order' p. 546.

85 'On occasions Casartelli would invoke the name of Bishop Milner: described by John Bossy as the 'foremost defender of hierarchical claims in the community', Milner was one who clearly knew how to put the laity in its place.' Aspden, 'The English Roman Catholic Bishops and the Social Order', p. 547.

86 William Bernard Ullathorne (1806–1889), Vicar Apostolic of the Western District.

87 Casartelli to Bishop of Middlesborough, Good Friday 1921; and Casartelli to Bishop of Southwark, Good Friday 1921; Casartelli Letters, 6001–6100, Box 164, SDA. Casartelli was prompted to say this because at the time he was reading Shane Leslie's *Henry Edward Manning. His Life and Labours* (London, 1921). An Appendix to the book deals with a meeting the bishops had held in Manning's absence, a fact that caused him to be very angry. Casartelli commented: 'It really does not tell much more than is told before; but I can't get rid of an unpleasant suspicion that it may have been added by 'order of authority.' Particularly page 511 we seem to have an implied censure of our historical Oscott meeting of 1917.' Casartelli to Bishop of Middlesborough 28 Mar. 1921, Casartelli Letters, 4201–4300, Box 164, SDA. For the significance of the Oscott meeting of 1917 see pp. 169–176, '1917: An *Annus Terribilis*.'

88 Casartelli to Archbishop of Liverpool, 14 Mar. 1912, Casartelli letters, 1401–1500, Box 158, SDA.

89 *Ibid.*

90 Casartelli to Archbishop of Liverpool, 12 Mar. 1912, 1401–1500, Box 158, SDA.

91 Bourne had replied thus: 'the action of the Nationalist Party in supporting the Second Reading of the Education Acts (Single-School Area) Amendment Bill was taken in direct opposition to the clearly- expressed opinion of the Cardinal Archbishop of Westminster, who regards the Bill as full of menace to the interest of religious education ... Mr. Dillon had no authority for saying that he spoke on behalf of the Catholics of England.' *The Tablet*, 16 Mar. 1912.

92 Casartelli to Bourne, 17 Mar. 1912, Casartelli Letters, 1401–1500, Box 158, SDA.

93 Casartelli to Canon O'Kelly, Passion Sunday, 1912, 1401–1500, Box 158, SDA.

94 Letter of Casartelli to Archbishop Ilsley of Birmingham, 29 April 1920, cited in Aspden, 'The English Roman Catholic Bishops' p. 547.

95 Casartelli to Archbishop of Liverpool, 19 April 1920. 5701–5800, Box 164, SDA.

96 Published in London, 1915.

97 CF., Jan. 1916.

98 An association of English Catholic laity. 'The greater number (though by no means all) of the Catholic aristocracy ... sympathised with them.' *The Catholic Encyclopaedia*, vol. 3, (London, 1908), p. 780. The Cisalpine Club had struggled with the Vicars Apostolic about a form of a suitable oath of allegiance to the Crown. McClelland writes: 'By the time of Catholic Emancipation in 1829, Cisalpinism (a peculiarly English variant of French Gallicanism or eighteenth-century German Febronianism had become marked by antipathy to the growing influence of the middle-class followers of O'Connell and by a resentment at the prominence being given to Irish ecclesiastical affairs in English planning and policy. The sense that Catholics were members of an international body with strong links to the faith and interest of fellow Catholics elsewhere was singularly absent from Cisalpine thought patterns ... While acknowledging the supremacy of the papacy in theological terms, it was concerned to preserve its independent life in matters of ecclesiastical organisation and control." 'The Formative Years, 1850–92', in V. A. McClelland and M. Hodgetts (eds.), *From Without the Flaminian Gate* (London, 1999), pp. 4–5.

99 CF., Jan. 1916.

100 Casartelli to Cardinal Gasquet 12 Jan. 1917, Gasquet Papers, 'Letters' (no other ref.,) DDA.

101 Casartelli to Canon Tynan, 19 Sept. 1917, Casartelli Letters, 4401–4500, Box 162, SDA.

102 Casartelli to Cardinal Gasquet, 10 Nov. 1917, Casartelli Letters, 4601–4700, Box 162, SDA.

103 Casartelli to Archbishop of Liverpool, 3 Oct. Casartelli Letters, 4501–4600, Box 162, 1917, SDA.

104 Casartelli, 'Reconstruction and Defence: A Sermon Preached at St Thomas of Canterbury's, Higher Broughton,' (J. McGrane, Gorton, Manchester.)

105 *Ibid.*, p. 5.

106 *Ibid.*, p. 6.

107 *Ibid.*, p. 6.

108 Casartelli to Bourne, 19 Oct. 1917, Casartelli Letters, 4501–4600, Box 162, SDA,

109 Began in 1905 as the successor to 'The Catholic Schools Committee'. Its purpose was to look after the interests of secondary and elementary Catholic education.

110 Casartelli to Bourne, 19 Oct. 1917, Casartelli Letters, 4501–4600, Box 162, SDA,

111 20 Oct. 1917, 4501–4600, Box 162, SDA.

112 Casartelli to Canon O'Kelly, 20 Oct. 1917, Casartelli Letters, 4501–4600, Box 162, SDA,

113 'All this comes of the silence of the Hierarchy, gagged by His Eminence.' Casartelli to Archbishop of Liverpool, 27 Oct. 1917, Casartelli Letters, 4501–4600, Box 162, SDA.

114 Casartelli to Archbishop of Liverpool, 6 Nov. 1917, Casartelli Letters, 4501–4600, Box 162, SDA.

115 *Ibid.*

116 Casartelli to Gasquet, 10 Nov. 1917, 4601–4700, Box 162, SDA,

117 'I know from letters that these are the feelings of my brother Bishops, – some being most outspoken.' *Ibid.*

118 Casartelli quoted the following, taken from a letter to him by the Archbishop of Liverpool: 'I object to these important matters being settled by *pourparlers* with Fisher or Lord Ed., Talbot. We were gagged before by answers from Lord Ripon, in the Cabinet at the time of the Birrell Bill. I have felt for some time that the Bishops' meetings have not been for a frank discussion and settlement of things by ourselves, but meetings merely to confirm the Cardinal's decisions. I have told the Cardinal he is getting out of touch with the Bishops. For that reason I have advocated regular executive meetings. But H. E. won't see it.' *Ibid.*

119 This was H. Moon, from Manchester. See *The Tablet*, 17 Nov. 1917, p. 634.
120 Casartelli to Canon O'Kelly, 17 Nov. 1917, Casartelli Letters, 4601–4700, Box 162, SDA.
121 Casartelli to Bishop of Northampton, 18 Nov. 1917, Casartelli Letters, 4601–4700, Box 162, SDA.
122 Casartelli to Archbishop of Liverpool, 17 Nov. 1917, Casartelli Letters, 4601–4700, Box 162, SDA. The teachers' meeting and the speeches made received full-page coverage.
123 Casartelli to Archbishop of Liverpool, 17 Nov. 1917.
124 Casartelli to Bishop of Northampton, 18 Nov. 1917.
125 Resolution of the Catholic Teachers' Guild at their AGM, Dec. 1917, reported in *The Tablet*, 5 Jan. 1918.
126 *The Tablet*, 5 Jan. 1918, Casartelli's letter to T. Meehan, Hon. Sec., of Catholic Teachers' Guild.
127 *The Tablet*, 2 Feb. 1918, T. Meehan to Casartelli.
128 *Ibid.*
129 *Ibid.*
130 Casartelli to Archbishop of Liverpool, 1 Dec. 1919, Casartelli Letters, 5601–5700, Box 163, SDA.
131 *Ibid.*
132 *Ibid.*
133 An account of this can be found in Oldmeadow, *Bourne*, vol. II, pp. 123–139, and Clifton, *Amigo Friend of the Poor*, pp. 43–50.
134 Casartelli to Bishop Hedley, 8 Dec. 1912, Casartelli Letters, 1801–1900, Box 159, SDA.
135 Casartelli to Cardinal Gasquet, 6 Dec. 1916, Casartelli Letters, 4001–4100, Box 161, SDA.
136 *Ibid.*
137 Casartelli to Amigo, 8 Dec. 1916, Casartelli Letters, 4001–4100, Box 161, SDA.
138 *Ibid.*
139 Casartelli to Amigo, 22 Jan. 1917, Salford File, AAS.
140 Casartelli to Whiteside, 8 Mar. 1917, Whiteside Papers, AAL.
141 *Ibid.*
142 Those absent were: the Archbishop of Cardiff and Bishop of Clifton, through illness; the Bishop of Middlesborough because of his age; and the Bishop of Plymouth, Casartelli does not say why, only, 'I presume for some other urgent reason.' Casartelli to Cardinal Gasquet, St Joseph's Day, 1917, Gasquet Papers, 'Letters,' DDA.
143 Casartelli Diaries, 18 Mar. 1917, SDA.
144 Casartelli to Gasquet, St Joseph's Day, 1917, Gasquet Papers, Letters, DDA.
145 *Ibid.* A copy of the *memorandum* is attached to Casartelli's letter.
146 Casartelli Diaries, 17 April 1917, SDA.
147 Casartelli to Gasquet, 10 Nov. 1917, Gasquet Papers, Letters, DDA.
148 See Oldmeadow, *Bourne*, II, pp. 125–139.
149 *Ibid.*, p. 125.
150 Rafael Merry del Val (1865–1930), served Benedict XV and Pius XI as Secretary of the Holy Office.
151 Casartelli to Merry del Val, 22 April 1917, Casartelli letters, 4201–4300, Box 161, SDA.
152 Casartelli to Bishop of Northampton, 3 May 1917, Casartelli Letters, 4201–4300, Box 161, SDA.
153 Casartelli to Mgr Brown of Southwark, 3 May 1917, Casartelli Letters, 4201–4300, Box 161, SDA.
154 Casartelli to Merry del Val, 22 April 1917, Casartelli Letters, 4201–4300, Box 161, SDA.
155 Casartelli to Cardinal Gasquet, 10 Nov. 1917, Casartelli Letters, 4601–4700, Box 162, SDA.
156 *Ibid.*

157 Casartelli to Bishop of Northampton, 18 Nov. 1917, Casartelli letters, 4601–4700, Box 162, SDA.

158 See Reginald J. Dingle, *Cardinal Bourne at Westminster* (London, 1934), chapter II, 'The Education Question', pp.13–44; *Congress Addresses by Cardinal Francis Bourne* (London, n.d.); Oldmeadow, *Bourne*, vol. II.

159 Maisie Ward, *The Wilfrid Wards and the Transition* vol. 2 (London, 1937) chapter XII, pp.212–239.

160 Margaret Fletcher, *O, Call Back Yesterday* (London, 1939), p. 135.

161 Adrian Hastings, *A History of English Christianity 1920–1990*, 3rd edition (London, 1991), p. 144.

162 Casartelli to Archbishop of Liverpool, 14 Mar. 1912, Casartelli Letters, 1401–1500, Box 158, SDA.

163 See Chapter Eight, 'The Catholic Federation: Federationism v Parochialism'.

164 *CF.*, May 1911.

165 Pastoral Letter, Lent 1920, 'The Holy Hour', ASEQ, Anns. XIV-XVIII, 1916–21, SDA.

166 Casartelli's elocution to the Diocesan Synod 1904, ASEQ, An. II, 1904–5, SDA.

167 *Ibid.*

CHAPTER EIGHT: THE LAY APOSTOLATE

1 Gioacchino Pecci (1810–1903), became pope in 1878.

2 L. C. Casartelli's Preface in C. D. Plater's *Retreats for the People* (London, 1912).

3 Kester Aspden, 'The English Roman Catholic Bishops and Politics, 1903–1943', (unpublished PhD thesis, University of Cambridge, 1999.), p. 28.

4 Cuthbert Hedley, *The Public Spirit of the Laity* (Catholic Truth Society, 1900), p. 2.

5 Herbert Vaughan, *The Work of the Catholic Laity in England* (Catholic Truth Society, 1899), p. 8.

6 Fr John Norris, headmaster of the Oratory School.

7 John Norris, *The Help of the Laity* (Catholic Truth Society, 1900).

8 In his 'Message' in the *Catholic Federationist*, Mar. 1913, Casartelli quoted the dictum, *fas est ab hoste doceri* ['it is quite lawful to learn from, and therefore to copy, the tactics of one's adversary'] and referred to, 'Masonic organisation in France which may go some way to explain how in that and other Continental countries a comparative handful of Freemasons has succeeded in monopolising the political and executive power over nations preponderatingly (*sic*) Catholic, also to show the efficacy of well-organised co-operative 'leavening' from within any body of men.'

9 Casartelli wrote to Mgr Brown of Southwark: 'I hope you will do your best for the Catenian Society whose growth I have watched from the beginning and whose success I have much at heart ... It is not in any way a 'secret society', although it has certain regalia and formulae which are found to have a certain attraction for business and professional men. [...] Certainly one of its main objects is to get Catholics to help one another in business – a perfectly legitimate object, as it seems to me, and one consistently carried out by Freemasons, by Dissenters, and by Scotchmen in general. Why should Catholics not take a leaf out of their book? [...] in many cases it has not only kept young men from Masonry, but has actually withdrawn them from its clutches by affording them just those attractions, social and otherwise, that draw men to Masonry in this country.' Casartelli to Mgr Brown, 17 Nov. 1911, Casartelli Letters, 1301–1400, Box 158, SDA.

10 Pastoral Letter, Feb. 1908, 'Amare et Servire', Acta Salfordiensia Episcopi Quarti, An. V, 1907–8, SDA. (Will be cited as 'Amare et Servire'.) In later years he referred to how he had 'ever looked upon [the Federation] as the chief work of my episcopate.' Diocesan Synod 1915, ASEQ, Anns. XII-XIII, 1914–16, SDA.

11 'Amare et Servire.'

12 'The German and Dutch Catholics, especially, as well as those of Belgium, particularly in the Flemish parts, were held up – and justly so – as models of perfect and wide-reaching systematisation of both clerical and lay activities in social and economic reform, as well as in the interests of the Catholic Church.' 'Bishop's Message', *CF.*, Feb. 1917.

13 'It is surely time that all Catholics, whether at home or abroad, should realise that in effective organisation alone is our hope for the future. Call it Federation, Association, or what you will, had French Catholics been organised on such lines, the history of the last forty years would have been different indeed.' 'Bishop's Message', *CF.*, Aug.. 1914.

14 'The Salford Diocesan Catholic Federation' in *The Month*, 113, pp. 465–476.

15 Peter Doyle, in 'The Catholic Federation', in W. J. Shiels and D. Wood (eds.), *Voluntary Religion* (1986), pp. 461–476.

16 Aspden, 'The English Roman Catholic Bishops and Politics', 1903–1943, p. 29.

17 Casartelli wrote on the occasion of announcing his intention to form the Federation: 'Here we see Catholics of all social classes and every political party united on one and the same platform, and above all, English and Irish Catholics banded together in defence of their common Faith and forgetting differences that never ought to have existed.' Letter to the Clergy and Laity, Whit Sunday 1906, ASEQ, An. III, 1905–6, SDA.

18 *Report of the Seventh Annual Conference of Catholic Colleges* (Ware, 1902), p. 36.

19 *Manchester Guardian*, 26 Nov. 1903.

20 T. Sharrock and T.F. Burns, 'The Salford Diocesan Catholic Federation', in *The Month*, 113, p. 470.

21 Philip Hughes, 'The Coming Century', in G. A. Beck, (ed.), *The English Catholics 1850–1950* (London, 1950), p. 39.

22 Casartelli wrote: 'I shall never feel properly happy until I get a branch in, at least, every one of the more important missions throughout the Diocese.' 'Bishop's Message', *CF.*, Feb. 1916.

23 Pastoral Letter, Feb. 1909, 'Faith and Good Works', ASEQ, An. VI. 1908–9, SDA. (Will be cited as 'Faith and Good Works'.)

24 *Ibid.*

25 Pastoral Letter, Nov. 1915, 'Dark Days', ASEQ, Anns. XII-XIII, 1914–16, SDA. (Will be cited as 'Dark Days'.)

26 *Ibid.* He spoke of how 'regret has been expressed that we are not as well provided as many of the denominations around us with organisations and agencies for training young men for civic service. This we hold to be entirely incorrect. We possess the best of all forms of organisation for this end in our admirable Diocesan Catholic Federation.'

27 Casartelli's Allocution to the Diocesan Synod, 1915.

28 'To have the same mind as the bishop'. Casartelli based this appeal on the teachings of Popes Leo XIII, Pius X and Benedict XV. See 'Appendix VI' in Diocesan Synod, 1915.

29 Casartelli Diaries, 6 Oct. 1915, SDA.

30 Casartelli Diaries, 6 Mar. 1916, SDA.

31 Casartelli Diaries, 22 Mar. 1916, SDA.

32 Casartelli Diaries, 22 May 1917, SDA.

33 Casartelli Diaries, 25 May 1917, SDA.

34 *CF.*, Sept. 1917.

35 *CF.*, June 1922.

36 See Casartelli to Canon Sharrock, 5 Nov. 1915, 3301–3400; & 30 Dec. 1915, 3401–3500, Casartelli Letters, Box 161, SDA.

37 Aspden, 'The English Roman Catholic Bishops and Politics. 1903–1943', p. 29.

38 Pastoral Letter, Oct. 1903, 'The Signs of the Times', ASEQ, An. I, 1903–4, SDA.

39 'Faith and Works'.

40 William Joynson-Hicks (1865–1932), later 1st Viscount Brentford.

41 Peter Doyle, 'The Catholic Federation 1906–1929', in W. J. Shiels and Diana Wood (eds.), *Voluntary Religion* (1986), p. 469.

42 See p. 263, n. 14.

43 John Redmond (1856–1918), leader of the Irish party. In 1910 he allied his party with the Liberals in order to achieve Home Rule for Ireland.

44 Address to the Manchester and Salford District Executive, 27 April 1908. Archdiocesan Archives Westminster, B05/14b-f. (Will be cited as 'Richardson's Address'.)

45 Letter of Hugh Fay of the Thomas Davis Branch of the United Irish League to Editor of the *Manchester Guardian*, 5 May 1908.

46 Richardson claimed that, 'Ever since the establishment of the Federation by His Lordship the Bishop there has been a determined mis-understanding by a certain number of people as to its aims, and amongst those who have partaken of this feeling the members of the United Irish League who have not joined the Catholic Federation … were amongst the most prominent.' He also acknowledged that many of the best members of the Catholic Federation were also members of the United Irish League (Richardson's Address).

47 *Ibid.*

48 The Thomas Davis Branch of the United Irish League was located in Manchester's commercial centre.

49 See Richardson's Address.

50 Patrick Lynch (1852–1921), a close associate of UIL and an old friend of Casartelli. He was the first priest Casartelli appointed to the Chapter (1903); this was quite possibly an attempt to create closer harmony with the United Irish League.

51 Casartelli to T. Sharrock, 15 April 1908, Casartelli Letters, B101–200, Box 157, SDA.

52 Casartelli to Tynan, 13 April 1908, Casartelli Letters, B101–200, Box 157, SDA.

53 'This meeting of Rectors and Representatives calls upon the Catholic electorate to offer Mr. Churchill their most unfailing opposition by their influence and their votes. We call upon the Catholics not to be betrayed a second time by Mr. Churchill, but to vote for Mr. Joynson-Hicks.' Quoted in P. J. Doyle, 'Manchester North-West, 1908. Federation v United Irish League' (unpublished manuscript). I am grateful to Mr. Doyle for a copy of this manuscript.

54 Casartelli Diaries 17 April 1908, SDA.

55 Casartelli Diaries 18 April 1908, SDA.

56 Casartelli to Rev. T. Sharrock, Holy Saturday 1908, Casartelli Letters, B101–200, Box 157, SDA.

57 Casartelli to Canon Beesley, Holy Saturday 1908, Casartelli Letters, B101–200, Box 157, SDA.

58 Casartelli to Canon Tynan, Holy Saturday 1908, Casartelli Letters, B101–200, Box 157, SDA.

59 Letter of Canon Richardson and T. F. Burns to the Editor of the *Manchester Guardian*, 8 May 1908.

60 Richardson's Address.

61 *Manchester Courier*, 21 April 1908.

62 *Ibid.*

63 Casartelli Diaries, 21 April 1908, SDA.

64 Winston Churchill to Miss Clementine Hozier, 27 April 1908, quoted in Randolph S. Churchill, *Winston S. Churchill 'Young Statesman 1901–1914'*, 2 vol. (London, 1967), II, p. 260.

65 Reported in MG., 16 April 1908. It would appear that Casartelli never forgave them for this action, for in 1916, during his visitation of St Cuthbert's parish, Withington, he noted in his Visitation Register: 'Was shocked to find *Catholic Herald* on sale at the church door, and even announced from the pulpit.' Casartelli's Visitation Register, 27 Feb. 1916, SDA.

66 Casartelli Diaries, 24 April 1908, SDA.

67 Casartelli to Miss Norris, 22 Oct. 1917, Casartelli Letters, 4501–4600, Box 162.SDA,

68 Casartelli to Canon O'Kelly, 18 June 1909, Casartelli letters, E401–500, Box 157, SDA.

69 Casartelli to Beesley, 22 June 1909, Casartelli letters, D401–500, Box 157, SDA.

70 The other five bishops were: Thomas Whiteside, Liverpool; William Gordon, Leeds; Thomas William Wilkinson, Hexham and Newcastle; Richard Lacey, Middlesborough; Robert Brindle, Nottingham.

71 The content of Casartelli's letter was:
    'That the Bishops should absolutely not go beyond drawing up a set of questions to be put before all Candidates, chiefly on the question of religious education.
    'That *all* replies should be published.
    'But that no directions or even advice as to voting should be given by either bishops or Federation: the most that could be prudently done would be to qualify replies as satisfactory or unsatisfactory; for the rest, the voters to be told to act according to their conscience.
    'That these questions should be drawn up jointly for the whole Province ... no other questions allowed (especially by Federation.)' Casartelli to Bourne, 14 Oct. 1909, Casartelli Letters, F501–600, Box 157, SDA.

72 Pastoral Letter of the Archbishop and Bishops of the Province of Westminster, on the duty of Catholics at the General Election 1910.' ASEQ, Anns. VI-VIII, 1909–11, SDA.

73 *Ad Clerum*, 23 Dec. 1909, ASEQ, Anns. VI-VIII, 1909–11, SDA.

74 Casartelli to T. Sharrock, 29 Dec. 1909, Casartelli Letters, Box 157, SDA.

75 *MG.*, 12 Jan. 1910.

76 Boulaye to Casartelli, 28 Jan. 1906, File 2, Box 182, SDA.

77 Casartelli to Lynch, 12 Jan. 1910, Casartelli Letters, G601–700, Box 157, SDA.

78 *MG.*, 13 Jan. 1910.

79 *Ibid.*, signed 'J. M.'

80 *MG.*, 8 May 1908.

81 *MG.*, 25 Mar. 1910.

82 Casartelli Diaries, 18 Sept. 1914, SDA.

83 Philip Hughes, 'The Coming Century', p. 39. n. 58.

84 Casartelli to T. F, Burns, 15 Nov. 1910, Casartelli letters, 801–900, Box 158, SDA.

85 Casartelli to T. Sharrock, 8 July 1909, Casartelli Letters, D301–400, Box 157, SDA.

86 Casartelli to Canon Sharrock, 30 Dec. 1915, Casartelli Letters, 3401–3500, Box 161, SDA.

87 *Ibid.*

88 Casartelli to Canon O'Kelly, 27 Jan. 1917, Casartelli Letters, 3601–3700, Box 161; 26 Nov. 1918, 5201–5300, Box 163; 15 Dec. 1920, 5901–6000, Box, 164, SDA.

89 See p. 197. See also, Casartelli to Canon Kelly, 15 Dec. 1920 & (no date), 5213, 5201–5300, Box 163, SDA.

90 Peter Lane, *The Catenian Association: 1908–1983* (London, 1982), p. 23

91 *Ibid.*, p. 23.

92 *Ibid.*, p. 16.

93 'Received a.m. deputation of 'Chums' (five including Mr. Lucan, R. and William O'Brien) re. this new organisation of Catholic business men for self-defence and in their common interests. Evidence of unfair competition by Freemasons, Dissenters, etc., want of support by Catholic architects.' Casartelli Diaries, 25 Sept. 1908, SDA.

94 Lane, *Catenian*, p. 10.

95 'Re., Catholic businessmen seeking your Grace's approval for the foundation in London of a circle of the (Catholic) Society called "Chums" ... An Association of Catholic business and professional men for mutual business assistance and social intercourse. The organis-ation has already succeeded in weaning a number of Catholics from Freemasonry, by substituting an organisation which supplies, from a Catholic point of view, many of the

advantages offered by Freemasonry. It is composed of men of all political shades of opinion and is thoroughly loyal.' Casartelli to Archbishop of Westminster, 26 Nov. 1909, Casartelli Letters, G601–706, Box 157, SDA.

96 Casartelli wrote to Mgr Brown regarding the Catenians: 'The more the Bishops and Clergy keep in touch with the Society, which is entirely loyal to ecclesiastical authority, the more they will be able to keep it on the right path.' Casartelli to Mgr Brown, Casartelli Letters, 1301–1400, Box 158, SDA.

97 Casartelli Diaries, 25 April 1908, SDA.

98 Lane, in his history of the Catenians, quotes a founding member: 'Bishop Casartelli was certainly responsible for the veto on the clergy being members. I was not present at the meeting but I was present at the second meeting with him where comment was made on the wisdom of his suggestion. It was by no means a surprising suggestion to those who knew him. He had found a great deal of opposition to his scheme of Catholic Federation from various parish priests. Time after time he championed the Catholic layman.' Lane, *Catenian*, p. 20.

99 Casartelli to Amigo, 7 May 1924, 'Salford File', Southwark Archdiocesan Archives. Nearly two years earlier Casartelli had refused the Knights of St Columba permission to establish themselves in his diocese: 'This evening a Mr. McGarry, evidently a very zealous Catholic (brother-in-law of Fr. Henshaw) called to see me re. Knights of Columbanus. Whilst extolling this work in USA, Italy, etc., told him definitely I could not agree to branch in this diocese, which would *faire concurrence* with the Catholic Federation and Catenians; no room for more.' Casartelli Diaries, 16 Sept. 1922, SDA. Fr. Henshaw was Casartelli's immediate successor as Bishop of Salford. He fully supported the Knights of St Columba but never mentioned once in an *Ad Clerum* or Pastoral Letter the Catholic Federation nor was there a branch in any of the parishes he served in.

100 John O'Donnell, a Manchester stockbroker and a founder member of the 'Manchester Chums.'

101 'Dark Days.'

102 T. F. Burns to Casartelli, Jan. 1917, File 2, Box 182, SDA.

103 Casartelli Diaries, 11 Jan. 1921.

104 Herbert Vaughan, Pastoral Letter, Feb. 1883, 'The true Basis of Catholic Politics.' Vaughan *Acta*, vol. 3, SDA.

105 Aspden, 'The English Roman Catholic Bishops,' p. 546.

106 Doyle, 'The Catholic Federation', p. 474. See Casartelli's letter to his father, 30 May 1875, 'Casartelli Letters', Ushaw College Archives. Casartelli Diaries, 24 Oct. 1875 & 7 Aug. 1876, SDA.

107 'Addressing a meeting under the auspices of the Catholic Women's League, held at the Midland Hotel, the Bishop of Salford (Dr. Casartelli) said he was rather afraid there was danger to be feared from the Labour party becoming strangled by the Socialist Party.' *Salford Reporter*, 15 June 1918.

108 *MG.*, 26 Dec. 1907.

109 René Waldeck-Rousseau (1846–1904), promulgated the Associations Laws in 1901. Twice minister of the interior. Émile Combes (1835–1921), Minister for Education, succeeded Waldeck-Rousseau as Minister for the Interior. He rigorously enforced the 1901 Association Laws.

110 *MG.*, 25 Jan. 1904.

111 *Ibid.*

112 This society was founded in Glasgow by John Wheatley who later became the Minister for Health in the first Labour Government.

113 *MG.*, 17 Dec. 1908.

114 Kester Aspden, 'The English Roman Catholic Bishops and the Social Order'.
115 Bourne, Pastoral Letter, Lent 1918, 'The Nation's Crisis', Westminster Archdiocesan Archives.
116 Pastoral Letter, Jan. 1910, 'What Shall it Profit a Man'?, ASEQ, An. VII, 1909–10, SDA.
117 *MG.*, 7 Sept. 1908.
118 *MG.*, 7 Aug. 1908.
119 Casartelli Diaries, 14 Oct. 1908, SDA.
120 *MG.*, 7 Sept. 1908.
121 *Ibid.* 17 Jan. 1908.
122 *CF.*, Feb. 1911.
123 See Peter Doyle, 'Charles Plater S. J. and the Beginnings of the Catholic Social Guild', in *Recusant History*, 21 (3) (1993), pp. 401–417.
124 *Catholic Social Guild Handbook*, (1910), p. 30.
125 *Ibid.*, p. 31.
126 *Catholic Social Work in Germany* (London, 1909) & *Retreats for the People* (London, 1912.)
127 Patrick Doyle, 'Accommodation or Confrontation: Catholic Response to the Formation of the Labour Party', in *North West Labour History*, 16 (1991–92), pp. 64–72.
128 T. F. Burns, 'The Catholic Working Man and Trade Unionism', in *C.S.G. Handbook* (1911).
129 See *CF.*, July 1914.
130 Charles Plater to Casartelli, 25 Dec. 1916, File 2, Box 182, SDA.
131 Casartelli to Mgr. Parkinson, 11 Feb. 1917, Casartelli Letters, 3601–3700, Box 161, SDA.
132 Casartelli to T. F. Burns, 11 Feb. 1917, Casartelli Letters, 3601–3700, Box 161, SDA.
133 Casartelli to Virginia Crawford, 23 May 1917, Casartelli Letters, 2401–4300, Box 161, SDA.
134 *Salford Reporter*, 15 June 1918.
135 T. F. Burns to Casartelli, 12 Nov. 1918, File 2, Box 182, SDA.
136 Casartelli to T. F. Burns, 30 Nov. 1918, Casartelli Letters, 5201–5300, Box 163, SDA.
137 Pastoral Letter, Lent 1919, quoted in *The Universe*, 14 Mar. 1919.
138 A copy of this document, dated 25 April 1919, is to be found in File 2, Box 182, SDA.
139 'Statement of Facts in Connection with the National Conference of Catholic Trade Unionists and Socialism,' File 2, Box 182, SDA.
140 Casartelli to Bourne, 16 May 1919, File 2, Box 182, SDA.
141 Bourne to Casartelli, 20 May 1919, File 2, Box 182, SDA.
142 T. F. Burns to Casartelli, 23 Sept. 1918, File 2, Box 182, SDA.
143 'F. Zanetti called *re.* standing for City Council as candidate of 'Centre Labour Party,' which I approved.' Casartelli Diaries, 13 Oct. 1919, SDA.
144 See Georgiana Putman McEntee, *The Social Catholic Movement in Great Britain* (New York, 1927), pp. 141–142.
145 See Bourne to Casartelli, 20 May 1919, File 2, Box 182, SDA.
146 Burns to Coates, 26 Feb. 1919, Vatican Secret Archives, Segreteria de Stato Ep. Moderna, A. 1920, R.81.F2.
147 Michael Clifton, *Amigo – Friend of the Poor* (Leominster, 1987), p. 108.
148 Casartelli to O'Kelly, 25 July 1919, Casartelli Letters, 5501–5600, Box 163, SDA.
149 Clifton, *Amigo*, p. 110.
150 Quoted in Riddell, 'The Catholic Church and the Labour Party', *Twentieth Century British History*, 8 (2) (1997), p. 170.
151 Ernest Oldmeadow, *Francis Cardinal Bourne*, vol. 2 (London, 1944), p. 207.
152 Casartelli to T. Sharrock, 22 Aug. 1914, Casartelli Letters, 4801–4900, Box 162, SDA.
153 'Bishop's Message', *CF.*, May 1924.
154 *Ibid.*

CONCLUSION

1 'The Signs of the Times', Pastoral Letter, Oct. 1903, *Acta Salfordiensia Episcopi Quarti*, An. I, 1903, Salford Diocesan Archives.

2 Casartelli Diaries, 13 June 1910, SDA.

3 *Salford Diocesan Almanac*, 1926, p. 36.

4 Quoted in J. G. Snead-Cox, *Life of Cardinal Vaughan*, 2 vol. (London, 1901), I, p. 458.

5 See Appendix Three for statistics of diocesan organisations begun in his episcopate.

6 Vaughan to Casartelli, 25 June 1877, Box 179, SDA.

7 Margaret Fletcher (1862–?), converted to Catholicism in 1897, founded the Catholic Women's League in 1906. Casartelli was one of the staunchest supporters of the League's journal *The Crucible*.

8 Margaret Fletcher, *O, Call Back Yesterday* (Oxford, 1939), p. 159.

9 Philip Hughes, 'The Coming Century', in G. A. Beck (ed.), *The English Catholics 1850–1950* (London, 1950), p. 39.

10 The increase in the number of Catholics who held public office (excluding the two Catholic Lord Mayors of Manchester) during Casartelli's episcopate was very small. Such positions would have been beyond the aspirations and concerns of the vast majority of the people of the diocese. The statistics are as follows (the previous number are in brackets): 6 County magistrates (4); 35 Borough Magistrates (18); 35 Municipal Councillors (24); 18 District Councillors (15); 35 Poor Law Guardians (32); 51 members of Education Authorities (49); 5 members of Infirmary Boards (1).

11 For example: Victoria Park, Whalley Range, Didsbury, Cheetham Hill, Crumpsall.

12 During his episcopate the diocese increased in the following manner: 24 new parishes; 2 male religious communities; 5 female religious communities; the foundation of 14 secondary and central schools; the accession of 90 to the number of clergy; a gain of 4,000 children over 13 years of age in elementary schools; a gain of 34,000 children in higher class schools; 2 new Rescue Homes; and the advent of 18 new Catholic organisations (see Appendix Three).

13 Mary Heimann, *Catholic Devotion in Victorian England* (Oxford, 1995), p. 3

14 *Relatio* 1912, S. Congr. Consist. *Relationes*, 705 (Salford), Archivo Segreto Vaticano.

15 *Relatio* 1922, ASV. See Appendix Three, p. 216 to compare statistics.

16 In 1912 there were 210 requests for dispensations for mixed-marriages, by 1922 this had risen to 1420. *Relationes* 1912 & 1922, ASV.

17 During the General Missions of 1922, 300 mixed-marriages (which had been contracted without a dispensation) were regularised according to Church law. *Relatio* 1922, ASV.

18 In the years that Casartelli was bishop Manchester had for the first time a Catholic Lord Mayor.

19 *The Times*, 2 Jan. 1935.

20 'Constitution on the Church in the Modern World', in W. M. Abbott (ed.), *The Documents of Vatican Two* (London, 1967), para. 1.

21 *Ibid*.

22 Jeffrey P. von Arx, 'Interpreting the Council: Archbishop Manning and the Vatican Decrees Controversy', in *Recusant History*, 26 (1) (2002), p. 229.

Bibliography

LIST OF CASARTELLI'S PUBLISHED WORKS
Books and pamphlets

Notes of a Course of Lectures on Commercial Geography (J. B. Ledsham, Manchester, 1881).

Commercial Education (John Heywood, London, 1882).

The Modern Languages Problem in Modern Education (John Heywood, London, 1888).

The Philosophy of the Mazdayasnian Religion under the Sassanids (Education Society's Press, Bombay, 1889).

Commercial Geography (Manchester, 1889).

Eastward Ho! Or Some Considerations on Our Responsibilities in the East (John Heywood, London, 1893).

Note sur la Terminaison Ambigue en Pehlevi '❤' (Extrait des Actes du Xe Congrès International des Orientalistes, session de Genève 1894) (Leiden, 1895).

A Forgotten Chapter of the Second Spring (Burns and Oates, London, 1895).

De L'Etat Actuel Des Etudes Supérieures dans le Clergé Anglais (Société Belge de Librairie, Brussels, 1896).

A Fragment of the Dinkart (Extrait des Mélanges Charles de Harlez) Leiden, 1895 (T. Sander & Co., Manchester, 1897).

The Study of Commercial History (T. Sander & Co., Manchester, 1897).

On Town Beauty (John Heywood, London, 1898).

Outre-Tombe: A Zoroastrian Idyll (Bombay, 1899).

The Trumpet of Jubilee (Cartwright & Rattray, London, 1901).

The Magi: A Footnote to Matthew 11.1 (Westminster Press, London, 1902).

Moods and Tenses, (St. William Press, Market Weighton, 1906).

Sketches From History (Benziger, New York, 1906).

Leaves From My Easter Garden (St. William's Press, Market Weighton, 1908). *Dante and Rosmini* (St. William's Press, Market Weighton, 1910).

Obituary Notice of H. Mills, *Journal of the Royal Asiatic Society* (March), 1919.

The Popes in the Divina Commedia (Sands and Co., London, 1921).

Catholic Truth Society Pamphlets

Catholic Missions (London, 1891).

The Three Greatest Books (London, 1897).

The Catholic Church in Japan (London, 1897).

The Litany of Loreto and its History (n.p., 1898).

The Church and The Printing Press (n. p., 1894).

The Religion of the Great Kings (London, 1909).

The Holy Rosary in the New Testament (London, n. d.).

The Stations of the Cross in Holy Writ (London, 1900).

The Spirit World (London, 1912).

Pax Christi: The Catholic Church and Peace (London, 1914).

Prefaces to books and encyclopaedia articles

Pagani, G. B. *The Life of Antonio Rosmini-Serbati* (George Routledge and Sons, London, 1906).

Anon., *The Sweet Miracle* (A Mystery Play, translated from the Portuguese and adapted from the dramatised version of Alberto d'Oliveira by the Sisters of Notre Dame.) (Sands and Co., London, 1910).

Ratti, Achille. *Climbs on Alpine Peaks* (T. Fisher Unwin, London, 1925).

Plater, C.D. *Catholic Social Work in Germany* (Sands and Co., London, 1909).

Plater, C. D. *Retreats For the People* (Sands and Co., London, 1912).

Caddell, Cecilia Mary. *The Cross in Japan: a History of the Missions of St. Francis and the Early Jesuits* (Burns and Oates, London, 1904).

Hull, E. R. *The Foundation of Character* (Sands and Co., London, 1910).

Quinlan, M. F. *My Brother's Keeper* (Catholic Truth Society, London, 1910).

Vaughan, J. S. *The Purpose of the Papacy* (Sands and Co., London, 1910).

Hohn, H. *Vocations* (R and T. Washbourne, London, 1910).

Curley, T. *The Catholic History of Oldham* (St. William's Press, Market Weighton, 1911).

Nesbitt, M. *Our Lady in the Church and Other Essays* (Longman, Green and Co., London, 1913).

Benson, H. E. *Vexilla Regis* (Longmans, Green and Co., London, 1914).

Hastings, J. *Encyclopaedia of Religion and Ethics* 12 vols. (T. and T. Clark, Edinburgh, 1908). *Celibacy* (Iranian), vol. 3; *Charm and Amulets* (Iranian), vol. 3; *Disease and Medicine* (Persian), vol. 4: *Dualism* (Iranian), vol. 5; *King* (Iranian), vol. 7; *Law* (Iranian), vol. 7; *Philosophy* (Iranian), vol. 9; *Saints and Martyrs* (Iranian), vol. 11; *Salvation* (Iranian), vol. 11; *Sassanians* vol. 11; *Sin* (Iranian), vol. 11; *Soul* (Iranian), vol. 11; *State of the Dead* (Iranian), vol. 11.

The Catholic Encyclopaedia (Caxton Publishing Co., New York, 1909). Ahrciman and Ormuzd, vol. 1; Avesta, vol. 2; Gentili, vol. 6.

Education papers and articles
(also see below 'Articles in the *Dublin Review*')

'A Catholic Head Master's Meeting', *Downside Review* (April), 1886.

'Catholics and University Education', *The Catholic Times*, 6 March 1896.

'The Problem of Foreign Pupils in our Catholic Schools', *Report of the Second Annual Conference of Catholic Colleges* (June 1897).

'The Pronunciation of Latin in our Schools', *Report of the Sixth Annual Conference of Catholic Colleges* (Cole, and Co., London, 1901).

'A Pedagogic and Educational Periodical for English Catholics', *Report of the Eighth Annual Conference of Catholic Colleges* (Cole and Co., London, 1903).

'Industrial Education in Catholic Missions', *Illustrated Catholic Missions* (April), 1903.

'A Problem of After-War Reconstruction: The Study of Foreign Languages', *Transactions of the Manchester Statistical Society* (1918–19).

'Catholic Secondary Schools and Our Universities', *Report of the 23rd Conference of Catholic Colleges* (Cole and Co., London, 1921).

'Our Silver Jubilee', *Report of the 25th Annual Conference of Catholic Colleges* (Cole and Co., London, 1921).

Articles (Oriental Studies)

'The Glory and Fall of Yima', *The Month* LXVII (224) (1883).

'Un manuscrit Karshuni du Musée de Liverpool', *Muséon*, 3 (1884).

'Un morceau de literature Dyak', *Muséon*, 4 (1885).

'Le Dinkart et son âge', *Muséon*, 3 (1884).

'New Europe - Romania, Servia, Bulgaria', *The Journal of the Manchester Geographical Society*, 1 (1895).

'After Death. From the Avesta', *The Month*, LV (256) (1885).

'The Teaching of Commercial Geography', *The Journal of the Manchester Geographical Society*, 2 (1886).

'Traité de Médecine Mazdéenne', *Muséon*, 5 (1886).

'The Semitic Verb in Pehlevi', *Babylonian and Oriental Review*, 1 (VI) (1886–1887).

'Etymology of the Name Zarathustra', *The Academy*, 31 (1887).

'The Discourses of Chrosroës' (I), *The Babylonian and Oriental Record*, (I) (VII) (1886–1887).

'A Parallel to the Pehlevi Jargon', *Babylonian and Oriental Record*, I (IX) (1886–1887).

'Two Discourses of Chrosroës' (II), *Babylonian and Oriental Record*, 2 (II) (1887–1888).

'The Semitic Suffix *Man* and its Origin' (III), *Babylonian and Oriental Record*, 2 (VI) (1887–1888).

'The Order of the Characters in Arabic Alphabet', *Babylonian and Oriental Record*, 3 (VI) (1888–1889).

'What Was Khvetuk-Das? and Other Papers', *The Babylonian and Oriental Record*, 3 (VIII) (1889).

'A Sidelight on the Khvêtûk-das Controversy', *Babylonian and Oriental Record*, 3 (IX) (1888–1889).

'Another Discourse of King Chrosroës', *Babylonian and Oriental Record* 3 (X) (1888–1889).

'Some Marriage and Funeral Customs of Ancient Persia' *The Babylonian and Oriental Record* 4 (V) (1889–1890).

'Oriental Testimonies Regarding Khvetuk-Das', *Babylonian and Oriental Record* 4 (V) (888–1889).

'Astôdans, and Avestic Funeral Prescriptions' *Babylonian and Oriental Record* 4 (VII) (1889–1890).

'Another Discourse of King Chosroes the Immortal-Souled', *The Babylonian and Oriental Record* 3 (X) (1889–1890).

'The Dog and Death', *The Babylonian and Oriental Record* 4 (XII) (1889–1890).

'Sâlûtar. La pierre-de-touche du cheval', (Extrait du *Muséon*) (1891).

Compte-Rendu du Congrès Scientifique International des Catholiques, Paris (1–6 April, Paris 1891).

'The Eagle of Etana-Gelgames and his Kindred in Folk Lore', *The Academy* (1891).

'The Literary Activity of the Parsis during the Past Ten Years in Avestic and Pehlevi Studies', *The Transactions of the Ninth International Congress of Orientalists* 2 (1892).

'Report on the Society's Examination on 'India' 1892', *Journal of the Manchester Geographical Society* 8 (1892).

'Tenth International Orientalist Congress at Geneva', *Journal of the Manchester Geographical Society* 10 (1894).

La Religion des Reis Achémenides d'après leurs Inscriptions', *Compte-Rendu du troisième Congrès Scientifique International des Catholiques, Brussels*, (3–8 September 1894).

'Geographical Missionaries Conference', *Journal of the Manchester Geographical Society* 13 (1897).

'Report on the Eleventh International Congress of Orientalists in Paris', September 5–12 1897, *Journal of the Manchester Geographical Society* 13 (1897).

'L'Idée du Péché chez les Indo-Eraniens de L'Antiquite', *Compte-Rendu du Quatrième Congres Scientifique Internal des Catholiques*, (Fribourg August 1897).

'Note on a Pehlevi Inscription in The Dublin Museum' (Extract from *Actes du Onzième Congrès International des Orientalistes*, (Paris 1897)

'Hindu Mythology and Literature' (I), *The Babylonian and Oriental Record*, IX (2) (1901).

'Hindu Mythology and Literature' (II), *The Babylonian and Oriental Record*, IX (3) (1901).

'Eranica', *Muséon* 21 (1902).

'The Temptation of Zoroaster', *Indian Antiquary* 32 (1903).

'The Literary Activity of the Parsis During the Past Ten Years in Avestic and Pehlevi Studies', *Asiatic Quarterly Review* (July) 1903.

'Obituary Notice. Friedrich Von Spiegel', *Journal of the Royal Asiatic Society* (1906).

'Essai sur la diffusion du Manichéisme dans l'empire romain', (n. p., 1907).

'Obituary of Ferdinand Justi', *Journal of the Royal Asiatic Society* (1907).

'The Zoroastrian Messiah', *The Hibbert Journal* 5 (October 1906 - July 1907).

'Hindu Mythology and Literature as Recorded by Portuguese Missionaries of the Early Seventeenth Century', *Anthropos* 1 (8) (1906–1908).

'Heart and Reins in Ancient Iran', *Journal of the Manchester Oriental Society* (1911).

'Religion of the Achaeminid Kings', *Journal of the Manchester Oriental Society* (1912).
'Early Zoroastrianism', *Journal of the Manchester Oriental Society* (1913–14).
Book review, *Journal of the Royal Asiatic Society* (1922).
'Avestan *urvan*, 'soul'', T. W. Arnold and R. A. Nicholson, (eds.), *A Volume of Oriental Studies Presented to Edward G. Browne* (Cambridge, 1922).
Book review, *Journal of the Royal Asiatic Society* (1923).
Book review, *Journal of the Royal Asiatic Society* (1924).
'The Dog and Death', *Journal of the Manchester Egyptian and Oriental Society* (1926).
'Note on the Probable Date of Zarathustra', (Bombay, n. d.) Oriental Essays, vol. I, Salford Diocesan Archives.
'The Persian Dante', (Extract from the *Dastur Hoshang Memorial Volume*) (Bombay, no date.) 'Oriental Essays', vol. II, SDA..
'The Société Scientifique of Brussels', (n. p. & n. d.) 'Miscellanea', vol. I, SDA.

Articles in The Dublin Review

'The Three Fausts', *The Dublin Review* II (1883).
'An Educational Lesson from Berlin', *The Dublin Review* XIX (II) (1888).
'Origins of the Church in Edessa', *The Dublin Review* XXI (II) (1889).
'The Art of Burial, *The Dublin Review*' CXIV (9) (1894).
'The English Universities and the Reformation', *The Dublin Review* CXVI (1895).
'The Catholic Church in Japan', *The Dublin Review* CXVI (1895).
'Our Diamond Jubilee', *The Dublin Review* 18 (1896).
'The Oriental Schools of Louvain. Two English Scholars and the Beginning of Oriental Studies at Louvain', *The Dublin Review* 19 (1896.).
'The Lombards', *The Dublin Review* CXXIX (1901).
'The English Pope', *The Dublin Review* CXXX (1902).
'The Magi: A Footnote to Mat. 11.1.', *The Dublin Review* CXXXI (1902).
'The First Gatha of the Avesta', *The Dublin Review* CXXXII(1903).
'Oxford and Louvain', *The Dublin Review* CXXXII (1903).
'The Ninth Gatha of the Avesta', *The Dublin Review* CXXXV (1904).
'The Plaint of the Kine', *The Dublin Review* CXXXIX (1906).

St. Bede's Magazine and Baeda

'Flowers From An Eastern Garden', *St. Bede's Magazine* (February) 1879.
'A Vedic Hymn to Ushas, Goddess of the Dawn', *St. Bede's Magazine* (April) 1879.
'The Language of The Afghans', *St. Bede's Magazine* (May) 1879.
'Lockyer's Sunset' (poem), *St. Bede's Magazine* (April) 1879.
'The Needs of Commercial Education', *St. Bede's Magazine* (February) 1880.
'Flowers From An Eastern Garden', *St. Bede's Magazine* (February) 1880.
'A Bright Morning in March' (poem), *St. Bede's Magazine* (March) 1880.
'Poet's Apology' (poem), *St. Bede's Magazine* (April) 1880.
'Student Life at the University of Louvain (I)', *St. Bede's Magazine* (April) 1880.

'Student Life at the University of Louvain (II)', *St. Bede's Magazine* (May) 1880.

'Flowers From An Eastern Garden', *St. Bede's Magazine* (May) 1880.

'Flowers From An Eastern Garden' *St. Bede's Magazine* (July) 1880.

'The Origins of the Afghans', *St. Bede's Magazine* (October) 1880.

'Flowers From An Eastern Garden', *St. Bede's Magazine* (January) 1881.

'Flowers From An Eastern Garden, *St. Bede's Magazine* (March) 1881.

'Tis Fifty Years Since', *Baeda* (1912).

Obituary of Fr Francis Hart, *Baeda* (1912).

Newspaper articles and reviews

The Tablet

'Catholicity and Pantheism', (review) *The Tablet*, 3 January 1874.

'Man and Apes', (review) *The Tablet*, 28 February 1874.

'Faraday's Lectures', (review) *The Tablet*, 14 March 1874.

'Holy Places' (review) *The Tablet*, 21 March 1874.

'Mgr. Menillord at Louvain', (letter) *The Tablet*, 7 June 1874.

'The Crisis in Belgium', (letter) *The Tablet*, 12 June 1874.

'Belgian Letter III', *The Tablet*, 2 June 1874.

'The Campaign Against Processions' (communiqué), *The Tablet*, 29 May 1875.

'Principia Dogmatico-Moralia Universae Theologiae Sacramentalis' (review) *The Tablet*, 29 May 1875.

'Louvain Letter', *The Tablet*, 20 November 1875

'Great wants in Catholic Literature I', *The Tablet*, 25 December 1875.

'Great Wants in Catholic Literature II', *The Tablet*, 13 January 1876.

'Great Wants in Catholic Literature III', *The Tablet*, 22 January 1876.

'Literary Work at Louvain during the last 12 Months', *The Tablet*, 31 March 1876.

'Alde Manuce' (review), *The Tablet*, 8 April 1876.

'Mis-translation of Prayers', (letter), *The Tablet*, 13 May 1876.

'Our Lord' or 'The Lord', (letter), *The Tablet*, 20 May 1876.

'The Hunting of the Snark', (review), *The Tablet*, 20 May 1876.

'Franz Hettinger on Dante', (review), *The Tablet*, 17 August 1876.

'Christian Poets' Philosophy', (review), *The Tablet*, 9 September 1876.

'Cardinal Franchi in Manchester', (communiqué), *The Tablet*, 23 September 1876.

'Curiosities of English Dialect', (review), *The Tablet*, 30 September 1876.

'Curiosities of English Dialect' (concluded) *The Tablet*, 7 October 1876.

'The Zend Avesta', (review), *The Tablet*, 7 October 1876.

'Druggists and Doctors' Prescriptions', (review), *The Tablet* 14 November 1876.

'Fr. De Smedt's Dissertations', (review), *The Tablet*, 16 December 1876.

'Furdusi and the Shah Nameh', (review), *The Tablet*, 14 October 1876.

'The Grand Duchy of Luxembourg', *The Tablet*, 13 January 1877.

'The Société Scientifique of Brussels' (review), *The Tablet*, 16 June 1877.

'Ancient and Modern Atomic Theories', (review), *The Tablet*, 30 June 1877.

'Gregory Bar-Hebraeus' (review), *The Tablet*, 21 July 1877.

'Revue des Questions Scientifiques' (review), *The Tablet*, 28 July 1877.

'Catholic Liberal Education', (letter), *The Tablet*, 19 January 1878.

'Catholic Liberal Education', (letter) *The Tablet*, February 9 1878.

Letter to Editor of *Revue Critique Internationale*, printed in *The Tablet*, 1 January 1881.

Letter to Editor, *The Tablet*, 15 January 1881.

'The Six Days of Creation', (letter), *The Tablet*, 25 June 1881.

'The Avesta', (letter), *The Tablet*, 10 December 1881.

'Six Days of Creation', (letter), *The Tablet*, November 19 1881.

'Statistics of the Religion of the World', (letter) *The Tablet*, 17 June 1882.

'Universality of the Deluge', (letter) *The Tablet*, 4 March 1884.

'Universality of the Deluge', (contd.) *The Tablet*, 15 March 1884.

'Universality of the Deluge', *The Tablet*, 12 April 1884.

'Universality of the Deluge', (concluded) *The Tablet*, 19 April 1884.

'The Dancing Procession at Echtermach', *The Tablet*, June 1884.

'Masters In Council', (letter), *The Tablet*, 23 January 1886.

'Stephen Langton and the Chapter of the Bible', (letter), *The Tablet*, 1 March 1890.

'Cardinal Newman and Gothic Architecture', (letter), *The Tablet*, 13 September 1890.

'Protestant Missions in India', (letter), *The Tablet*, 15 August 1891.

'Purcell's Life of Manning', (letter), *The Tablet*, 28 march 1896.

'Private Tutor', (letter), *The Tablet*, 21 May 1898.

'Higher Education at Louvain', (letter), *The Tablet*, 11 February 1899.

Obituary of Charles de Harlez, *The Tablet*, 22 July 1899.

'A Monument to Adrian IV', (letter), *The Tablet*, 3 November 1900.

'A Monument to Adrian IV', (letter), *The Tablet*, 1 December 1900.

'Central Idea of Everyman', (letter), *The Tablet*, 27 December 1902.

'Leo XIII and the Parsees', (letter), *The Tablet*, 12 July 1902.

'Margaret Clements in Louvain', (letter), *The Tablet*, 16 May 1903.

'St. Ursula's Convent at Louvain', *The Tablet*, 30 May 1903.

'Dante's Moral Character', (letter), *The Tablet*, 6 June 1903.

'The Congo and Western Australia', (letter), *The Tablet*, 2 July 1904.

'Louvain, 1745 and 1914: A Contrast', *The Tablet*, 12 September 1914.

'The Beginnings of Louvain', 26 September 1914.

'The Saviour and Victim of Europe', *The Tablet*, 31 October 1914.

'More About Louvain Library', *The Tablet*, 30 January 1915.

'Le Muséon', *The Tablet*, 27 March 1915.

'Syrian Catholics', *The Tablet*, 27 March 1915.

'The War and National Repentance', *The Tablet*, 14 August 1915.

'Victor Brants', *The Tablet*, 11 December 1915.

'A Faked Article', *The Tablet*, 18 November 1916.

'Shakespeare's Catholic Tone', *The Tablet*, 27 May 1916.

'Matthew Bridges', *The Tablet* 16 June 1917.

'The Question of Luxembourg', *The Tablet*, 27 October 1917.

'St. Michael's Church', *The Tablet*, 1 December 1917.

'Professor Colinet', *The Tablet*, 15 December 1917.

'A Prophecy of Leo XIII', *The Tablet*, 23 November 1918.

'The New Pope. By One Who Knows Him', *The Tablet*, 11 February 1922.

The Catholic Opinion (merged with the *Catholic Times* in February 1876)

'Sedes Sapientiae', (letter to the Editor), *The Catholic Opinion*, 14 January 1874.

'St. Patrick Champion of Ireland', *The Catholic Opinion*, 18 March 1874.

'Books by the Nuns of Kenmare', (review), *The Catholic Opinion*, 18 March 1874.

John Pearl's Lay Sermons I: 'What the Bible Teaches About Itself and the Church', *The Catholic Opinion*, 24 December 1873.

John Pearl's Lay Sermons II: 'The Bible and Conversion', *The Catholic Opinion*, 31 December 1873.

John Pearl's Lay Sermons III: 'Unpolitical Politics', *The Catholic Opinion*, 14 January 1874.

John Pearl's Lay Sermons IV: 'Politics and Education', *The Catholic Opinion*, 28 January 1874.

John Pearl's Lay Sermons V: 'A Church and A Bible', *The Catholic Opinion*, 11 February 1874.

John Pearl's Lay Sermons VI: 'What Is The Bible'? *The Catholic Opinion*, 25 February 1874.

John Pearl's Lay Sermons VII: 'John's Pilgrimage', *The Catholic Opinion*, 23 September 1874.

John Pearl's Lay Sermons VIII: 'The Relics at Aachen', *The Catholic Opinion*, 30 September 1874.

John Pearl's Lay Sermons IX: 'Forgotten Watchwords', *The Catholic Opinion*, 21 October 1874.

John Pearl's Lay Sermons X: 'Mr. Gladstone and Our Loyalty', *The Catholic Opinion*, 9 December 1874.

John Pearl's Lay Sermons XI: 'Mr. Gladstone's Mistake and Somebody Else's', *The Catholic Opinion*, 16 December 1874.

John Pearl's Lay Sermons XII: 'Fixing the Limit', *The Catholic Opinion*, 23 December 1874.

John Pearl's Lay Sermons XIII: 'Other Theories – Loyalty', *The Catholic Opinion*, 20 January 1875.

John Pearl's Lay Sermons XIV: 'Before and After', *The Catholic Opinion*, 27 January 1875.

John Pearl's Lay Sermons XV: 'Before and After' contd., *The Catholic Opinion*, 10 February 1875.

John Pearl's Lay Sermons XVI: 'Odd Difficulties', *The Catholic Opinion*, 17 February 1875.

John Pearl's Lay Sermons, XVII: 'Consolation for Catholics', *The Catholic Opinion*, 24 February 1875.

Difficulties of the Day I: 'Introduction', *The Catholic Opinion*, 24 November 1875.

Difficulties of the Day II: 'Catholic and Protestant Countries', *The Catholic Opinion*, 1 December 1875.

Difficulties of the Day III: 'Catholic and Protestant Countries' (contd.) *The Catholic Opinion*, 8 December 1875

Difficulties of the Day IV: 'Objections to the Preceding Articles', *The Catholic Opinion*, 15 December 1875.

Difficulties of the Day V: 'Conversion and the Peace of the Families', *The Catholic Opinion*, 22 December 1875.

Difficulties of the Day VI: 'The Church and Her Adversaries', *The Catholic Opinion*, 29 December 1875.

Difficulties of the Day VII: 'Moody and Sankeyism', *The Catholic Opinion*, 5 January 1876.

Difficulties of the Day VIII: 'Moody and Sankeyism' contd., *The Catholic Opinion*, 19 January 1876.

Difficulties of the Day IX: 'The Education of Women', *The Catholic Opinion and Times*, 16 February 1876.

Difficulties of the Day X: 'The Education of Women' (continued) *The Catholic Opinion and Times*, 23 February 1876.

Difficulties of the Day XI: 'The Education of Women', (concluded) *The Catholic Opinion and Times*, 1 March 1876.

Difficulties of the Day XII: 'Education and the Church', *The Catholic Opinion and Times*, 8 March 1876.

Difficulties of the Day XIII: 'Epilogue', *The Catholic Opinion and Times*, 15 March 1876.

Manchester Guardian

'The Nine Joys of Our Lady', *Manchester Guardian*, 19 January 1874.

'Italian Epitaph', *Manchester Guardian*, 26 January 1874.

'Portin', *Manchester Guardian*, 16 February 1874.

'Rush Bearing', *Manchester Guardian*, 23 February 1874.

'Lancashire Use of Brass', *Manchester Guardian*, 23 March 1874.

'Lancashire Pronoun', *Manchester Guardian*, 13 April 1874.

'Jacksnipe and Bilsnipe', *Manchester Guardian*, 13 April 1874.

'Buile Hill', *Manchester Guardian*, 18 May 1874.

'Witchert', *Manchester Guardian*, 25 May 1874.

'Portin II', *Manchester Guardian*, 25 May 1874.

'Balby Heardses', *Manchester Guardian*, 9 June 1874.

'Funeral Garlands', *Manchester Guardian*, 12 June 1874.

'Future Tense in Lancashire', *Manchester Guardian*, 14 September 1874.

'Mayor of Ardwick' (query), *Manchester Guardian*, 12 June 1876.

'Cardinal Franchi at St. Bede's' (communiqué), *Manchester Guardian*, 20 September 1876.

'De Quincey', *Manchester Guardian*, 20 January 1887.

'Earthquake', *Manchester Guardian*, 3 November 1893.

'The Earthquake', *Manchester Guardian*, 19 December 1896.

Letter to the Editor, *Manchester Guardian*, 13 May 1899.

'Congo Atrocities', *Manchester Guardian*, 31 March 1904.

'The Congo and Western Australia', (letter) *Manchester Guardian*,
2 July 1904.
'Scholarship Students', *Manchester Guardian*, 19 October 1905.
'Blessing the House', *Manchester Guardian* 25 March 1913.
'Letter to the Editor', *Manchester Guardian*, 8 August 1915.
'Letter to the Editor', *Manchester Guardian*, 19 October 1915.
'Letter to the Editor', *Manchester Guardian*, 18 August 1917.

The Harvest
'A Relic of Manchester in Catholic Days: The Old Christmas Carol',
The Harvest, I (4) (1888).
'Dante', *The Harvest*, VII (75) (1893).
'A Manchester Bishop in Central Africa', *The Harvest*, VIII (84) (1894).
'Our Missionaries to Uganda', *The Harvest* VII (93) (1895).
'A Children's Story', *The Harvest* (November 1917).
'Whalley', *The Harvest* (December) 1917.
'The Duke of Norfolk and the Salford Diocese', *The Harvest* XXX (353) (1917).
'Joseph Gillow', *The Harvest* (March) 1921.
 'Whalley Abbey', *The Harvest*, XXXVI (432) (1923).
Obituary of Ernest Annacker', *The Harvest* XXXVII (439) (1924).
'Bishop Turner' *The Harvest* XIV (166, 168, 169) (1901).

The Catholic Federationist
Each month Casartelli wrote a 'Message' for this newspaper which was the organ of
the Catholic Federation. Copies are available in the Salford Diocesan Archives. Between
November 1912 and July 1913 Casartelli translated an article for the *Federationist* by
Bishop Bonomelli, entitled 'Strikes and Strike-Makers'.

Miscellaneous
'Recent Earthquakes', *Geological Magazine*, April 1867
'Volcanic Disturbance in Mediterranean', *Geological Magazine*, May 1867.
'Pre-adamite Man', *World of Science*, 7 September 1867.
'Word-Love I & II', *The Lamp*, April 1871.
'A Long Lost Church', *The Lamp*, April 1871.
'The Will of God', *The Lamp*, April 1871.
'The Even-Song of the Flowers', *Rosarian*, August 1871.
'Vandalism', *The Isle of Man Times*, 23 August 1873.
'Louvain Literary Letter', *The Weekly Register*, 8 April 1876.
'Contributions to Catholic Folk Lore', *The Belfry*, October 1876.
'Oriental Studies: Gregory Bar-Hebraems', *The Belfry*, January 1877.
'Le Chat Hypocrite: Traduit du Samouit', *Revue Catholique*, 15 June 1877.
'Lettere Britanniche', *L'Aurora*, 5 April 1881.
'Lettere Britanniche', *L'Aurora*, 12 April 1881.
'Lettere Britanniche', *L'Aurora*, 24 April 1881.

285

'Lettere Britanniche', *L'Aurora*, 3 July 1881.

'The Jubilee at Louvain', *The Weekly Register*, 17 May 1884.

'Recollections of Northern India', *Illustrated Catholic Missions*, No. 12, April 1887.

'Notes on Manchester Rainfall during the Twelve Years 1878–1889', *The Journal of the Manchester Geographical Society* 7 (1890).

'A Month's Meteorological Observation and Notes of the Great Storm, St. Joseph's Observatory, Belize', *Journal of the Manchester Geographical Society* 9 (1893).

'Alleged Crime in Sicily', *Manchester Evening News*, May 7 1913.

'St. Dominic and Dante, *Blackfriars*, (August 1921).

'Whalley Abbey', (letter to the Editor), *The Times*, 12 July 1923.

'Sermon on the Priesthood', (June 1901) Miscellanea vol. I, SDA.

'Sermon on Latter-day Christianity', (July 1900) Miscellanea vol. I, SDA.

PRIMARY SOURCES

A. Manuscripts

Archdiocesan Archives Birmingham
    Illsley *Acta*
Archdiocesan Archives Liverpool
    Whiteside *Acta*
    Whiteside Papers
Archdiocesan Archives Southwark
    Salford File
Archdiocesan Archives Westminster
    Vaughan *Acta*: V.1/63. 1–259
    Bourne *Acta*: Bo 5/14 b-f; 25b; 25d; Bo 1/135B; Bo 1/178;
    Hierarchy Meeting Minutes
Arundel Castle Archives
    Papers of the 15th Duke of Norfolk:
        MD 2116–2118; MD 1900; MD 2078; MD2084; MD 2121
Archivo Segreto Vaticano
    Segreteria di Stato Ep. Moderna, A. 1920 R.81.F2.
Brompton Oratory Library, London
    Francis Bourne's Pastoral Letters
Colindale Newspaper Archive
    The Catholic Opinion
    The Catholic Times
Downside Abbey Archives
    Gasquet Papers: Gasquet 'Letters' (no further ref.); Gasquet Letters 1885–1904, No. 938; Gasquet Family Papers and Personal History, No. 887
Grieve Family Papers, Whalley (private collection)
John Rylands Library
    Moulton Papers: JRL. MA. MOU. II.
    Minute Book of the Manchester Egyptian Society, EOS/1/1

Minute Book of the Manchester Oriental Society, EOS/2/1
Minute Book of the Manchester Egyptian and Oriental Society EOS/3/1
Manchester Central Reference Library
    Belgian Refugees M138
    Manchester Statistical Society, Box 519
    Dante Society, Misc. 323/box 515
Manchester County Record Office
    Papers of the Manchester Geographical Society
National Library of Wales, Aberystwyth
    Hedley Papers: Boxes 23, 52, 53, 55
Propaganda Fide Archives, Rome
    A. 1903. Vol. 259. Rub. 102. pp. 247 – 254.
Salford Diocesan Archives, Burnley
    Casartelli Papers: 'Miscellanea', vols. 1 & 2;'Oriental Essays', vols. 1 and 2
    Casartelli Diaries (unmarked box)
    Casartelli *Acta*: bound volumes 1903 – 1925.
    Casartelli's Visitation Register
    Boxes 157 – 165: Casartelli Letters (n.b. Box 160 missing)
    Box 179: Vaughan Correspondence
    Box 182: Catholic Federation File; Non-Catholic Societies File
    Box 187
    Box 193
Salford Diocesan Chapter Archives, Cathedral House, Salford
    Chapter Minutes
Salford Local History Library
    Census Returns 1861
St Bede's College, Manchester
    College Diary, New Series: Vols. 1 – 4.
    College Scrapbook compiled by Mgr Hill.
St Edmund's College, Cambridge
    Boxes 2–4; 7 and 8
St. Gabriel's Hall, University of Manchester
    Minutes Book 1
University of Louvain Archives
    Copies of various manuscripts (no ref.)
University of Manchester Archives
    VCA/6/C12/1–2
Ushaw College Archives
    Casartelli Letters

B. Printed sources

Casartelli, L. C. 'Catholic Liberal Education', a letter to the Editor of the Tablet, 29 January 1878.

Casartelli, L. C. 'The Needs of Commercial Education', St Bede's Magazine 9 (February) (1880).

Casartelli, L. C. 'Commercial and Technical Education in Manchester', St Bede's Magazine 18 (January) (1881).

Casartelli, L. C. Commercial Education (John Heywood, London, 1882).

Casartelli, L. C. 'The Teaching of Commercial Geography', The Journal of the Manchester Geographical Society 2 (1886).

Casartelli, L. C. 'A Catholic Head Masters' Meeting', Downside Review 5 (1886).

Casartelli, L. C. The Modern Languages Problem in Modern Education (London: John Heywood, 1888).

Casartelli, L. C. 'An Educational Lesson From Berlin', Dublin Review 19 (2) (April) 1888.

Casartelli, L. C. Commercial Geography (Manchester: Co-Operative Printing Society, 1889)

Casartelli, L. C. Eastward Ho! Or Some Considerations on our Responsibilities in the East (London: John Heywood, 1893).

Casartelli, L. C. 'The English Universities and the Reformation', Dublin Review 117 (16) (October) 1895.

Casartelli, L. C. A Forgotten Chapter in the Second Spring (London: Burns and Oates, 1895).

Casartelli, L. C. 'De l'Etat Actuel des Études Supérieures dans le Clergé Anglais' (Société Belge de Librairie, Brussels 1896).

Casartelli, L. C. The Study of Commercial History (Manchester: T. Sowler and Co., 1897).

Casartelli, L. C. 'Charles de Harlez: In Memoriam', The Tablet, 22 July 1899.

Casartelli, L. C. 'The First Bishop of Salford', (3 parts) The Harvest 14 (166, 168, and 169) (1901)

Casartelli, L. C. Dante and Rosmini (Market Weighton: St. William's Press, 1910).

Casartelli, L. C. Sketches in History (London: R. and T. Washbourne, 1906).

Casartelli, L. C. ''Tis Fifty Years Since', Baeda 1912.

Casartelli, L. C. 'The Duke of Norfolk and the Salford Diocese', The Harvest 30 (March) 1917.

Casartelli, L. C. 'A Problem of After-War Reconstruction: The Study of Foreign Languages', Transactions of the Manchester Statistical Society 1918–19.

Casartelli, L. C. 'Catholic Secondary Schools and our Universities', Report of the 23rd Annual Conference of Catholic Colleges (London: Cole and Co., 1919).

Casartelli, L. C. 'Our Silver Jubilee', Report of the 25th Annual Conference of Catholic Colleges (London: Cole and Co., 1921).

Plater, C. Retreats for the People, with a preface by L. C. Casartelli, (London: Sands and Co., 1912).

SECONDARY SOURCES

A. Printed books

Archer, A. *The Two Catholic Churches* (London: SCM Press, 1986).

Archer, R. L. *Secondary Education in the Nineteenth Century* (London: Frank Cass, 1996).

Arnstein, Walter L. *Protestant versus Catholic in Mid-Victorian England: Mr. Newdegate and the Nuns* (London: University of Manchester, 1982).

Arthur, J. *The Ebbing Tide* (Leominster: Gracewing, 1995).

Arx, J. von *Varieties of Ultramontanism* (Washington, DC: Catholic University of America, 1998).

Aspden, Kester *Fortress Church* (Leominster: Gracewing 2002).

Ashton, T.S. *Economic and Social Investigations in Missouri, 1833–1933*, 2nd edn (London: The Harvester Press, 1977).

Aubert, R. *History of the Church*, vol. IX (London: 1981).

Banfield, Edwin *The Italian Influence on English Barometers from 1780* (Trowbridge: Baros Books, 1993).

Barker, R. *Education and Politics 1900–1951* (Oxford: Oxford University Press, 1972)

Beck, G. A. (ed.), *The English Catholics* (London: Burns and Oates, 1950).

Bedoyere, De La Michael *The Life of Baron Von Hügel* (London: J. M. Dent, 1951).

Benson, R. H. *Vexilla Regis* (London: Longmans, Green, 1914).

Bolton, C.A. *Salford Diocese and its Catholic Past* (Manchester: 1950).

Bossy, John *The English Catholic Community 1570–1850* (London: Dartman, Longman, and Todd, 1975).

Bourne, Francis *Congress Addresses* (London: Burns and Oates, n.d.).

Bradly, James E. and Muller Richard A. *Church History. An Introduction to Research, Reference Works and Methods* (Grand Rapids, MI: William B. Eerdmans, 1995).

Briggs, Asa *Victorian Cities* (Harmondsworth: Penguin Books, 1990).

Briggs, Asa *Victorian Things* (Harmondsworth: Penguin Books, 1990).

Broadley, M. J. *A History of St. Mary's Roman Catholic Church Oswaldtwistle* (Accrington, 1997).

Brodie Brosnan, J. *The Sacrifice of the New law* (London: Burns and Oates, 1926)

Brown, T. Nigel L. *The History of the Manchester Geographical Society: 1884–1950* (Manchester: Manchester University Press, 1971).

Brown, William Francis. *Through Windows of Memory* (London: Sands, 1946).

Bruton, F. A. *A Short History of Manchester and Salford* (Manchester: Sheratt and Hughes, 1924).

Buchanon, T. (ed.), *Political Catholicism in Europe, 1918–1965* (Oxford: Clarendon Press, 1996).

Butler, Cuthbert *The Life of Bishop Ullathorne*, 2 vols. (London: Burns and Oates, 1912).

Casartelli, J. *A Short Description of the Human Eye* (Manchester: J. Sale, 1868).

Chadwick, Owen *The Victorian Church 1860– 901* vol. 2 (London: SCM, 1997).

Chadwick, Owen *A History of the Popes 1830–1914* (Oxford: Clarendon Press, 1998).

Churchill, Randolph S. *Winston S. Churchill*, vol. 2 (London: Heinemann, 1967).

Clark, Peter *Zoroastrianism. An Introduction to an Ancient Faith* (Brighton: Sussex Academic Press, 1998).

Clark, P. F. *Lancashire and the New Liberalism* (Cambridge: Cambridge University Press, 1971).

Clifton, M. *Amigo: Friend of the Poor* (Leominster: Fowler Wright, 1987).

Coman, P. *Catholics and the Welfare State* (London: Longman, 1977).

Comby, Jean *How To Understand the History of Christian Mission* (London: SCM Press, 1996).

Congar, Yves M. J. *Lay People in the Church* (London: Geoffrey Chapman, 1965).

Crews, Clyde F. *English Catholic Modernism. Maude Petre's Way of Faith* (London: Burns and Oates, 1984).

Crichton, J. D. et al. *English Catholic Worship: Liturgical Renewal in England Since 1900* (London: Geoffrey Chapman, 1979).

Cruickshank, M. *Church and State in English Education* (London: Macmillan, 1964).

Daniel-Rops, H. *The Church in the Age of Revolution* (London: Dent, 1965).

Daniel-Rops, H. *A Fight For God* (London: Dent, 1965).

Davies, A. *Leisure, Gender and Poverty. Working-Class Culture in Salford and Manchester 1900 – 1939* (Milton Keynes: Open University Press, 1992).

Davies, Andrew and Fielding, Steven (eds.), *Workers' Worlds, Cultures and Communities in Manchester and Salford 1880–1939* (Manchester: Manchester University Press, 1992).

Denzinger, E. *El Magisterio de la Iglesia* (Barcelona: Herder, 1963).

Dessain, C. S. and Gornall T. *The Letters and Diaries of John Henry Newman*, vol. XXVII (Oxford: Clarendon Press, 1975).

Dingle, Reginald J. *Cardinal Bourne at Westminster* (London: Burns and Oates, 1934).

Doyle, Peter 'The Catholic Federation' in *Voluntary Religions*, Shiels W., and Wood D. (eds.), (Ecclesiastical History Society, 1981).

Drinkwater, F. H. *Educational Essays* (London: Burns and Oates, 1951).

Eaton, M., Longmore J. and Naylor A. (eds.), *Commitment to Diversity Catholics and Education in a Changing World* (London: Cassell, 2000).

Edwards, Gerard. *The Catholic Truth Society in the Diocese of Salford* (Liverpool: Mersey Mirror, 1992).

Evennett, H. D. *The Catholic Schools of England and Wales* (Cambridge: Cambridge University Press, 1944).

Evennett, H. D. 'Catholics and the Universities', in Beck, G. A. (ed.), *The English Catholics 1850–1950* (London: Burns and Oates, 1950).

Fiddes, E. *Chapters in the History of Owens College and of Manchester University* (Manchester: Manchester University Press, 1937).

Fielding, S. 'The Church and the People: Catholics and Their Church in Britain *circa* 1880–1939', in Fielding S. (ed.), *Warwick Working Papers in Social History* (Warwick: University of Warwick, 1988).

Fielding, S. *Class and Ethnicity* (Milton Keynes: Open University, 1993).

Fletcher, Margaret *O Call Back Yesterday* (Oxford: Blackwell, 1939).

Ford, C. S. *Pastors and Polemicists. The Character of Popular Anglicanism in South-East Lancashire, 1847–1914* (Manchester: Chetham Society, 2002).

Fussell, P. *The Great War and Modern Memory* (London: Oxford University Press, 1975)

Gilley, Sheridan 'The Roman Catholic Church in England 1780–1940' in *A History of Religion in Britain,* Sheridan Gilley, et al. (Oxford: Blackwell, 1994).

Gillow, Joseph *A Bibliographic Dictionary of the English Catholics* (London: Burns and Oates, n.d.)

Gladstone, W. E. *The Vatican Decrees on Civil Allegiance: A Political Expostulation* (London, 1874).

Greenall, R. L. *The making of Victorian Salford* (Lancaster: Carnegie Publishing, 2000).

Gregory, Adrian *The Silence of Memory. Armistice Day 1919–1946* (Oxford: Berg, 1994).

Gwynn, D. *The Second Spring 1818–1852* (London: Burns and Oates, 1942).

Gwynn, D. *Father Luigi Gentili and His Mission (1801–1848)* (Dublin: Clonmore and Reynolds, 1951).

Hamer, Edna *Elizabeth Prout* (Bath: Downside Abbey, 1994).

Hastings, Adrian (ed.), *Bishops and Writers* (Hertfordshire: Anthony Clark, 1977).

Hastings, Adrian *A History of English Christianity* (London: Collins, 1991).

Heimann, M. *Catholic Devotion in Victorian England* (Oxford: Oxford University Press, 1995)

Heimann, M. 'Stereotypes in Catholic Devotion' in Tallet F. and Atkin N., *Catholicism in Britain and France since 1789* (London: Hambledon Press, 1996).

Hickey, John *Urban Catholics. Urban Catholicism in England and Wales from 1829 to the Present Day* (London: Geoffrey Chapman, 1967).

Hilton, J. A. *Catholic Lancashire From Reformation to Renewal* (Chichester; Philimore, 1994).

Holmes, D.J. *More Roman Than Rome* (London: Burns and Oates, 1978).

Holmes, J. D. 'English Catholics and Higher Education at the End of the Nineteenth Century' in Davies M. (ed.), *Newman and Education* (Rugeley: Spode House, 1980).

Holmes, J. D. *The Papacy in the Modern World* (London: Burns and Oates, 1981).

Hooper, F. and Graham G. *Commercial Education at Home and Abroad* (New York: Macmillan and Co., 1901).

Jedin, H. (ed.), *Ecumenical Councils of the Catholic Church* (London: Burns and Oates, 1960).

Jenkins, Roy *Sir Charles Dilke A Victorian Tragedy* (London: Collins, 1958).

Johnson, Paul (ed.), *20th Century Britain* (London: Longman, 1994).

Johnson, T. and Hagerty J. *The Cross on the Sword* (London: Geoffrey Chapman, 1996).

Kerr, Ian *John Henry Newman* (Oxford; Oxford University Press, 1988).

Kerr, Ian *Newman the Theologian* (London: Collins, 1990)

Kerr, Ian *The Achievement of John Henry Newman* (London: Collins, 1990).

Kidd, A. *Manchester* (Keele: Keele University Press, 1983).

Kidd, A. J. and Roberts K.W. *City, Class and Culture* (Manchester: Manchester University Press, 1985).

King, Alex *Memorials of the Great War in Britain. The Symbolism and Politics of Remembrance* (Oxford: Berg, 1998).

Klein F. *Diary of a French Army Chaplain* (London: Longmans, 1915).

Lane, P. *The Catenian Association* (London: Burleigh Press, 1982).

Lawson, T. and Silver, H. *A Social History of Education in England* (London: Methuen, 1973).

Lea, Lady Herbert (trans.) *St John Baptist de Rossi* (London: Burns and Oates, 1906).

Leetham, Claude R. *Luigi Gentili. A Sower for the Second Spring* (London: Burns and Oates, 1965).

Leslie, Shane (ed.) *Letters of Herbert Cardinal Vaughan to Lady Herbert of Lea 1867–1903* (London: Burns and Oates, 1942).

Leslie, Shane *Cardinal Gasquet* (London: Burns and Oates, 1953).

Manning, H. E. 'Caesarism and Ultramontanism', *The Tablet* (3 January 1874).

Markus, R. A. 'Saint Augustine on the "Just War"', in Shiels, W. J. (ed.), *The Church and War* (Ecclesiastical History Society, 1983).

Martin, C. *English Life in the First World War 1914–1918* (London: Wayland, 1974).

Matthew, H. C. G. (ed.), *The Gladstone Diaries* vols. VIII and IX (Oxford: Clarendon Press, 1982, 1986).

Matthew, David *Catholicism in England* (London: Longmans, Green, 1936).

McClelland, V. A. *Cardinal Manning His Public Life and Ministry 1865–1895* (London: Oxford University Press, 1962).

McClelland, V. A. *English Roman Catholics and Higher Education* (Oxford: Clarendon Press, 1973).

McClelland, V. A. and Hodgetts M. (eds.), *From Without the Flaminian Gate* (London: Darton Longman and Todd, 1999).

McCormack, Arthur. *Cardinal Vaughan* (London: Burns and Oates, 1966).

McEntee, G. P. *The Social Catholic Movement in Great Britain* (New York: Macmillan, 1927).

McInally, M. *Edward Ilsley, Archbishop of Birmingham* (London: Burns and Oates, 2002.)

Mcleod, Hugh. 'Building the Catholic Ghetto: Catholic Organisations 1870–1914' in Shiels W. and Wood, D. (eds.), *Voluntary Religions* (Ecclesiastical History Society, 1981).

McLeod, Hugh *Religion and Society in England, 1850–1914* (London: Macmillan, 1996).

Messinger, G. S. *Manchester in the Victorian Age* (Manchester: Manchester University Press, 1985).

Milburn, David *A History of Ushaw College* (Durham: Ushaw College, 1964).

Misner, Paul *Social Catholicism in Europe from the Onset of Industrialisation to the First World War* (London: Darton, Longman and Todd, 1991).

Moloney, T. *Westminster, Whitehall and the Vatican* (London: Burns and Oates, 1985).

Moulton, J. H. *Early Zoroastrianism* (London: Williams and Norgate, 1913).

Moulton, W. F. *James Hope Moulton* (London: Epworth Press, 1919).

Murphy, J. *Church, State and Schools in Britain, 1800 – 1970* (London: Routledge, 1971).

Neuner, J. and Dupuis J. *The Christian Faith* (Dublin: The Mercier Press, 1976).

Neville, Graham *Radical Churchmen* (Oxford: Clarendon Press, 1998).

Newman, J. H. *Letter to the Duke of Norfolk on the Occasion of Mr. Gladstone's Expostulation* (London: D. M. Pickering, 1875).

Newman, J. H. *Certain Difficulties Felt By Anglicans in Catholic Teaching* (London: Longmans, Green, 1885).

Newman, J. H. *The Idea of a University* (London: Longmans, Green, 1907).

Nichols, Aidan *Catholic Thought Since the Enlightenment* (Leominster; Gracewing, 1998).

Nichols, Aidan *Dominican Gallery* (Leominster; Gracewing 1997).

Nicholls, D. and Kerr F. *John Henry Newman: Reason, Rhetoric and Romanticism* (Bristol: The Bristol Press, 1991).

Norman, Edward *Anti-Catholicism in Victorian England* (London: George Allen and Unwin, 1968)

Norman, Edward *The English Catholic Church in the Nineteenth Century* (Oxford: Clarendon Press 1984).

Norman, Edward *Roman Catholicism in England from the Elizabethan Settlement to the Second Vatican Council* (Oxford: Oxford University Press, 1985).

Nowell-Smith, Simon *The House of Cassell 1848–1958* (London: 1958).

O'Dea, John *The Story of the Old faith in Manchester* (Manchester: 1910).

Oldmeadow, E. *Cardinal Francis Bourne*, 2 vols (London: Burns and Oates, 1940).

O'Neil, R. *Herbert Vaughan* (London: Burns and Oates, 1995).

Pagini, Fr *Life of the Rev. Aloysius Gentili* (London: Richardson and Son, 1851).

Palin, M. (ed.), *University of Manchester Faculty of Theology Seventy-Fifth Anniversary Papers* (Manchester: Faculty of Theology, 1980).

Panaino, A. *Encyclopaedia Iranica* vol. 5 (Costa Mesa, CA: Mazda Publishers, 1992).

Parsons, G. and Wolffe, J. *Religion in Victorian Britain*, 5 vols. (Manchester: Manchester University Press, 1988)

Pax, D. G. *Popular Anti-Catholicism in Mid-Victorian England* (Stanford University Press, California 1992).

Pereiro, J. *Cardinal Manning, an Intellectual Biography* (Oxford: Clarendon Press, 1998).

Plater, C. *Catholic Soldiers* (London: Longmans, Green, 1919).

Pollard, J. F. *The Unknown Pope: Benedict XIV and the Pursuit of Peace* (London: Geoffrey Chapman, 1999).

Purcell, E. S. *Life of Cardinal Manning* 2 vols. (New York: Macmillan, 1896).

Quinn, Dermot *Patronage and Piety: The Politics of English Roman Catholicism, 1850 – 1900* (Stamford, CA: Stamford University Press, 1993).

Rea, Anthony *Manchester's Little Italy. Memories of the Italian Colony of Ancoats* (Manchester: Neil Richardson, 1988)

Rea, Anthony *Italians in Manchester* (Aosta: Musumeci Editore, 1990).

Sharp, J. *Reapers of the Harvest* (Dublin: Veritas Publications, 1989).

Slugg, J. T. *Reminiscences of Manchester Fifty Years Ago* (Manchester: J. E. Cornish, 1881).

Smith, J. C. *Zeppelins Over Lancashire* (Manchester, 1991).

Snead-Cox. J. G. *The Life of Cardinal Vaughan*, 2 vols. (London: Burns and Oates, 1910).

Speight, K. *A Short Account of the First Fifty Years of the Manchester Dante Society*, (Manchester: Morris & Yeaman 1957).

Sweeney, G. *St. Edmund's House, Cambridge: the First 80 Years* (Cambridge: St Edmund's House, 1980).

Vaughan, Kenelm *The papacy and the Bible: A Controversy* (Alex. Ireland and Co., 1874 n.p.)

Walsh, Michael *St. Edmund's College Cambridge 1896–1996* (Cambridge: St Edmund's College, 1996).

Ward, B. *The Sequel to Catholic Emancipation*, 2 vols. (London: Longmans, Green, 1915).

Ward, M. *The Wilfrid Wards and the Transition*, 2 vols. (London: Sheed and Ward, 1934).

Ward, W. *The Life of John Henry Newman*, 2 vols. (London: Longmans, Green, 1912).

Watkin, E. J. *Roman Catholicism in England From the Reformation to 1950* (London: Oxford University Press, 1957).

Wetton, Jenny *Scientific Instrument Making in Manchester 1790–1870* (Manchester: Museum of Science and Industry, 1993).

Wilkinson, A. *The Church of England and the First World War* (London: SCM Press, 1978).

Wilkinson, A. *Dissent or Conform?* (London: SCM Press, 1986).

Wilson, J. Anselm *The Life of Bishop Hedley* (London: Burns and Oates, 1930).

Winter, Jay *Sites of Memory, Sites of Mourning the Great War in European Cultural History* (Cambridge: Cambridge University Press, 1995).

Worrall, B.G. *The Making of the Modern Church. Christianity in England Since 1800* (London: SPCK, 1991).

Wraith, B. 'A Pre-Modern Interpretation of the Modern: the English Catholic Church and the 'Social Question' in the Early Twentieth Century', in Swanson, R. R. (ed.), *The Church Retrospective* (Boydell Press: Studies in Church History, vol. 33. Ecclesiastical History Society, 1997).

Zaehner, R. C. *The Dawn and Twilight of Zoroastrianism* (London: Weidenfeld and Nicolson, 1961).

B. Published articles

Anon, 'Classical and Modern: Cardinal Vaughan's Ideal', *Baeda* XII (1) (Easter) 1937.

Arx, J. P. von 'Manning's Ultramontanism and the Catholic Church in British Politics', *Recusant History* 19 (3) 1989.

Arx, J. P. von 'Interpreting the Council: Archbishop Manning and the Vatican Decrees Controversy', *Recusant History* 26 (1) 2002.

Aspden, Kester 'The English Roman Catholic Bishops and the Social Order: 1918–1926', *Recusant History* 25 (3) 2001.

Atkinson, H. 'September 1894 to 1899', *Baeda* XII (1) (Easter) 1937.

Bolton, C. A. 'Cardinal Vaughan as Educator', *The Clergy Review* (28) 1947.

Burge, T. A. 'Conference of Catholic Colleges', *Ampleforth Journal* July 1896.

Campbell, Debra 'The Catholic Evidence Guild; Towards a History of the Laity', *The Heythrop Journal* (30) 1989.

Carnoy, A. 'Monseigneur Louis-Charles Casartelli', *Annuaire de L'Université Catholique de Louvain 1920–1926*.

Casartelli, Joseph 'Rainfall at Longsight', *Proceedings of the Manchester Literary and Philosophical Society* (2) 1862.

Cashman, J. 'The 1906 Education Bill: Catholic Peers and Irish Nationalists,' *Recusant History* 18 (4) 1987.

Connelly, G. 'The Transubstantiation Myth: Towards a New Popular History of Nineteenth Century Catholicism in England', *Journal of Ecclesiastical History* 35 (1) 1984.

De Felice, Paul 'Reconstructing Manchester's Little Italy', *Manchester Region Historical Review* (12) 1998.

Devlin, Carol A. 'The Eucharistic Procession of 1908: The Dilemma of the Liberal Government', *Church History* (63) 1994.

Doyle, Patrick 'Religion, Politics and the Catholic Working Class', *New Blackfriars* May 1973.

Doyle, Patrick 'Accommodation or Confrontation; Catholic Response to the Formation of the Labour Party', *North West Labour History* (16) 1991/2.

Doyle, Peter 'Charles Plater and the Origins of the Catholic Social Guild,' *Recusant History* 21 (3) 1993.

Doyle, Peter 'The Education and Training of Roman Catholic Priests in Nineteenth Century England', *Journal of Ecclesiastical History* (35) 1984.

Fielding, S. 'Irish Politics in Manchester, 1890–1914', *International Review of Social History* (33) 1988.

Freeman, T. W. 'The Manchester Geographical Society 1884–1984', *Journal of the Manchester Geographical Society* 1984.

Gunn, S. 'The Ministry, the Middle-Class and the 'Civilising Mission' in Manchester, 1850–1880', *Social History* 21 (January) 1996.

Hagerty, J. M. 'The Diocese of Leeds During the First World War', *Northern Catholic History* (337) 1996.

Hamer, Sr Dominic Savio 'A Phase of the Struggle for Catholic Education: Manchester and Salford in the mid-Nineteenth Century', *Recusant History* 23 (1) 1996.

Holmes, J. D. 'Louis Charles Casartelli, Bishop of Salford 1903–1925', *Ushaw Magazine* 243 (85) 1974.

Holmes, J. D. 'English Ultramontanism and Clerical Education', *The Clergy Review* (62) July 1977.

Horwood, Thomas 'Public Opinion and the 1908 Eucharistic Congress,' *Recusant History* 25 (1) 2000.

Hunter-Blair, O. 'The Founder of St Bede's', *Baeda* (new series) 12 (1) (Easter) 1937.

Kane, P. M. 'The Willing Captive of Home? The English Catholic Women's League, 1906–1920', *Church History* 60 (3) 1991.

Machin, G. I. T. 'The Liberal Government and the Eucharistic Procession of 1908', *Journal of Ecclesiastical History* 34 (4) 1983.

Manley, G. 'Manchester Rainfall since 1765: further comments, meteorological and social', *Memoirs and Proceedings of the Manchester Literary and Philosophical Society* (117) 1974–75.

Marmion, John 'Catholic Manchester', *Priest and People* 1 (4) 1987.

Mason, Francis M. 'The Newer Eve: The Catholic Women's Suffrage Society in England, 1911 – 1923', *Catholic Historical Review* (72) 1986.

McClelland, V. A. 'Bourne, Norfolk and the Irish Parliamentarians: Roman Catholics and the Education Bill of 1906', *Recusant History* 23 (2) 1996.

McClelland, V. A. 'The Universities Catholic Board and the Chaplain, 1895–1939', *Ampleforth Journal* 1 (Spring) 1973.

Morrisey, H. 'Bishop Casartelli', *The Ushaw Magazine* 103 (March) 1925.

O'Brien, H. F. 'A New Boy of 1879', *Baeda* (new series) 12 (1) (Easter) 1937.

O'Connor, M. 'Joseph Louis Casartelli' *The Harvest* 13 (152) (May) 1900.

O'Dea, W. 'Sir Daniel McCabe, D.L. K.S.S., J.P.', *The Harvest* 33 (386) (November) 1919.

Rafferty, O.P. 'The Jesuit College, Manchester', *Recusant History* 20 (2) 1990.

Riddell, Neil 'The Catholic Church and the Labour Party, 1918–1931,' *Twentieth Century British History* 8 (2) 1997.

Sharrock, T. and Burns, T. F. 'The Salford Diocesan Catholic Federation', *The Month* 113.

Snape, M. 'British Catholicism and the British Army in the First World War', *Recusant History* 23(2) 2002.

Tanner, L. 'The Debt to O'Donnell', *Catena* 63 (642) (April) 1983.

Vaughan, Herbert 'The Evangelisation of Africa', *The Dublin Review* (3rd series) January–April 1879.

Wilkin, C. 'I Remember', *Baeda* XII (1) (Easter) 1937.

Zanetti, F. 'Our Duty as Citizens', *The Harvest* 18 (218) 1905.

Zanetti, F. 'The Late Bishop of Salford', *The Harvest* 38 (451) 1925.

C. Unpublished theses

Aspden, Kester 'The English Roman Catholic Bishops and Politics, 1903–1943' (PhD thesis, University of Cambridge, 1999).

Doyle, Peter 'The Episcopate of Alexander Goss of Liverpool, 1856–1872: Diocesan Organisation and Control after the Restoration of the Roman Catholic Hierarchy' (PhD thesis, University of Liverpool, 1981).

Fanning, M. 'The 1906 Liberal Education Bill and the Roman Catholic Reaction of the Diocese of Salford' (Undergrad. dissertation, Exeter College, University of Oxford, 1996).

Hamer, E. 'Martha and Mary: A Study of Elizabeth Prout (1820–1864) in the Context of the Passionist Mission to England in the Working Classes of the Manchester Area', (PhD thesis, University of Manchester, 1992).

OTHER SOURCES

A. Newspapers

Daily Dispatch
The Catholic Federationist
Catholic Opinion
Catholic Times
Manchester Courier
Manchester Guardian
The Harvest
Salford Reporter
The Tablet

B. Reference works

The Catholic Encyclopaedia, (New York: Robert Appleton, 1912).
Catholic New Encyclopaedia, (Washington, DC: Catholic University of America, 1967).
Chambers Biographical Dictionary (Edinburgh, 1984).
The Dictionary of Catholic Biography (London: Robert Hale, 1961).
A New Dictionary of Christian Theology (London: SCM Press, 1983).

C. Miscellaneous

1851 Census Surname Index (10) Public Record Office, Ref. 0107/2220.
Census Returns 1861, Manchester Central Reference Library.
Manchester of Today 1888, Manchester Central Reference Library.
Report of the Annual Conference of Catholic Colleges (1902 – 1924). Copies of these reports are available at the Salford Diocesan Archives.
Slater's Directory, 1855.

D. Unpublished manuscripts

Patrick Doyle, 'Manchester North West, 1908. Federation v. U.I.L.'
Patrick Doyle, 'The Essence of Catholic Politics'
Snape, M. 'British Catholicism and the British Army in the First World War.'

Index

⚜